Environmental Politics

Domestic and Global Dimensions

Environmental Politics

Domestic and Global Dimensions

Third Edition

Jacqueline Vaughn Switzer
Northern Arizona University

Bedford/St. Martin's
Boston ◆ New York

For Bedford/St. Martin's

Executive Editor for History and Political Science: Katherine E. Kurzman
Developmental Editor: Amy McConathy
Senior Editor, Publishing Services: Douglas Bell
Production Supervisor: Joseph Volpe
Project Management: Publisher's Studio
Cover Design: Zenobia Rivetna
Cover Photo: Windpower plant near Palm Spring, CA. Photo © Stefan Schott/Panoramic Images, Chicago
Composition: Stratford Publishing Services, Inc.
Printing and Binding: Haddon Craftsman, an R.R. Donnelley & Sons Company

President: Charles H. Christensen
Editorial Director: Joan E. Feinberg
Director of Marketing: Karen R. Melton
Director of Editing, Design, and Production: Marcia Cohen
Manager, Publishing Services: Emily Berleth

Library of Congress Catalog Card Number: 00-104007

Manufactured in the United States of America.

6 5 4 3 2 1
f e d c b a

For information write: Bedford/St. Martin's, 75 Arlington Street, Boston, MA 02116 (617-399-4000)

ISBN: 0-312-25590-X

Acknowledgments

Chapter-Opener Photo Credits Introduction: Jacqueline Vaughn Switzer; Chapters 2, 4, and 7: Martin Nie; Chapter 1: *Time,* April 22, 1970. Julian Wasser/Time Magazine. Copyright © 1970 Time, Inc. Reprinted by permission; Chapter 3: From *U.S. News & World Report,* January 27, 1997, p. 32. Chick Harrity, U.S. News & World Report. Reprinted by permission; Chapter 5: Niall Benvie/CORBIS; Chapters 6, 11, and 12: Joseph Sohm, ChromoSohm, Inc./CORBIS; Chapter 8: David Ostergren; Chapter 9: Judyth Platt, Ecoscene/CORBIS; Chapter 10: Chad Loberger. **Text Credits** Table 5.1: Spent Nuclear Fuel Stored at U.S. Commercial Power Plants, by State. From USA Today, December 31, 1998, p. 6A. Copyright © 1998, USA Today. Reprinted by permission; Chapter 12, footnote 30: Mike Robbins quote from "A Place for Feelings" in *Audubon* magazine's editorial, May–June 1996, p. 4. Copyright © NASI, 1996.

For Clovis Hill, who taught me how to write

Preface

As a native southern Californian, I grew up with smoggy skies, urban sprawl, and the fumes from too many automobiles and trucks on an ever-expanding freeway system, although at the time, I did not think of that scenario in environmental terms. In 1969, I watched as big globs of gooey oil washed up on the beaches of Santa Barbara; a year later, my friends from University of California at Santa Barbara (UCSB) and I celebrated the first Earth Day there. In Los Angeles, I participated in the struggles of the South Coast Air Quality Management District to develop an air pollution control plan that would satisfy the Environmental Protection Agency and then worked with scientists at Southern California Edison to find ways to comply with the enormously complex and expensive regulatory maze. In moving from southern Oregon to northern Arizona in 1997, I became more aware of the regional nature of many of our nation's most contentious environmental problems. In Oregon, community leaders shared concerns over spotted owls and marbled murrelets and over the decline of their timber-based economies. In Arizona, the haze over the Grand Canyon and water issues dominate the debate, especially on the Indian lands that form a patchwork over the Colorado Plateau.

These experiences have framed my views about the environment and how we attempt to develop policies that will solve the problems that affect us on a global basis. No one model can provide a complete assessment of all the factors that affect policy making, but the process model is a useful paradigm for exploring environmental policy and politics. It focuses attention on the interaction of policy-making institutions such as Congress, the president and the executive branch, and the courts as they compete for influence in formulating and implementing policies. Focusing on process also provides a way to see how nongovernmental actors interact with formal institutional powers. Ultimately, a process model permits us to understand how policies are made and how they can be tailored to more effectively address the problems at which they are aimed. Ecological science has made clear the stakes: we are experimenting on a global scale with the natural systems that make life possible. Some mistakes may be irreversible, at least in a human scale of time. There is no greater collective need than to improve our capacity to make good environmental policies.

Although much of the focus of the book is on the development of environmental policy in the United States, considerable attention is also paid to the globalization of environmental politics. The chapters often refer to environmental *regimes* — international agreements that may take the form of conventions or protocols — that have been created in an attempt to solve many of the transboundary problems that the book identifies. References are also made to the international body responsible for most regime formation in environmental issues, the United Nations (UN). Following the United Nations Conference on the Human Environment, held in Stockholm in June 1972, the UN General Assembly established the UN Environment Programme (UNEP), which has become the lead agency for many of the regimes discussed throughout this book.

Many people interested in the future of our nation and our planet may have only a "headline news" awareness of environmental problems. This book tries to provide a more comprehensive, objective view of issues that have been mired in controversy for decades while avoiding the rhetoric that often distorts the environmental protection debate. In that sense, *Environmental Politics* is designed to serve as a complement to other books that can provide the reader with additional background on the nature of the public policy process, public administration, political history, natural resources, or environmental studies.

The introduction to the third edition of *Environmental Politics* begins with the story of changing attitudes and policies toward the preservation of Yosemite National Park in California. While most of the public considers Yosemite to be a national icon that represents a natural treasure, the introduction explains how this has not always been the case. Chapter 1 follows with an overview of environmental history to provide background on the early beginnings of concern about the environment, followed by an explanation of the participants in the environmental debate in Chapter 2. Chapter 3 introduces the process by which environmental policy is made at the federal, state, and local levels, identifying key agencies and nongovernmental organizations involved in legislation, regime formation, and rule making. Chapters 4 through 8 introduce the essential issues related to the protection of land, waste management, energy, water, and air quality. Although many of the problems associated with environmental protection are overlapping and interrelated, these sections bring the reader up to date on the most critical issues and provide an evaluation of what progress has been made. Chapters 9 shifts in emphasis to the issues facing the Global Commons, including transboundary pollution (especially across the U.S. borders with Mexico and Canada), the role of international regimes with environmental concerns, such as the World Trade Organization (WTO), and the protection of the atmosphere and oceans. In Chapter 10, the focus is on endangered species, biodiversity, and forests, while Chapter 11 explores the problems associated with managing population growth, from both U.S. and global perspectives. Chapter 12 looks at the issues that are emerging for twenty-first century environmental politics, among them the role of science and politics, collaborative decision making, the debate over genetically engineering products, and world trade. The third edition now includes three appendices: a table covering major U.S. environmental legislation from 1947–2000, a summary of major international environmental agreements of the twentieth century, and a listing of environmental film resources.

Any one of these topics merits a complete, book-length treatment of its own, and the end of each chapter includes suggestions for further reading. It is hoped that this "taste" of key environmental issues will lead the reader to develop an appetite for further study and research. Taken as a whole, however, the goal is that all readers — whether students, citizen activists, or government officials — emerge with a better understanding of the totality and scope of environmental politics.

The third edition of *Environmental Politics* has been thoroughly updated to include some of the most recent environmental policy disputes, ranging from the regulation of personal watercraft as an air pollution control strategy to the deregulation of the nation's electric utilities. Each chapter's "Another View, Another Voice" feature has been redesigned to focus attention on individuals and organizations that have played an important role in environmental policy making, from the international to the local arenas. Finally, in the six chapters that include discussions on new or developing environmental concerns in other nations, a new feature, "The Global Dimension" focuses attention on environmental issues from an international perspective, highlighting topics like world energy consumption and the shrinking waters of the Aral Sea.

ACKNOWLEDGMENTS

An author reaches a third edition only because there was a first edition, and I remain indebted to Don Reisman, now at Resources for the Future, who was responsible for the acquisition of the original manuscript almost ten years ago, when he worked at St. Martin's Press. Beth Gillett took on responsibility for the second edition, and Katherine Kurzman, Amy McConathy, and James Headley served as shepherds for this third volume. I appreciate the continuing confidence of Bedford/St. Martin's in my work and in the value of this book. I wish also to thank the following individuals, who reviewed portions of the manuscript in preparation: Phillip Brick, Whitman College; Robert Higgins, Rutgers University; Sheldon Kamieniecki, University of Southern California; Matthew Lindstrom, Siena College; and Clifford Wirth, University of New Hampshire. I also benefited from the loyalty and patience of three graduate assistants at Northern Arizona University, and I promised to mention them in the book; they are Jonny Jemmings, Ed Sharkey, and Cecily Smith. I continue to express my appreciation to the colleagues who have adopted the book and used it in their own classrooms and to my students, old and new, who serve as my most critical reviewers, term after term. This book remains, as always, my gift to you.

JACQUELINE VAUGHN SWITZER

Contents

About the Author

Jacqueline Vaughn Switzer is an associate professor in the department of political science at Northern Arizona University, where she specializes in public policy and administration. Professor Switzer holds a Ph.D. in political science from the University of California, Berkeley, where she also attended the Graduate School of Public Policy. She taught previously at the University of Redlands and Southern Oregon University. Professor Switzer has a broad spectrum of nonacademic experience, including as an aide to a member of the California state legislature, as a program coordinator in the district attorneys' offices in two counties, and as a partner in a political consulting firm. Her environmental background stems from her work with the South Coast Air Quality Management District in southern California and as a policy analyst for Southern California Edison. Professor Switzer's previously published books include the coauthored American government textbook, *The Play of Power,* and *Green Backlash: The History and Politics of Environmental Opposition in the United States.*

Introduction

National Parks, while revered for their preservation of scenic beauty and wildlife, have also played another important role in America's history: they serve as representations of our changing values about wild places.

— Karen Sorensen is a Berkeley, California, writer whose family has camped and hiked in Yosemite for decades.[1]

For many, Yosemite National Park symbolizes not only the natural beauty of America, but also the ways in which politics and policymakers affect how and what we seek to preserve. The story of Yosemite tells us much about how time changes the way we feel and act — it is thus a mirror of the policy process that is the foundation for this book.

Frederick Law Olmsted, one of the country's first professional landscape architects, was among the voices who sought the preservation of Yosemite.[2] In 1864, Congress had granted Yosemite to California as a public park, with Olmsted as commissioner to manage the valley. A year later, he reported that "few persons can see such scenery as that of the Yosemite and not be impressed by it in some slight degree." He wanted its beauty and serenity to be protected, in part so that all members of the public, rich and poor alike, would have access to Yosemite for "refreshing rest and reinvigoration to the whole system." To do that, he called for the preservation and maintenance of Yosemite "as exactly as is possible of the natural scenery; the restriction . . . of necessary accommodation of visitors, of all artificial constructions and the prevention of all constructions markedly inharmonious with the scenery or which would unnecessarily obscure, distort or detract from the dignity of the scenery."[3]

However, Olmsted's plea went unheeded; for many in the late nineteenth and early twentieth centuries, Yosemite was simply a natural resource waiting to be used. Several hundred thousand sheep grazed in its meadows on the valley floor, while shepherds burned natural vegetation and trees to increase the land available for forage. Beginning around 1912, loggers began producing more than a billion board feet of lumber within the park on private land that the government could not afford to purchase.

◁ ***John Muir first saw Yosemite Valley from the rim in July 1869, when he "shouted and gesticulated in a wild burst of ecstasy" at the sight of Yosemite Falls, "all a-tremble with the thunder tones of the falling water."[4]***

Yosemite became a mecca for tourism even before the turn of the century, when stagecoaches and pack animals brought people and supplies to the park — so many that by the late 1800s, nine hotels had been built in the area. In the late 1920s, the opening of an all-year highway brought thousands of visitors to the park in vehicles that drove across meadows and parked and camped wherever space was available. The first airplane landed on the valley floor in 1919, and by 1925 the "Old Village" included several photography studios, a store, a church, a dancing/movie pavilion, and saloons. Yosemite Valley also boasted of a zoo of various cages and enclosures that housed bears and deer, and an elk herd was established, even though elk were not native to the region.

Outdoor sports and activities were heavily promoted in the late 1920s and 1930s in what was then called "The Switzerland of the West." A toboggan run was built, and the firm that managed the park, the Curry Company, flooded a sixty-thousand-square-foot parking lot to create the largest outdoor ice skating rink in the West. Visitors could go dogsleding, take a sleigh ride, or ski at the Badger Pass Ski Lodge, built in 1935. The promotion of Yosemite as a winter attraction even included a proposal to host the 1932 Winter Olympics in the park — a proposal backed by the park's superintendent. Congress had declared Yosemite a national park in 1891 — nearly thirty years after Olmsted's report — but in the next one hundred years, it was far from what Olmsted had envisioned.

Promoters and entrepreneurs looked at Yosemite as a moneymaking attraction, not as a place for contemplation. One popular proposal supported by California's governor authorized an engineering survey to build a tramway from the valley up to the top of Glacier Point. A wealthy real estate developer attempted to get U.S. Department of Interior officials to allow him to build an electric elevator that would be studded to the face of the sheer cliff below Glacier Point, while another proposal would have placed a searchlight atop the valley cliffs to "illuminate, in various colors" the waterfalls, domes, cliffs, and a fountain.

Although none of these proposals was ever approved by the federal government, they illustrate the changing values associated with the preservation of, not only Yosemite, but of the natural environment itself. Today, an environmental ethic has become a thread in the fabric of American life, as it is in many other nations around the world. Cutting a tunnel through a giant sequoia tree so a stagecoach could pass through to Yosemite was common in the late nineteenth century; today, protesters chain themselves to ancient redwoods to protect them. Before World War II, Yosemite's park rangers dumped garbage on specially built platforms lit by floodlights so visitors sitting in nearby bleachers could watch bears feed. In 1999, the Yosemite Fund, a nonprofit organization founded to support the park, allocated six thousand dollars toward the purchase of 260 additional bear-proof dumpsters to discourage the animals from foraging in campgrounds.

In one sense, it could be said that these changes represent a sort of environmental mood swing as we first exploit our natural resources and then try to find ways to protect and preserve them. To understand how and why this happens, it is first important to develop an overview of the policy-making process and the people who have a stake in policy outcomes. One way of doing so is through Anthony Downs's 1972 model, called the "issue-attention cycle."[5] According to Downs, the public's interest in an issue, such as the preservation of natural resources, goes through a cycle of ebb and flow — a process that is continuous, but not always predictable. Initially, a condition must be recognized as a problem; subsequent steps to solve that problem make up the policy process. Public policies are those developed by the arms of government, like the National Park Service or other agencies.

There are many approaches to policy study, including political systems theory,[6] group theory,[7] elite theory,[8] institutionalism,[9] and rational choice theory.[10] To better understand how politics has affected environmental policy, this book uses the five steps in the sequential model adapted from the work of political scientist James Anderson.[11] Yosemite National Park can be used as a case study to illustrate how the model works.

1. *Problem identification and agenda formation:* In this stage, policy issues are brought to the attention of public officials in a variety of ways. Some are uncovered by the media; others become prominent through crisis or scientific study. Organized groups may demonstrate or lobby officials to focus attention on the problem, or they may enlist celebrities to bring it to the government's attention on their behalf. Some problems may exist without being recognized except by a few isolated individuals or groups, who clamor to have their voices heard. Other problems are so immediate or visible that there is an immediate call for resolution. Once identified, problems are said to be part of the *policy agenda.*

Yosemite has long been a park that has been loved to death. Visitation has climbed steadily and is nearing five million visitors per year, leading to traffic congestion and air pollution, as wild areas such as meadows become crisscrossed with bike trails and footpaths that threaten native species on the valley floor. Over the years, growing demands for employee housing and visitor accommodations have totally altered the character of the park. Park officials have been aware of these problems for decades, and thus Yosemite has maintained a place on the National Park Service (NPS) policy agenda. Its location on the agenda, however, changes as other issues take precedence, such as the wildland fires in Yellowstone National Park in 1988 or declining air and water quality in Shenandoah National Park.[12]

2. *Policy formulation:* After a problem is identified as worthy of government attention, policymakers must develop proposed courses of action to solve it. Policy formulation may involve a variety of actors, which will be covered in more detail in Chapter 3. Some policies come directly from the president, such as President Bill Clinton's designation of the Grand Staircase–Escalante National Monument in 1996. Other policies, such as the approval of a state's air quality plan, are developed by regulatory agencies like the federal Environmental Protection Agency (EPA). Congress and state legislatures are often the source of policy initiatives, including Oregon's landmark "bottle bill," which established cash refunds for recycled products. Interest groups often place pressure on legislators or provide their expertise on matters that are scientifically or technically complex. The control of toxic substances, for example, is made more difficult because of

issues of scientific uncertainty. Groups like the Lead Industries Association have gone to court to question whether the EPA was reasonable in its attempt to create an appropriate margin of safety.[13]

In the case of Yosemite, policy formulation was not a swift process. Environmental organizations like the Natural Resources Defense Council, the Sierra Club, and the National Parks and Conservation Association bemoaned the state of the park for decades, with little success until 1980, when the NPS finalized the Yosemite General Management Plan. The plan was designed to provide specific direction regarding how the park was to be managed in order to preserve its resources. Its broad goals were to remove nonessential buildings and facilities from Yosemite Valley, restore large areas of the valley to natural conditions, and relocate visitor accommodations and employee housing away from environmentally sensitive or hazardous areas.[14] The plan was an example of the alternatives considered by NPS leaders to solve the problems identified in prior years.

3. *Policy adoption:* The acceptance of a particular policy is a highly politicized stage, often involving legislation or rule making, that legitimizes the policy. This is usually referred to as the authorization phase of policy making, and it often occurs outside the public's direct view. Hearings on competing proposals, meetings among stakeholders, and the publication of new standards of regulation may be conducted with minimal public participation or media attention. The process of making a choice among competing alternatives (such as different bills in the Congress) has been studied extensively by political scientists, who often refer to this area as the *decision sciences.*

Although important policy outcomes may be the result of informal, intuitive judgments, there are three theories of decision making that are generally used to try and explain policy adoptions. The rational-comprehensive theory is used to explain the procedures used to maximize the attainment of specific goals. These goals are intended to solve problems that can be clearly identified and defined. It is the process of problem definition that makes this approach quite difficult.

Incrementalism, in contrast, involves making relatively limited changes — fine tuning — rather than major alterations in policy. Incrementalism is built on the premise that there is no single "right" answer to problem solving, but rather a limited number of potential choices. This type of decision making tends to be conservative and is unlikely to lead to innovative solutions.

Multiple advocacy calls for the use of a "broker" who brings together a wide range of (often conflicting) alternatives and opinions. Leaders listen to the various arguments and ideas as they are presented, hopefully with a neutral perspective. While this format allows for greater participation by a number of actors, not all actors are equal in their resources, powers, or level of information about the nature of a problem.

One of the difficulties faced by NPS officials in adopting the 1980 plan was that although it was clear some decision was needed on future park management, there was disagreement among NPS officials, environmental groups, and members of the public as to how the plan's goals ought to be prioritized. The problems, especially those related to visitor congestion, were interlinked, and resources to solve the park's myriad problems were limited. The result was the development of four more plans over the next five years: the Concessions Services Plan, the Draft Yosemite Housing Plan, the Yosemite Falls Project, and the Yosemite Lodge Design Concept Plan.

4. *Policy implementation:* To put an agreed-on policy into effect, this fourth stage involves conflict and struggle as the administrative machinery of government begins to turn. Affected groups must now turn their attention from the legislative arena to the bureaucracy and, in some cases, the judicial branch to get the policy to work. Usually implementation is conducted through a complex administrative process, which may force agencies to make decisions based on very broad, ambiguous legislative intent. Implementation may become politicized and may force agencies to compete against one another for government resources and attention. The interest groups that were instrumental in getting the policy problem identified and placed on the policy agenda may become enmeshed in the implementation process, making further demands on the bureaucracy. Contending interests will push their own agendas forward, often at the expense of the initial policy they sought to have adopted.

Recognizing the need for a more comprehensive plan and inundated with pleas from various park users, NPS officials issued the Draft Yosemite Valley Implementation Plan at the end of 1997. The plan presented four alternatives for carrying out the provisions of the 1980 General Management Plan. This document formed the implementation strategy — a much more explicit and clearly designed proposal that set forth the steps that would need to be taken to meet the broad goals of the 1980 plan. The section dealing with concession services, for example, called for an increase in food service seating through the redesign of indoor spaces and increased outdoor seating in order to alleviate crowding and better meet the needs of visitors. It also recommended reducing the density of tent cabins, making a slight reduction in lodging units, and changing the mix of room types. By specifying what problems were to be addressed and when, the actual implementation began to take place. Piece by piece, the NPS began to work on projects that had long been ignored, often because of a lack of funds. Trampled meadow areas were roped off to protect native grasses; popular trails began to be repaired. However, major battles erupted over the more controversial elements of the plan, such as the removal of nonessential employee housing. There was agreement that employee housing ought to be relocated — rather, the issue focused on the proposed site for the construction of new facilities. One alternative had been released in July 1992 and had been heavily criticized; another was released for public comment in 1996. In this instance, policy implementation of one of the 1980 plan's basic goals — the relocation of employee housing away from environmentally sensitive areas — was stalled.

5. *Policy evaluation:* An ongoing process, this stage involves various determinations as to whether the policy is effective. This appraisal may be based on studies of program operations, systematic evaluation, or personal judgment, but

whatever the method, the evaluation may start the policy-making process all over again. Public policies are usually evaluated by the agencies that administer them or, occasionally, at the request of Congress or the president. Policy evaluation takes a number of forms. Researchers may use cost:benefit analysis to determine whether the amount of money being spent on a project is matched by the value obtained. They may conduct an evaluation midway through the implementation process so that changes can be made or errors corrected. However, policy evaluation also takes many other forms. Elected officials may make a determination about how well a policy is doing based on the comments they receive from their constituents or from organized groups attempting to lobby their support or responding on the basis of partisan concerns.[15]

For Yosemite, it often seemed as though virtually everyone was doing an evaluation on the progress of the 1980 plan and its subsequent revisions and additions. In 1998, for example, the Natural Resources Defense Fund noted that the park's beauty and natural values were being seriously threatened by visitation and vehicles. A senior policy analyst remarked that "too many visitors to the park experience it while sitting in traffic and driving around in search of parking. Visitors often find the views from world-famous points impaired by haze created by the exhaust from thousands of cars."[16] Others criticized the numerous and confusing proposals that had been presented. Some elements of the implementation proposal were halted or delayed because too many people had too many opinions about how best to preserve the park's resources.

However, the elements of this model of policy making are not separate, distinct events: policy making is an organic, even messy, process of defining and redefining problems; formulating and implementing policies and then reformulating them; and moving off and back on the policy agenda.

It took two crises in Yosemite — a massive rockfall in 1996 and raging flood waters in January 1997 — to force park management and the public to recognize the problem once again and for the NPS to move the restoration of Yosemite back on the public policy agenda. The 1996 event obliterated much of the landscape in a popular hiking and interpretative area, smashing bridges over the Merced River and destroying trails. The January 1 flood — the largest in over an eighty-year period of record — damaged or destroyed most employee housing areas and about half the visitor accommodations at Yosemite Lodge, which had been built on a flood plain. The resulting damage was so massive (Interior Secretary Bruce Babbitt initially estimated the cost to fully repair and restore the park at nearly $180 million) that it became clear that officials had no choice but to develop a new proposal to restore the park's natural environment. Not only did the flooding put Yosemite back on the NPS policy agenda, it also provided an opportunity for the government to readdress the issues identified in the 1980 plan.[17]

After extensive public comment and environmental analysis, the provisions of the previous proposals and the Draft Yosemite Valley Implementation Plan were rolled into still another initiative, which was announced by Interior Secretary Babbitt in December 1998 — the Yosemite Valley Plan. The secretary noted, "We have listened to public response . . . and we got the message loud and clear"; one environmental group praised the process and Secretary Babbitt, crediting him with giving "the Yosemite Valley planning process a much needed spark."[18] The decision-making process is far from over, and no doubt there will be continued debate over how extensively Yosemite National Park should be preserved or developed. Regardless of whether you have spent days in the park's wilderness areas or simply heard about its beauty, it is useful to understand how the policy process has changed Yosemite's mission and direction. Nearly 150 years ago, gold rush–era explorer and journalist James Mason Hutchings first shared his impressions with readers of the *Mariposa Gazette,* questioning if the area would remain in its isolated and wild state.

> After completing our series of views of this beautiful and wildly romantic valley, we looked a last look upon it, with regret that so fine a scene should be only the abode of wild animals and Indians, and that many months, perhaps years, would elapse before its silence would again be broken by the reverberating echoes of the rifle, or the musical notes of the white man's song.[19]

NOTES

1. Karen Sorensen, "The Way We Were," *Approach, 7,* no. 1 (Spring/Summer 1999): 8.
2. Olmsted's contributions are many, including his plan and development of New York City's Central Park. His efforts to preserve scenic vistas are chronicled in several biographies, including Albert Fein, *Frederick Law Olmsted and the American Environmental Tradition* (New York: Braziller, 1972); Charles C. McLaughlin, *The Formative Years* (Baltimore, MD: Johns Hopkins University Press, 1977); Elizabeth Stevenson, *Flo: A Biography of Frederick Law Olmsted* (New York: Macmillan, 1977); and Cynthia Zaitzevesky, *Frederick Law Olmsted and the Boston Park System* (Cambridge, MA: Belknap Press, 1982).
3. Frederick Law Olmsted, "The Yosemite Valley and the Mariposa Big Trees," *Landscape Architecture, 43* (1952): 12–25.
4. Harold Gilliam, "Yosemite in a New Dimension," in *Above Yosemite,* ed. Robert Cameron (San Francisco: Cameron and Company, 1983), 7.
5. Anthony Downs, "Up and Down with Ecology — The 'Issue-Attention Cycle,'" *The Public Interest,* 28 (Summer 1972): 38–50.
6. See David Easton, *A Systems Analysis of Political Life* (New York: John Wiley, 1965).
7. See Earl Latham, *The Group Basis of Politics* (New York: Octagon Books, 1965), and a more contemporary discussion of the roles of groups in Frank R. Baumgartner and Beth L. Leech, *Basic Interest: The Importance of Groups in Politics and Political Science* (Princeton, NJ: Princeton University Press, 1998).
8. See Thomas R. Dye and L. Harmon Zeigler, *The Irony of Democracy,* millennial ed. (Fort Worth, TX: Harcourt Brace, 2000).
9. Institutionalism is defined as the study of the more formal and legal aspects of government decisions. It is assumed that the structure, rules, and procedures of institutions (such as Congress or state legislatures) will affect policy making.
10. See Anthony Downs, *An Economic Theory of Democracy* (New York: Harper and Row, 1957).
11. James E. Anderson, *Public Policymaking: An Introduction,* 4th ed. (Boston: Houghton Mifflin, 2000). While Anderson's text is one of the more readable and up-to-date explanations of the policy process, several others are also worth mentioning. See, for example,

Thomas R. Dye, *Understanding Public Policy* (Englewood Cliffs, NJ: Prentice-Hall, 1992), and Charles E. Lindblom and Edward J. Woodhouse, *The Policy-Making Process,* 3rd ed. (Englewood Cliffs, NJ: Prentice Hall, 1993).

12. There have been ongoing clashes within the park system over how best to manage its resources, as described in depth in Richard West Sellars, *Preserving Nature in the National Parks: A History* (New Haven, CT: Yale University Press, 1997).

13. 647 F. 2d 1130 (D.C. Cir. 1980).

14. *1980 Yosemite General Management Plan* (Washington, DC: National Park Service).

15. Anderson, *Public Policymaking,* 261–288.

16. Remarks of Charles M. Clusen, Senior Policy Analyst, Natural Resources Defense Council, December 7, 1998, available at <http://www.nps.gov/yose/news_98/vip-nrdc.html>.

17. See "Interior Department Estimates Cost to Repair Flood Damage at Yosemite National Park at $178 Million," press release, January 31, 1997, cited at <http://www.nps.gov/pub_aff/press/yoflood.html>. See also Gary Smillie, Bill Jackson, and Mike Martin, "Yosemite Valley Flood, January 1–3, 1997," available at <http://www.aqd.nps.gov/yosevf.html>.

18. "The Plan for Yosemite Valley," *Approach, 7,* no. 1 (Spring–Summer 1999): 1.

19. The *Mariposa Gazette* article is believed to have been published on August 9, 1855, and was found in Hutchings's scrapbook, which was recently donated to the Yosemite Museum. Cited in *Approach, 7,* no. 2 (Autumn–Winter 1999), 11.

FOR FURTHER READING

James E. Anderson. *Public Policymaking: An Introduction,* 4th ed. Boston: Houghton Mifflin, 2000.

Stanford E. Demars. *The Tourist in Yosemite, 1855–1985*. Salt Lake City, Utah: University of Utah Press, 1991.

Steven J. Holmes. *The Young John Muir: An Environmental Biography*. Madison: University of Wisconsin Press, 1999.

Sally M. Miller, ed. *John Muir in Historical Perspective*. New York: Peter Lang, 1999.

John Muir. *Our National Parks*. Boston: Houghton Mifflin, 1901.

Thomas R. Vale. *Walking with Muir across Yosemite*. Madison: University of Wisconsin Press, 1998.

EARTH DAY

CHAPTER 1

A Historical Framework for Environmental Protection

The days of photo-op environmentalism are over.
— President Bill Clinton, announcing his new environmental policy[1]

Most contemporary observers regard Earth Day, 1970, as the peak of the American environmental movement, and the events of April 22 were indeed historic. An estimated twenty million Americans participated: New York Mayor John Lindsay closed Fifth Avenue to traffic during the event, and a massive rally was held in Union Square. Speeches and songs were heard at the Washington Monument, and virtually every college town, from Berkeley to Madison, held teach-ins and demonstrations. Philadelphia held a week-long observance, with symposia by environmental leaders and scientists, including Maine's Senator Edmund Muskie, author Paul Ehrlich, and consumer activist Ralph Nader. The event was highlighted by the appearance of the cast of the Broadway musical *Hair*. In San Francisco, the day was marked by symbolic protests, as a group calling itself Environmental Vigilantes dumped oil into the reflecting pool in front of Standard Oil. In Tacoma, Washington, nearly a hundred high school students rode down the freeway on horseback urging drivers to give up their automobiles.

A review of American history, however, shows that concern about the environment surfaced in the nation's infancy and has been a recurrent theme throughout the past three hundred years. One interesting aspect of that history is that some individuals or events appear to have had a momentary influence on policy development and then virtually disappeared from our historical consciousness. For example, Gifford Pinchot, an advisor to Theodore Roosevelt and leader of the conservation movement during the early twentieth century, had a tremendous impact on policy making during that period, but his name is unknown to most

◁ ***On April 22, 1970, more than 1,500 college campuses observed Earth Day with special events like the launch of this hot air balloon at Cerritos Junior College in California, teach-ins, and protests against oil spills, air pollution, and toxic chemicals.***

contemporary members of the environmental movement. There is no Pinchot National Park or building in Washington, nor is the date of his birth celebrated. Like a shooting star, his role was transitory and ephemeral. Similarly, although women's organizations were responsible for bringing urban environmental issues such as solid waste and water quality to the policy agenda, that function ended when it was replaced by the struggle for suffrage.

Equally perplexing are the effects of a number of environmental disasters and crises that made headlines. Some, like the thirty-million-gallon oil spill caused by the sinking of the supertanker *Torrey Canyon* off the coast of England in 1967, have been upstaged by more recent events such as the oil spill resulting from the grounding of the *Exxon Valdez* in Alaska. The radiation leak at the Soviet Union's Chernobyl plant in April 1986 has become synonymous with concerns about nuclear power and is likely to serve as a catalyst for international protests for years to come.

The development of an environmental policy agenda can be viewed in two ways. First, it is a history of ideas, a philosophical framework about our relationship to nature and the world. This history is punctuated with names ranging from Thomas Malthus and Charles Darwin to Karl Marx and Francis Bacon, along with modern commentary from Barry Commoner, Garrett Hardin, and Paul Ehrlich. Second, it is a factual history, made up of events, individuals, and conditions. This chapter focuses on factual history to identify five distinct periods in the development of policies to protect the environment.

GERMINATION OF AN IDEA: FROM THE COLONIAL PERIOD TO 1900

Even before the states were united there was an awareness of the need to limit the use of the new land's natural resources. As early as 1626, the members of the Plymouth Colony passed ordinances regulating the cutting and sale of timber on colony lands. Other colonial leaders recognized the importance of preserving the region's resources, prohibiting the intentional setting of forest fires, and placing limits on deer hunting. In 1681, William Penn, proprietor of Pennsylvania, decreed that, for every five acres of land cleared, one must be left as virgin forest.[2] In 1691, Massachusetts Bay leaders began to set aside "forest reservations" — large stands of pines valued for their use as ships' masts. Forest preservation became an entrenched principle of colonial land management as early as the seventeenth century.[3]

During the eighteenth century, the nation was consumed with the building of a new government, but individual states made efforts to preserve the resources within their boundaries. Massachusetts in 1710 began to protect coastal waterfowl and in 1718 banned the hunting of deer for four years. Other states, such as Connecticut (1739) and New York (1772), also passed laws to protect game.[4] Political leaders at the beginning of the nineteenth century expressed interest in studying soil erosion; both Washington and Jefferson wrote of their concerns about the lands at their estates. With the opening of the Erie Canal in 1825 bringing pine forests within the reach of eastern markets, states were forced to confront the issue of timber poaching — one of the first environmental crimes.[5]

By midcentury, the public began to be interested in preserving natural resources. George Perkins Marsh's 1864 book, *Man and Nature,* captured attention with its call for the protection of songbirds and the use of plantings to prevent soil erosion.[6] In 1866, German scientist and philosopher Ernst Haeckel coined the term *ecology,* and the subject became a thriving research discipline.[7] Still, there was no philosophy of protection that dominated either American or European thought. Studies of the popular literature of the 1870s led some historians to conclude that the environmental movement came alive with the advent of sportsmen's magazines. In October 1871, *The American Sportsman,* a monthly newspaper, marked a watershed in environmental history when it became the first publication to interrelate the subjects of hunting, fishing, natural history, and conservation. Two years later, *Forest and Stream* advocated the protection of watersheds, scientific management of forests, uniform game laws, and abatement of water pollution.[8] Diminishing supplies of fish in the Connecticut River resulted in the development of the fish culture industry and the formation in 1870 of the American Fisheries Society, the first biological society to research a diminishing natural resource. A year later the U.S. Fish Commission was created, the first federal agency responsible for the conservation of a specific natural resource.[9]

Adventure and exploration enhanced the public's interest in the environment throughout the nineteenth century. Lewis and Clark's transcontinental journeys, beginning in 1804, and John Wesley Powell's descent down the Colorado River, in 1869, increased Americans' awareness of the undiscovered beauty of the frontier.[10]

Tremendous urban population growth between 1870 and the turn of the century led to new environmental problems, including contamination of drinking water sources and garbage and sewage dumping. The problems were most evident in the cities of the Northeast and Midwest, where the population increases were the most rapid. Although New York remained the nation's largest city, nearly tripling its population over the thirty-year period, Chicago had the biggest percentage increase, nearly sixfold. Similarly, Philadelphia, St. Louis, and Boston nearly doubled the sizes of their populations. Although industrial development did not reach the West Coast's cities as quickly, San Francisco, which served as the major shipping port, doubled its population between 1870 and 1890. The biggest increase was in Los Angeles, which grew to over twenty times its size from 1870 to 1900. American cities became centers of industry, and industry, with its accompanying population growth, meant pollution. By 1880, New York had 287 foundries and machine shops and 125 steam engines, bone mills, refineries, and tanneries. By the turn of the century, Pittsburgh had hundreds of iron and steel plants. Chicago's stockyards, railroads, and port traffic filled the city with odors and thick, black smoke.[11]

Pollution problems caused by rapid industrial growth resulted in numerous calls for reform, and women became key leaders in cleaning up the urban environment. Upper-class women with extended periods of leisure time, believing that "the housekeeping of a great city is women's work," formed civic organizations dedicated to monitoring pollution and finding solutions to garbage and sanitation problems. The first of these groups, the Ladies' Health Protective Association, was founded in 1884 with the goal of keeping New York City's streets free of garbage. The Civic Club of Philadelphia, formed in 1894, began by placing trash receptacles at key intersections. Other groups were organized in Boston (the Women's Municipal League) and St. Louis (the Women's Organization for Smoke Abatement).[12]

The nation's environmental awareness was enhanced by the actions of specific individuals. George Catlin first proposed the idea of a national park in 1832.[13] Henry David Thoreau spoke poetically in 1858 of his return to a natural world.[14] George E. Waring built the first separate sewer system in Lenox, Massachusetts, in 1876 and was a pioneer in the study of sanitary engineering. Waring, known as "the apostle of cleanliness," crusaded about the impact of garbage on public health and was responsible for the beginnings of contemporary solid waste science.[15] Later, after the turn of the century, progressive reformers like Dr. A. Wilberforce Williams brought advice on hygiene and sanitation to the urban black community.[16]

The concept of preserving natural areas came from a variety of sources. In 1870, a group of explorers recommended that a portion of the upper Yellowstone River region be set aside to protect its geothermal features, wildlife, forests, and unique scenery. The result, the establishment of Yellowstone National Park in 1872, was the beginning of a pattern of preserving large undisturbed ecosystems. The public endorsed the idea, and Congress responded by creating Sequoia, Kings Canyon, and Yosemite National Parks in 1890, followed by Mount Rainier National Park in 1899. Interest in trees and forests was an important element of preservationism, symbolized by the proclamation of the first Arbor Day on April 10, 1872. The event was the culmination of the work of J. Sterling Morton, editor of Nebraska's first newspaper, and Robert W. Furia, a prominent nursery owner who later became governor. The two men convinced the Nebraska state legislature to commemorate the day with tree plantings to make Nebraska "mentally and morally the best agricultural state in the Union." More than one million trees were planted the first year, and Nebraska became known as the "Tree Planter's State" in 1895. With the Forest Reserve Act of 1891, the U.S. Congress set aside forest lands for preservation for the first time. Several years later President Grover Cleveland ordered lands to be protected because few states were willing to protect their forests from logging.

The founding of the Sierra Club by John Muir in 1892 marked the beginning of interest in a more broadly based environmental organization.[17] Although the early organizations have been called "pitifully weak" in membership and finances, these early groups had a strong sense of determination. Most groups debated the scientific management of resources rather than organizing to protect them. But the idea of preserving land and natural resources was germinating within American society.[18]

PROGRESSIVE REFORMS AND CONSERVATIONISM: 1900–1945

Despite these whispers of ideas and early efforts, most environmental historians place the beginning of an actual "movement" at the turn of the century, when conservationism became a key element of the Progressive Era. The term *conservation* sprung from efforts by pioneers such as Frederick H. Newell, George Maxwell, and Francis G. Newlands to construct reservoirs to conserve spring flood waters for later use during the dry season. The concept behind conservation was "planned and efficient progress."[19]

In the United States, the infant environmental movement split into two camps: preservationists and conservationists. Under the leadership of Gifford Pinchot, the conservationists, influenced by forest management practices in Europe, believed that sustainable exploitation of resources was possible. The preservationists, led by John Muir, sought to preserve wilderness areas from all but recreational and educational use. Pinchot, a Yale graduate who trained at the French Forest School and later received an appointment as forester on the seven-thousand-acre North Carolina estate of George W. Vanderbilt, became the nation's most publicized environmentalist. In 1898, he became chief of the Division of Forestry (later renamed the U.S. Forest Service) and, as a personal friend of Theodore Roosevelt, had tremendous influence over the development of conservation policy through his connections in Washington, D.C. He convinced Roosevelt of the need to preserve forests and to use scientific forestry techniques to manage them.[20] In contrast, John Muir, who spent much of his life in California's Sierra Nevada, championed the protection of the Yosemite Valley and crusaded against the development of Yosemite's Hetch Hetchy reservoir, which he viewed as misuse of the region's natural resources.[21]

Generally, the conservationists' position won, at least at the national level. Before the turn of the century, there had been little federal consideration for conservation. The zenith can be traced to May 13–15, 1908, when a thousand national leaders met to attend a White House Conference on Resource Management, coordinated by Pinchot. This meeting was one of the first official agenda-setting actions in environmental policy making.[22] At the end of the conference, the leaders asked the president to create a National Conservation Commission to develop an inventory of all natural resources. Roosevelt did so, appointing Pinchot as its chairman. By mid-1909, forty-one states had created similar organizations.[23] Pinchot organized the Conservation Congresses, which convened to discuss the familiar subjects of forest, soil, and water problems and management and eventually expanded to include issues such as public control of railroads, regulation of speculation and gambling in foodstuffs, coordination of governmental agencies, and creation of better rural schools.[24] The Congresses provided an opportunity for debate among federal, state, and local conservation leaders but were heavily politicized. Bitterness and internal struggles brought an end to the annual events in 1917. Of prime importance to many conservation leaders was the "public land question." The possibilities of unlimited economic growth in the West caused President Theodore Roosevelt to appoint a Public Lands Commission in 1903. While many hoped the commission would promote orderly growth, there was also concern that the old practice of disposing nonagricultural lands to private owners would give way to public ownership and management.[25] During the presidencies of Theodore Roosevelt, William Howard Taft, and Woodrow Wilson, new national forests were created by Congress, which also passed laws to protect historic sites and migratory birds and enacted the National Park Service in 1916.

The Progressive era is noted also for the birth of conservation organizations such as the National Audubon Society, in 1905; the National Parks Association, in 1919; and the Izaak Walton League, in 1922. Pinchot organized the National Conservation Association in 1909, with the group's primary interests being limited to water power and mineral leasing, reflecting an extension of Roosevelt's policy. The group disbanded in the 1920s. Progressive Era reforms were focused on *efficiency,* striving to make better use of natural resources. The reformers were not radicals in the traditional political sense, so Progressive conservation posed only a modest threat to the existing distribution of power in the United States.[26]

As the term *conservation* broadened, it gradually lost its initial meaning. Roosevelt began to refer to the conservation of human health, and the National Conservation Congress devoted its entire 1912 session to "the conservation of human life." While conservationists focused attention on the sustainability of natural resource use, progressives in urban areas began to work for new laws and regulations to reduce pollution and protect public health. Cities were the first to regulate air pollution; the first clean air laws were enacted in the late 1800s. Public health advocates and activists such as Alice Hamilton and Jane Addams provided the impetus for state and local regulatory programs to improve water quality, provide for sanitation and waste removal, and reduce workers' exposure to toxic chemicals.[27]

During the 1930s, the environmental movement again became a battle between conservation and preservation. As a result, environmental leaders redoubled their efforts to preserve scenic areas. In 1935, Aldo Leopold founded the Wilderness Society to protect public lands, and the National Wildlife Federation (1936) served as the first of the conservation education organizations, sponsoring National Wildlife Week in schools beginning in 1938. Conservation organizations were closely allied with the four major engineering societies: the American Society of Civil Engineers, the American Society of Mechanical Engineers, the American Institute of Electrical Engineers, and the American Institute of Mining Engineers, all of which spearheaded the drive for efficiency. The Great Depression brought the federal government into new areas of responsibility, including environmental policy. Federal conservation interest intensified with the growth of agencies with specific resource responsibilities, beginning with the Tennessee

Valley Authority in 1933, the Soil Conservation Service in 1935, and the Civilian Conservation Corps, which from 1933 to 1942 gave productive work to two million unemployed young men.

RECREATION AND THE AGE OF ECOLOGY: POST–WORLD WAR II TO 1969

After World War II, Americans' interest in the environment shifted to a new direction. Concern about the efficient scientific management of resources was replaced with desire to use the land for recreational purposes. Over thirty million Americans toured the national parks in 1950. The parks were, in the words of one observer, "in danger of being loved to death," since roads and services were still at prewar levels.[28] National Park Service (NPS) Director Conrad Wirth presented Congress with a "wish list" of park needs that came to be known as Mission '66 — a ten-year improvement program that would coincide with the fiftieth anniversary of the NPS. That plan served as the blueprint for massive growth in both national parks and recreational areas during the next twenty years.[29] Habitat protection became the focus of groups like the Defenders of Wildlife, founded in 1947 to preserve, enhance, and protect the diversity of wildlife and its habitats. In 1951, The Nature Conservancy began to acquire, either through purchase, gift, or exchange, ecologically significant tracts of land, many of which are habitats for endangered species.

The 1960s brought a battle between those who supported industrial growth and those who worried about the effects of pollution caused by growth. It was a decade when an author's prose or a single event could rouse the public's indignation. The 1960s marked the beginning of legislative initiatives that would be fine-tuned over the next thirty years and of tremendous growth in environmental organizations.

Two authors brought public attention to environmental problems during this decade. Rachel Carson, in her book *Silent Spring,*[30] and Paul Ehrlich, in *The Population Bomb,*[31] warned the world of the dangers of pesticides and the population explosion, respectively. Several authors served up "doom-and-gloom" predictions of the problems facing the planet, and there was a spirit of pessimism regarding the environmental situation. In January and February 1969, two oil spills five and a half miles off the coast of Santa Barbara, California, hit a public nerve like never before. Only eight days into his administration, President Richard Nixon was faced with an environmental crisis for which he was totally unprepared. The media captured the essence of the spills with images of birds soaked in gooey, black oil and pristine, white beaches soiled with globs of oil that washed up with each tide.[32] (See "Another View, Another Voice: Robert H. Boyle: The Hudson River Fishermen's Association.")

Legislatively, the 1960s heralded a period of intense activity (see Appendix A). In a carryover of issues from the postwar period, parks and wilderness remained high on the public's and legislature's agendas. By 1960, the number of

Another View, Another Voice

ROBERT H. BOYLE
The Hudson River Fishermen's Association

In the early 1960s, *Sports Illustrated* writer Robert H. Boyle moved to New York and became friends with a small group of fishermen who lived along the Hudson River, part of a community that supports one of the nation's oldest commercial fisheries. Like the sports anglers and aquarium enthusiasts, Boyle studied the flora and fauna of the Hudson and became a serious researcher of the region's waterways. He also came into contact with a fledgling environmental organization, called the Scenic Hudson Preservation Conference, that was attempting to stop Consolidated Edison, the state's principal electric utility, from building a pump storage facility nearby. The site, Storm King Mountain, was known for its beauty and scenic vistas, but Boyle's research had also identified it as one of two principal spawning grounds for Atlantic Coast striped bass. After years of hearings, petitions, and negative publicity, the utility company agreed to abandon the project and donated the land as a park.

The victory at Storm King Mountain was due in part to a 1966 meeting in Boyle's home that convened to discuss issues of increasing importance to the participants—the decline in fish stock, the growing pollution, and odors of decay from industrial waste that had turned the river into an open sewer. Boyle, a writer and naturalist, brought together an airline pilot, an ecologist, a photographer, a grave digger, an orthodontist, a prison guard, an entomologist, an oceanographer, and a marine biologist. The group, which became the Hudson River Fishermen's Association, held in common the conviction that the government could not be trusted to protect the environment. Termed "blue-collar environmentalism," the association's members shared the belief that the Hudson River was public property, to serve as their livelihood or a place of recreation, and that its protection was akin to the protection of basic democratic values.

Their secret weapons (at a time when there were virtually no federal environmental laws) were two late nineteenth-century statutes: the 1899 Federal Refuse Act and the New York Rivers and Harbors Act of 1888, which banned the discharge of pollutants into navigable waters. Boyle had unexpectedly discovered the laws while researching an article, and he was even more surprised to find that there was a bounty provision. A person who reported violations of the laws was allowed to keep half the penalty charged against the polluter.

On March 20, 1966, there was standing room only at the first public meeting of the association—and the crowd consisted of roofers, carpenters, commercial fishermen, and residents of the area who worked in the factories along the Hudson. They were willing to risk their jobs to report illegal dumping into and pollution of the river that they thought of as their own backyard. Two years later, using the 1899 act as the basis for their arguments, they filed their first suit against Penn Central Railroad, which for years had openly discharged diesel oil waste directly into the river basin. In 1969, the railroad lost the case, and paid a fine of four thousand dollars, half of which went to the Hudson River Fishermen's Association—the first time a private organization had ever received a bounty under the seventy-year-old statute. Over ten thousand "Bag a Polluter" postcards were distributed by the association, outlining the provisions of the Refuse Act and urging recipients to take action against polluters in their area by reporting violations to federal authorities. In 1970, a local high school class alerted the association to the New York National Guard's attempts to dump debris in a local marshland.

In England, landowners hired riverkeepers to monitor local trout streams against poachers—an idea Boyle had envisioned for the Hudson and every other major waterway. In 1983, the association hired its first riverkeeper, John Cronin, to patrol the river and investigate citizen complaints. Four years later, a new organization, Riverkeeper, joined with the Pace University School of Law to establish an environmental law clinic, which now brings suits against private corporations, municipalities, and agencies that violate pollution laws. Today, there are nearly forty members of the Water Keeper Alliance monitoring U.S. lakes, bays, and rivers; the first Canadian program began in 1999 on the Petitcodiac River in New Brunswick. Under chief prosecuting attorney Robert F. Kennedy, Jr., the organization has brought more than 150 legal cases, including a historic settlement with the Exxon Corporation that brought the group international attention. Robert Boyle is now president of the Board of Directors of Riverkeeper, and John Cronin still serves as riverkeeper, devoting all his time to advocacy work on the Hudson.

For More Information

For more information on Riverkeeper, call (800) 21-KEEPER, e-mail <info@riverkeeper.org>, or visit its website at <www.riverkeeper.org>.

national park visitors had grown to seventy-two million, and Congress responded by creating the Land and Water Conservation Fund to add new wilderness areas and national parks. Congress also expanded recreational areas with the passage of the National Wilderness Act in 1964 and the Wild and Scenic Rivers and National Trails Acts in 1968. President Lyndon Johnson, as part of his environmental policy, which he called "the new conservation," sought congressional support for urban parks to bring the land closer to the people.[33] Johnson's wife, Lady Bird, spearheaded the drive to improve the nation's roadways through her highway beautification program and sought, and found, congressional support for the 1965 passage of the Highway Beautification Act.[34]

Although there were several legislative precursors during the 1940s and 1950s, many of the hallmark pieces of pollution legislation were enacted during the 1960s, with the signing of the first Clean Air Act in 1963 (amended as the Air Quality Act in 1967) and of the Water Quality Act in 1965. The Endangered Species Preservation Act (1966) marked a return to the federal interest in animal and plant habitat that had begun earlier in the century. The National Environmental Policy Act (NEPA), signed by President Nixon in 1970, served as the foundation for policy initiatives that were to follow throughout the next twenty years.

Political leadership on environmental issues during the 1960s focused on several individuals, and environmental organizations began to grow. Senator Edmund Muskie of Maine was among the most visible, but he became the target of considerable criticism, especially when he became a leading contender for the Democratic presidential nomination. A 1969 report by Ralph Nader's consumer organization gave Muskie credit for his early stewardship in the air pollution battle but accused the senator of subsequently losing interest.[35] Other leaders, such as Senator Henry Jackson of Washington (who chaired the Senate Interior and Insular Affairs Committee and was largely responsible for shepherding NEPA through Congress) and Representative John Dingell of Michigan, were primarily involved in the legislative arena. Not only did the number of environmental groups expand during the 1960s, but existing ones experienced tremendous growth. New organizations like the African Wildlife Foundation (1961), the World Wildlife Fund (1961), the Environmental Defense Fund (1967), and the Council on Economic Priorities (1969) broadened the spectrum of group concerns. Meanwhile, the Sierra Club's membership grew tenfold from 1952 to 1969, and the Wilderness Society expanded from twelve thousand members in 1960 to fifty-four thousand in 1970.[36] One of the most compelling themes to emerge from the decade of the 1960s was that the federal government must take a more pervasive role in solving what was beginning to be called "the environmental crisis." The limited partnership between the federal government and the states was insufficient to solve what was already being spoken of in global terms.

EARTH DAYS AND DEREGULATION: 1970–1988

In August 1969, Wisconsin Senator Gaylord Nelson (profiled in Chapter 3) was on his way to Berkeley when he read an article in *Ramparts* magazine about the anti–Vietnam War teach-ins that were sweeping the country. Nelson, who was one of the few members of Congress who had shown an interest in environmental issues, thought a similar approach might work to raise public awareness about the environment. In September, he proposed his idea during a speech in Seattle. Later that fall he incorporated a nonprofit, nonpartisan organization, Environmental Teach-In, pledging $15,000 of his own funds to get it started.[37] In December 1969, Nelson asked former Stanford student body president Denis Hayes to serve as national coordinator for what was to become Earth Day on April 22, 1970. Hayes, who postponed plans to enter Harvard Law School, worked with a $190,000 budget, purchasing a full-page ad in the *New York Times* to announce the teach-in. Not everyone was supportive. President Nixon, who had presented a thirty-seven-point environmental message to Congress a few months earlier, refused to issue a proclamation in support of Earth Day. Instead, the White House issued proclamations for National Archery Week and National Boating Week.[38]

Certainly 1970 marked a watershed year for new environmental organizations, with the founding of the Center for Science in the Public Interest, Citizens for a Better Environment, Environmental Action, Friends of the Earth, the League of Conservation Voters, Natural Resources Defense Council, and Save the Bay. Greenpeace and Public Citizen were formed the following year. This period marks the beginning of a turnaround in leverage, as business and industry mobilized to slow the pace of environmental legislation (see Chapter 2). Environmental organizations were no longer able to monopolize the policy debate to serve their own interests. The range of environmental issues had become so extensive that organized environmental groups were unable to act effectively in all areas. Even more important, many issues had become matters, not for public debate and legislative action, but for administrative choice, an area in which politics was dominated by technical issues that placed a premium on the financial resources necessary to command expertise. This gave considerable political advantage to administrators and private corporate institutions, which employed far more technical personnel than did environmental organizations.

The American public's attitude about the environment has never been very stable, and the decade of the 1970s is a perfect example. When George Gallup asked respondents in his national survey to identify the most important problem facing the nation in November 1967, the environment did not even make the list, nor did it appear when the question was asked in three surveys in 1968 or another survey in 1969. The Vietnam War and the economy overshadowed other concerns of Americans during that period. Not until May 1970 (after Earth Day) did the topic appear as an issue, when it ranked second and was mentioned by 53 percent of those responding. By June 1970, the subject had dropped off the list, replaced in the number one spot by the campus unrest caused by the Vietnam War. Pollution and ecology returned to the list in March 1971 (ranked sixth, with only 7 percent of respondents naming these as the most important problem); by June 1971, these two topics ranked tenth. Environmental issues reemerged as a topic of concern in August and October 1972 and in March 1973, when the subject ranked sixth. But in May 1973, although pollution was ranked as the fifth most important problem facing the nation, it began to be overshadowed by another problem — the energy crisis, which ranked thirteenth. In January 1974, Gallup found that the public considered the energy crisis to be its most important problem, being selected by 46 percent of the public. By July that ranking dropped to number four, mentioned by 4 percent of those surveyed — a figure that stayed relatively constant throughout the rest of the decade.

President Nixon, whose position on environmental protection often reflected public opinion, used the signing of NEPA in 1970 to declare the next ten years as "the environmental decade" and instructed his staff to rush the issue of new legislative proposals. With his creation of the Environmental Protection Agency (EPA) by executive order in 1970, Nixon moved ahead in the race with Congress to take advantage of the public's mood.

In the meantime, Congress too was firmly on the environmental protection bandwagon, enacting more than twenty major pieces of legislation, many of which were refinements of earlier bills. Other laws, such as the Marine Mammal Protection Act (1972), the Federal Environmental Pesticides Control Act (1972), the Resource Conservation and Recovery Act (1976), and the Toxic Substances Control Act (1976), brought the federal government into new areas of environmental protection.

As had been the case in the 1960s, unexpected events periodically refocused attention on the environment.[39] The 1973 Arab oil embargo pushed energy to the top of the policy agenda, although a succession of presidents had sought to make the United States "energy independent." President Jimmy Carter pushed through most of his energy conservation program while turning down the White House thermostat and wearing a sweater indoors. Nuclear power, which was being touted as a cleaner, more reliable alternative to foreign oil, suffered a major setback in 1979 when cooling water at the Three Mile Island nuclear power plant, near Harrisburg, Pennsylvania, dipped below safe levels and triggered a meltdown. Although no radioactive fuel escaped and no one was injured, the accident cast a shadow of doubt over the entire nuclear energy program.

During the summer of 1978, media coverage of incidents near the Love Canal in Niagara Falls, New York, reawakened American concerns over toxic waste. The abandoned canal had been used as a dumping ground for waste during the 1940s by the Hooker Chemicals and Plastics Corporation, which filled in the site and sold it to the Niagara Falls Board of Education for $1. A school was then built near the site, which was located in the midst of a residential area. When local health officials found higher-than-normal rates of birth defects, miscarriages, and other medical problems among Love Canal residents, President Carter ordered the federal government to purchase the 240 homes nearest the site, eventually spending more than $30 million in relocation costs.[40]

Similar incidents occurred in 1979 in West Point, Kentucky, where seventeen thousand drums of leaking chemicals were discovered, and in 1983 in Times Beach, Missouri, where high levels of dioxin were thought to have contaminated the entire town. The Hudson River was found to be contaminated by more than a million pounds of polychlorinated biphenyls (PCBs), and well water in the West was contaminated with cancer-causing trichloroethylene (TCE). The impact of publicity surrounding Love Canal and similar disclosures can be seen in public opinion polls. In July 1978, Resources for the Future (RFF) surveyed Americans' attitudes at a time when the inflation rate topped 10 percent and an endangered fish, the tiny snail darter, had stopped progress on the Tellico Dam. The RFF survey found that environmental public support continued to hold firm, with the number of people who felt "we are spending too little on environmental protection" increasing despite widespread economic problems.[41]

Just as the 1969 Santa Barbara oil spill had galvanized public opinion, the December 3, 1984, leak of deadly methyl isocyanate gas at a Union Carbide plant in Bhopal, India, reawakened interest in environmental disasters. The leak, which killed more than two thousand people and injured two hundred thousand, was brought closer to home when it was revealed that an identical Union Carbide plant was located in Institute, West Virginia. The public and governmental outcry resulted in a shutdown of the plant for several months for inspections and safety checks. These events also caused a shifting of legislative gears as interest changed to toxic and hazardous waste and the health impacts of pollution. With congressional enactment of the Resource Conservation and Recovery Act and the Toxic Substances Control Act in the 1970s, the foundation was laid for the Comprehensive Environmental Response, Compensation, and Liability Act ("Superfund") in 1980 (reauthorized in 1986) and the Hazardous and Solid Waste Amendments in 1984. Concerns about health found their way into the Safe Drinking Water Act Amendments of 1986 (an expansion of the 1974 law) and the Federal Insecticide, Fungicide, and Rodenticide Act Amendments of 1988.

But the 1980s brought an increase in the pessimistic attitudes Americans had toward the efforts that had been made in the previous decade. A Cambridge Reports survey from 1983 to 1989 found that respondents believed that the overall quality of the environment was worse than five years before, with a sharp increase in pessimism beginning in 1987.[42] When the question of "most important problem" was asked again during the 1980s by a Gallup poll, energy often made the list of most important problems, although the environment did not. A separate Gallup survey conducted in September 1989 found that 66 percent of the respondents said they were "extremely concerned" about the pollution of sea life and beaches from the dumping of garbage, medical wastes, and chemicals into the ocean, with the same percentage also expressing extreme concern about the pollution of freshwater rivers, lakes, and other sources of drinking water. Fifty percent of those surveyed said they were extremely concerned about air pollution, and 41 percent expressed concern over the disposal of household garbage and trash.[43]

The 1980s environmental policy agenda was molded most by the administration of President Ronald Reagan, whose main concern was to reduce the amount of governmental regulation (see Chapter 3). Reagan's budget cuts and personnel decisions and a weakening of the previous decade's legislative efforts had a profound effect on policy for the next ten years. Despite those changes, public concern over environmental degradation has risen substantially in recent years, commanding support from large majorities. What was less clear at the end of the 1980s was the strength of the public's commitment to environmental protection.[44]

GLOBAL AWARENESS AND GRIDLOCK: THE 1990s

In 1992, the Gallup International Institute's *Health of the Planet* survey showed that concern about the environment was not limited to wealthy industrialized nations of the Northern Hemisphere. In half of the twenty-two nations surveyed, environmental problems were rated as one of the three most serious problems, and only small percentages of people in any nation dismissed environmental issues as not serious. The survey found that air and water pollution were perceived as the most serious environmental problems affecting nations, with the loss of natural resources mentioned most often by residents of other nations.[45]

After declaring himself "the environmental president" after his 1988 campaign, George Bush was faced, not only with the Reagan legacy of environmental slash and burn, but also with a host of newly discovered environmental problems and crises, many of which had a global focus. Two major pieces of legislation enacted during the Bush administration were the Clean Air Act Amendments of 1990 and the 1992 Energy Policy Act, both of which represented a break in the legislative gridlock that had characterized Congress under Republican administrations. Environmental organizations, many of which experienced a decline in membership growth after the initial burst of activity in the early 1970s, received a booster shot with Earth Day 1990. The Gallup organization classified about 20 percent of the American public as hard-core environmentalists — those who call themselves strong environmentalists and feel that major disruptions are coming if we do not take drastic environmental actions, even at the cost of economic growth.[46]

Perhaps the most important development is the globalization of environmental protection. The 1992 Earth Summit refocused the need for environmental issues to be viewed globally, rather than locally. It also provided dramatic evidence of the need for international cooperation to solve the larger issues of global warming, transboundary pollution, and biodiversity and raised the critical question of whether the industrialized world is willing to pay for environmental protection in developing countries. It also spotlighted the North/South split (the split between nations of the Northern and Southern Hemispheres) between industrialized and developing nations — a controversy not resolved by the end of the decade.

The inauguration of President Bill Clinton and Vice President Al Gore marked yet another turning point in environmental politics. The vice president was widely known as an aggressive advocate of environmental regulation and author of a best-selling call to environmental arms, titled *Earth in the Balance*.[47] Although the environment never surfaced as a key issue in the 1992 presidential campaign, Clinton administration officials immediately called for peaceful coexistence between environmentalists and business as the administration prepared its legislative agenda. Early in 1993, the Clinton administration proposed sweeping changes in public lands policies, including raising grazing fees and imposing hard-rock mining royalties and below-cost timber sales in national forests, as part of a budget bill aimed at reducing the federal deficit. The proposals were immediately attacked by members of Congress from Western states, many of whom were Democrats or represented states where Clinton had won in 1992; as a result the president quickly retreated and shifted his attention to other policy initiatives.

In October 1993, the administration's initiative to add grazing-fee hikes and new environmental safeguards for grazing lands to the Interior Department appropriations bill failed when the Senate was unsuccessful in ending a filibuster of the bill by Republicans and Western Democrats. The proposals were eventually dropped from the bill, but not until Western Senators blasted the administration as launching a war on the West. However, while the Senate resisted changes, the media gave increasingly favorable attention to Secretary Bruce Babbitt's efforts to get Westerners to pay fair prices for using public lands and to increase environmental protection. Babbitt's agenda of reorienting the Bureau of Reclamation away from dam building and toward water conservation, amending the Endangered Species Act to increase habitat preservation, and updating mining and logging policies raised tremendous opposition among some in the West, while encouraging many others who believed such changes to be long overdue. Babbitt argued that public lands policy should be guided by the idea of "dominant public use," requiring the preservation of ecosystems, rather than "multiple use," in which logging, mining, and ranching interests dominate. Babbitt argued that dominant public use requires policymakers to look at the needs for biodiversity, watershed protection, and landscape, as well as the opportunities for extractive industries, and to set priorities accordingly.[48] However, by the time Congress adjourned in 1994, the only conservationist legislation that had been enacted created two new national parks in California, Death Valley and Joshua Tree, and a third protected area, the Mojave Desert.

In 1994, Republican candidates in a number of Western states were successful in running against Babbitt and Clinton's Western lands reforms. The Republicans effectively integrated attacks on Democrats for launching a war on the West with antitax, anti-Washington, and antiregulation rhetoric. The election in 1994 of a Republican Congress shifted the attention to the economic costs and regulatory burdens of environmental protection. There was a growing belief that environmental politics had been guided by popular opinion rather than by science. Critics pointed to sweeping governmental regulations enacted during the Reagan and Bush administrations to reduce concentrations of toxic compounds in water, air, and land even when there was little scientific evidence of risk to humans. Congress, responding to highly publicized concerns about the dangers of asbestos, radon, and toxic waste dumps, quickly wrote legislation that has resulted in costing the government and business an estimated $140 billion a year. Even William Reilly, the EPA administrator under Bush, has said that action in the past was "based on responding to the nightly news. What we have had in the United States is environmental agenda-setting by episodic panic."[49]

When the American economy was relatively healthy, few bothered to question the cost:benefit ratio for such expenditures. But with resources growing increasingly scarce and with the federal government placing a new emphasis on domestic problems like crime, drugs, health care, and the urban infrastructure, this questioning of environmental priorities seemed long overdue. The 1994 House Republican *Contract with America,* written by Newt Gingrich and other Republican House leaders, outlined a set of national issues for House Republican candidates to run on and, after the Republicans won, played a major role in shaping the policy agenda. Among other things, the contract promised to "roll back government regulations and create jobs."[50] Frank Lutz, the Republican pollster who worked with Gingrich in creating the *Contract with America,* told his clients that "Americans believe Washington has gone too far in regulating and they want to turn the clock and paperwork back." Party strategist William Kristol suggested that Republicans immediately identify regulatory "excesses," and he organized a meeting entitled, "What to Kill First: Agencies to Dismantle, Programs to Eliminate, and Regulations to Stop." William Niskanen, head of the Cato Institute, called on Congress to "rein in what I call the 'Nanny State.' Stop telling states where to set speed limits. . . . Stop telling businesses about whether and when employees and customers may smoke."[51] Heritage Foundation analysts published "real life 'horror' stories of individuals who have lost their property or had their business harmed because of overzealous government regulators" and offered the following agenda for reforming regulation: force environmental agencies to base their evaluations of proposed regulations on sound scientific criteria; place a ceiling on the estimated total cost of all regulations promulgated by the agency; force regulators to account for the costs of their proposals, whenever possible; insist that regulators rely on markets rather than red tape; and enact legislation specifying exactly when the federal government must compensate property owners for regulatory takings.[52]

The *Contract with America* did not mention the environment directly, but it included numerous provisions aimed at reducing regulation and promoting economic development rather than preservation. These provisions included requirements that Congress fund the regulatory mandates imposed on states and that agencies perform cost:benefit analyses before issuing regulations, reduce paperwork requirements, compensate landowners for costs resulting from regulation, and formulate a regulatory budget of compliance costs being imposed on business. Republicans in Congress sought to reduce environmental regulation through cutting EPA and Interior Department budgets, attaching riders to appropriations bills that reduced specific protections, and introducing major rewrites of the leading environmental laws.

However, Republican efforts to reduce environmental regulation were short-lived. To begin with, environmental groups challenged the new Republican agenda in the spring of 1995. The largest environmental organizations proposed an Environmental Bill of Rights, to be signed by Americans throughout the nation and presented to Congress and the White House.[53] President Clinton began vetoing appropriations bills with provisions aimed at reducing environmental protection and saw his popularity climb. That encouraged more vetoes and more challenges to the Republican agenda, and by 1996, the Republicans had abandoned their attacks on environmental laws and programs. Clinton skillfully positioned himself between the Republican radicals and popular environmental programs during the 1996 presidential campaign, and his reelection was, in part, the result of his willingness to challenge the congressional Republicans' deregulatory agenda. Bruce Babbitt had become one of the most popular members of the Clinton administration, and he led the criticism of the Republican Congress, which contributed greatly to the president's political rehabilitation in 1996. He was most effective at drawing attention to the Republican Congress's environmental agenda, particularly when he charged that some Republicans were seeking to sell off the national parks. Babbitt's shift from public lands issues in the West to national environmental issues defused criticism of him from inside the administration and in the environmental community.[54] Congress and the White House came together to pass new pesticide and safe drinking water laws in the summer of 1996, which were widely heralded as examples of the potential of bipartisan environmentalism. But the demands for more environmental protection and less burdensome regulation are not easily satisfied, a factor that characterized environmental politics in Clinton's second term.

President Clinton began his second term on the heels of a Harris public opinion poll that showed (despite Republican claims to the contrary) that Americans continue to favor strong environmental policies and do not support reducing the powers of the EPA. Researchers found that over half those surveyed believe that the EPA is needed now more than when it was founded.[55] The study confirmed the findings of another Harris Poll conducted just a few months earlier that found 60 percent of the public opposed to the Republicans' efforts at environmental deregulation, which indeed had failed miserably during Clinton's first term.[56] By 1998, the Harris Poll "feel good index," which measures how people feel about their lives, noted substantial increases in the number of respondents who felt good about the quality of the air, water, and environment where they live and work.[57]

Against this backdrop, many assumed that the president would capitalize on rising public support for environmental protection by proposing new initiatives or the reform of older laws like the Endangered Species Act and Superfund. But Clinton's administration became so engrossed in dealing with scandal and impeachment proceedings that the last four years of his term as president are marked by few notable environmental achievements. The business of retaining the presidency in times that were tumultuous both nationally and globally left Clinton neither time nor congressional support for proposals that environmental groups had long hoped would be passed. Despite his 1993 pledge, Clinton and Vice President Al Gore were more often seen at largely symbolic photo opportunities with the press than at bill-signing ceremonies in the White House.

Clinton and Gore observed Earth Day in April 1998 by traveling to Harper's Ferry, West Virginia, to help volunteers maintain America's longest footpath, the 2,157-mile-long Appalachian Trail. The president used the occasion to urge Congress to "end its attacks on the environment and help build on America's conservation legacy."[58] Later that year they went to the New River in North Carolina to formally designate fourteen American Heritage Rivers.

While the president used the Council on Environmental Quality to trumpet an accelerated cleanup of toxic waste sites and a reduction of paperwork at the EPA,[59] there were several initiatives that hit a dead end. For example, the administration's efforts at issuing more stringent air quality standards were struck down by a federal court in 1999. The EPA had tried to issue new regulations for particulate matter and ozone, but the court ruled that the standards had not been based on public health concerns and thus constituted an unconstitutional delegation of power to the agency by Congress.[60] Attempts to strengthen right to know laws about toxic chemical releases were overshadowed by research that showed existing laws to be ineffective. In mid-1999, a study by the Environmental Working Group showed that almost four of every ten factories tracked by the EPA over a two-year period were guilty of significant violations of air quality regulations. The study noted that although major violations were punishable by fines that could have ranged into the millions of dollars, government officials had disregarded guidelines for setting the amounts, and in some cases, offending firms paid no penalty at all. The report blamed the EPA for poor oversight and state regulators for enforcement failures.[61] A 1999 EPA study also found that, rather than meeting the administration's goals of a reduction in toxic chemical releases, the amount of toxic chemicals released into the environment by industrial plants had actually increased. The report attributed the increase to factories sending their metal wastes to landfills instead of to recycling centers, thus ending years of steady decline in toxic chemicals entering the environment.[62] But the president did herald the fact that the administration had established a Brownfields National Partnership, which brought together the resources of more than a dozen federal agencies to help thousands of communities clean up abandoned pieces of land that had been contaminated by previous industrial use. Moreover, in October 1999, Clinton used his weekly radio address to announce that, effective January 1, 2000, new rules would significantly lower the amount of twenty-seven dangerous chemicals, including dioxin, that companies could use before reporting discharges to the public.

Clinton could point to some victories in the area of natural resource protection. For example, the federal government agreed to acquire mining property near Yellowstone National Park and to decontaminate the site from the effects of earlier mining activities. Among the more noteworthy preservation accomplishments was the acquisition of the largest privately owned stand of ancient redwoods in the Headwaters Forest in northern California—a deal negotiated among the landowner, the federal government, and the state. The president also sought funds to continue the restoration of the South Florida ecosystem and to purchase fifty thousand additional acres of land on the northern edge of Everglades National Park—issues important to the region's politically powerful leaders.

On a global level, the administration called on a reluctant Congress for more bilateral and multilateral environmental assistance to address issues such as biodiversity and to fund contributions to the United Nations' environmental agencies. In the area of global climate change, the United States participated in negotiations calling for cuts in greenhouse gas emissions, which became formalized as the Kyoto Protocol in December 1997, but by the end of the decade there was little sign that the projected reductions would be realized.

Clinton's "common sense environmental reforms," such as helping American business compete more effectively in the global market through environmental technology, were not new, and they lacked the luster of even the Bush administration's environmental efforts. The president had, for the most part, piggybacked on proposals that preceded his administration, thus disappointing environmental leaders who had supported the Clinton-Gore ticket as a potential for reawakening the nation's environmental conscience. Those hopes became lost in issues that, by the end of 1999, had pushed the environment almost to the bottom of the political agenda: sexual scandals, impeachment, conflict in the Balkans, and violence in the workplace and the schools.

Most observers have commented that, although there was some disappointment that the Clinton-Gore ticket failed to live up to its advance billing as proactive on environmental protection, the administration was able to stop the Republican-controlled Congress from dismantling controversial laws like the Endangered Species Act or cutting agency budgets, as had been feared. The Clinton administration was able to build on the groundwork laid by congressional leaders and environmental organizations. His goal, Clinton said, was to block attempts to roll back safeguards for the nation's food, water, and air: "I want an America in the year 2000 where no child should have to live near a toxic waste dump, where no parent should have to worry about the safety of a child's glass of water, and no neighborhood should be put in harm's way by pollution from a nearby factory."[63]

NOTES

1. Bill Clinton, "Remarks Announcing A New Environmental Policy." *Weekly Compilation of Presidential Documents, 29,* No. 6 (1993): 159.

2. Roderick Nash, *American Environmentalism,* 3rd ed. (New York: McGraw-Hill, 1990), xi. Nash has published numerous works on American environmental history, including *The American Conservation Movement* (St. Charles, MO: Forum, 1974); *Wilderness and the American Mind* (New Haven, CT: Yale University Press, 1982); and *The Rights of Nature: A History of Environmental Ethics* (Madison: University of Wisconsin Press, 1988).

3. The colonial period is also covered in David Cushan Coyle, *Conservation* (New Brunswick, NJ: Rutgers University Press, 1957).

4. Nash, *American Environmentalism,* xi.

5. Coyle, *Conservation,* 8–9, 21.

6. George Perkins Marsh, *Man and Nature; or Physical Geography as Modified by Human Action* (New York: Scribner, 1864). See also David Lowenthal, *George Perkins Marsh: Versatile Vermonter* (New York: Columbia University Press, 1958).

7. Donald Worster, *American Environmentalism: The Formative Period, 1860–1915* (New York: Wiley, 1973), 3.

8. One of the historians who has researched the sportsmen's movement is John E. Reiger, *American Sportsmen and the Origins of Conservation* (Norman: University of Oklahoma Press, 1986).

9. Ibid., 53.

10. The biographical materials on these early pioneers provide an excellent background on the formation of the early conservation movement. See, for example, George T. Morgan, Jr., *William B. Greeley, A Practical Forester* (St. Paul, MN: Forest History Society, 1961); and Wallace Stegner, *Beyond the Hundredth Meridian: John Wesley Powell and the Second Coming of the West* (Boston, MA: Houghton Mifflin, 1954).

11. Another one of the major contributors to the field of American environmental history is Joseph Petulla, *Environmental Protection in the United States* (San Francisco, CA: San Francisco Study Center, 1987), 13–30.

12. Suellen Hoy, "Municipal Housekeeping: The Role of Women in Improving Urban Sanitation Practices," in *Pollution and Reform in American Cities 1870–1930,* ed. Martin Melosi (Austin: University of Texas Press, 1980), 173–198. See also the spring 1984 issue of *Environmental Review* for a summary of the contributions of women in the environmental movement.

13. See Harold McCracken, *George Catlin and the Old Frontier* (New York: Dial, 1959), for a biographical perspective on one of the frontier environmentalists.

14. There are two ways to gauge the impact of Thoreau on the development of the environmental movement, especially his sojourn at Walden Pond. One is to read his own words, such as *The Annotated Walden* (New York: Potter, 1970) and *Consciousness in Concord* (Boston, MA: Houghton Mifflin, 1958). There have been numerous attempts to characterize this complex individual, including these by the following biographers: Milton Meltzer and Walter Harding, *A Thoreau Profile* (New York: Crowell, 1962); Sherman Paul, *The Shores of America: Thoreau's Inward Exploration* (Urbana: University of Illinois Press, 1959); and Robert Richardson, *Henry Thoreau: A Life of the Mind* (Berkeley: University of California Press, 1986).

15. The urban sanitation issue became one of the cornerstones of urban environmentalism. See George Rosen, *A History of Public Health* (New York: MD Publications, 1958).

16. See Suellen Hoy. *Chasing Dirt: The American Pursuit of Cleanliness* (New York: Oxford University Press, 1995), 117–120.

17. There are few comprehensive studies of the early organizations except for those produced by the groups themselves. See, for example, Michael Cohen, *The History of the Sierra Club 1892–1970* (San Francisco, CA: Sierra Club, 1988).

18. For more information on this early period, see Henry Clepper, *Origins of American Conservation* (New York: Ronald Press, 1966); and Peter Wild, *Pioneer Conservationists of Western America* (Missoula, MT: Mountain Press, 1979).

19. Samuel P. Hays, *Conservation and the Gospel of Efficiency* (Cambridge, MA: Harvard University Press, 1959), 5.

20. Pinchot writes of his efforts in *The Fight for Conservation* (New York: Harcourt Brace, 1910), and *Breaking New Ground* (New York: Harcourt Brace, 1947). Biographers who have identified his critical role in the Progressive movement include Martin Fausold, *Gifford Pinchot, Bull Moose Progressive* (Syracuse, NY: Syracuse University Press, 1961); M. Nelson McGeary, *Gifford Pinchot: Forester-Politician* (Princeton, NJ: Princeton University Press, 1960); and Harold T. Pinkett, *Gifford Pinchot: Private and Public Forester* (Urbana: University of Illinois Press, 1970).

21. In contrast to Pinchot, Muir's views are found in his book, *Our National Parks* (Boston, MA: Houghton Mifflin, 1901), and *The Yosemite* (New York: Century, 1912). One of the most widely researched environmental pioneers, Muir has been the subject of dozens of biographers, including Michael P. Cohen, *The Pathless Way: John Muir and the American Wilderness* (Madison: University of Wisconsin Press, 1984); Stephen Fox, *John Muir and His*

Legacy (Boston, MA: Little, Brown, 1981); Frederick Turner, *Rediscovering America: John Muir in His Time and Ours* (New York: Viking, 1985); and Linnie M. Wolfe, *Son of the Wilderness: The Life of John Muir* (New York: Knopf, 1945).

22. Nash, *American Environmentalism,* 84.

23. Hays, *Conservation and the Gospel of Efficiency,* 132.

24. The activities of the Conservation Congresses are outlined in Grant McConnell, "The Conservation Movement — Past and Present," *Western Political Quarterly, 7,* no. 3 (September 1954): 463–478.

25. Hays, *Conservation and the Gospel of Efficiency,* 69.

26. Many historians and analysts of the Progressive period have downgraded its importance to contemporary environmentalism. See Geoffrey Wandesforde-Smith, "Moral Outrage and the Progress of Environmental Policy: What Do We Tell the Next Generation about How to Care for the Earth?" in *Environmental Policy in the 1990s,* ed. Norman J. Vig and Michael E. Kraft (Washington, DC: Congressional Quarterly Press, 1990), 334–335.

27. For a discussion of the evolution of public health and environmental protection, see Robert Gottlieb, *Forcing the Spring: The Transformation of the American Environmental Movement* (Washington, DC: Island Press, 1993).

28. For a summary of the development of the parks and wilderness areas, see Dyan Zaslowsky and the Wilderness Society, *These American Lands* (New York: Henry Holt, 1986).

29. There is a wealth of historical information on the National Park Service and its programs, including William C. Everhart, *The National Park Service* (New York: Praeger, 1972); Ronald A. Foresta, *America's National Parks and Their Keepers* (Washington, DC: Resources for the Future, 1984); Alfred Runte, *National Parks: The American Experience* (Lincoln: University of Nebraska Press, 1982); David J. Simon, ed., *Our Common Lands* (Washington, DC: Island Press, 1988); and *Investing in Park Futures: A Blueprint for Tomorrow* (Washington, DC: National Parks and Conservation Association, 1988).

30. Rachel Carson, *Silent Spring* (Greenwich, CT: Fawcett, 1962). For biographical material on the woman who is largely credited with reviving the contemporary environmental movement, see Paul Brooks, *The House of Life: Rachel Carson at Work* (Boston, MA: Houghton Mifflin, 1972); Carol Gartner, *Rachel Carson* (New York: Ungar, 1983); H. Patricia Hynes, *The Recurring Silent Spring* (New York: Pergamon Press, 1989); and Philip Sterling, *Sea and Earth: The Life of Rachel Carson* (New York: Crowell, 1970).

31. Paul Ehrlich, *The Population Bomb* (New York: Ballantine, 1968).

32. For an account of this event, see Carol Steinhart and John Steinhart, *Blowout: A Case Study of the Santa Barbara Oil Spill* (Belmont, CA: Wadsworth, 1972). An extensive bibliography on the spill was compiled by Kay Walstead, *Oil Pollution in the Santa Barbara Channel* (Santa Barbara: University of California, Santa Barbara Library, 1972).

33. Zaslowsky, *These American Lands,* 37.

34. See Lewis L. Gould, *Lady Bird Johnson and the Environment* (Lawrence: University of Kansas Press, 1988).

35. John C. Esposito, *Vanishing Air* (New York: Grossman, 1970), 292.

36. Samuel P. Hays, "From Conservation to Environment," *Environmental Review, 6* (Fall 1982): 37.

37. Jack Lewis, "The Spirit of the First Earth Day," *EPA Journal, 16,* no. 1 (January–February 1990): 9–10.

38. See John C. Whitaker, *Striking a Balance: Environment and Natural Resources Policy in the Nixon-Ford Years* (Washington, DC: American Enterprise Institute, 1976), 6.

39. Samuel P. Hays, *Beauty, Health and Permanence: Environmental Politics in the U.S., 1955–1985* (Cambridge: Cambridge University Press, 1987), 61.

40. See Lois Gibbs, *Love Canal* (Albany: State University of New York Press, 1983); and Adeline Gordon Levine, *Love Canal: Science, Politics and People* (Lexington, MA: Heath, 1982).

41. Robert Cameron Mitchell, "The Public Speaks Again: A New Environmental Survey," *Resources, 60* (September–October 1978): 2.

42. David Rapp, "Special Report," *Congressional Quarterly,* January 20, 1990, 138.

43. "Household Waste Threatening Environment; Recycling Helps Ease Disposal Problem," *Gallup Report 280,* January 1990, 30–34.

44. See Riley E. Dunlap, "Public Opinion in the 1980s: Clear Consensus, Ambiguous Commitment," *Environment, 33,* no. 8 (October 1991): 9–15, 32–37.

45. Press release, "Environment Given Priority over Economic Growth in Both Rich and Poor Nations," Washington, DC, George H. Gallup International Institute, May 4, 1992. See also Riley E. Dunlap, George H. Gallup, Jr., and Alec M. Gallup, *The Health of the Planet Survey* (Washington, DC: George H. Gallup International Institute, May 1992).

46. George Gallup, Jr., and Frank Newport, "Americans Strongly in Tune with the Purpose of Earth Day 1990," *The Gallup Poll Monthly,* April 1990, 6.

47. Albert Gore, *Earth in the Balance* (Boston: Houghton Mifflin, 1992).

48. Margaret Kriz, "Quick Draw," *National Journal,* November 13, 1993, 2711–2716, quote on 2713.

49. Keith Schneider, "New View Calls Environmental Policy Misguided," *New York Times,* March 21, 1993, 1.

50. See Ed Gillespie and Rob Shellhas, eds., *Contract with America* (New York: Times Books, 1994): 125–141. For a discussion of the history and evolution of the *Contract with America,* see Elizabeth Drew, *Showdown: The Struggle between the Gingrich Congress and the Clinton White House* (New York: Simon and Schuster, 1996), 28–34.

51. Quoted in Cindy Skryzycki, "Hill Republicans Promise a Regulatory Revolution," *Washington Post,* January 4, 1995, A1.

52. Craig E. Richardson and Geoff C. Ziebart, *Red Tape in America: Stories from the Front Lines* (Washington, DC: Heritage Foundation, 1995), v.

53. B. J. Bergman, "Standing Up for the Planet," *Sierra,* March/April 1995, 79–80.

54. Tom Kenworthy, "In Smooth Water Now," *Washington Post National Weekly Edition,* December 11–17, 1995.

55. "Harris Poll: Americans Want Conservation Laws," *Columbia University Record, 21,* no. 13 (January 19, 1996): 29.

56. "Poll Shows Opposition to Easing Environmental Rules," available at <http://www.pond.com/~hhorning/sfund/sfund/polls.html>, March 18, 2000.

57. Humphrey Taylor, "Nation's 'Feel Good Index' Rises Sharply," *The Harris Poll #26,* June 3, 1998.

58. White House Press Release, "President Clinton: Saving America's Natural Treasures," April 22, 1998.

59. "Protecting the Environment: President Clinton and Vice President Gore," available at <http://www.whitehouse.gov/CEQ/accomp.html>, March 18, 2000.

60. *American Trucking Association v. U.S. Environmental Protection Agency,* 175 F3d 1027 (D.C. Cir., 1999).

61. Traci Watson, "Study: 4 of 10 Factories Violated Clean Air Act," *USA Today,* May 20, 1999, 3A.

62. "Toxic Chemical Release Rises," *Arizona Republic,* May 23, 1999, A28.

63. "Protecting the Environment: President Clinton and Vice President Gore."

FOR FURTHER READING

Richard N. L. Andrews. *Managing the Environment, Managing Ourselves: A History of American Environmental Policy*. New Haven, CT: Yale University Press, 1999.

Gary C. Bryner. *Environmental Movements in the 21st Century*. Lanham, MD: Roman and Littlefield, 2000.

Robert Engberg and Donald Wesling, eds. *John Muir: To Yosemite and Beyond*. Salt Lake City: University of Utah Press, 1999.

Mary Graham. *The Morning after Earth Day: Practical Environmental Politics*. Washington, DC: Brookings Institution Press, 1999.

Benjamin Kline. *First along the River: A Brief History of the U.S. Environmental Movement*, 2nd ed. San Francisco, CA: Acada Books, 2000.
Aldo Leopold. *For the Health of the Land: Previously Unpublished Essays and Other Writings*. Covelo, CA: Island Press, 1999.
Carolyn Merchant, ed. *Green vs. Gold: Sources in California's Environmental History*. Covelo, CA: Island Press, 1998.
Gifford Pinchot. *Breaking New Ground: Commemorative Edition*. Washington, DC: Island Press, 1998.
Charles T. Rubin. *The Green Crusade: Rethinking the Roots of Environmentalism*. Lanham, MD: Rowman and Littlefield, 1998.

I'd rather see a Cow
than a Condo .....

CHAPTER 2

Participants in the Environmental Debate

We can't be extreme enough in this day and age, when we're losing the earth so rapidly. People want a movement that's strong, tough, and unbending. We won't always win, but we shouldn't lose because we're willing to compromise.
— Martin Litton, former Sierra Club director[1]

On October 21, 1998, a group calling itself the Earth Liberation Front (ELF) sent an e-mail message to KCFR-FM public radio in Denver, in which it claimed responsibility for a series of seven fires on Vail Mountain. The message read:

> On behalf of the lynx, five buildings and four ski lifts at Vail were reduced to ashes on the night of Sunday, October 18. Vail, Inc. is already the largest ski operation in North America and now wants to expand even further. The 12 miles of roads and 885 acres of clearcuts will ruin the last, best lynx habitat in the state. Putting profits ahead of Colorado's wildlife will not be tolerated. This action is just a warning. We will be back if this greedy corporation continues to trespass into wild and unroaded areas. For your safety and convenience, we strongly advise skiers to choose other destinations until Vail cancels its inexcusable plans for expansion.[2]

The group's action caused $12 million in damage to the ski resort—the costliest act of ecoterrorism in the United States. At issue was an 885-acre expansion project, which environmental group leaders claimed would interfere with plans to reintroduce the North American lynx to the state. A federal court had turned down a request for an injunction from the Colorado Environmental Coalition, Defenders of Wildlife, and the Sierra Club to halt the project on grounds that the U.S. Forest Service had failed to consider the project's impact on wildlife.

◁ *Signs like this one in a field outside Durango, Colorado, are becoming more common as farmers and environmental groups show their opposition to urban sprawl into rural and agricultural areas.*

The ELF was founded in Great Britain in 1992 by a splinter group of Earth First! members who were said to be frustrated at the pace of species protection. They claimed responsibility for a series of actions, ranging from spraying red paint on the Mexican consulate in Boston in 1997 to protest the treatment of peasants in Chiapas, Mexico, to setting fires at U.S. Agriculture Department buildings in Olympia, Washington, and the "freeing" of 310 animals from a Wisconsin fur farm in collaboration with the Animal Liberation Front, another radical group. The ELF surfaced again in January 1999 when the group said it was responsible for a fire that destroyed the corporate headquarters of U.S. Forest Industries in Medford, Oregon. This time, the ELF sent a fax that stated: "To celebrate the holidays, we decided on a bonfire. . . . This action is a payback and it is a warning, to all others responsible we do not sleep and we wont [*sic*] quit."[3]

The radical beliefs and tactics of groups like the ELF and Earth First! are an important part of the environmental debate. Radical organizations shun traditional structure and administrative rules, preferring militant action, termed "monkeywrenching" and "ecotage," to the traditional political strategies used by mainstream environmental organizations. Many subscribe to the school of ecological thought termed *deep ecology* by Norwegian philosopher Arne Naess. Deep ecology is philosophically based on Naess's seven tenets. A rejection of the "shallow ecology movement," it focuses on the fight against pollution, resource depletion, and the consumption of goods by people living in developed countries.[4]

There have been flare-ups of radical environmental activity since the early 1970s, although it is often difficult to trace acts of violence to specific groups or individuals. Generally, their actions are shunned by both environmental organizations and groups associated with the environmental opposition. But the mainstream groups also use the radicals as a foil, realizing that the posturing and activities of such groups cause their own agendas to be perceived as much more reasonable and acceptable in contrast.

This chapter uses the concept of group theory as a way of explaining how interest groups influence public policy and of deciphering the actions of the primary actors and stakeholders in the debate over the environment and natural resources. Adherents to this approach believe that political decisions are the result of the struggles among competing interests with access to the political process. Key to understanding group theory is the assumption that some groups will have more political access than others because of superior financial resources, leadership, organization, or public support for their cause.[5] Although this book does not attempt to delve into the theoretical debate over *how much* influence various groups have in the making of environmental policy or to apply the pluralist tradition of American politics to other countries to explain their environmental politics, it does describe their role in the environmental debate. The chapter begins with an overview of the major mainstream U.S. environmental organizations, followed by a discussion of the environmental justice movement and the development of an environmental opposition. "The Global Dimension" section shifts to a discussion of international actors, ranging from nongovernmental organizations to the green party movement and to the international organizations that attempt to protect the environment on a global scale. The chapter touches briefly on these participants' strategies, successes, and failures and provides a summary of their participation in the policy-making process.

U.S. ENVIRONMENTAL ORGANIZATIONS

In the one hundred years since the founding of the first American environmental associations, there has been a gradual evolution of the movement. Seven of the ten most powerful groups (known collectively as the "Group of Ten") were founded before 1960. Most have influential local or regional chapters and have broadened their interests from land and wildlife issues to broader, "second-generation" issues, which are not necessarily site- or species-specific.[6]

These mainstream organizations have as a common strategy an emphasis on lobbying, although their specific focus often varies. The Sierra Club, the Wilderness Society, and the National Parks and Conservation Association, for example, have tended to emphasize the preservation of public lands for future generations, while groups such as the National Wildlife Federation and Izaak Walton League, with a large percentage of sports enthusiasts and hunters within their constituency, are more involved with habitat preservation for wildlife. Some groups, such as the American Lung Association, are primarily interested in pollution and its impact on public health. But they sometimes work with nature-oriented groups on issues such as air pollution.

When the Environmental Defense Fund (EDF) was founded in 1967, a new breed of organization joined these mainstream groups. EDF and, later, the Natural Resources Defense Council made environmental litigation an art form, moving group strategy from the legislative to the judicial arena. These groups have benefited from the citizen suit provisions in virtually every federal environmental statute since the 1970 Clean Air Act. The provisions allow "any person" to sue private parties for noncompliance with the law and to sue, not only for injunctive relief, but also for civil penalties. This allows those who sue to recover the cost of attorneys' fees and "mitigation fees" in lieu of, or in addition to, civil fines. The groups often receive from offending companies direct transfer payments, which help fund their operations and projects, making litigation an attractive group strategy (see Chapter 3).[7]

Other mainstream groups, although smaller in size and resources, conduct research or grass-roots campaigns. Two of the most prominent are Environmental Action and the League of Conservation Voters. Founded in 1970, Environmental Action, which merged with the Environmental Task Force in 1988, conducts lobbying, research, education, and organizing efforts. The group developed a "Dirty Dozen" campaign to spotlight the environmental records of members of Congress and has actively lobbied against utility companies and for bottle-deposit legislation. Also founded in 1970, the League of Conservation

Voters has two goals: to help elect pro-environment candidates and to monitor congressional performance. It is not the group's members that give it clout, but its annual report, the *National Environmental Scorecard,* which ranks the voting records of each member of Congress on environmental legislation.

Some environmental organizations are characterized by their emphasis on a single issue. These groups rarely shift from their area of concern to another issue, although some overlap is developing. Clean Water Action, founded in 1971, conducts research and lobbies on issues related to drinking water and groundwater resources. Recognizing the interrelatedness of pollution, Clean Water Action also became involved in the passage of the 1986 Superfund legislation and the 1990 Clean Air Act Amendments. The Clean Air Network is an umbrella organization that brings together national and grass-roots groups to promote implementation of the Clean Air Act and oppose efforts by industry to weaken its provisions. The Defenders of Wildlife work, as their group's name implies, to protect wildlife habitats through education and advocacy programs. Founded in 1947, the group is now working to strengthen the Endangered Species Act and develop funding for wildlife refuges.

Among the more recently created environmental organizations are those, often with a purely regional base of operation, seeking to preserve individual species. Many of these groups were organized in the 1980s after the initial burst of momentum in the environmental movement had passed. Although these groups limit their activities to individual species, they often form coalitions to preserve natural habitats and wildlife ranges. Their membership is typically smaller (ten thousand to forty thousand) and may include researchers dedicated to scientific study of the species. Typical of such groups are Bat Conservation International, founded in 1982, and the Mountain Lion Preservation Foundation, founded in 1986. Both of these organizations emphasize education as well as research and habitat studies. The Mountain Lion Preservation Foundation, for example, has developed an aggressive media campaign in California to educate the public on the habitat needs of this animal, as well as lobbying for a permanent state ban on the hunting of the mountain lion (also known as the cougar, puma, or panther).

Property-oriented groups, such as The Nature Conservancy and Ducks Unlimited, represent examples of long-standing organizations that focus their efforts on management and preservation. Both of the groups mentioned here have invested private funds for purchasing lands that are then reserved for wildlife habitats. One of the older environmental groups, Ducks Unlimited, with chapters throughout the United States, was founded in 1937 by hunters seeking to preserve wetland habitats. The Nature Conservancy, founded in 1951, has privately purchased land for habitat protection throughout the United States as well as global ecological preserves that are home to endangered species.

Another subgroup is comprised of organizations that originated or are based in the United States, have members throughout the world, and have broadened their interests to more global concerns. The largest international environmental organization, Greenpeace, was founded in 1969, as the Don't Make A Wave Committee, by a small group of Sierra Club members and peace activists. Greenpeace drew its name from a rented boat used to protest nuclear weapons testing in the Aleutian Islands. Its initial effort was the Save the Whales campaign, which was later expanded to include other sea animals such as the Steller sea lion and dolphins. Since then, Greenpeace has extended its concerns to issues ranging from the use of chlorine bleach during paper processing to nuclear disarmament and weapons testing to toxic pollution to nuclear power to drift nets to protection of the Antarctic. Greenpeace activities have often bordered on the radical, as was the case in 1989 when a Greenpeace ship protested a Trident missile test and was rammed by a U.S. Navy vessel. The group is known, too, for its ability to use the media to its advantage, as demonstrated when its activists are pictured in small boats placing themselves between whales and whaling ships.

Environmental organizations have periodically attempted to put aside their individual interests and have formed coalitions in an attempt to advance their collective interests. In 1946, the Natural Resources Council of America was formed to bring together conservation organizations to serve as an information-sharing body and sponsor policy briefings and surveys of public opinion on issues such as energy needs and conservation. Coalitions have also been formed to lobby specific pieces of legislation, such as the National Clean Air Coalition, which came together during debate over the 1977 and 1990 Clean Air Act Amendments. Consensus reports are becoming more commonplace, such as the 1985 publication of *An Environmental Agenda for the Future* and the 1989 *Blueprint for the Future,* which was prepared to assist the Bush administration in developing environmental policy. Such reports also give groups the appearance of more clout, since legislators perceive them as presenting a unified front.

The membership of environmental organizations has ebbed and flowed over the past three decades, often in response to the government's environmental initiatives or electoral change. With the flurry of environmental legislation enacted in the late 1960s and early 1970s, the membership of the organizations grew enormously. When energy replaced the environment as a key issue during the Carter administration, the groups' direct mail campaigns generally yielded just enough members to replace those who failed to renew. But two of Reagan's appointees, Secretary of the Interior James Watt and Environmental Protection Agency Administrator Anne Burford, were perceived as a threat to the movement, which resulted in a surge in membership as environmental organizations warned potential members of what might happen if they did not have the funds to closely monitor Reagan administration policies. The Wilderness Society's membership grew by 144 percent between 1980 and 1983, with the Sierra Club increasing by 90 percent and the Defenders of Wildlife and Friends of the Earth by 40 percent each. Another surge took place at the turn of the decade, when the national environmental lobby's U.S. membership exceeded three million and attention was focused on Earth Day 1990. But by the early 1990s, even though the environment appeared to be a core value for most Americans, membership decreased again, with many of the groups reducing staffing, closing field offices, and narrowing their program focus to just a few, key issues. Despite the loss of members among the largest organizations, small, grass-roots groups appeared to be gaining in strength, with their concentration on local or regional issues. (See "Another View, Another Voice: Audie Bock: Green Party Legislator.")

THE ENVIRONMENTAL JUSTICE MOVEMENT

From the early 1960s through the 1980s, the majority of the mainstream environmental organizations focused on issues related to natural resource management and preservation, along with efforts to control air and water pollution. Their leadership (and support) came primarily from middle- and upper middle-class whites, and surveys found that members of environmental groups were considerably better educated, more likely to have white-collar jobs, and more likely to have high incomes in comparison to the larger population.[8]

At the same time, the civil rights movement had become a fixture in American politics, with a focus on bringing jobs and social justice to poor communities and improving the economic conditions of minorities and people of color. Often community leaders made a trade-off between bringing jobs and industry into neighborhoods faced with high unemployment and the cost of exposing workers and their families to industrial pollution and toxic hazards, a condition political scientist Robert Bullard refers to as "job blackmail." Bullard notes that, eventually, there was a convergence of environmentalism and the civil rights movement that called for a balancing of economic development, social justice, and environmental protection.[9] In cities like Los Angeles, African-American and Latino groups formed in the mid-1980s to fight the siting of municipal and hazardous waste incinerators in poor, largely minority neighborhoods. Native American groups have organized against landfills on their reservations, which are not subject to federal or state environmental laws, and farm workers in California's Central Valley protested the hazardous waste landfill and a proposed incinerator in one tiny community.[10]

These community struggles developed a political focus from two hallmark events. In 1987, the United Church of Christ Commission for Racial Justice published a controversial study, *Toxic Wastes and Race in the United States: A National Report on the Racial and Socio-Economic Characteristics of Communities with Hazardous Waste Sites,* which concluded that the poor and members of racial minority groups were being treated inequitably in the siting of such facilities. The report was followed in October 1991 by the First National People of Color Environmental Leadership Summit in Washington, D.C. The meeting produced a set of Principles of Environmental Justice that called upon people of color to secure their economic and social liberation, which had been denied them as a result of the "poisoning of our communities and land and the genocide of our peoples."[11] In calling for environmental justice, the summit's leaders demanded

Another View, Another Voice

AUDIE BOCK
Green Party Legislator

"Vote Green, Not Machine." With those words as her campaign slogan, an Oakland, California, woman became the first member of the Green Party to be elected to the California legislature, in April 1999. Audie Bock, who holds a B.A. degree from Wellesley College and a master's degree from Harvard, works as a part-time college instructor and is a single parent. She says she joined the Green Party after volunteering for Ralph Nader's 1996 presidential campaign and that she wanted to work together "with others who want to change the back-scratch, business-as-usual approach of big politics."

Bock's victory was a political surprise to those who follow the conventional wisdom of partisan politics. For six years she had lived in the predominantly black district she represents, where the voter registration figure is 65 percent for Democrats and only 1.2 percent for the Green Party. Her major opponent was the former mayor of Oakland, Elihu Harris, who had previously served six terms in the state legislature. But the career politician faced a five-way primary election, and many believe he did not have a grasp of the disaffection of the area's voters, who chose Bock by only 327 votes in the runoff election. Other pundits faulted the Democratic party itself, which sent out mailers to voters in predominantly African-American neighborhoods offering them a free chicken dinner if they went to the polls. Some called the controversial tactic a bribe with racial overtones, intended to entice black voters to the polls.

Bock ran on a platform that called for better schools, cleaner air and water, and quality health care, transportation, and housing—traditional political values. "Our living standard has declined because we are not educating our kids, caring for our sick, and maintaining our urban environment," she says. "It's time to reverse the trend."[1] Her antiestablishment profile attracted votes from Republicans, Democrats, and other third-party supporters. But does the vote reflect a "green" constituency? Despite the claims of the Green Party of California that the election was "a victory for democracy," it is doubtful Bock capitalized on the Green Party platform of ecological wisdom, social justice, grass-roots democracy, and nonviolence.

In the United States, the Green Party USA has worked hard to establish a base of political support through grass-roots organizing, and is active in forty-six states. Party efforts have focused on local and community issues—not all of them directly related to the environment—including homelessness and equal rights, in addition to recycling and toxic dumping. Initially, the Green Party found its greatest political success in New England; by 1990, the party's leaders realized that the loose network structure was inadequate. A restructuring took place in 1991, establishing a Green Congress and national annual

(continued)

Green Gathering. As of May 1999, sixty-eight Green Party members held elected office in seventeen states; the majority were members of city councils or local boards.

Audie Bock's victory marked a watershed for the Green Party USA since her election gave the movement national attention and electoral momentum. By finally electing one of its members to a state legislature, the Party claimed victory as well. But the unique character of the legislative district, the manipulations of Democratic leaders, and the special circumstances surrounding her bid for state office are more likely a political aberration than a mandate for change. As one observer put it, "Something like this could only happen in California!"

More important, Bock found that her first term was made more difficult because of the partisan nature of the state's legislature. Basic housekeeping tasks like issuing a press release or setting up a website were frustrated by the fact that no one was assigned to assist a nonaligned third-party legislator—she had difficulty even finding a meeting room because even building space is allocated on a partisan basis. A bill she had sponsored to create a resource center on workplace safety for young people was defeated even though there was no organized opposition and it had broad support from a coalition of employers, labor groups, students and educators. But Bock learned a hard lesson—a message that politics, not policy, prevailed and that Democratic legislators would not allow her to build a record of accomplishment to use as a base for a reelection bid. Bock said that the message was loud and clear; still, she refused to align herself with either mainstream party, while realizing that her maverick status would also require some compromise. "Everyone has to be willing to negotiate."[2]

For More Information

For more information on the Green Party USA, contact its national clearinghouse at PO Box 1134, Lawrence, MA 01842, or call (978) 682-4353. The group's website is at <http://www.greens.org/gpusa>.

Notes

1. "Assemblymember Audie Bock Talks about the Greening of the California Legislature," *Public Affairs Report* (September 1999): 2.

2. Ibid.

the right to participate as equal partners in environmental decision making, free from any form of discrimination or bias. But it also placed a responsibility on individuals to make personal and consumer choices in their life-styles that minimized the use of natural resources and produced as little waste as possible.

Subsequently, national civil rights leaders criticized environmental organizations and political decisionmakers for "environmental racism"—a term used to describe the fact that "whether by conscious design or institutional neglect, communities of color in urban ghetttos, in rural 'poverty pockets,' or on economically impoverished Native American reservations face some of the worst environmental devastation in the nation."[12]

There was a variety of responses to these charges. Civil rights organizations like the National Association for the Advancement of Colored People and the American Civil Liberties Union have begun working side-by-side with mainstream environmental organizations such as the Natural Resources Defense Council. Larger environmental groups, such as the Sierra Club and the Wilderness Society, have made attempts to diversify their governing boards and staff, with a corresponding "trickling down" to state governments, which, in turn, have begun to enact some form of environmental justice laws.[13] In 1994, President Bill Clinton issued an executive order that instructed federal agencies to integrate environmental justice into their ongoing missions and EPA administrator Carol Browner announced that she would make environmental equity a part of her agency's decision-making processes.

There is, however, a discordant note among those who believe that the environmental justice movement is facing challenges it cannot overcome. Brookings Institution scholar Christopher H. Foreman Jr. has argued that many of the goals of the environmental justice movement—such as community empowerment, social justice, and public health—are difficult for federal officials to address using the environment as a policy "hook." He also believes that such advocacy directs community attention away from the problems that pose the greatest risks and "may therefore have the ironic effect of undermining public health in precisely those communities it endeavors to help." He cautions that there are significant political hurdles to be overcome as well, such as a lack of congressional support and the infeasibility of attempting to ban new siting in and near low-income communities and communities of color. Many leaders concur with Foreman's conclusion that what is really at stake, not only in the environmental justice movement but in the environmental movement itself, is what he calls "an abiding hunger for livable communities."[14]

ENVIRONMENTAL OPPOSITION IN THE UNITED STATES

The Progressive Era ideals of the conservation movement had almost universal support throughout the early twentieth century, although the early groups were still dominated by business organizations, which were much more influential in the political arena. As the goals of the movement began to expand from conservation to environmentalism in the late 1960s and early 1970s, so, too, did the potential impact on business and industry, which had never really felt threatened before. The development of an organized environmental opposition involved three interests, farmers and ranchers, organized labor, and industry, and has recently coalesced into three grass-roots opposition movements: wise use, property rights, and county supremacy.

The initial concern of farmers and ranchers was the tremendous influx of city dwellers who sought the tranquility of rural life after World War II. "Recreationists," as they were called, brought tourist dollars to rural economies badly in need of them, but they also brought with them litter, congestion, and noise. Urban visitors seldom paid much attention to property lines, and major battles developed over public access along the California coastline and through inland wetlands. Farmers who were used to controlling predators on their private property were suddenly facing raptor protection programs and angry wildlife enthusiasts who sought preservation of wolves and coyotes. Agricultural land use also came under fire, as environmental groups sought to legislate farm practices relating to pesticide use, soils, and irrigation. As development, including oil pipelines and utility transmission lines, began to intrude onto rural areas, farmers felt even more threatened. The two issues that have most galvanized farmers have been proposals to restrict the use of agricultural pesticides and herbicides and agricultural use of water. In the case of pesticide use, rural interests have formed a coalition with chemical companies and their associations, bringing together such disparate groups as the American Farm Bureau Federation and the National Agricultural Chemical Association, along with the National Association of State Departments of Agriculture, the Association of American Plant Food, Pesticide and Feed Control Officers, the National Association of County Agents, and the Christmas Tree Growers Association.[15] But the land-use issue has become even more controversial as a result of the Sagebrush Rebellion and the development of the grass-roots environmental opposition movements discussed later in this chapter.

Organized Labor

There are a number of environmental issues that have had an impact on workers, who have often been forced to take sides in the policy debate. On the one hand, organized labor has traditionally supported attempts to make a safer workplace and working conditions. Most labor unions have also supported programs that involve occupational health issues, such as exposure to airborne particulates and toxic chemicals. The United Steelworkers of America, for example, has long supported clean air legislation, an environmental problem caused, to some extent, by the steel industry.[16] Farm workers in California have been active participants in federal pesticide legislation, and cotton dust exposure led the Amalgamated Clothing and Textile Workers Union to lobby the Occupational Safety and Health Administration to develop rules to protect workers in textile mills.

Labor has often opposed pollution control efforts (and more recently, implementation of the Endangered Species Act) that affect job security. The United Auto Workers union has consistently supported environmental regulations except when they affect the auto industry. The fear of loss of jobs because of environmental regulations has permeated many regions of the United States, often when the real reason for job loss is technological change and innovation. Environmentalists working within the energy industry unions have repeatedly argued that energy conservation has no negative impact on jobs and is, in fact, beneficial to workers.[17]

Industry Interests

Industry interests have traditionally opposed environmental rules for two reasons: the cost of complying with regulations threatens a company's ability to make money, and there is little incentive for voluntary compliance. Sometimes, their opposition results from disagreement over the goals or means used to protect the environment. Yet industry leaders recognize that they (and their employees and their families) breathe the same polluted air and face the same toxic contamination as the rest of America. Industry's role has been described as "marked not by agreement on values but by tactics of containment, by a working philosophy of maximum feasible resistance and minimum feasible retreat."[18]

Businesses were initially slow to recognize the potential impact of the environmental movement on their operations, characterizing the activities of most groups as no more than a fad. But officials within the pulp and paper industry began, in the late 1950s, to understand how desires for more recreation land would likely mean a call for reduction in logging activities and expansion of wilderness area designations. Eventually, other industry leaders became alarmed at the rapid pace of environmental legislation, which accelerated during the late 1960s and into the 1970s. They countered by forming trade associations and nonprofit research groups or think tanks to further their aims, pouring millions of dollars into education and public relations. The American Forest Institute, for example, was specifically created to justify the need for increased, rather than reduced, timber production. The oil industry has been especially hard hit as the environmental movement gained more clout. Companies have been ordered by the courts to pay for special cleanups or fines and have faced lengthy and costly litigation as a result of compliance suits brought by environmental groups.[19]

Today, industries affected by environmental regulations rely on a threefold approach in their opposition to environmental groups. One, there is a continuation of the public relations campaigns that began in the early 1960s to paint industry with an environmentally green bush. Chevron Oil, for example, ran advertisements in national publications promoting its "People Do" projects to protect the habitat of endangered species to counter the public backlash that results after every oil spill, and Dow Chemical Company's efforts included sponsorship of the 1990 Earth Day activities in the company's hometown of Midland, Michigan.[20]

Two, virtually every sector of the economy relies on a stable of federal and state lobbyists to review legislation that could potentially have an impact on its operations. Although federal law prohibits them from contributing directly to candidates, corporations can form political action committees, which funnel campaign contributions directly to legislators as a way of enhancing their access to the political system. Companies and trade associations also employ their own scientists, economists, and policy experts to refute the claims made by environmental groups, and usually have more financial resources to devote to this strategy than do grass-roots groups.

Three, once programs reach the implementation stage, most industry interests regroup to press their case through the administrative maze. Since many of the implementation decisions are made by low-level administrators, or in a less public arena than Congress, industry has been much more successful in molding programs at this phase of the policy process. EPA rule development has frequently been hampered by companies who argued that information about products and processes constituted trade secrets or are proprietary. Industry lawyers have also launched a flurry of lawsuits aimed at regulations and enforcement actions.

Perhaps the biggest change in industry's role in opposing environmental legislation is that these efforts have now shifted toward industry's taking an active, rather than a reactive stance, forming coalitions to enhance their overall effectiveness. During debate on the 1990 Clean Air Act Amendments, for example, utility lobbyists brought with them to Washington dozens of amendments designed to reduce the cost of compliance with proposed acid rain legislation. The Clean Air Working Group, the major industry coalition, actively fought each amendment proposed by environmental groups.[21]

Some industry groups have become more responsive to environmental concerns as negative publicity surrounding their emissions have generated adverse public relations. The chemical industry, which for years was accused of intransigence, decided in the late 1980s to move toward a pollution prevention approach as a way to improve the marketability of its products. They were active in the debate over the 1990 Clean Air Act Amendments, and politicians gave the industry's lobbyists credit for drafting its own legislation rather than just opposing what was on the table. Monsanto Company's Charles Malloch told fellow industry representatives that such initiative was imperative at the rulemaking phase of the Clean Air Act. "Anyone sitting on their hands waiting for the regs to come out is way behind the eight ball."[22] Similarly, the Alliance for Responsible Atmospheric Policy and the Nuclear Energy Institute coordinate the efforts of hundreds of companies, speaking with one voice for their interests and using their financial resources and technical expertise to counter efforts by environmental groups to strengthen existing environmental protection rules.[23]

Grass-Roots Opposition

In 1988, a different type of environmental opposition surfaced as an outgrowth of a meeting of 250 groups at the Multiple Use Strategy Conference, sponsored by the Center for Defense of Free Enterprise. One of the group's leaders, Ron Arnold, applied the phrase "wise use" (originally used by conservationist Gifford Pinchot) in describing twenty-five goals to reform the country's environmental policies, including opening up national parks and wilderness areas to mineral exploration, expanding visitor facilities in the parks, and restricting application of the Endangered Species Act.[24] Now, grass-roots opposition is focused on three movements led by large umbrella organizations: wise use, property rights, and the county supremacy movement. The umbrella groups serve as a clearinghouse for information and share a deep antigovernment sentiment and opposition to efforts by government and environmental groups to further regulate the use of public and private lands and natural resources. Although some of their efforts are supported by private interests, ranging from the Mountain States Legal Foundation to agricultural groups and oil, timber, and mining companies, there is a strong grass-roots component of individuals who perceive the government to be intruding into their lives by telling them what they can do with their private property or how lands and resources within the public domain ought to be used. It is difficult to estimate the membership of these groups, since so many individuals are members simply because they belong to another group that has supported one or more of the umbrella groups' tenets. The four million members of the American Farm Bureau Federation (AFBF), for example, are counted as members of the wise use movement simply because the AFBF has endorsed some wise use policies.

The Sagebrush Rebellion began in the 1970s as an effort by wealthy ranchers and others to gain control of public lands in the West. The movement had proponents in government in the 1980s, particularly Interior Secretary James Watt. The movement was reinvigorated in the early 1990s as the wise use and county supremacy movements garnered attention. Although there are similarities between the wise use movement and the Sagebrush Rebellion of the late 1970s and early 1980s, one difference between the two is that the current efforts are marked by steps to broaden the base of support beyond purely western issues. Like other political movements, the groups employ a wide variety of strategies and tactics to push their agenda forward. For example, the annual September "Fly In For Freedom" lobbying effort in Washington, D.C., sponsored by the Alliance for America, brings in representatives from diverse groups, who are urged to wear work clothes — with special attention to gloves, boots, hard hats, and bandannas — when they rally. The Blue Ribbon Coalition, which represents motorized recreational interests, tracks legislation and alerts its members to contact their congressional representatives when a bill affects their members. Some of the more militant opposition groups, like the Sahara Club, boast of vandalizing property or disrupting environmental group activities. In addition to cattle ranchers resisting higher grazing fees, the grass-roots efforts tap into gulf shrimpers opposing the use of turtle-excluding devices, Alaskans seeking to expand oil drilling, and private property owners from eastern states battling the National Park Service over boundary disputes. The three movements are well organized, tapping into an electronic network that keeps even the most isolated adherents in touch with one another.[25] Sporadic violence has occurred, aimed at federal agency facilities and employees.

From a political standpoint, the grass-roots opposition has had moderate success legislatively. During President Clinton's first term, it stalled proposed grazing fee increases and was able to get congressional approval for a brief moratorium on listings under the Endangered Species Act. Organizations like the Mountain States Legal Foundation and the Individual Rights Foundation have led the legal fight against federal lands. Between 1991 and 1995, fifty-nine western counties passed ordinances that claimed authority to supercede federal environmental and land use laws and regulations, and thirty-four counties in Nevada, California, Idaho, New Mexico, and Oregon had passed ordinances challenging federal control of local lands.[26] The resolutions declared that federal land in the county actually belonged to the state and that the county alone has the authority to manage it. Although the resolutions are not technically law, local officials were enforcing them as though they were. The Justice Department challenged the ordinances as illegal and sought an injunction to ban their enforcement.

The courts have dealt a serious blow to county supremacy groups by striking down ordinances that would have given counties the right to determine how public lands within their boundaries would be used (see Chapter 4). Most individuals involved in the property rights movement are mired in a legal system that takes years to resolve issues, reducing their ability to accomplish their goals. The grass-roots movements have as much success as they do because they have been led by *policy entrepreneurs,* charismatic individuals who have capitalized on the public's distrust of the government's natural resource policies, as well as mistrust of the federal government in general, and turned that distrust into self-perpetuating organizations. Although they have often been at odds with most environmental organizations, some opposition group leaders appear to be seeking common ground and compromise as a more effective way of affecting environmental policy during an era when the vast majority of Americans still adhere to a protectionist ethic. But the wise use movement's adherents are highly motivated; moreover, they are well organized through a network of web pages, e-mail, and grass-roots chapters and continue to press their concerns forcefully.

THE GLOBAL DIMENSION

Concern about the environment is universal, and although this chapter has thus far focused on the development of the environmental movement and opposition groups in the United States, the environmental debate involves a number of international actors. Some international activism paralleled what was taking place in the United States, beginning with the founding of the Commons, Open Spaces and Footpaths Preservation Society in Britain in 1865. There appears to be a trend in industrial nations that ties the development of environmental awareness to business cycles; in Britain, for example, support for environmental protection has been strongest toward the end of periods of sustained economic expansion. With greater economic prosperity, people shift their interest from immediate material needs to the nonmaterial aspects of their lives. As a result, economic advances in the late 1960s and early 1970s led to a tremendous growth spurt in the membership of existing nature groups and the formation of new groups, paralleling activity in the United States during that same period.[27]

Nongovernmental organizations (NGOs) now play a key role in environmental policy making in both industrialized and developing countries. The term is used to describe all organizations that are neither governmental nor for-profit, and may include groups ranging from rural people's leagues and tribal unions to private relief associations, irrigation user groups, and local development associations. NGOs can be classified as grass-roots organizations (membership-oriented, often in developing nations), service NGOs (supporting the development of grass-roots groups), or policy-specific (environment, human rights, family planning). One characteristic many of the groups have in common is that they are often parochial — concerned almost exclusively about environmental issues in their region. A typical example is the group Dasohli Gram Swarajya Mandal, which began a logging public awareness campaign in India in 1964 that led to the Chipko Andalan movement. Chipko, which means "to cling to," literally is composed of India's tree huggers, Himalayan Indians who launched protests over logging. Indian environmentalists developed political clout over the issue of proposed dams and hydroelectric projects, but have often limited their activism to specific projects. Not only do these groups help shape policy, but they play a major role in generating demands within individual countries for governments to comply with and implement the global agreements they have signed.

NGOs are growing in both number and influence, particularly in developing nations. Unlike their counterparts in Northern Hemisphere countries, NGOs in the south perform somewhat different functions. They often fill a vacuum left by ineffective or nonexistent government programs or extend the reach of resource-poor national governments. They may also forge links with NGOs whose issues are decidedly nonenvironmental, such as the networking that is beginning to occur with human rights and economic development NGOs. Last, NGOs in developing countries may serve as an independent voice for public participation, either in opposition to a government program or by placing pressures on government to create new programs.[28] (See Table 2.1.)

Studies of NGOs indicate that they are evolving in three directions: the southern NGOs are seeking greater autonomy from those in the north; NGOs are forming international networks and coalitions to keep abreast of issues; and they are performing new roles in legal defense and policy research. The first trend appears to be the most critical as Southern Hemisphere NGOs seek to distance themselves from their dependence on their northern partners. Long dependent for financial support on their northern donors, these groups now seek the transfer of the technical expertise they need to gain independence. They hope to set their own environmental protection agendas rather than have the terms of their activities dictated by

Table 2.1 Major International Environmental/Developmental Nongovernmental Organizations (NGOs)

Basel Action Network (BAN)
Climate Action Network (CAN)
Consumers International (CI)
Earth Council
Earthwatch Institute
Environmental Liaison Centre International (ELCI)
European Environmental Bureau (EEB)
Forest Stewardship Council (FSC)
Friends of Nature
Friends of the Earth International (FoEI)
Greenpeace International
International Chamber of Commerce (ICC)
International Confederation of Free Trade Unions (ICFTU)
International Planned Parenthood Federation (IPPF)
International Solar Energy Society (ISES)
International Union for the Conservation of Nature (IUCN)
Pesticide Action Network (PAN)
Sierra Club
Society of International Development (SID)
Third World Network (TWN)
Water Environment Federation (WEF)
Women's Environment and Development Organization (WEDO)
World Business Council for Sustainable Development (WBCSD)
World Federalist Movement (WFM)
World Wide Fund for Nature (WWF)

Source: Adapted from materials from the Fridtjof Nansen Institute, 2000.

outside sources whom they perceive to be less familiar with local problems. Technological advances such as facsimile machines and computer-linked networks have allowed groups to coordinate their efforts on a global scale, and they have steadily increased their presence in the diplomatic world as well. NGOs held a parallel conference at both the 1972 and 1992 United Nations environmental meetings, and several organizations were accredited by the United Nations to participate in the preparatory meetings leading up to the Earth Summit. Although these trends indicate that NGOs are growing in both numbers and importance, their influence on global environmental protection is still limited by a lack of stable funding sources and political sophistication.

Only a handful of organizations have begun to address the global issues of concern to many of the mainstream organizations in the United States, such as global warming and stratospheric ozone depletion. Friends of the Earth International, for example, has affiliates throughout the world, as does Greenpeace.

NGOs are especially important in regions where environmental concern has only recently begun to emerge, as evidenced by the founding of a Russian affiliate of Greenpeace. Without the support of an international organization and its resources, environmental activists in the republics of the former Soviet Union would have little voice for their efforts to draw international attention to decades of environmental degradation.

Cultural differences are the major factor behind the variations in how environmental interests become structured or operate. In democratic nations, the pluralist system legitimizes interest group membership. But acceptable tactics in one nation may be considered unacceptable or even criminal in others.

In nondemocratic countries such as the People's Republic of China, the government crackdown on Western influences has made it difficult even for NGOs such as the World Wildlife Fund to have much of an impact, leaving little room for environmental groups, domestic or foreign. International pressure and the government's expanded involvement in international trade and politics have led to substantial advances in China's environmental policies, and small groups, such as Friends of Nature, have been successful at lobbying against clear-cutting of old-growth forests.[29]

The most cohesive and powerful environmental movements are found in western Europe, where public opinion polls have shown that support for the environment is especially strong and continues to grow. Coalition building is a common strategy, with umbrella groups monitoring proposed legislation and lobbying. Group activism has frequently been focused on the issues of nuclear power and nuclear weapons, leading to massive public protests in 1995 when the French government resumed weapons testing in the South Pacific. The environmental movement in Europe is best characterized as diverse, with each group developing its own structure, strategy, and style.[30]

Green Political Parties

Unlike the environmental movement in the United States, which has failed to capture (or be captured by) one of the two major political parties, green parties have formed in dozens of countries, with the major ones identified in Table 2.2. They vary considerably in strength and impact on their respective political systems, in membership, and in the percentage of the electorate they represent. International green parties are often difficult to track, since they frequently change their names or form new alliances with other groups to bolster their political clout. The term *green party* is sometimes used generically, and many groups represent a broader social movement or consist of activists focused on a single issue. In Hungary, for example, "greens" were called "blues" in reference to the Blue Danube Circle (those opposed to the building of the Nagymaros Dam), and in Poland, the largest environmental organization was not a party per se, but the Polish Ecology Club.[31]

Table 2.2 Major Green Political Parties, by Region

Africa	
Benin	Parti Ecologiste Beninois
Burkina Faso	Les Verts du Berkina
Cameroon	Defense de l'Environnement Camerounais
	Cameroun Vert
	Mouvement des Ecologistes du Cameroun
	Association Ecologique du Cameroun
Cote d'Ivoire	Parti pour la Protection de l'Environnement Association Ecologie
Egypt	Egyptian Green Party
Gabon	Front des Ecologistes Gabonais
Guinée	Parti des Ecologistes Guineens
Madagascar	Union National pour la Democratie et le Developpement
	Rassemblement des Verts de Madagascar
Niger	Rassemblement pour un Sahel Vert
Senegal	Parti Africain Ecologiste-Sebegal
South Africa	Green Party
Asia, Australia, and Oceana	
Australia	Australian Greens
Hong Kong	Green Power
India	Green Party of Kerala
New Zealand	Green Party of Aotearoa
Pakistan	Green Party of Pakistan
Philippines	Philippine Greens
Caribbean and Latin America	
Bolivia	Movimiento Poder Verde
Chile	Instituto de Ecologia Politica
Ecuador	Horizonte Verde
French Guyana	Les Verts Guyane
Guatemala	Green Party
Martinique	Verts Martinique
Mexico	Partido Verde Ecologista de Mexico
Uruguay	Partido del Sol
Europe	
Austria	Die Grunen
Bulgaria	Bulgarian Green Party
Cyprus	Cyprus Green Party
Czech Republic	Strana Zelenych
Denmark	De Gronne
England and Wales	Green Party
Estonia	Eesti Rohelised
Finland	Vihrea Liitto

Table 2.2 (continued)

Europe	
France	Les Verts
Germany	Die Grunen
Greece	Politiki Oikologia
Hungary	Zold Alternativa
Ireland	Comhaontas Glas
Italy	Federazione dei Verdi
Luxemburg	Dei Greng
Netherlands	De Groenen
	GroenLinks
Norway	Miljopartiet de Gronne
Portugal	Os Verdes
Russia	Green Party of St. Petersburg
Scotland	Scottish Green Party
Spain	Confederacion de Los Verdes
Sweden	Miljopartiet de Grona
Switzerland	Grune
	Les Verts
	I Verdi
Ukraine	Ukrainian Green Party
North America	
Canada	Canadian Greens
United States	Green Party USA

The first green party was the United Tasmania Group, which contested the local elections in the Tasmanian region of Australia in 1972. Although the party was unsuccessful in the ten elections it contested before its dissolution in 1976, it was instrumental in placing the environment at the top of the Australian political agenda. The major wave of green party activity has been in Europe, primarily because the structure of European political systems allows political parties, even small ones, a role in policy making. During the 1970s, one of the first green parties to form was in Germany, where a loose coalition of groups, the Bund Burgerinitiativen Umweltschutz (BBU), organized massive demonstrations opposing nuclear energy but exercised little political power. Over the past two decades, the German greens have formed several electoral alliances, becoming what many believe is the most powerful environmental force in Europe. Their increasing role in national politics has come despite the death of one of their most influential leaders, Petra Kelly, in 1992. Although the German green party has been split internally, with some factions seeking to move even closer toward the political center, it has gradually dropped some of the demands made in the party's infancy. In 1996, for example, the party agreed to lift a ten-year boycott of computers, which was exemplary of how out of touch with prevailing social attitudes some of the group's demands had been.

The achievements of the German greens has not been matched elsewhere, however. Initially, green parties' successes seemed to be limited to getting their members elected at the local and regional levels. In countries such as Sweden, where legislative seats are allotted based on a threshold level of representation, green parties have struggled to attract the necessary numbers of voters or often have been shut out of the process entirely. Even in those countries with proportional representation, most green parties have had little support, in large part because they modeled their strategy on the atypical German model. The "fading of the greens," as the phenomenon has been called, is not an indication of the lack of the public's environmental interest or its saliency as a political issue. One observer has argued that in one sense the national green parties simply outlived their usefulness once the major political parties adopted the greens' issues as their own. In addition, many environmental activists, sensing that structural barriers limited their ability to attain status as a potent political entity, shifted their energies toward affecting legislation and policy through the NGOs (described earlier).

INTERNATIONAL GOVERNMENTAL ORGANIZATIONS

The concept of protecting the global environment through some form of international regime or institution did not occur until well into the twentieth century. The United Nations (UN) Charter of 1945, for instance, did not include any mention of the environment in its mission. Although there were forty or more international environmental agreements signed prior to World War II, most international governance was conducted through regional commissions. In 1909, for example, the United States and Canada formed the International Joint Commission to deal with transboundary issues between their shared three-thousand-mile border, and a similar treaty was signed in 1906 between the United States and Mexico.

Since then, international governmental organizations (IGOs) have become important participants in the global effort to protect the environment. The United Nations has increasingly served as a diplomatic platform for the negotiation of international agreements. In 1949, the UN held its first environmental conference on the Conservation and Utilization of Resources. Five years later, it sponsored the Conference on Conservation of Living Resources of the Sea, which resulted in the International Convention for the Prevention of Pollution of the Sea by Oil.

The UN entered a second phase of international environmental protection on January 17, 1972, when its General Assembly passed a Resolution on Development and Environment that criticized highly developed nations for improper planning and inadequate coordination of industrial activities that had led to serious environmental problems worldwide. In language highly critical of the United States, the UN General Assembly called upon the industrialized nations to provide additional technological assistance and financing, starting a decades-long debate over who should bear the cost of environmental cleanup in developing nations.[32]

Today, environmental IGOs have begun to bring together the often competing issues of environmental protection and economic development. They can be structurally divided into two types: organizations and programs developed under the auspices of the UN and IGOs made up of states or national government bodies. The primary UN body charged with natural resource protection is the UN Environment Programme (UNEP), which was conceptualized at the 1972 Stockholm Conference on the Human Environment. The UNEP was established in 1973 and is facilitated by a secretariat in Nairobi—a significant siting, as it is the only major global United Nations agency headquartered in a developing country. It is governed by a fifty-eight-member Governing Council, made up of representatives elected by the UN General Assembly and based on geographic region. The mission of the agency is set forth in ten-year-long work plans known as the Montevideo Programmes. Each work plan sets out the tasks and goals the UNEP expects to achieve; the 1992–2002 work plan identifies eighteen areas for global environmental action.

The UNEP has been widely criticized for becoming too bureaucratic and unwieldy and for problems with its financial management. It is primarily funded through voluntary contributions from member nations, and throughout the 1990s it faced a financial crisis that many observers believed could not be overcome. A subsequent compromise reorganization created a smaller advisory body that is charged with reviewing the UNEP's administrative structure and making recommendations for change.

In the last decade of the twentieth century, the issues of environment and development have become even more closely intertwined. The Commission on Sustainable Development (CSD), established in 1993 as a body within the UN Economic and Social Council, has the primary responsibility for implementing the recommendations that were produced from the 1992 United Nations Conference on Environment and Development in Rio de Janeiro. The recommendations, known as Agenda 21,[33] encourage national and subnational governments to integrate environmental and economic concerns, but the CSD has no legal authority and has only the power to make recommendations. Another major IGO, the UN Development Programme (UNDP) is more active on the issues of development and trade.

Most funding for global efforts to protect the environment comes from the Global Environmental Facility (GEF), which was originally established in 1991 as a pilot project under the organizational umbrella of the World Bank. It has now become the largest multilateral source of funding for grants to individual countries for environmental projects. It, too, has been criticized because it focuses its funding priorities on only four areas: climate change, the conservation of biological diversity, the protection of international waters, and ozone depletion. Most of the GEF's grants have been made to developing countries based on recommendations by its own scientific panel of experts. In contrast, there are a handful of IGOs that affect natural resource policy that are made up of states or national government bodies. The most visible is the European Union Environment Agency, which serves as a regional IGO.

International governmental organizations are critical to global environmental protection for a number of reasons. They allow problems like water or air pollution to be approached from an integrated perspective, rather than unilaterally. By standardizing policies such as acid deposition emissions, they recognize the importance of transboundary issues. They provide a forum for the diplomatic negotiation of issues, such as whaling, and serve as a clearinghouse for information and scientific research. The drawback of IGOs is that they have limited powers and virtually no enforcement capabilities. When a nation fails to abide by an international regime, such as the Convention on International Trade in Endangered Species of Wild Fauna and Flora, there is little an IGO can do except attempt to apply the force of public opinion to the rogue state. However, forums like the UN are critical because without them, there would be no singular body or mechanism for disputes to be aired or problems to be addressed. Efforts to reform IGOs and make them stronger have failed to date, largely because of a lack of financial support and a fear by some developed nations that they might force industrialized countries to turn over valuable technology to poorer nations. A more likely future for IGOs is the continuing development of regional bodies and agreements, such as those which have been created as a result of the North American Free Trade Agreement and the General Agreement on Tariffs and Trade.[34]

In addition, other major UN-based IGOs, like the Food and Agriculture Organization (FAO), United Nations Children's Fund (UNICEF), and the UN Population Fund (UNFPA), are assuming a more active role in environmental/development issues. Each of these IGOs is now interacting with the UNEP and the UNDP to coordinate global environmental initiatives. (See Table 2.3.)

Table 2.3 Major International Environmental/Developmental Intergovernmental Organizations (IGOs)

Commission for Environmental Cooperation (CEC)
Commission on Sustainable Development (CSD)
European Union Environment Agency (EUEA)
Food and Agriculture Organization (FAO)
Global Environmental Facility (GEF)
Intergovernmental Panel on Climate Change (IPCC)
International Atomic Energy Agency (IAEA)
International Council for the Exploration of the Sea (ICES)
International Fund for Agricultural Development (IFAD)

Table 2.3 (continued)

International Labour Organization (ILO)
International Maritime Organization (IMO)
International Monetary Fund (IMF)
International Oil Pollution Compensation Fund (IOPCF)
United Nations Children's Fund (UNICEF)
United Nations Development Programme (UNDP)
United Nations Education, Scientific, and Cultural Organization (UNESCO)
United Nations Environment Programme (UNEP)
United Nations Industrial Development Organization (UNIDO)
United Nations Population Fund (UNFPA)
World Bank
World Food Programme (WFP)
World Health Organization (WHO)
World Meteorological Organization (WMO)
World Trade Organization (WTO)

NOTES

1. "Last Words," *Sierra,* January–February 1998, 124.

2. "Text of Vail Fire Message," Associated Press Headlines, October 23, 1998, cited at <http://dailynews.yahoo.com/headlines/ap////?s=v/ap/19981023/us/vail_fire_text2>.

3. For various perspectives on the Vail incident and the ELF, see Alex Markels, "Backfire," *Mother Jones,* March–April 1999, 60–64, 78–79; Steven K. Paulson, "Environmental Activists Criticized," Yahoo! News, October 23, 1998; Jan Faust, "Earth Liberation Who?" ABC News.com, October 22, 1998; Michael Lovell, "Lynx at Heart of Vail Fire Case," Yahoo! News, October 23, 1998; Robert Weller, "Group Claims It Caused Fires," ABC News.com, October 22, 1998; Michelle Nijhuis, "ELF Strikes Again," *High Country News,* February 1, 1999, 3.

4. For an explanation of the concept of deep ecology, see Arne Naess, *Ecology, Community and Lifestyle* (Cambridge: Cambridge University Press, 1989), and Bill Devall and George Sessions, *Deep Ecology* (Salt Lake City, UT: Gibbs Smith, 1985). For more on radical environmentalism, see Robert Hunter, *Warriors of the Rainbow: A Chronicle of the Greenpeace Movement* (New York: Holt, Rinehart and Winston, 1979); Paul Watson, *Sea Shepherd* (New York: Norton, 1982); Rick Scarce, *Eco-Warriors: Understanding the Radical Environmental Movement* (Chicago: Noble Press, 1990); and Dave Foreman, *Confessions of an Eco-Warrior* (New York: Harmony Books, 1991).

5. For the classical tenets of group theory, see David Truman, *The Governmental Process* (New York: Knopf, 1951), and Earl Latham, *The Group Basis of Politics* (New York: Octagon Books, 1965).

6. Riley E. Dunlap and Angela G. Mertig, "The Evolution of the U.S. Environmental Movement from 1970 to 1990: An Overview," in *American Environmentalism: The U.S. Environmental Movement, 1970–1990,* ed. Riley E. Dunlap and Angela G. Mertig (Washington, DC: Taylor and Francis, 1992), 4.

7. See Michael S. Greve, "Private Enforcement, Private Rewards: How Environmental Suits Became an Entitlement Program," in *Environmental Politics: Public Costs, Private Rewards,* ed. Michael S. Greve and Fred L. Smith Jr. (New York: Praeger, 1992), 105–109.

8. Craig R. Humphrey and Frederick H. Buttel, *Environment, Energy and Society* (Belmont, CA: Wadsworth, 1982).

9. Robert D. Bullard, ed. *Confronting Environmental Racism: Voices from the Grassroots* (Boston: South End Press, 1993), 15–39. See also Marcia Coyle, "When Movements Coalesce," *National Law Journal*, September 21, 1992.

10. See, for example, Allan Schnaiberg, *The Environment: From Surplus to Scarcity* (New York: Oxford University Press, 1980); Robert D. Bullard, *Dumping in Dixie: Race, Class, and Environmental Quality* (Boulder, CO: Westview Press, 1990); Bunyan Bryant and Paul Mohai, eds., *Race and Incidence of Environmental Hazards* (Boulder, CO: Westview Press, 1992); Richard Hofrichter, ed., *Toxic Struggles: The Theory and Practice of Environmental Justice* (Philadelphia: New Society, 1993); Bunyan Bryant, ed., *Environmental Justice: Issues, Policies, and Solutions* (Covelo, CA: Island Press, 1995); and David E. Camacho, ed., *Environmental Injustices, Political Struggles: Race, Class, and the Environment* (Durham, NC: Duke University Press, 1998).

11. United Church of Christ Commission for Racial Justice, *Proceedings: The First National People of Color Environmental Leadership Summit* (New York: United Church of Christ Commission for Racial Justice, 1993), xiii–xiv.

12. Bullard, *Confronting Environmental Racism,* 17.

13. Robert D. Bullard, "The Environmental Justice Movement Comes of Age," *Amicus Journal, 16,* no. 1 (Spring 1994): 32–37.

14. Christopher H. Foreman Jr., *The Promise and Peril of Environmental Justice* (Washington, DC: Brookings Institution Press, 1998), 3, 133.

15. Samuel P. Hays, *Beauty, Health and Permanence: Environmental Politics in the United States 1955–1985* (Cambridge: Cambridge University Press, 1987), 295.

16. See United Steelworkers of America, *Poison in Our Air* (Washington, DC: United Steelworkers of America, 1969).

17. See Frederick H. Buttel, Charles C. Geisler, and Irving W. Wiswall, eds., *Labor and the Environment* (Westport, CT: Greenwood Press, 1984), 1–2.

18. Hays, *Beauty, Health and Permanence,* 308.

19. Mark Ivey, "The Oil Industry Races to Refine Its Image," *Business Week,* April 23, 1990, 98.

20. See Art Kleiner, "The Three Faces of Dow," *Garbage,* July–August 1991, 52–58.

21. The battle among the groups is outline in Gary Bryner, *Blue Skies, Green Politics: The Clean Air Act of 1990 and Its Implementation,* 2nd ed. (Washington, DC: Congressional Quarterly Press, 1995). See also Richard E. Cohen, *Washington at Work: Back Rooms and Clean Air* (New York: Macmillan, 1992), and George Hager, "For Industry and Opponents, A Showdown Is In the Air," *Environment '90* (Washington, DC: Congressional Quarterly Press, 1990), 10.

22. Bryan Lee, "Washington Report," *Journal of the Air and Waste Management Association,* 41, no. 8 (August 1991): 1022.

23. For an overview of strategies used by various industries, see George W. Ingle and Beverly Lehrer, "The Chemical Manufacturers Association," *Chemtech, 15* (February 1985); 71–73; Bruce A. Ackerman and William T. Hassler, *Clean Coal, Dirty Air* (New Haven, CT: Yale University Press, 1981); Kim Goldberg, "Logging On," *Columbia Journalism Review, 32* (November–December 1993): 19–20; and Chris Crowley, "With Environmental Opposition to Projects, Fight Fire with Fire," *The Oil and Gas Journal,* 90, no. 31 (August 31, 1992): 30–31.

24. Alan M. Gottlieb, ed., *The Wise Use Agenda* (Bellevue, WA: Free Enterprise Press, 1989).

25. For different views of the grass-roots movements, see Ron Arnold, *Ecology Wars: Environmentalism As If People Mattered* (Bellevue, WA: Free Enterprise Press, 1987); David Helvarg, *The War against the Greens: The "Wise Use" Movement, the New Right, and Anti-Environmental Violence* (San Francisco: Sierra Club Books, 1994); John Echeverria and Raymond Booth Eby, eds., *Let the People Judge: Wise Use and the Private Property Rights Movement* (Washington, DC: Island Press, 1995); Philip D. Brick and R. McGreggor Cawley, eds., *A Wolf in the Garden: The Lands Rights Movement and the New Environmental Debate*

(Lanham, MD: Rowman and Littlefield, 1996); and Paul R. Ehrlich and Anne H. Ehrlich, *The Betrayal of Science and Reason* (Washington, DC: Island Press, 1996).

26. Keith Schneider, "A County's Bid for U.S. Land Draws Lawsuit," *New York Times,* March 9, 1995, A1.

27. David Vogel, "Environmental Policy in Europe and Japan," in *Environmental Policy in the 1990s,* ed. Norman J. Vig and Michael E. Kraft (Washington, DC: Congressional Quarterly Press, 1990), 262.

28. John McCormick, "The Role of Environmental NGOs in International Regimes," in *The Global Environment: Institutions, Law, and Policy,* ed. Norman J. Vig and Regina S. Axelrod (Washington, DC: Congressional Quarterly Press, 1999), 52–71; Thomas Princen and Matthias Finger, eds., *Environmental NGOs in World Politics* (London: Routledge, 1994).

29. See Lester Ross, "The Politics of Environmental Policy in the People's Republic of China," in *Ecological Policy and Politics in Developing Countries,* ed. Uday Desai (Albany: State University of New York Press, 1998, 47–64; and John Leicester, "A 'Green' Movement Takes Root in China," *San Francisco Examiner,* November 29, 1998, A22.

30. See Russell J. Dalton, *The Green Rainbow: Environmental Groups in Western Europe* (New Haven, CT: Yale University Press, 1994), and John McCormick, *British Politics and the Environment* (London: Earthscan, 1991).

31. Anna Bramwell, *The Fading of the Greens: The Decline of Environmental Politics in the West* (New Haven, CT: Yale University Press, 1994).

32. Marvin S. Soroos, "Global Institutions and the Environment: An Evolutionary Perspective," in *The Global Environment,* ed. Norman J. Vig and Regina S. Axelrod (Washington, DC: Congressional Quarterly Press, 1999), 27–51.

33. United Nations, *Agenda 21: Report of the United Nations: Conference on Environment and Development* (New York: United Nations, 1992).

34. For an overview of IGOs and their role in environmental protection, see Oran Young, *International Governance: Protecting the Environment in a Stateless Society* (Ithaca, NY: Cornell University Press, 1994); Lamont C. Hempel, *Environmental Governance: The Global Challenge* (Washington, DC: Island Press, 1996); and Ronnie D. Lipschutz with Judith Mayer, *Global Civil Society and Global Environmental Governance: The Politics of Nature from Place to Planet* (Albany: State University of New York Press, 1996).

FOR FURTHER READING

John Barry. *Rethinking Green Politics.* Thousand Oaks, CA: Sage Publications, 1999.

Mary Joy Breton. *Women Pioneers for the Environment.* Boston: Northeastern University Press, 1998.

David E. Camacho. *Environmental Injustices, Political Struggles: Race, Class, and the Environment.* Durham, NC: Duke University Press, 1998.

Andrew Dobson. *Justice and the Environment.* New York: Oxford University Press, 1999.

Christopher H. Foreman Jr. *The Promise and Peril of Environmental Justice.* Washington, DC: Brookings, 1998.

Ronald T. Libby. *Eco-Wars: Political Campaigns and Social Movements.* Irvington, NY: Columbia University Press, 1999.

Leslie Paul Thiele. *Environmentalism for a New Millennium.* New York: Oxford University Press, 1999.

Norman J. Vig and Regina S. Axelrod, eds. *The Global Environment: Institutions, Law, and Policy.* Washington, DC: Congressional Quarterly Press, 1999.

CHAPTER 3

The Political Process

"Al, read your book."
— chant at environmental group rally

In 1992, then-U.S. Senator Al Gore published his book, *Earth in the Balance: Ecology and the Human Spirit,* as part of what he called "a personal journey that began more than twenty-five years ago, a journey in search of a true understanding of the global ecological crisis and how it can be resolved."[1] The book describes "the dangerous dilemma that our civilization now faces" and chronicles Gore's alarm at rising levels of carbon monoxide in the atmosphere, the deteriorating ozone layer, the rapid destruction of the world's rainforests, and his analysis of "where we've gone wrong." Gore states:

> I have come to believe that we must take bold and unequivocal action: we must make the rescue of the environment the central organizing principle for civilization. Whether we realize it or not, we are now engaged in an epic battle to right the balance of our earth, and the tide of this battle will turn only when the majority of people in the world become sufficiently aroused by a shared sense of urgent danger to join an all-out effort.[2]

Gore's "Global Marshall Plan" outlined five strategic goals: stabilizing the world's population, the rapid creation and development of environmentally appropriate technologies, a comprehensive and ubiquitous change in economic accounting, the negotiation and approval of a new generation of international agreements, and the establishment of a cooperative plan for educating the world's citizens about our global environment.[3]

Unfortunately, however, by the close of the twentieth century, Gore's plan had gathered dust, his lofty goals barely remembered by an American public that had just witnessed a presidential impeachment, the embarrassingly almost daily mea culpas of

On September 18, 1996, President Clinton, joined by Vice President Al Gore, bypassed Congress and used his presidential power of executive order under the 1906 Antiquities Act to designate 1.7 million acres of land in southeastern Utah as the Grand Staircase–Escalante National Monument.

legislators, and the focusing of a nation's attention on a stained blue dress. Gore's hope of rousing public opinion to recapture an environmentalism of the spirit was shattered by the all too familiar tawdriness of American politics. Somewhere between idea and implementation, protecting the environment had been relegated to the political back burner.

Chapters 1 and 2 provided an overview of the political context in which environmental policy is made, outlining the historical development of environmental consciousness and awareness and identifying the key stakeholders who participate in the environmental debate. James Anderson's model characterizes those activities and actors as the first and second stages of the policy-making process: problem identification/agenda setting and policy formulation. This chapter continues with an explanation of the third stage, policy adoption, and then moves to the fourth stage, policy implementation. The discussion begins with an analysis of the two agencies with the principal responsibilities for stewardship of the environment in the United States, the Department of the Interior and the EPA, and the role of presidential leadership. The chapter discusses the role of Congress and key legislative committees and the function of the courts in the adoption and implementation of environmental policy. (Agencies with more narrow environmental jurisdiction, such as the U.S. Forest Service, Bureau of Land Management, and National Park Service, are discussed more fully in subsequent chapters relating to their functions.) The chapter then provides a brief overview of the role of state and local governments and explores how these entities approach problem identification and policy formulation, adoption, and implementation. Finally, Chapter 3 concludes with a discussion of the role of the media, which often frames the way in which problems are identified and how they become part of the political agenda. The media also takes part publicizing (or ignoring) policies as they make their way through the political process. Along with the other major political forces, like the president and Congress, the policy-making process becomes dynamic and complex as public opinion, scientific discovery, and partisanship create American environmental policy.

THE EXECUTIVE BRANCH AGENCIES

Despite the prolonged public interest in conservation and environmental protection outlined in Chapter 1, the federal government's involvement is actually relatively recent. During the first hundred years after the nation's founding, both the president and Congress were much more deeply involved with foreign affairs, paying little attention to internal domestic problems until the growth of the country literally demanded it. The creation of a federal environmental policy was sporadic and unfocused, with responsibility for the environment scattered among a host of agencies.[4] Today, the Department of the Interior, established by congressional legislation in 1849, and the EPA, created by executive order in 1970, have jurisdiction over the implementation of most of the nation's environmental policies. This constitutes the fourth stage of the policy process, according to Anderson's model.

Under its first secretary, Thomas Ewing, the Department of the Interior was given domestic housekeeping responsibilities different from today's cabinet-level department. Initially, the department controlled the General Land Office, Office of Indian Affairs, Pension Office, and Patent Office, as well as supervised the Commissioner of Public Buildings, Board of Inspectors, the Warden of the District of Columbia Penitentiary, the census, mines, and accounts of marshals of the U.S. courts. Gradually, a shift occurred as the agency's responsibilities were transferred to other agencies within the executive branch. Eventually, the need to manage newly discovered public resources, especially land and mineral rights, led to the development of several agencies that later came under the Department of the Interior's umbrella, as seen in Table 3.1. The secretary of the interior is nominated by the president and confirmed by the Senate, as are the agency directors.

The EPA, in contrast, is an independent agency in the executive branch; it is headed by an administrator, a deputy, and nine assistant administrators, all nominated by the president and confirmed by the Senate. The EPA has responsibility for administering a broad spectrum of environmental laws. In one sense, it is a regulatory agency, issuing permits, setting and monitoring standards, and enforcing federal laws, but it also gives grants to states to build waste water treatment and other facilities.

The president also receives policy advice on environmental matters from the Council on Environmental Quality (CEQ), created as part of the 1970 National

Table 3.1 Agencies of the U.S. Department of the Interior

Agency	*Established*
Bureau of Indian Affairs	1824*
Bureau of Land Management	1946†
Bureau of Reclamation	1902
Minerals Management Service	1982
National Park Service	1916
Office of Surface Mining Reclamation and Enforcement	1977
U.S. Geological Survey	1879
U.S. Fish and Wildlife Service	1940‡

*Originally in War Department; transferred to Interior in 1849.
†Combined the responsibilities of the General Land Office, created in 1812, and the Grazing Service, established in 1934.
‡Combined the responsibilities of the Bureau of Fisheries, established in 1871, and the Bureau of Biological Survey, created in 1885.

Environmental Policy Act. Its members recommend policy to the president and to some degree evaluate environmental protection programs within the executive branch and environmental impact statements prepared by federal agencies. The CEQ has no regulatory authority; its recommendations are purely advisory. The CEQ's staff and budget were reduced under both Reagan and Bush, and the agency's primary task became the preparation of an annual report on the environment. Although the EPA and Interior Department are responsible for most policy implementation, they share jurisdiction with a number of other federal agencies, as seen in Table 3.2.

Sometimes an agency may have powers and an interest level comparable to that of the Department of the Interior or EPA, as is the case with the Nuclear Regulatory Commission, which authorizes the construction of nuclear power plants and supervises their operation. Other agencies, such as the Federal Aviation Administration (FAA), may not have environmental concerns as their primary mission but may be affected by regulations or legislation implemented by other agencies. Thus, the FAA was consulted in 1990 when air-quality officials within the EPA began to consider legislation that would govern the amount of particulates released in aircraft exhaust emissions.

Table 3.2 Other Federal Agencies and Commissions with Environmental Policy Jurisdiction

Department	***Agency/Commission***
Agriculture	Agriculture Stabilization and Conservation Service
	Soil Conservation Service
Commerce	National Bureau of Standards
	National Oceanic and Atmospheric Administration
Defense	Army Corps of Engineers
Energy	Federal Energy Regulatory Commission
	Office of Conservation and Renewable Energy
Health and Human Services	Food and Drug Administration
	National Institute for Occupational Safety and Health
Labor	Mine Safety and Health Administration
Transportation	Federal Aviation Administration
	Federal Highway Administration
	Materials Transportation Bureau
	National Transportation Safety Board
	U.S. Coast Guard
Commissions/Regulatory Agencies	
Consumer Product Safety Commission	
Federal Maritime Commission	
Federal Trade Commission	
Nuclear Regulatory Commission	

The process of implementing environmental policy is complicated by interest groups, which are playing an increasingly significant role at this stage of policy development. Industry, especially, has made great strides in crafting policies that parallel their needs. Industry groups have often appeared to "give up" their interests at the policy adoption or legislative stage, only to come back stronger than ever during the implementation phase. Generally, this strategy has been successful in influencing environmental legislation. During the policy formulation and adoption phase, which is highly visible and public, industry (ever mindful of its public image) has often accepted or provided only token resistance to proposed legislation that would negatively affect it. Instead, industry has done its best to circumvent costly or logistically difficult environmental regulations when they reach the implementation stage — the responsibility of bureaucratic organizations and agencies such as the EPA.

One way in which environmental groups have been kept out of the implementation process is through industry efforts to remove rule making from the public domain. The kinds of complex, time-consuming procedures that are typical of the rule-making process provide a shield to regulated industries against government intervention and a legitimate basis for resisting demands for information that might be obtained by competitors. The rule-making process involved with the implementation of the seven-hundred-page 1990 Clean Air Act Amendments is exemplary of this problem. The EPA was required to complete 150 regulatory activities, including one hundred rule makings, during the first two years after passage of the amendments — an unheard of time frame. Surprising nearly everyone, the agency issued most of the regulations on time. To put the process in perspective, consider that in the past the EPA has issued seven or eight major regulations *per year* on all phases of environmental law — from pesticides to solid waste to air and water pollution. Although the issue of nitrogen oxide emissions (one of two acid rain–causing chemicals) took only two pages of the act itself, the regulations crafted by the EPA are several hundred pages long.

Participation by interest groups is made even more difficult by the short comment periods (usually thirty or sixty days) necessitated by the scheduling. From the perspective of those interested in influencing the rule, the tight deadlines mean that the agency has likely already made up its mind and that comments will not bring about many changes in direction.[5] Implementation is also hampered by the complexity of the rule-making process itself. Although the Resource Conservation and Recovery Act (RCRA) was enacted in 1976, it took the EPA four years to implement the first rules under the act. In the meantime, state governments held their own agonizingly slow rule makings or waited until federal funds were made available, giving industry more time to muster its defenses.[6]

The responsibility for implementing policy has often been left to agencies and commissions that are ill equipped for the task. In 1979, for example, when RCRA rule making was finally underway, the process was considered so technical and complex that both the EPA and the environmental community suffered from a lack of expertise. Most of the comments that were received on the individual rules were from companies subject to them.[7] During the implementation of the 1990 Clean Air Act Amendments, the EPA was forced to hire outside consultants, many of them drawn from industry, to draft preliminary rules, especially those dealing with airborne toxins, on which the EPA's expertise is notoriously lacking.

Finally, policy implementation is an incremental process. It is made in a series of small steps, each one dependent on the previous one. The process is time-consuming and seldom results in any major legislative or policy advances. The history of water-quality legislation, for example, is one of fine-tuning rather than abrupt or dramatic change. Congress has been unwilling to orchestrate a complete revamping of the legislation initially passed in 1965, and as a result, agencies such as the EPA have followed suit. There have been no major advances in water-quality issues, and none are expected until the legislation is reauthorized.

PRESIDENTIAL LEADERSHIP

Historically, the president has had a limited role in environmental politics, with much of the power delegated to the executive branch agencies. Not until Richard Nixon's tenure began in 1969 did the environment become a presidential priority, and even then, Nixon was reluctant to act. After years of study and staff negotiations, Nixon agreed to a federal reorganization plan calling for an independent pollution control agency, which later became the EPA.

The agency opened its doors under the stewardship of William Ruckelshaus, a graduate of Harvard Law School and former Indiana assistant attorney general. Although he had virtually no background in environmental issues, Ruckelshaus had the support of Nixon's attorney general, John Mitchell, and was confirmed after only two days of hearings. On the day of his selection as administrator, Ruckelshaus was briefed by Nixon, who gave him the impression that he considered the environmental problem "faddish."[8] Ruckelshaus came to the EPA with three priorities: to create a well-defined enforcement image for the agency, to carry out the provisions of the newly amended Clean Air Act, and to gain control over the costs of regulatory decision making.[9] In setting up the agency, Ruckelshaus decided each regional organization within the EPA should mirror the full agency's structure, with staff capabilities in every program area and delegation of responsibility to regional offices, creating an organizational structure that gave the agency a rare capability to make decisions, move programs ahead, and motivate people to produce high volumes of work.[10] Inside the EPA, morale was high, in large part resulting from the accessibility of Ruckelshaus to his staff. Outside, he became a forceful spokesperson for the public interest and was well respected by both sides in the environmental debate. Early on, Ruckelshaus concentrated on air and water pollution, assigning three-quarters of his staff to that task. As a result, there was an improvement in noncompliance with air-quality standards in most cities, and the agency effected a change from aesthetic concerns about the recreational uses of water to health concerns.[11]

Nixon's efforts to give credibility to the Department of the Interior were not nearly as successful. It appears that the creation of the EPA relegated the Department of the Interior to backseat status as far as environmental issues were concerned. A succession of secretaries came and went (see Table 3.3) while the EPA administrators garnered publicity and notoriety. Despite these efforts, there is some doubt as to how much Nixon really cared about the environment as an issue. Some staff members believed the Nixon reorganization experts were neither proponents nor opponents of environmental reform; their specialty was management and organization. They focused on the environment because that was the area in which political pressures were creating a demand for action.

Typical is the case of Walter Hickel, whom Nixon chose in late 1968 as the new interior secretary, setting off a storm of protest. Hickel, who had grown up in Kansas and lived on a tenant farm during the Depression, was a Golden Gloves boxer who loved to fight. As governor of Alaska, he was accused of being a pawn of the U.S. Chamber of Commerce and of the oil industry. After four days of defensive hearings, his nomination was confirmed. Hickel's bold style was his undoing; he offended the president in a rambling letter about Nixon's policies (eventually leaked to the press) after the Kent State shootings. The gaffe came at a time when the president's staff was considering the reorganization proposal that would have elevated Hickel to head the new Department of Natural Resources. He was fired Thanksgiving Day, 1970.[12]

To Nixon's credit, it should be noted that it was under his administration that the United States first began to take a more global approach to environmental protection. Ruckelshaus was successful in convincing Nixon of the important role the United States could play at the UN Conference on the Human Environment in June 1972 in Stockholm. Although the United States was not totally in agreement with the priorities of the United Nations Environment Programme, which grew out of the Stockholm conference, Nixon persuaded Congress to pay the largest share (36 percent) of the new secretariat's budget.[13]

Table 3.3 Environmental Agency Leadership, 1970–2000

President	*Secretary of the Interior*	*EPA Administrator*
Nixon	Rogers Morton (1971–74)	William Ruckelshaus (1970–73)
Ford	Rogers Morton (1974–75)	Russell Train (1973–77)
	Stanley Hathaway (1975)	
	Thomas Kleppe (1975–77)	
Carter	Cecil Andrus (1977–81)	Douglas Costle (1977–81)
Reagan	James Watt (1981–83)	Anne (Gorsuch) Burford (1981–83)
	William Clark (1983–85)	William Ruckelshaus (1983–85)
	Donald Hodel (1985–89)	Lee Thomas (1985–89)
Bush	Manuel Lujan, Jr. (1989–92)	William Reilly (1989–92)
Clinton	Bruce Babbitt (1993–)	Carol Browner (1993–)

When Gerald Ford took over as president upon Nixon's resignation, he made few changes in the way environmental policy was being conducted. Russell Train remained head of the EPA under Ford and served in that position until Ford was defeated by Jimmy Carter in 1976. Carter kept most of Nixon's other environmental appointees, including Interior Secretary Rogers Morton. For the most part, the crush of environmental programs that marked the Nixon years slowed considerably under Ford for three reasons. One, the energy shortage created by the 1973 Arab oil embargo pushed pollution off the legislative agenda for several years (see Chapter 6). A second factor was a growing concern that the cost to industry to comply with EPA standards was slowing the economy at a time when expansion was needed. Last, the environmental momentum of the early 1970s faded by 1976, and Ford did little to refuel it. Congressional initiatives expanded the EPA's authority with the Safe Drinking Water Act of 1974, the Toxic Substances Control Act of 1976, and the Resource Conservation and Recovery Act of 1976 (legislation discussed in later chapters), but Ford's unsuccessful presidential campaign made him an observer, rather than a participant, in the policy-making process. The environmental slate for Gerald Ford is a clean, albeit empty, one.

In 1976, groups such as the League of Conservation Voters gave presidential candidate Jimmy Carter high grades for his environmental record as governor of Georgia, although his campaign focused more on other issues, such as human rights and the economy. President Carter openly courted environmental groups during his single-term administration, and he counted on their support to carry him through to reelection in 1980, when he lost to Ronald Reagan. He received high marks from environmental groups who believed he would emphasize environmental issues in his administration, but he initially offended one of the environmental movement's heroes, Maine Senator Edmund Muskie. Carter began by choosing Douglas Costle to head the EPA over the objections of Muskie. Costle, a Seattle native, attended Harvard and the University of Chicago Law School and had worked at the Office of Management and Budget under Nixon. His main environmental credential was a stint as Commissioner for Environmental Affairs in Connecticut, but he had a strong financial management background from working at the Congressional Budget Office.

Under Costle, the EPA became the first federal agency to adopt Carter's plan of zero-based budgeting. Costle's main aim in taking over the agency was "to convince the public that EPA was first and foremost a public health agency, not a guardian of birds and bunnies."[14] Taking Costle's lead, Congress responded by passing the Superfund authorization in late 1980, establishing a $1.6 billion emergency fund to clean up toxic contaminants spilled or dumped into the environment. The result was a major shift in the agency's regulatory focus from conventional pollutants to toxics. This allowed the agency room to grow and justification for a 25 percent budget increase at a time when the president was preaching strict austerity.

Carter had a number of environmental achievements during his term, including passage in 1980 of the landmark Alaska National Interest Lands Conservation

Act, or Alaska Land Bill, which brought millions of acres of pristine wilderness under federal protection. As part of his attempt to gain group support, Carter convinced Congress to consider a windfall profits tax on oil to fund solar research and pushed stronger energy conservation measures.[15] But the inability of Congress to develop a comprehensive energy policy under his administration has led most observers to conclude that Carter was not an especially effective leader in environmental policy or in protecting the environment.

The eight years of Ronald Reagan's administration mark a stormy chapter in environmental politics. Critics believe that he almost single-handedly destroyed the progress that had been made in the area of pollution control. Supporters point to his legislative achievements and say the picture was not so bleak after all, but critics argue that those successes came as a result of congressional initiative, not from Reagan. During his stints as governor of California and then as president, Reagan was heavily influenced by probusiness interests like Colorado brewer Joseph Coors, who urged him to take a more conservative approach to environmental regulation. Coors and his allies were represented in Reagan's inner circle by Nevada Senator Paul Laxalt, and they focused their attention on the appointment of a conservative secretary of the interior who would show prudent respect for development interests, especially in the West.[16]

Their candidate was James Watt, a Wyoming native who had served as a legislative aide to Senator Milward Simpson. He had served as a member of the Nixon transition team in 1968 to help Walter Hickel through his confirmation hearings as secretary of the interior and was then appointed deputy secretary for water and power. In 1977, he founded the Mountain States Legal Foundation, a conservative anti-environmental regulation law firm, and was later connected to the leadership of the Sagebrush Rebellion (see Chapter 2). Although some of Reagan's advisors preferred Clifford P. Hansen, former Governor and Senator from Wyoming, for the Department of the Interior slot, Watt's rhetorical style and ability to bring in dollars as a conservative fundraiser for Reagan gave him a decided edge. He was a spokesperson for the New Right, among those who believed Reagan was drifting too close to the political center.[17]

Watt divided people into two categories — liberals and Americans — and called the Audubon Society "a chanting mob."[18] He perceived environmentalists as "dangerous and subversive,"[19] suggesting they sought to weaken America and to undermine freedom. He called them extremists and likened them to Nazis. More telling, however, was the comparison of Watt to his predecessor, Cecil Andrus, who had said, "I am part of the environmental movement and I intend to make the Interior Department responsive to the movement's needs."[20] Watt discovered he had great independence in molding the agency to conform to his policy interests. Among his first directives, he ordered a moratorium on any further National Park acquisitions and announced his intention to open up federal lands to mining and logging. He proposed to permit leasing of 1.3 million acres off the California coast for offshore oil and gas exploration and auctioned off 1.1 billion tons of coal in the Powder River Basin of Montana and Wyoming, actions that infuriated environmentalists. By summer 1981, Watt had made enough enemies that the Sierra Club, National Wildlife Federation, and Audubon Society gathered more than one million signatures seeking Watt's ouster. Together, ten organizations urged President Reagan to fire Watt, issuing a stinging indictment that purported to show how he had subverted environmental policy.

His supporters, however, point out that under Watt, the federal government spent more than one billion dollars to restore and improve the existing national parks, and 1.8 million acres were added to the nation's wilderness system. Watt's vision was to develop America's energy resources and to remove what many perceived as excessive regulation of business, efforts at which he was successful.[21] But by late 1982, Watt was under heavy criticism for his actions, although he was blunt enough to say out loud what many in the Reagan administration were thinking. Reagan called Watt's record "darn good"[22] but urged him to reconcile with environmental groups, to whom he had stopped speaking just six weeks into his job. They continued to criticize him for refusing to touch more than one billion dollars in the Land and Water Conservation Fund, which had been set aside for national park acquisition, and for spending only about half of the amount of funds for land acquisition appropriated by Congress.[23]

Watt's bluntness turned out to haunt him after he banned the Beach Boys from performing on the Capital Mall, embarrassing the president and the first lady (a great admirer of the musicians), who rescheduled the concert. Then, in a speech before Chamber of Commerce lobbyists, Watt recalled that an Interior Department coal advisory panel was comprised of "a black, a woman, two Jews and a cripple," a remark widely criticized in the press. Eventually this made Watt a major liability to Reagan, who then asked for his resignation. Shortly thereafter, to head the Department of the Interior Reagan appointed William Clark, a man whose term was as undistinguished as Watt's had been tumultuous. Clark served less than a year and a half and was replaced by Donald Hodel, another moderate.

Reagan's appointment of Anne (Gorsuch) Burford as Administrator of the Environmental Protection Agency proved to be even more of an embarrassment than Watt. Burford, a former member of the Colorado legislature, became one of the youngest of Reagan's appointees despite her lack of administrative experience. She began her term as administrator by reorganizing the agency, abolishing divisions only to reestablish them later. The EPA's highly politicized staff members demoralized careerists, and the agency was constantly under siege both from environmental groups (who believed Burford's appointment signaled Reagan's support for industry interests) and from members of Congress. More telling, perhaps, was the loss of a fifth of the EPA's personnel and the major cuts in the agency's budget that began in 1980.[24]

Under Burford, the Office of Enforcement was dismantled, and personnel within the agency found their positions downgraded. Environmental professionals were often passed over for promotion by political appointees, and neither of the two original associate administrators served more than one hundred days.[25] The Reagan administration became embroiled in further controversy when several top EPA administrators, including the agency's general counsel, were investigated or accused of conflict of interest, perjury, giving sweetheart deals to polluters who had influential political ties, and other misdeeds. By the end of his third year in office, more than twenty senior EPA employees had been removed from office and several key agency officials had resigned under pressure.[26]

The biggest fall was Burford's. In fall 1982, John Dingell, chairman of the House Committee on Energy and Commerce, initiated an investigation of alleged abuses in Superfund enforcement and sought EPA documents as part of the case. Dingell subpoenaed Burford to appear to provide the committee with the documents, but on the basis of Justice Department advice, she declined to do so, citing the doctrine of executive privilege. In December 1982, the House voted to declare her in contempt of Congress. Eventually a compromise was struck that allowed the committee to examine nearly all the documents they sought, and the contempt citation was dropped.

The contempt charge was coupled with charges of EPA mismanagement of cleanup operations after discovery of the toxic chemical dioxin in roadways at Times Beach, Missouri. The project had been handled by EPA Assistant Administrator for Hazardous Waste, Rita Lavelle, who was eventually fired by Reagan. Lavelle was the only EPA official to face criminal charges, and she was convicted of perjury and obstructing a congressional investigation. She was sentenced to six months in prison and fined $10,000. The incident cast further doubt on Burford's ability to manage the agency, and she resigned March 9, 1983. At a press conference two days later, Reagan said he believed that it was he, not Burford, who was the real target of Congress's action. He said that he never would have asked for her resignation.[27] Congress did not let up even after Burford resigned. At the end of August 1984, a House Energy and Commerce Oversight Committee concluded that from 1981 to 1983, "top level officials of the EPA violated their public trust by disregarding the public health and environment, manipulating the Superfund program for political purposes, engaging in unethical conduct, and participating in other abuses."[28]

To return the agency to some semblance of credibility, Reagan called upon the EPA's first administrator, William Ruckelshaus, who returned to coordinate salvage operations. Ruckelshaus restored morale to the middle-level EPA staff, reversed the adversarial posture of EPA toward Congress and the media, and brought in new and experienced administrators to replace political appointees.[29] During his second stint as administrator, Ruckelshaus revised the standards for the lead content in gasoline and declared an emergency ban on ethylene dibromide (EDB), a pesticide widely used in grain and food production. Ruckelshaus served until after Reagan's reelection, when the President appointed his third EPA administrator, Lee Thomas.

Thomas, a South Carolina native, became the first nonlawyer to head the agency. He had previously worked in the Federal Emergency Management Administration and headed the Times Beach Task Force that led to Rita Lavelle's firing. When Lavelle left, Thomas took over her position as coordinator of hazardous waste, Superfund, and RCRA programs. Seen as a career EPA employee, he redefined the agency's mission. On the one hand, he focused attention on localized concerns such as medical waste and the garbage crisis that was threatening urban areas. At the same time, he brought attention to global concerns like the weakening of the ozone layer and chlorofluorocarbons (CFCs). Thomas made sure that the EPA became an active participant in international forums and returned the environment to the policy agenda.[30] Another major achievement was the full restoration of the EPA's reputation for strong enforcement, especially after the agency reached a 1985 agreement with Westinghouse Corporation to spend $100 million to clean up toxic waste at its Indiana facilities. This was followed in 1986 by an agreement with Aerojet General to clean up a toxic dump near Sacramento (estimated to cost the company $82 million) and in 1988 by a $1 billion cleanup agreement with Shell Oil and the U.S. Army at the Rocky Mountain arsenal near Denver.

Many environmentalists believed George Bush's campaign promise to be "the environmental president" when he appointed William Reilly to head the EPA in 1989. Reilly, who had previously served as head of the U.S. branch of the World Wildlife Fund, was the first environmental professional to serve as administrator. He had also established a reputation as a moderate while serving with the Washington, D.C.–based Conservation Foundation. The Sierra Club took a wait-and-see attitude, declaring that Reilly was "clearly tagged to be the administration's good guy in a very tough job."[31] Reilly's agenda was different from those of the Reagan appointees. In several early speeches and articles, he reiterated the need for pollution prevention as "a fundamental part of all our activities, all our initiatives, and all our economic growth," making it the theme of EPA's Earth Day celebrations in April 1990.[32] He also pointed to science and risk assessment "to help the Agency put together a much more coherent agenda than has characterized the past 20 years."[33] Reilly and Bush were jointly praised for having broken the legislative gridlock that characterized clean air legislation since the amendments had last been revised in 1977 (see Chapter 8).

Some observers believe, however, that Reilly's efforts were often derailed by members of the White House staff, especially by then Chief of Staff John Sununu, who ridiculed EPA pronouncements on global warming and wetlands preservation, and by budget director Richard Darman, who once called Reilly "a global rock star."[34] Sununu was criticized by environmentalists, who believe he blocked serious international negotiations on global warming. Reilly was caught up in White House politics again in June 1992 when a memo to President Bush on negotiations at the Earth Summit was leaked to the press; some insiders believe that Vice President Dan Quayle's office was responsible.

Bush's other appointees were given mixed reviews, from Michael Deland, head of the Department of Environmental Quality (DEQ) and an ardent environmentalist, to James Watkins, Bush's secretary of energy, who won praise for his commitment to alternative energy and energy conservation policy, although critics of the administration felt that his views had not been translated into substantive policy change. The appointment of Manuel Lujan, Jr., a former congressional representative from New Mexico, as secretary of the interior, was criticized by environmental groups that believed he favored the logging and mining interests of the West. Lujan's critics became even more alarmed when Lujan agreed in October 1991 to convene the so-called Endangered Species "God Squad" to review the denial of timber permits on Bureau of Land Management (BLM) property because they threatened the habitat of the Northern spotted owl, a species that had been declared threatened the previous year. But the secretary's supporters argued that he was taking a more reasonable approach to the Endangered Species Act and simply invoking a mechanism provided for under law. Equally controversial was the president's wetlands policy. By redefining what constitutes a wetland, the administration had exempted thousands of acres of land from federal protection — a move that pleased the business community and angered environmentalists who took the matter to court.

Did Bush live up to his claims as "the environmental president"? In his 1991 message on environmental quality, Bush pointed to adoption of an international agreement on CFCs, enactment of the Oil Pollution Act of 1990, enactment of an environmentally progressive farm bill, and his commitment to environmental stewardship. He noted that in 1990, the EPA's enforcement staff had a record of felony indictments that was 33 percent higher than that of 1989. His America the Beautiful tree-planting initiative hoped to add one billion new trees annually over the next ten years.[35] In December 1990, he established the President's Commission on Environmental Quality to build public/private partnerships to achieve concrete results in the area of pollution prevention, conservation, education, and international cooperation. Critics counter that under Vice President Dan Quayle, the Council on Competitiveness thwarted congressional intent by preventing agencies from issuing regulations required by environmental laws. House Subcommittee on Health and the Environment Chairman Henry Waxman accused the council of "helping polluters block EPA's efforts" through its regulatory review process.[36] Proving that almost everything he does offends someone, Bush was criticized by both environmentalists and conservatives.

Voters had a clear choice on environmental issues in the 1992 presidential election. While Bush proposed giving greater consideration to protecting jobs in enforcing the Endangered Species Act, Bill Clinton ran on an environmentalist's dream platform. One of the key provisions of the Clinton campaign was a promise to limit U.S. carbon dioxide emissions to 1990 levels by the year 2000 to halt global warming — an issue for which Bush was soundly criticized for not supporting at the Earth Summit. Clinton also pledged to create recycling and energy conservation incentives, to set national water pollution runoff standards, and to support a forty-miles-per-gallon fuel standard. In direct contrast to Bush, Clinton promised to restore to the UN Population Fund monies that had previously been cut off and to oppose drilling in the Arctic National Wildlife Refuge. These viewpoints, along with his appointments to executive branch agencies, gave environmentalists room for hope and a sense of renewed executive branch leadership.

Clinton faced a unique situation during his first term. During his first two years as president, he worked with a Democratic Congress, while the sea change congressional elections of 1994 made a historic transfer of power of both houses to the Republicans, effectively bottling up the few legislative initiatives the administration tried to make. Even during the first two years, Clinton's environmental successes were minimal. Clinton's White House staff initially set the tone by eliminating the Council on Competitiveness, which both Bush and Reagan had used to sidestep EPA regulations, and by proposing to replace the CEQ with a new White House environmental policy office. The CEQ was a statutory agency of Congress, not subject to presidential fiat and, therefore, could not be abolished. But it was merged in 1994 with the new Office of Environmental Policy, headed by Gore protégé Kathleen McGinty. The president also appointed a Council on Sustainable Development, made up of business leaders, representatives from environmental groups, and government officials, which issued a 1996 report calling for a change from conflict to collaboration to maximize environmental protection. Less than a month into his administration, Clinton also endorsed a Senate bill to create the Department of the Environment, elevating the EPA to cabinet-level status. Similar legislation had been introduced each session since 1989, but never gained sufficient support, especially when the Republicans took control of Congress. His Office of Environmental Justice, established in 1994 by executive order, was the first effort by any administration to deal with the issue.

Clinton's first term was marked by the signing of only two environmental measures of any significance — the 1994 California Desert Protection Act and bipartisan-supported revisions in safe drinking-water amendments in 1996. In both cases, the groundwork for passage had been laid by Congress, and both measures reflect legislative momentum rather than presidential leadership. The majority of the nation's most important domestic environmental problems — grazing fees on public lands, designations of wetlands, storage of hazardous and nuclear waste, reauthorization of Superfund legislation — remained trapped in the legislative gridlock of a divided government. Environmentalists criticized the administration for switching sides and accepting a logging compromise in 1995 that opened old-growth forests to salvage timber cuts and for compromising with automakers on implementation of the 1990 Clean Air Act Amendments. Industry groups were just as upset with the White House. There were some small preservationist victories, such as the reintroduction of wolves into Yellowstone National Park and continuation of protection of the Arctic National Wildlife Refuge and the Tongass National Forest in Alaska. The 1997 Interior Department appropriations bill avoided the controversies that plagued the 1996 bill and actually increased overall spending for the department because of emergency funds for fighting Western fires.[37] However, the first Clinton term was hard on the EPA, resulting in staff cutbacks for research by one-third and a shift toward external rather than in-house research. One report on the agency found that the agency's ability to produce sound environmental studies had been diminished and that the "quality of science produced in EPA has plummeted into a state of crisis."[38]

In the area of global environmental politics, Clinton had promised to accelerate and expand U.S. involvement in international preservation efforts, expecting support from Gore and a new legion of activist Democratic members to implement a wide-ranging but unfocused plan. The president failed to establish a timetable to meet proposals to reduce emissions of greenhouse gases, but Clinton can be credited with his prompt signing of the biodiversity treaty that had been adopted at the Earth Summit in 1992. Clinton followed up by establishing a National Biological Service to survey American species — a program that immediately became the target of Republican budget slashers. Clinton also followed up on a campaign promise to restore support for international family planning programs and the Global Environmental Facility, a fund to help developing countries meet their global environmental obligations under international treaties, but these programs also were slashed by the new Republican majority in Congress. Clinton promised early in his first term that the United States would take the lead in addressing global climate change, and he proposed an energy tax in 1993 as part of his deficit reduction plan, but he abandoned both of those efforts in the face of strong opposition from the Republican-controlled Congress. These policy failures undermined the United States' leadership in global environmental diplomacy that seemed so certain when the Clinton-Gore ticket was first elected. By 1996, the administration had given modest support to legally binding limits on greenhouse gases, to be set sometime after the year 2005, and had failed to rally support to ratify the biodiversity convention.[39]

Clinton's administration will be remembered as one in which the president was successful in blocking Republicans who sought a major regulatory overhaul for laws covering issues such as wetlands, mining reform, and the Endangered Species Act and who tried to use the budget process to reduce environmental regulations and agency activities.[40] But environmental policy did not become a priority of the administration until blocking congressional environmental protection rollbacks became politically potent. Despite his efforts to reinvent government and make regulation more efficient, Clinton met with resistance virtually every time he sought collaborative agreements on environmental problems.[41] He had largely abandoned global environmental concerns, while his promises to protect Social Security, education, and health care from Republicans became core issues. As one political scientist, Martin Nie, has noted, "Clinton found himself to be not 'the candidate of change' in regard to the environment, but the defender of the environmental status quo."[42]

CONGRESSIONAL POLICY MAKING

The most striking thing about environmental policy making in Congress is its fragmentation. James Anderson refers to this issue in his discussion of majority building in Congress as a part of the policy adoption phase of policy making.[43] The authorizing committees have primary responsibility for writing environmental laws. In the House, the Resources Committee is the primary focus of bills dealing with public lands and natural resources. The Commerce Committee has broad jurisdiction over energy, environmental regulation, and health. The Transportation and Infrastructure Committee has responsibility for water projects. Several other committees regularly get involved in environmental issues: Agriculture, Government Reform and Oversight, International Relations, Science, and Small Business. Then there are committees that have a say in how much money is raised from special environmental taxes (the Ways and Means Committee), how much is spent on environmental programs in general (the Budget Committee), and how funds are distributed to specific agencies and programs (the Appropriations Committee). Each committee is further divided into subcommittees that create additional overlaps. The Senate is almost as fragmented for environmental policy, with a similar set of budget-related committees (the tax committee is Finance rather than Ways and Means). The Energy and Natural Resources and the Environment and Public Works committees are the major players, but the Agriculture, Commerce, Foreign Relations, Governmental Affairs, and Small Business committees are also regular participants in major environmental initiatives.

The House and Senate leaders also play primary roles in environmental policy, as they set the agenda for their chambers and determine what issues will be given priority. The House leaders have taken a particular interest in environmental regulation, vowing to reduce its cost and intrusiveness. The House Government Reform and Oversight and Senate Governmental Affairs, as well as the other committees, have given particular scrutiny in oversight hearings and investigations to the Interior Department and the EPA. The chairs of committees play enormously important roles in deciding what bills are moved through the process and what committee resources are aimed at what issues.

Although Congress has primary responsibility for policy formulation and adoption, the nature of the institution has hampered that role. Congress's current inability to develop an overall national environmental policy has been termed "environmental gridlock,"[44] referring to the contrast between the institution's rapid pace and initiative during the 1960s and 1970s in comparison with the body's current inability to move forward with a legislative agenda. There are a number of reasons to explain current congressional inaction:

1. The fragmentation of the committee system decentralizes both power and the decision-making process. Environmental issues do not "belong" to any one committee within Congress. Eleven of the Senate's standing committees and fourteen of those in the House claim some environmental jurisdiction. Depending on the title of a particular piece of legislation and the subject matter, there is a great deal of latitude in deciding which committee(s) should have jurisdiction. For example, a bill dealing with global warming could be heard by the Senate's Agriculture, Appropriations, Commerce, Science and Transportation, Energy and Natural Resources, or Environment and Public Works committee, since each claims some degree of jurisdiction over that subject. Similarly, in the House, the

same bill might be heard by either the Agriculture, Appropriations, Foreign Affairs, or Committee on Technology and Competitiveness committee. When environmental issues are "hot," a certain rivalry exists that causes competition among committees as to which one will have the greatest chance of influencing the bill's content.

2. The pressures of an increasing number of "green" groups and industry interests have made it more difficult to build congressional consensus. The same committee fragmentation that is a characteristic of the modern Congress also gives interest groups more access to the legislative process. If a group feels one committee is less accommodating to their interests, they may seek a more favorable venue before another committee or subcommittee. At any one point in the legislative process, there may be dozens of groups vying for members' attention, and environmental groups have lost the power advantage they once enjoyed at the problem-identification stage of the policy process.

3. Members of Congress often lack the time and expertise needed to produce sophisticated legislation. One of the criticisms of Congress is that it is "an assembly of scientific amateurs enacting programs of great technical complexity to ameliorate scientifically complicated environmental ills most legislators but dimly understand."[45] Nowhere is this incapacitation better viewed than in the congressional hearings on the 1990 Clean Air Act Amendments. Many of the more technical aspects of the legislation, such as those applicable only to utility oil-fired boilers, were so obtuse that several members left it up to their staff to dicker with industry lobbyists over the feasibility of proposed controls. Similarly, when debate on highly sophisticated bills dealing with stratospheric ozone depletion becomes a battle of one expert's research against another, many members of Congress are at a loss about whom to believe. The result is often legislation that is watered down or intentionally vague. The hectic pace of lawmaking also has an impact on congressional policy making. Staff members taking notes on the 1990 Clean Air Act Amendments hurriedly jotted down proposed amendments, the authors of which were often unsure of exactly where they would fit in the mammoth bill. Lobbyists, watching the markup process, found that their notes from committee sessions often differed from those of staff, and it was not unusual to see the two groups huddling over pages of red-lined, handwritten legislation.

4. Localized reelection concerns override a "national" view of environmental policymaking. It is difficult for a member of Congress from northern California to convince a colleague from an urban district in New York of the relative importance of a bill barring timber exports to Japan. As reelection pressures mount (especially in the House, where the fever strikes every two years), bargaining becomes an essential style of policy making. Members with little personal interest in an issue could often care less about the legislative outcome, and only by bargaining for something of value to their own district do they have a reason to become involved. Votes on pork barrel projects such as dams and parklands, for example, are often based on the "you-scratch-my-back-I'll-scratch-yours"

principle, with no thought given to consistency or even to the regional impact of the decision. Local concerns determine which grants get funded and which do not, and legislators in positions of seniority, especially members of the powerful Appropriations Committees, are particularly adept at bringing projects and facilities "back home."

5. The election of a Republican Congress in 1994, 1996, and 1998 seriously challenged the existing structure of environmental law, and political ineptitude dashed any chance of improving environmental law. Republican leaders sought to rewrite the major laws, reduce the resources of the EPA and other agencies, and reshape the regulatory process so that agencies would be much less likely to intrude on industrial and commercial activities, but the extreme, antiregulatory agenda was blocked by moderates within the Republican Party who joined with Democrats and, eventually, by White House vetoes. The failure of the Republican regulatory relief effort was ultimately its failure to take into account widespread public support for environmental, health, and safety regulation. This strong underlying support caused a split among Republicans and gave the Clinton administration the incentive to block congressional efforts to cut regulation.

As a result, the most recent congressional sessions are noteworthy for their lack of partisan environmental legislation, especially in comparison to prior years. The Republicans could claim few victories, such as the 1995 closure of the Office of Technology Assessment (OTA). Congress had established OTA in 1972 to provide its committees with neutral analyses of scientific and technical issues but defunded the $22 million program as part of an antiregulatory sweep in the 104th Congress. That same year, Congress voted to close the U.S. Bureau of Mines, which was created in 1910 in response to concerns about health and safety conditions in the nation's mines. Although Congress terminated all of the bureau's programs, many of its functions were simply transferred to the U.S. Geological Survey, the Department of Energy, and the Bureau of Land Management.

The 105th Congress was noteworthy for what the Republican majority could *not* do — gather sufficient support for the Omnibus National Parks and Public Lands Act of 1998. The bill combined several noncontroversial measures with dozens of others that environmental organizations opposed because they would have threatened wilderness areas and were considered environmentally destructive. The National Parks and Conservation Association called the measure "bloated" and claimed its defeat as a major environmental victory, while the president of the Wilderness Society noted that "the result sends a resounding message to members of Congress who supported this assault: don't mess around with our environmental protections."[46]

The 106th Congress began in 1999 with presidential impeachment its main order of business, and environmental issues were far down on the president's political agenda. With Interior Secretary Bruce Babbitt under investigation and President Clinton's attention diverted to foreign policy issues, the administration and Congress seem to have reached a mutual agreement to turn their attention to other matters. Even as candidates began to emerge for the presidential election in

2000, there was little talk of air quality, global warming, or biodiversity among candidates, who seemed unsure of the hot button issue for the November election. As was predicted by Downs's issue-attention cycle (discussed in the Introduction), the environment lay in a dormant twilight stage of public interest, with policymakers avoiding any new initiatives until after the new president would be inaugurated and a new Congress seated in January 2001. Then, the policy process would begin again, with new political actors identifying problems, placing them on the policy agenda, formulating, adopting, implementing, and evaluating what needs to be done about the environment in the twenty-first century. (See "Another View, Another Voice: Gaylord Nelson: 'Father Earth.'")

COURTS AND ENVIRONMENTAL POLITICS

The courts have two primary functions in the making of environmental policy: to exercise their authority for judicial review and to interpret statutes through cases brought to them. In doing so, they use the Constitution to determine the legality of actions of the executive and legislative branches and define the meaning of laws that are often open to differing interpretations. Often courts have the authority to determine who has access to the judicial process and may play an activist role in policy making through their decisions.

Before the passage of the major environmental laws of the 1970s, most courts' involvement in environmental issues was limited to the adjudication of disputes between polluting industries and citizens affected by pollution under the common law of nuisance. The result in most cases was a cease-and-desist order and, perhaps, a fine. The new generation of environmental laws opened up a variety of opportunities for private parties, usually environmental groups, to use the courts to compel agencies to take actions mandated by statutes or to sue polluters when government officials failed to enforce the law. Administrative requirements for environmental assessments of projects funded or carried out by federal agencies under the National Environmental Policy Act (NEPA) spawned hundreds of lawsuits challenging agency actions. Studies of NEPA litigation show that the willingness of the courts to review agency decisions, especially in the early 1970s, resulted from a number of factors, including public support for the environment, a tendency toward strict enforcement of statutory procedural requirements, and most importantly, timing. NEPA was enacted at a time when the courts were generally tightening their review of agency decision making and increasingly taking a "hard look" at agency actions.[47]

Several important environmental decisions came about during this period of judicial activism. Interpreting congressional intent in the opening words of the 1970 Clean Air Act, the U.S. Supreme Court upheld a district court order that instructed the EPA to prevent the "significant deterioration" of air quality in regions that had already met federal standards.[48] A 1973 decision by the District of Columbia Circuit Court forced the EPA to prepare plans to reduce ozone and

Another View, Another Voice

GAYLORD NELSON
"Father Earth"

Hundreds of American political figures have been involved with the process of environmental policymaking, but it is doubtful that any is as revered as Gaylord Nelson, a former Wisconsin senator who is fondly known as "Father Earth" for his role in establishing the first Earth Day in 1970.

Nelson was born June 4, 1916, in Clear Lake, Wisconsin. He received a bachelor's degree from San Jose State University in California and then returned to Wisconsin, where he received his law degree from the University of Wisconsin Law School in 1942. During World War II, he served as a first lieutenant in the U.S. Army and then again returned to Wisconsin, after the war's end, to practice law for over a decade. From 1959 to 1962, Nelson served as governor of his home state, and it was under his administration that the state began purchasing land for recreation, parks, and wildlife areas under a penny-a-pack tax on cigarettes. The Outdoor Recreation Acquisition Program, the first of its kind in the nation, purchased over one million acres under his leadership.

Nelson ran successfully for the U.S. Senate in 1962, serving an eighteen-year career and developing a reputation as one of the most environmentally conscious legislators of our time. While in the Senate, he introduced the first legislation in Congress to require automobile fuel efficiency standards, control strip mining, ban the use of DDT and Agent Orange, and ban the use of phosphates in detergents. He was a sponsor of the 1964 Wilderness Act, as well as legislation to protect natural areas throughout the nation. But he was troubled by the lack of concern for the environment that he found among his colleagues in Congress. He notes: "It was clear that until we somehow got this matter into the political arena — until it became part of the national political dialogue — not much would ever be achieved. The puzzling challenge was to think up some dramatic event that would focus attention on the environment."[1]

His first attempt was in 1963, when Nelson persuaded President John Kennedy to give the environment national visibility by going on a nationwide conservation tour, but the five-day presidential event did not succeed in making the environment a national political issue. In 1969, when Nelson was on a speaking tour, he read an article on the teach-ins that were being conducted all across the country to protest the Vietnam War. In a speech in Seattle that September, he announced plans for a national environmental teach-in sometime in 1970, and the national media publicized what would soon be known as Earth Day. He hired a former Stanford University student body president to coordinate the event, using $10,000 of his own funds as seed money. "Earth Day was a gamble," he says, "but it worked."[2]

In 1995, President Clinton awarded Nelson the Presidential Medal of Freedom — the nation's highest civilian award. In presenting the medal, Clinton remarked: "Twenty-five years ago this year, Americans came together for the very first Earth Day. . . . And they came together, more than anything else, because of one American — Gaylord Nelson. As the founder of Earth Day, he is the grandfather of all that grew out of that event. . . . He also set a standard for people in public service to care about the environment and to try to do something about it."

Today, Nelson serves as Counselor to the Wilderness Society and continues to speak to college students on campuses all over the United States. "We have a long way to go to protect Mother Earth," he says, "but I am an optimist, and I take heart from the efforts underway to instill a conservation ethic in our children."[3] As Earth Day is observed for its thirtieth year in 2000, Gaylord Nelson serves as a reminder of how one person in public service can make a difference that will be remembered for generations to come.

Notes

1. "Earth Day History," available at <http://carthday.wilderness.org/history>.
2. "Gaylord Nelson Will Speak at Beloit College on Earth Day," Beloit College, press release.
3. Ibid.

carbon monoxide (key components of smog) for cities using transportation control measures.[49] The legal concept of "standing" — the right of an individual or group to bring an issue before a court — was greatly expanded as well. The constitutional basis for standing is found in Article III, which gives courts the authority to decide "cases and controversies," and has been historically interpreted to mean that an individual had the right to bring a suit only when there was a clear showing that the person had been harmed, in terms of either personal injury or loss of property. Thus, most suits against polluting industries could be brought only by citizens actually affected by the pollution. Environmental groups found it difficult to qualify as litigants in most suits because environmental harm was not considered by most courts to be personal in nature, so litigation was infrequent.[50] Gradually, however, the courts began to allow members of environmental groups to sue on behalf of the public interest, increasing the number of lawsuits against industries, and later against agencies, that failed to comply with environmental laws and regulations.[51]

There is much evidence to conclude that the courts are now becoming the arena of choice for resolving all types of environmental disputes. On the one hand, environmental groups have been particularly successful in using the courts to compel enforcement of environmental regulations. A suit by the Coalition for Clean Air against the South Coast Air Quality Management District, the agency responsible for controlling stationary sources of air pollution in the Los Angeles Basin, compelled the agency to move forward on preparing a State Implementation Plan (SIP) to meet federal air-quality standards. Coalition members criticized the agency for stalling on the preparation of the EPA-mandated plan, and only legal action got the plan moving forward.

On the other hand, it is usually to industry's advantage to litigate environmental regulations because the process has the net effect of stalling the implementation of new rules. Industry can demur during the policy formation and adoption stage, thereby avoiding the bad press that comes from intrusive lobbying, in hopes of moving the courts closer to their position.[52] Judicial challenges to agency actions have come to dominate the process of issuing regulations. Thousands of jobs for lawyers have been created. Virtually every major agency decision will be highly scrutinized. Regulatory officials must anticipate a lawsuit anytime they take an action of any consequence. It is difficult to assess the benefits that have come from more careful agency action with the disadvantages of a regulatory process that is slow, expensive, and cumbersome.

STATE AND LOCAL POLICY MAKING

For most of the past thirty years, the federal government has been given low marks in its efforts to deal with the most serious environmental problems: water and air pollution, the handling of municipal and hazardous wastes, the protection of endangered species and habitats, and the management of public land resources, from wilderness areas to forests, grazing areas, minerals, and energy. The prevailing pattern has been fragmentation, and efforts to integrate federal, state, and local policymakers have been inconsistent and often unsuccessful.[53]

Beginning in the 1950s, states developed resource management agencies, most often to deal with forests or mining activities on state lands. However, the overall state interest in environmental problems like pollution was minimal. The local government contribution came from concerns about public health and air pollution, a function that local health departments gradually conceded to government scientists. In contrast, jurisdiction over water pollution was taken away from health officials and made a separate agency in most cities.[54]

Federal mandates, which began to proliferate in the late 1960s and 1970s, forced states to create environmental agencies on a single-media basis, such as state air-quality boards or water commissions. It was clear, however, that the federal government expected the states to be the implementing agencies, while the federal agencies provided funds for planning, monitoring, management, and technical studies.[55]

Gradually, three patterns of state initiative emerged. Some states, such as New York and Washington, created "superagencies" or "little EPAs" for purposes of administrative efficiency. In some cases, this was done for political acceptability, rather than to integrate an entire program of environmental management.[56] Minnesota, for example, created its Pollution Control Agency (PCA) in 1967 and shifted responsibility for water pollution control to it and out of the state health department, giving the PCA air and solid waste authority as well. Most of these consolidated programs include a citizen board, which often comes under criticism because of a perception that its members lack sufficient technical expertise. A second pattern was to create a totally new environmental agency focusing on pollution control. Illinois, for example, created a powerful, full-time, five-member Pollution Control Board with a full research staff, the Institute for Environmental Quality. In states like California where environmental quality issues are highly politicized, the single media approach still reigns, with separate agencies for solid waste, coastal protection, air, and water pollution. The heads of each agency are frequently selected not so much for their technical background as for their partisanship, and as a result, leadership changes hands with the election of a new governor and party.

As the technical competence of state government grew, so too did an "environmental presence," which business and industry interests found unacceptable. They turned to the federal government for regulatory relief and federal preemption of state authority.[57] The New Federalism, which actually began with the State and Local Fiscal Assistance Act of 1972, is exemplified by the Reagan administration's philosophy of "getting government off the backs of the people."[58] Reagan's belief in a reduction in the scope of federal activity, privatization, and the devolution of policy and fiscal responsibility to the states resulted in an EPA unwilling to serve as policy initiator or congressional advocate. To fill that void, state officials began to band together to lobby collectively. In the area of air quality, for example, eight states formed the group Northeast States for Coordinated Air Use Management (NESCAUM) to actively lobby for reauthorization of the Clean Air Act in 1987 when the EPA was no longer its congressional policy advocate. The group prepared legislative proposals, technical support, and documentation for its position, termed "a complete role reversal, with states serving as policy initiators."[59]

During the 1980s, states were characterized as being somewhat passive in their environmental leadership, with implementation of the 1986 Superfund amendments often cited as an example. One study found very low levels of compliance with the law, with some states in complete ignorance of the requirements of the statute.[60] However, other researchers have concluded that there is an "unevenness" in compliance with environmental regulations for a number of reasons, and that states are now taking a much more active role than they did during the 1980s and early 1990s. Among the reasons used to explain why some states approach environmental protection more comprehensively than others is the "severity argument" — that those states with the most concentrated population growth and urbanization (and therefore the most severe pollution problems) take the most active role in dealing with them. This may also be tied to states where the environmental movement has been strong and has pressured local officials to enact environmental regulations more stringent than those of the federal or state government, as is the case in several Western states.

The "wealth argument" states that there is a direct relationship between the state's resource base and its commitment to environmental protection. States with budget surpluses or other resources may use those funds directly for environmental mandates, as compared to states where monies are extremely limited and where environmental problems compete with issues like education, crime control, and health care. The "partisanship argument" is that states with a Democratic-leaning legislature are more likely to work toward environmental protection than those that are Republican controlled.[61]

One reason for the change in state-level response appears to be the expansion of state bureaucracies and the enhanced taxing powers they enjoy. Those bureaucracies have become more professionalized and stimulated as state political parties have become more competitive, which forces state officials to respond to their constituencies. Termed a resurgent "statehouse democracy," these forces are coupled with an increase in unfunded mandates from the federal governments which force, or even allow, states to develop their own answers to solving environmental problems.[62]

Others argue that, despite efforts at developing cooperative arrangements between what the federal government wants states to do and what states are willing or able to do, there is still a need for strong federal oversight and funding. Without the presence of the federal government, states' willingness to operate with environmental programs does vary dramatically. When policy cues involve highly detailed, domain-specific knowledge, vertical or "picket fence" federalism may develop vertical working relationships. Coercive controls, in contrast, appear to be the least effective approach for federal officials attempting to secure compliance.[63]

Many states and communities have made tremendous progress in developing their capacity to pursue environmental protection goals. States have experimented with innovative ways of integrating pollution control programs to ensure that emissions are actually reduced rather than simply transformed from one form to another. In 1997 San Diego's City Council devised a plan to protect hundreds of thousands of acres of land in Southern California. The plan won the support of developers and environmentalists and was heralded by many as a model for national efforts to protect diversity.[64] However, there have been problems as well. EPA officials have regularly complained that some states have not effectively enforced environmental laws, announcing in 1997 a plan to give states more freedom to develop innovative regulatory programs. The plan was withdrawn a few weeks later when critics charged that the proposal would permit states to circumvent federal laws and regulations by claiming that they were simply experimenting with new approaches.[65]

The one issue on which the Clinton administration and the Republican Congress have agreed is the need for the federal government to be more sensitive to the financial burdens it imposes on states when it enacts environmental and other laws. In March 1995, Congress passed and President Clinton signed the Unfunded Mandates Reform Act, which made it more difficult for the federal government to impose regulatory responsibilities on state and local governments without appropriating money for them. Bills that include unfunded mandates on states and localities are subject to special procedural provisions that permit members of Congress to block passage of the bills until specific votes are taken. Passage of the bill signaled a new willingness of Congress and the White House to begin to rethink the relationship between the federal and state governments in the formulation and implementation of environmental policy.

THE MEDIA AND THE ENVIRONMENT

The media play two important roles in bringing environmental problems to the attention of both the public and policymakers. One, they report events and conditions that they consider to be "newsworthy" and in doing so, may help to convert a problem to an item on the policy agenda. For example, just before the turn of the twenty-first century, a number of national publications began increasing their coverage of urban sprawl, designating it as one of the primary environmental problems that political leaders would need to deal with in the new millennium.[66] Several journalists cited the example of Las Vegas, the nation's fastest-growing community, and how rapid growth (a house is built there every fifteen minutes) is creating an enormous unsatisfied demand for parks and water delivery systems. As a result, the visible "problem" that many urban citizens had long been complaining about reached the policy agenda. A similar situation took place in Seattle, where the *Seattle Times* ran a series of "Front Porch" stories on coping with sprawl in the Puget Sound region.

Political scientists Roger Cobb and Charles Elder distinguish two types of agendas: a systemic agenda and a governmental agenda.[67] The systemic agenda includes those issues which are perceived by members of the political community as being worthy of public attention and are part of the jurisdiction of governmental authority. The systemic agenda is primarily made up of discussion items; often, there are few distinct or specific answers to a perceived problem. While the environment is most commonly thought to be a problem dealt with on all levels of government, the media often focuses on issues that are more localized or regional. In the case of Las Vegas, local newspapers published extensive reports on the need for an infrastructure of roads, schools, and other facilities to match the massive level of residential home building. As a result, home builders, property owners, and new residents began discussing potential impacts and solutions.

Cobb and Elder define the governmental agenda as those problems to which political leaders decide to give their more serious attention. Not all problems identified by the media will make their way to the governmental agenda, especially if there is little public knowledge of the issue. Although the issue of what to do about nuclear waste has been recognized for decades by environmental organizations as key and has been widely publicized by the press, many believe it is not yet important enough to have reached the stage where policy-makers are willing to devote substantial legislative action to solving it.

This represents the second major role of the media's coverage of the environment. If an issue or problem is not yet widely recognized by the public, the media can make it more salient, that is, worthy of attention. The most common way in which this function is performed by the media is through long-term, comprehensive coverage, including follow-up stories and features. James Anderson notes that, in this sense, the discretion the media have is not so much to tell people or leaders what to think, as what to think about.[68]

In recent years, there has been widespread criticism of the media's failure to accurately cover environmental issues, often with unintended consequences. In 1989, the television program *60 Minutes* reported on Alar, a chemical pesticide used on apples, using as the basis for the segment a study conducted by the Natural Resources Defense Council (NRDC). Alar was widely used by the apple industry to enhance the color of apples, increasing their redness. The NRDC said that Alar posed an extraordinary threat to children (because they eat more apples than adults), and shortly thereafter, the Environmental Protection Agency declared Alar a "probable" carcinogen and banned its use. What generated the criticism, however, was the fact that the NRDC had hired a Washington, D.C.–based public relations firm, Fenton Communications, to promote its Alar report to the CBS news department, a tactic that led to questions about not only the veracity of the report but how the media handled the story.[69]

One researcher has characterized environmental reporting as "muddled," especially in the case of media coverage of chemicals, which "consistently ha[s] been alarmist. A television newscast may present a perfectly accurate report stating that people who live near a place where toxic chemicals have been handled are frightened: the report then skips over the slow-moving subject of whether there is a logical basis for fright."[70]

Because of the perception of media inaccuracy, one observer has noted that "some state environmental regulators would undoubtedly rather contend with a big oil spill than talk to a reporter. After all, the way the news business is heading these days, the chances are good that a print or television journalist delving into a pollution problem will be on the hunt for scandal."[71] This has been true in a number of instances, including a Minneapolis television station that alleged the state's Natural Resources Department squandered taxpayer funds by conducting employee training sessions at posh resorts; the station was criticized for its sensationalized coverage by the state's watchdog Minnesota News Council.[72]

Sometimes, the media affects the agenda-setting process by choosing which stories to cover and which to ignore, a process that leads to what researchers Peter Bachrach and Morton Baratz have called nondecision making.[73] The suppression of discussion may not always be deliberate, but it may also be enough to keep a problem from agenda status. In 1989, for instance, a steam tube ruptured in the McGuire nuclear facility outside Charlotte, North Carolina, and the plant's operators quickly shut the reactor down. Local television crews arrived within minutes, followed by national media and preparations for a community evacuation. Network newscasters reported "a terrifying nuclear 'accident'" even though the event was over in less than an hour and no radiation was released either inside or outside of the plant. The widely publicized incident was the subject of months of public hearings, and local and national environmental organizations demanded that the nuclear facility be closed. In contrast, a petroleum refinery in Pasadena, Texas, exploded that same year. Over three hundred workers were injured and twenty-three were killed. Although the nightly news carried helicopter footage of the fiery blaze, the story subsequently vanished from the media.[74] The difference is reflective of the media's (and public's) perceptions about energy and fears about anything nuclear.

However, the media has brought a number of environmental problems to the governmental agenda that might never had been considered serious problems without highly visual coverage. Many Americans associate marine oil pollution with the nightly news reports that showed dying birds stuck in the oily goo that leaked from offshore oil leaks in Santa Barbara, California, in 1969. Sensitivity toward the plight of endangered species is a result of extensive coverage of whales, dolphins, and other marine mammals, especially when there are highly charged images of overfishing. When the media does not have direct access to these images, they often rely on videos or photographs provided by interest groups, which are more than willing to share graphic illustrations of clear-cut forests, uranium mine tailings, or plumes of smokey pollutants rising from industrial smokestacks.

The media covers the environment because it is politically attractive to do so, according to J. Clarence Davies. He argues that environmental issues are of less concern and receive less media attention in developing countries because people who are compelled to continually worry about whether they will be able to secure the basic necessities of life are likely to have less time or inclination to fret about pollution. In that sense, Davies believes, the underlying reason for attention to pollution in the United States is affluence. Increasing production has contributed to or intensified actual pollution, and as the standard of living has increased, the public has been permitted the luxury of being able to be concerned about it.[75] Without media coverage of environmental problems, most Americans would undoubtedly continue to believe that pollution and other issues were no longer serious and, thus, not worthy of government action.

NOTES

1. Al Gore, *Earth in the Balance: Ecology and the Human Spirit* (New York: Houghton Mifflin, 1992), 1.
2. Ibid., 269.
3. Ibid., 293–360.
4. For the historical background of the nation's earliest attempts at environmental protection, see U.S. Department of the Interior, *Creation of the Department of the Interior* (Washington, DC: U.S. Department of the Interior, 1976), and Donald C. Swain, "Conservation in the 1920s," in *American Environmentalism,* 3rd ed., ed. Roderick Nash (New York: McGraw-Hill, 1990), 117–125.
5. Henry V. Nickel, "Now, the Rush to Regulate," *The Environmental Forum, 8,* no. 1 (January–February 1991): 19.
6. See Joseph Petulla, *Environmental Protection in the United States* (San Francisco, CA: San Francisco Study Center, 1987), 98–99.
7. For a comprehensive discussion of the process by which the RCRA was created, see Marc K. Landy, Marc J. Roberts, and Stephen R. Thomas, *The Environmental Protection Agency: Asking the Wrong Questions,* expanded ed. (New York: Oxford University Press, 1994), 89–132.
8. Alfred A. Marcus, *Promise and Performance: Choosing and Implementing an Environmental Policy* (Westport, CT: Greenwood Press, 1980), 87.
9. Ibid., 85.
10. John Quarles, *Cleaning Up America: An Insider's View of the EPA* (Boston: Houghton Mifflin, 1976), 34.
11. Steven A. Cohen, "EPA: A Qualified Success," in Sheldon Kamieniecki et al., *Controversies in Environmental Policy* (Albany: State University of New York Press, 1986).
12. Quarles, *Cleaning Up America,* 17–19.
13. John McCormick, *Reclaiming Paradise: The Global Environmental Movement* (Bloomington: Indiana University Press, 1989), 110.
14. Landy, Roberts, and Thomas, *The Environmental Protection Agency,* 41.
15. See C. Brant Short, *Ronald Reagan and the Public Lands* (College Station: Texas A&M University Press, 1989), 47.
16. Lou Cannon, *President Reagan: The Role of a Lifetime* (New York: Simon and Schuster, 1991), 530–531.
17. Short, *Ronald Reagan,* 57.
18. Cannon, *President Reagan,* 531.
19. Jonathan Lash, Katherine Gillman, and David Sheridan, *A Season of Spoils: The Reagan Administration's Attack on the Environment* (New York: Pantheon Books, 1984), 231.
20. Ron Arnold, *At the Eye of the Storm: James Watt and the Environmentalists* (Chicago: Regency Gateway, 1982), 94.
21. Ibid., 93.
22. Cannon, *President Reagan,* 532.
23. Lash, Gillman, and Sheridan, *Season of Spoils,* 287–297.
24. Needless to say, Burford's account of the personnel loss and her subsequent fall from grace is somewhat different. She attributes the changes to natural attrition within the agency. See Anne Burford with John Greenya, *Are You Tough Enough?* (New York: McGraw-Hill, 1986).
25. See Richard E. Cohen, "The Gorsuch Affair," *National Journal,* January 8, 1983, 80.
26. Haynes Johnson, *Sleepwalking through History: America in the Reagan Years* (New York: W. W. Norton, 1991), 170.
27. *Public Papers of the President of the United States: Ronald Reagan, 1983* (Washington, DC: Government Printing Office, 1984), 388–389.
28. Johnson, *Sleepwalking,* 171.
29. Landy, Roberts, and Thomas, *The Environmental Protection Agency,* 252.
30. Ibid., 256.

31. Tom Turner, "Changing the Guards," *Mother Earth News,* May–June 1989, 56.

32. William K. Reilly, "Pollution Prevention: An Environmental Goal for the '90s" *EPA Journal, 16,* no. 1 (January–February 1990): 5.

33. "A Vision for EPA's Future," *EPA Journal,* 16, no. 6 (September–October 1990): 5.

34. "William Reilly's Green Precision Weapons," *The Economist,* March 30, 1991, 28.

35. Executive Office of the President, Council on Environmental Quality, *The 21st Annual Report of the Council on Environmental Quality* (Washington, DC: Government Printing Office, 1991).

36. "Quailing over Clean Air," *Environment, 33,* no. 6 (July–August 1991): 24.

37. Allan Freedman, "After Interior's Smooth Ride, Some Issues Left Behind," *Congressional Quarterly Weekly Report,* October 5, 1996, 2858..

38. Gary Lee, "Agency Takes a Hit from One of Its Own," *Washington Post,* June 27, 1997, A27.

39. Robert L. Paarlberg, "A Domestic Dispute: Clinton, Congress, and Environmental Policy," *Environment,* October 1996, 16–28.

40. See Colin Campbell and Bert A. Rockman, eds., *The Clinton Presidency: First Appraisals* (Chatham, NJ: Chatham House Publishers, 1996).

41. One notable exception was the administration's acceptance of the Safe Harbor program, initiated by the Environmental Defense Fund and the National Cattlemen's Beef Association. Under a safe harbor agreement, a landowner commits to restoring or enhancing habitats for endangered species, and the government pledges not to "punish" the landowner by placing any new restrictions on the land if their actions result in the natural introduction of endangered species. See <http://www.edf.org/safeharbor>.

42. Martin Nie, "It's the Environment, Stupid! Clinton and the Environment," *Presidential Studies Quarterly, 27,* no. 1 (Winter 1997): 39–51.

43. James Anderson, *Public Policymaking,* 4th ed. (Boston: Houghton Mifflin, 2000), 152–155.

44. Michael E. Kraft, "Environmental Gridlock: Searching for Consensus in Congress," in *Environmental Policy in the 1990s,* ed. Norman J. Vig and Michael E. Kraft (Washington, DC: Congressional Quarterly Press, 1990), 103–124.

45. Walter A. Rosenbaum, *Environmental Politics and Policy,* 2nd ed. (Washington, DC: Congressional Quarterly Press, 1991), 83.

46. See "House Kills Bloated Parks and Lands Bill," National Parks and Conservation Association news release, October 7, 1998, and "Bad Parks Bill Defeated!" October 7, 1998, available at <http://www.wilderness.org/hottopics/omnibusparksdefeat.html>.

47. Frederick R. Anderson, *NEPA and the Courts* (Baltimore, MD: Johns Hopkins University Press, 1973), 17.

48. *Sierra Club v. Ruckelshaus,* 344 F.Supp. 2253 (1972).

49. *Natural Resources Defense Council v. EPA,* 475 F. 2d 968 (1973).

50. Werner F. Grunbaum, *Judicial Policy Making: The Supreme Court and Environmental Quality* (Morristown, NJ: General Learning Press, 1976), 4.

51. The case that is generally regarded as opening the door to environmental group litigation is *Scenic Hudson Preservation Conference v. Federal Power Commission,* 453 F. 2d 463 (2nd Cir. 1971). The local conservation group challenged the application of New York Edison Company to build a power plant on Storm King Mountain in the Hudson River valley and was granted standing by the Second Circuit Court under the Federal Power Act, which directs the Federal Power Commission to consider the impact of proposed projects.

52. See Lettie M. Wenner, *The Environmental Decade in Court* (Bloomington: Indiana University Press, 1982).

53. Barry G. Rabe, *Fragmentation and Integration in State Environmental Management* (Washington, DC: The Conservation Foundation, 1986), 17.

54. J. Clarence Davies, *The Politics of Pollution* (New York: Pegasus, 1970).

55. See Samuel P. Hays, *Beauty, Health, and Permanence: Environmental Politics in the United States, 1955–1985* (Cambridge: Cambridge University Press, 1987), 441.

56. Rabe, *Fragmentation,* 31.

57. Hays, *Beauty, Health, and Permanence,* 433.

58. For an explanation of the emerging trends of state innovation, see Barry G. Rabe, "Power to the States: The Promise and Pitfalls of Decentralization," in *Environmental Policy: New Directions for the Twenty-First Century,* 4th ed., ed. Norman J. Vig and Michael E. Kraft (Washington, DC: Congressional Quarterly Press, 2000), 32–54.

59. Edward Laverty, "Legacy of the 1980s in State Environmental Administration," in *Regulatory Federalism, Natural Resources, and Environmental Management,* ed. Michael S. Hamilton (Washington, DC: American Society for Public Administration, 1990), 68–70.

60. Susan J. Buck and Edward M. Hathaway, "Designating State Natural Resource Trustees under the Superfund Amendments," in *Regulatory Federalism, Natural Resources, and Environmental Management,* ed. Michael S. Hamilton (Washington, DC: American Society for Public Administration, 1990), 83–94.

61. James P. Lester, "A New Federalism?" in *Environmental Policy in the 1990s,* ed. Norman J. Vig and Michael E. Kraft (Washington, DC: Congressional Quarterly Press, 1990), 59–79.

62. Rabe, "Power to the States," 33–34.

63. Denise Scheberle, *Federalism and Environmental Policy: Trust and the Politics of Implementation* (Washington, DC: Georgetown University Press, 1997), 12–16.

64. William K. Stevens, "Conservation Plan for Southern California Could Be Model for Nation," *New York Times,* February 16, 1997, A12.

65. John H. Cushman Jr., "EPA Withdraws Plan Giving States More Say in Enforcement," *New York Times,* March 2, 1997, A13.

66. See, for example, William Fulton and Paul Shigley, "Operation Desert Sprawl," *Governing,* August 1999, 16–21.

67. Roger W. Cobb and Charles D. Elder, *Participation in American Politics: The Dynamics of Agenda-Building,* 2nd ed. (Baltimore, MD: Johns Hopkins University Press, 1983).

68. Anderson, *Public Policymaking,* 100.

69. For one conservative perspective on the media's coverage of environmental issues, see Andrea Arnold, *Fear of Food: Environmental Scams, Media Mendacity, and the Law of Disparagement* (Bellevue, WA: Free Enterprise Press, 1990).

70. Gregg Easterbrook, *A Moment on the Earth: The Coming Age of Environmental Optimism* (New York: Viking, 1995), 230.

71. Tom Arrandale, "Trust and the Press," *Governing,* November 1999, 78.

72. Ibid.

73. Peter Bachrach and Morton Baratz, *Power and Poverty* (New York: Oxford University Press, 1970), 44.

74. Easterbrook, *A Moment on Earth,* 493.

75. J. Clarence Davies, *The Politics of Pollution,* 2nd ed. (Indianapolis, IN: Bobbs-Merrill, 1975), 7.

FOR FURTHER READING

Cecil D. Andrus and Joel Connelly. *Cecil Andrus: Politics Western Style*. Seattle, WA: Sasquatch Books, 1998.

Ken Conca and Geoffrey Debelko. *Green Planet Blues: Environmental Politics from Stockholm to Kyoto,* 2nd ed. Boulder, CO: Westview Press, 1998.

David F. Linowes. *Creating Public Policy: The Chairman's Memoirs of Four Presidential Commissions*. Westport, CT: Praeger, 1998.

Denise Scheberle. *Federalism and Environmental Policy*. Washington, DC: Georgetown University Press, 1997.

Ken Sexton et al., eds. *Environmental Decisions: Strategies for Governments, Businesses and Communities*. Washington, DC: Island Press, 1999.

Dennis L. Soden, ed. *The Environmental Presidency*. Albany: State University of New York Press, 1999.

Edward P. Weber. *Pluralism by the Rules: Conflict and Cooperation in Environmental Regulation*. Washington, DC: Georgetown University Press, 1998.

Todd Wilkinson. *Science under Siege: The Politicians' War on Nature and Truth*. Boulder, CO: Johnson Books, 1998.

Oran R. Young, ed. *Global Governance: Drawing Insights from the Environmental Experience*. Cambridge, MA: MIT Press, 1998.

CHAPTER 4

Public and Private Lands

A land ethic reflects the existence of an ecological conscience, and this in turn reflects a conviction of individual responsibility for the health of the land.
— Aldo Leopold, *A Sand County Almanac*[1]

Long before land use issues were on the public's environmental agenda, the discovery of gold in California in 1849 and the subsequent gold rush became the foundation for the nation's mining policies. When California was admitted as a state a year later, the area, which was under control of the military, still had no federal regulation of land use, even though officially miners were considered trespassers on public lands. The overriding theme, according to Christopher Klyza, was one of economic liberalism. From 1848 to 1866, the military appears to have ignored mining activities, even though the miners themselves realized that some regulations were necessary to fill the legal vacuum.[2]

Responding to miners' efforts to strengthen property-rights claims yet cause as little disruption to mining activities as possible, Congress enacted one general mining law in 1866, followed by amendments in 1870 which allowed a person or group to patent up to 160 acres and to purchase the claims for $2.50 an acre. Congress recodified the provisions of the 1866 and 1870 laws with the 1872 Mining Law, later signed by President Ulysses S. Grant. The purpose of the law was simple — to encourage the expansion and settlement of the West. At the time, miners, who were confident of the fortunes that they could make in the largely unexplored Western lands, used pick axes, shovels, and pans to look for mineral treasures. There was little consideration for the environmental impacts of mining — a problem that developed in the twentieth century as the industry used more highly mechanized equipment and dumped mining waste into rivers and streams.

◁ ***Congress, which has statutory authority to protect and preserve public lands like this wilderness area in northern Arizona, often struggles to balance environmental and land-planning goals with other governmental program responsibilities.***

Since that time, environmental organizations have sought to reform the law because of what many considered the "federal giveaway" of the statute. Arkansas senator Dale Bumpers has referred to the 1872 law as "a license to steal," but so far, despite repeated introductions of mining law reform bills in both houses of Congress, the legislation remains unchanged.

At issue are the provisions of the law that still allow mining on public lands for minimal fees. The Natural Resources Defense Council (NRDC) estimates that $2 to $3 billion worth of minerals are extracted from public lands each year — subsidized, financially and environmentally, by taxpayers. Another group, the Mineral Policy Center, believes that $245 billion have been mined "at give-away prices" since the mining law was passed in 1872.[3]

Although environmental groups have sought reform for decades, their interests have been outweighed by those of the mining industry. However, in August 1996, the issue resurfaced on the political agenda when Crowne Butte Mines, a subsidiary of a Canadian company, applied to purchase twenty-seven acres of public land near Yellowstone National Park. On the lands was a closed mine that had been used sporadically since the late 1800s. The company would have purchased the land, and the minerals beneath it, for only $135 under the terms of the 1872 law. The property is now estimated to contain $650 million in gold, silver, and copper reserves — revenues on which the company would have paid no royalties whatsoever. Environmental organizations like the NRDC were also concerned that the cyanide-based chemical extraction process and use of heavy machinery would cause irreparable damage to the Yellowstone ecosystem.

Instead, the Clinton administration negotiated an agreement to purchase the site in exchange for the surrender of Crowne Butte's mining rights, payment of a cleanup fee of over $22 million, and a land swap giving the company federal land worth $65 million. Despite the publicity surrounding the agreement, Congress still refuses to enact legislation that would provide fair compensation to the taxpayer for the value of minerals extracted from public lands, establish long-term monitoring of all mine sites, and set standards for regulating water quality, with special provisions for environmentally sensitive areas.[4]

The Crowne Butte example illustrates how difficult it can sometimes be to get a problem placed on the policy agenda. Although there is almost total agreement on the need for the General Mining Law to be amended and for appropriate environmental safeguards to be placed on public lands, efforts to do so have been unsuccessful for over a century, Mining policy has not captured the interest of the general public, and a strong lobbying effort by extractive resource industries has put pressure on Congress to leave the law alone. Environmental organizations have focused on other issues, while powerful Western lobbyists have kept the law intact.

Mining is only one public land use issue on today's policy agenda and, as the rest of this chapter will show, it is often ignored in favor of more publicized, visible problems like conditions within our national parks and wilderness areas. This chapter outlines the challenges now facing the federal government as it seeks to manage public lands. There are several continuing debates that will be explored, including the perspectives of the stakeholders involved with each issue. It also summarizes governmental regulation of private lands, one of the most contentious issues of the twenty-first century.

THE PUBLIC LANDS

When the United States was in its infancy, "public lands" referred to the entire area west of the thirteen original colonies. The government, however, was not interested in being in the land business and began selling millions of acres to private owners as quickly as possible. The disposal process started with the Ordinance of 1785, which allowed the sale of parcels of land to the highest bidder at a minimum price of one dollar per acre, with a 640-acre minimum. The disposal process did not end until 1934, when President Franklin Roosevelt signed the Taylor Grazing Act, which ended private settlement and established grazing districts on the remaining federal lands. By then more than one billion acres of public land had been brought under private ownership, with 170 million acres remaining under public domain.

The federal government slowed its marketing approach to public land in 1872 when it established Yellowstone National Park. This shift in both attitude and policy — from selling land to preserving it — was mainly the result of the Progressive Era and the pleas of Thoreau and Emerson for government intervention to protect natural areas. Under growing pressure from the conservation movement, Congress began to tighten up the government's somewhat cavalier attitude toward land in the public domain. With passage of the 1891 Forest Reserve Act (repealed in 1907), the federal government began to set aside forest land to protect future timber supplies. Subsequent legislation in 1906 gave the president authority to withdraw federal lands from settlement and development if they had national or historic interest, and the 1920 Mineral Leasing Act authorized leases, rather than outright sales, of public lands for extraction of oil, gas, coal, and other minerals.

Congress has designated five major uses for public lands under its control: wilderness (lands set aside as undeveloped areas), national forests (areas reserved to ensure a continuous supply of timber, not exclusive of other uses), national parks (which are open to the public for recreational use and closed, for the most part, to resource development), national wildlife refuges (which provide a permanent habitat for migratory birds and animals), and rangelands (open for livestock grazing on a permit basis).

Today, the federal government holds responsibility for managing over 650 million acres of public lands: the Bureau of Land Management (BLM), the U.S. Forest Service, the U.S. Fish and Wildlife Service, the National Park Service (NPS), and the Department of Defense. Each agency has its own clientele, some of which overlap, and its own agenda in how it implements federal law. The conflicts created by shared jurisdiction are epitomized by the term *multiple use,* which refers to those federal lands that have been designated for a variety of purposes, ranging from grazing to recreation. By its very name, a multiple-use designation means that groups compete for the permitted right to use the land. A second component of the multiple-use policy is sustained yield, which means that no more forage or timber may be harvested than can be produced.

Several legislative efforts demonstrate the government's continued commitment to the multiple-use concept. Congress enacted the Multiple-Use Sustained-Yield Act (MUSYA) of 1960 and, four years later, the Classification and Multiple Use Act. These two pieces of legislation recognized that land held within the public domain might be used for activities other than logging and grazing, although the laws were minimally successful in changing patterns of use that had existed for decades. When the Federal Land Policy and Management Act was enacted in 1976, it reiterated the government's position on multiple use. The legislation required full public participation in land management decisions and specified that all public lands under federal management were to continue under federal ownership unless their sale was in the national interest. Critics of multiple use, however, call the policy a charade, arguing that it is a smokescreen used by the federal government to justify the exploitation of public lands and resources by favored commodity interests.[5]

"THE BEST IDEA AMERICA EVER HAD": THE NATIONAL PARKS

In the policy process, one of the most difficult tasks is finding a way to stimulate government to take action, and equally perplexing is the question of why some problems are acted upon while others are not. Anderson's model of the policy process notes that, oftentimes, government does not take action until the public considers a situation troubling or it causes discontent. If the public thinks that a condition is normal, inevitable, or its own responsibility, then nothing is likely to happen because that condition is not perceived as a problem. Conditions do not become public problems, Anderson says, until they are defined as such, articulated by someone, and then brought to the attention of government.

Such is the case of America's national park system. Early naturalists and explorers of the West sought some form of preservation for the scenic wonders they discovered in the latter half of the nineteenth century. Led by John Muir, preservationists believed that only by setting aside areas of wilderness where no commercial or industrial activity was permitted could their value be preserved forever. His influence and the pressure he brought to bear on the government were responsible for Yosemite being designated as a national park in 1890.

When President Woodrow Wilson signed the National Park Service Act in 1916, he brought thirty-six national parks under a single federal agency, in what was termed by former British ambassador to the United States James Bryce as "the best idea America ever had." The concept of a national park has now been copied by more than 120 other nations worldwide. Since it was created, the U.S. system has been enlarged to nearly 400 sites, including 230 sites that represent historical or cultural events and places of significance, such as the theater where President Abraham Lincoln was assassinated and Hawaii's leprosy settlement. Many environmental groups are critical of the addition of such monuments to the

NPS system when the infrastructure within the parks is in need of maintenance and so many parks have personnel shortages. Facilities at Ellis Island, New York, are in need of repair, and temporary concrete barriers had to be installed in Glacier National Park where the road's stone restraining wall has crumbled. Campgrounds, trails, roads, sewer lines, and other park facilities are swamped with growing numbers of users.[6]

While there is little dispute that the country's existing national park system is in trouble and needs vast amounts of additional resources, Congress has been pressured by environmental organizations to continue adding more and more lands and historical sites as protected areas. Perceiving a "problem," members of Congress responded to groups' lobbying by enacting the 1994 California Desert Protection Act, which created more than 7.5 million acres of federally protected land in the California desert. This was the largest land withdrawal since the Alaska National Interest Lands Conservation Act of 1980 (ANILCA) and the largest wilderness law in any of the lower forty-eight states. The act included the creation of three national parks, totaling nearly four million acres: Joshua Tree, Death Valley, and East Mojave. The first two parks had been managed as wilderness areas by the NPS for more than a decade.[7] In the final days of the 104th Congress, in September 1996, members passed a seven-hundred-page omnibus parks bill that they had been considering for months. The legislation included federal funds to help purchase the Sterling Forest on the border of New Jersey and New York, creation of a trust to preserve the Presidio in San Francisco, creation of a tall-grass prairie reserve in Kansas, a swap of lands in Utah for a ski resort, and dozens of other projects affecting forty-one states.[8]

Later that year, President Clinton bypassed the legislative process entirely by using one of the few elements of presidential power still under his control — the executive order. On September 18, 1996, he designated 1.7 million acres of land in southeastern Utah as the Grand Staircase–Escalante National Monument, creating the largest national monument in the lower forty-eight states. Invoking the 1906 Antiquities Act, under which objects of "historic or scientific interest" can be set aside by executive order without congressional approval, Clinton attempted to woo back environmental supporters who admitted they were disappointed with his choice of priorities and the lack of attention being paid to issues and legislation they considered to be integral to a comprehensive environmental policy.[9] In January 2000, Clinton used the same power to create the Grand Canyon–Parachant and Agua Fria National Monuments in Arizona and the California Coastal National Monument.

Environmental organizations claimed one last victory during the Clinton administration with the defeat of the Omnibus Parks and Public Lands Act of 1998. The measure, which was opposed by a strong coalition of conservation groups, would have eliminated protections for certain wilderness areas, would give and sell away national park lands, and would have encouraged increasing logging on national forests. It would have restricted the president's ability to create national monuments as Clinton had done in Utah but did include some provisions to build new visitor centers and create a network of National Discovery Trails across the United States. The bill was rejected by the House in a bipartisan, 302–123 vote.

While Congress has perceived the need for expansion as the parks' priority, the NPS has perceived a totally different problem. The park service administration has followed through on its plans to place a greater emphasis on natural resource protection, and in 1998, agency officials began devising a Natural Resources Initiative that would strengthen system-wide resource management, giving it a higher priority and additional staff, funding, and program direction. Existing policies had been criticized by groups like the National Parks and Conservation Association, which maintained that the NPS already had the capability, since the time of its establishment, to conduct routine inventory on entire ecosystems and to monitor its own natural resources.[10] The result is that the difference in the perception of what constitutes a problem has placed Congress in the more powerful role, by granting it control of the NPS budget for infrastructure improvement and planning and by citing constituent concerns as the legitimate rationale for expanding the number of parks.

It is the cultural icons like Yellowstone and Yosemite where most of today's policy confrontations take place; however, these are symptomatic of similar problems throughout the park system. In the nation's oldest park, Yellowstone, the NPS is still reeling from the controversy over its handling of the summer 1988 fire and extensive forest fires in 1996 that consumed more than 5.7 million acres as examples of mismanagement and confusion over how the parks should be run. The fires were a result of decades of fire-suppression efforts and timber-harvesting policies, as dead and dying trees accumulated in forests over a hot, dry summer.[11]

The federal government responded with the Federal Wildland Fire Management Policy and Program Review — an attempt to ensure that policies are uniform and programs are cooperative and cohesive. The policy created an "umbrella" that joined together the Departments of the Interior and Agriculture, together with tribal governments, states, and other jurisdictions with responsibility for the protection and management of natural resources on lands they administer.[12] One element of the policy is the use of prescribed fire — the deliberate application of fire to wildlands to achieve specific resource-management objectives, such as reducing fuel hazards and increasing specific responses from fire-dependent plant species, such as the regeneration of aspen. However, federal officials admit that these efforts must include education efforts to expose the public to accurate information on the environmental, social, and economic benefits that result when prescribed fire is used.[13]

Throughout the national park system, an unanswered question lingers over the management of scenic and historical sites. In Yosemite, a long-standing issue during the 1970s and 1980s concerned the activities of the concessionaire, Yosemite Park & Curry Company. Under the terms of the 1965 Concessions Policy Act, concessions were supposed to be limited to those "necessary and appropriate" to the parks' purposes. The vagueness of the legislation brought beauty parlors, banks, and video arcades to Yosemite along with more compatible enterprises like lodging and restaurants. Environmental groups, park officials, and legislators criticized the thirty-year franchise granted to the company, which allowed it to pay only 75 cents of every $100 in gross sales to the federal government, an arrangement one Wilderness Society member called "the sweetheart of all deals." The revenues subsequently were deposited in the federal treasury, with only a small percentage sent back to Yosemite for projects like infrastructure repairs. In 1992, when the franchise expired, a fierce bidding war involving five companies led to major changes in the concessions at the park. The contract was awarded to Delaware North Company, based in Buffalo, New York. Now the concession agreement requires the company to return $20 for every $100 in sales, with much of the income returned to the park for improvements.[14]

Yosemite has also been the subject of considerable criticism because of what was perceived to be a lack of planning and management, despite the finalization of the park's General Management Plan (GMP) in 1980. The provisions of the GMP were outlined in the Draft Yosemite Valley Implementation Plan, which incorporated the 1992 Concessions Services Plan, the 1996 Draft Yosemite Valley Housing Plan, and the 1997 Yosemite Lodge Design Concept Plan. The latter proposal became necessary when floods in January 1997 damaged 100 percent of employee housing in two areas and about 50 percent of visitor accommodation units at Yosemite Lodge. The broad goals of the GMP are to reduce motor vehicle traffic in Yosemite Valley, restore large areas of the valley to natural conditions, remove nonessential buildings and facilities, and relocate visitor accommodations and employee housing away from environmentally sensitive or hazardous areas.[15]

Although the media and environmental leaders heralded the proposals, which included a demonstration plan for 1999–2001 to use seventeen buses expected to carry about 75,000 passengers a year,[16] park officials ran into other, competing values. In May 1998, a coalition of mountaineering and environmental groups such as Friends of Yosemite Valley filed a federal suit to stop construction of repairs on Yosemite Lodge and the building of new employee housing. The suit contended that the NPS had ignored the cultural and historical value of an area known as Camp 4. The site has been a gathering place for climbers in Yosemite Valley since before World War II.[17] Rock climbing enthusiasts were also angered by a U.S. Forest Service ban on the use of permanent fixed anchors for rock climbing in wilderness portions of national forests, affecting an estimated forty wilderness areas with major rock-climbing opportunities.[18]

The two actions mobilized sufficient criticism that the Department of Agriculture delayed implementation of the nationwide ban, pending issuance of a final policy. The department opted instead to use the negotiated rule-making process, prompting Access Fund president William R. Supple III to note that climbers "will continue to fight any irrational and arbitrary ban on this essential component of the climber's safety system."[19] Subsequently, a district court judge issued a temporary injunction to halt the building of the housing near the rock climbers' gathering area, ruling that NPS officials may have failed to consider alternative sites, standards that must be met under the National Environmental Policy Act.

This case exemplifies the problem of competing values and differences in the perception of problems plus the difficulty of developing a policy that meets the needs of a variety of interests. On the one hand, the General Management Plan was lauded for its vision and attention to environmental concerns. At the same time, the plan was perceived as ignoring the needs of another users' group — rock climbers. Some members of Congress used the incidents to buttress their perception that the NPS is being poorly managed, and to seek to control the agency through actions such as the Parks Act. NPS officials then responded somewhat defensively, challenging their vision of how the national parks ought to be managed over congressional partisanship and conflicting interest group demands. Since legislative bodies are asked to deal with thousands of policy problems each year, only a small fraction of them will receive serious consideration. Anderson argues that because of limitations on their time and resources, policymakers will choose to act on only a few problems, which then constitute the policy agenda. When there is substantial disagreement over the best solution to a problem, as is the case with the national parks, policymakers may choose not to put the item on the agenda, deciding instead to deal with other priorities or issues where the choices are more clear. (See "Another View, Another Voice: Geoffrey Barnard: President, the Grand Canyon Trust.")

GRAZING RIGHTS AND WRONGS

In 1934, the Taylor Grazing Act established a federal Division of Grazing to work with the General Land Office to establish grazing districts, set fees, and grant permits for use. The two agencies later merged to become the BLM. Fees are calculated on the basis of an Animal Unit Month (AUM) — the amount of forage required to feed a cow and her calf, a horse, or five goats or sheep for a month. Access to federal lands is fixed to base property ownership, so that those who own the greatest amount of property get priority for federal grazing privileges.[20] Grazing is also permitted on many national wildlife refuges and within some national parks. When the Taylor Act went into effect in 1936, the fee was five cents per AUM, although the U.S. Forest Service and BLM have often differed in the rates they charged. Congress passed legislation in 1978 to require a uniform grazing fee, which reached a high of $2.36 per AUM in 1980. Shortly thereafter, the Public Rangelands Improvement Act required fees to be set by a formula that took into account production costs and beef prices.[21]

Another View, Another Voice

GEOFFREY BARNARD

President, the Grand Canyon Trust

For a first-time visitor, it is difficult to absorb the experience of the Grand Canyon. Terms like majestic, incomparable, breathtaking, and awesome do not begin to capture the beauty and expanse of "America's favorite canyon." The responsibility for preserving the richness of such a place lies primarily with the National Park Service. The organization protects and restores the canyon country of the Colorado Plateau — its spectacular landscapes, flowing rivers, clean air, diversity of plants and animals, and areas of beauty and solitude. Barnard's dream: "I want the future to be seriously changed for the better by our work."[1]

Such an ambitious mission requires experience, leadership, and vision on a scale with the canyon itself. Barnard was born in Berkeley, California. Barnard's parents were early members of the Sierra Club, providing him with what he calls "almost a birth-right interest in the environment."[2] He took his first backpack trip at age six and remembers his parents' involvement in conservation battles in California, Minnesota, and Canada.

Barnard could not avoid the specter of communism that brought the space race, nuclear war, and fallout shelters into every American's home at night during the late 1950s and early 1960s, and he followed his family's urging that he study "the hard sciences" by enrolling in Stanford's School of Engineering. "I was never an engineer at heart," he notes. "I circulated environmental petitions to put ugly power lines underground near campus and drew the scorn of my engineering colleagues." He finished his electrical engineering degree and went on to get an MBA at Stanford, "to get a broader education and to see how the world really works."[3]

Barnard suspects that Stanford's alumni office (eternally competitive with Harvard in comparing the starting salaries of their graduates) was underwhelmed when he reported the $125 a month he received when he responded from his Peace Corps station on an island in Peru's Lake Titicaca. After the Peace Corps, he spent a year in Latin America before returning to the United States and joining The Nature Conservancy. From 1972 to 1995, he served in a series of management positions and initiated projects such as Parks in Peril, which brought emergency protection to the most threatened parks in Latin America and the Caribbean. He conducted one of the first debt-for-nature swaps to fund environmental programs in Ecuador and participated in the development of the first national environmental trust fund in Latin America.

Now he heads an NGO that maintains three offices, with a staff of twenty and an annual operating budget of $1.7 million and $2 million in assets.

(continued)

Barnard's description of his place? "I have no aspirations for public recognition of me personally. I view myself much more as a coach than a quarterback. My role is to have the right staff in place with the right skills, funds, and technical resources to succeed. I motivate, urge, paint visual images of a better environmental future. I am eternally optimistic."[4]

For More Information

For more information on the Grand Canyon Trust, contact its headquarters at 2601 North Fort Valley Road, Flagstaff, AZ 86001, or call (520) 774-7488. You can visit its website at <www.grandcanyontrust.org>.

Notes

1. Geoffrey Barnard, interview by author, October 9, 1998.
2. Ibid.
3. Ibid.
4. Ibid.

Environmental organizations want the federal government to bring the charges more in line with what it costs to graze animals on the private market, rather than subsidizing ranchers. Ranchers rely on the subsidies as a way of providing their industry with a stable source of forage for their livestock. They also believe that public subsidies keep the cost of meat at a reasonable level for consumers and help to sustain the economic base for the rural West.

In addition to the financial subsidies provided by the federal grazing program, critics point to the ecological damage caused by livestock. Overgrazing is claimed to have led to erosion and stream sedimentation in riparian habitats and to have devastated populations of game birds, song birds, and fish. In one study, the General Accounting Office (GAO) found that more U.S. plant species are wiped out or endangered by livestock grazing than by any other single factor. Livestock are also major consumers of one of the West's most precious resources — water — which is needed to irrigate hay and other crops. Grazing also forces out populations of wildlife that cannot compete for forage and water.[22]

Besides fee increases, several solutions have been proposed to deal with the grazing issue. Some environmental groups have lobbied for a complete prohibition against grazing on federal lands. Others believe that agencies like the BLM simply need more funds to repair overgrazing damage and to monitor land use. A third option, proposed by the Sierra Club, would be to allow grazing on those lands that have not been abused, but to ban the practice on those that are already in unsatisfactory condition. That option is viewed as an acknowledgment that conservationists' achievements are not keeping up with chronic abuse of public lands.

The powerful livestock lobby has dominated the grazing issue. One GAO report found that "the BLM is not managing the permittees, rather, permittees are managing the BLM."[23] Occasionally, environmental groups have been successful in forcing the federal government to analyze the impact of grazing, as was the case in 1974 when the Natural Resources Defense Council won a landmark suit that forced the BLM to develop 144 environmental impact statements on grazing. But in response, ranchers fought back in a Rocky Mountain West movement during the late 1970s, which environmentalists called "The Great Terrain Robbery," better known as "The Sagebrush Rebellion."

During the late 1970s, several Western groups were formed by conservatives and ranchers dissatisfied with the policies of the BLM. The movement had three objectives: to convince state legislators to pass resolutions demanding that BLM and Forest Service lands be transferred from the federal government to individual states, to create a financial war chest for legal challenges in the federal courts, and to develop a broad public education campaign to get Western voters to support the movement. The rebellion was portrayed as a "states' rights" issue, although it became obvious that what the organizers really wanted was to eliminate the federal government from having any say in how ranchers used the land. The Sagebrush Rebellion was the first organized and politically viable challenge to the environmental movement since the early 1950s. One observer, however, believes that, although there was a rebellion for a time, only one side showed up to fight.[24]

The movement was successful in gaining favorable legislation in Arizona, New Mexico, Utah, and Wyoming, but by 1982 it had fizzled as a significant factor in western politics, especially in urban areas. Efforts to join the rebellion failed in Idaho, Montana, Oregon, South Dakota, and Washington and were ended by gubernatorial veto in California and Colorado. Supporters believed that the election of Ronald Reagan in 1980, and his subsequent appointment of James Watt as secretary of the interior, would enhance their efforts, and there was certainly a more conservative approach to land policy taken during his administration. In 1982, Watt ordered his staff to investigate the disposal of federal lands, and Congress introduced bills to sell public lands as a way of reducing the federal deficit.

By late 1982, the Sagebrush Rebellion came under siege from those who believed the states were ill equipped to manage public lands properly. Government officials such as former Interior Secretary Cecil Andrus and Arizona governor Bruce Babbitt, members of the hunting and fishing lobby, and organized environmental organizations such as the Sierra Club and Audubon Society all criticized the movement as insensitive to the preservation of public lands. Under an umbrella group called Save Our Public Lands, the preservation lobbyists targeted Watt until he became a major liability to Reagan and was forced to resign in late 1983. Eventually, legal funds dried up, congressional legislation withered, and Reagan backed away from the cause.

The movement was reinvigorated in the early 1990s as the wise use and county supremacy movements garnered attention. Organizations such as the Mountain States Legal Foundation and the Individual Rights Foundation have led the legal fight against federal lands. Counties passed ordinances challenging federal control of local lands, and state legislators proposed bills calling for state ownership of federal lands.[25] The Western states' rebellion reached Washington, D.C., in 1995 when the Republicans became a majority in Congress. The Republican agenda of a smaller federal government fit well with calls for the devolution of power to local government and transfer of federal lands to states. The Clinton administration's public land policies became a high priority of the new leaders of Congress. When President Clinton named Bruce Babbitt as interior secretary, the former governor found himself in a position to reform public lands policy, particularly grazing policy. In 1990, 1991, and 1992, the House passed grazing fee increases (as high as $8.70 per AUM), but the bills died in the Senate or were stripped from the bills in the conference committees.[26]

The Clinton administration then entered the grazing-lands reform debate through the budget process, proposing to raise the grazing fee from $1.92 to $5.00 per AUM as part of its fiscal stimulation package. Western Senators quickly opposed the administration's initiative and the president just as quickly retreated, dropping his demands for public land reform and reduction of subsidies. The failure of congressional reform prompted a series of twenty meetings throughout the West convened by Secretary Babbitt and others, which culminated in a March 1994 Department of the Interior proposal to raise the grazing fee, broaden public participation in rangeland management, and require environmental improvements on rangelands. The proposal, called Rangeland Reform '94, went into effect in August 1995. Rangeland Reform '94 created Resource Advisory Councils (RACs) — comprised of ranchers, conservationists, and other stakeholders to help create grazing policy — authorized permit holders to not use land for up to ten years for conservation purposes and to graze fewer animals than permitted without losing leases, allowed federal officials to consider a permittee's past performance when determining future permits, required grazing land improvements to be owned by the federal government, raised fees to approximately $3.68 per AUM and subsequent fees to be negotiated, and required changes in grazing practices to ensure recovery and protection of endangered species and protect rangelands.

As Rangeland Reform '94 was evolving through the administrative process, opponents in Congress tried to enact legislation to overturn it. In May 1995, Senator Pete Domenici (R-New Mexico) and Representative Wes Cooley (R-Oregon) introduced their Public Grazing Act of 1995.[27] The Senate version was reported out of the Energy and Natural Resources Committee in June. Negotiations continued, and a substitute bill, the Public Rangelands Management Act, was reported by the committee in November and passed by the Senate in March 1996.[28] The Senate bill would have placed BLM and Forest Service grazing lands under one law, removed the national grasslands from the national forest system, lengthened grazing permits from ten to twelve years, limited the application of National Environmental Policy Act (NEPA) reviews to land use plans and not grazing permits, given ranchers more control over management of the lands that they use and more influence in agency decision making, created local advisory councils of ranchers and other interests (but not the "interested public"), and increased fees by 30 percent. The House Resources Committee approved a similar bill in April 1996, but opposition from Democrats and moderate Republicans kept it from reaching the House floor. In June 1996, House Parks Subcommittee Chair Jim Hansen (R-Utah) attached the grazing bill to the omnibus parks bill that had been passed by the Senate in May. Babbitt threatened that the president would veto the entire parks bill if the grazing provisions were attached, and House leaders stripped them before the parks bill was brought for a final, successful vote.

Wise use advocates had achieved few of their policy goals during Clinton's second term. However, they had successfully placed their concerns on the policy agenda, and federal agencies, environmentalists, and members of Congress were all scrambling to anticipate their attacks on public lands policy and their defense of the traditional West.

TRENDS IN LAND USE AND MANAGEMENT

Given these examples of current land use controversies, what does this tell us about trends in how America's land use policies have developed?

First, attitudes about the management of public lands have evolved slowly in the United States, from a policy of divestiture and conservation to one of preservation. Those attitudes reflect the changing consciousness about the environment, which has had its peaks and valleys throughout U.S. history. When citizens are concerned about land use, they demand to be involved and participate fully. When they are apathetic, decisions get made without them.

Second, land use policies are tempered by politics. Frustrated by their attempts to influence presidential policy making, environmental groups have often turned to Congress or the president in hopes of exploiting regional and partisan rivalries. Many of the legislative mandates given to the agencies responsible for land management are vague and often contradictory, and Congress has seldom seemed eager to be more explicit in its direction. This is partly the result of congressional sidestepping of many of the more controversial conflicts in resource use. Should deserts be opened up to all-terrain vehicles or left in a pristine condition where no one can enjoy them? Should the national parks be made more accessible so that they can accommodate more visitors, or should traffic be limited to not destroy their scenic beauty through overuse? Should private property owners be told by governmental regulatory agencies how their land can be used? The answers to those questions depend largely on which member of Congress, in what region of the country, is answering them.

Third, the future of public lands appears to have a price tag attached. Although there is a general sense that Americans want to preserve wilderness areas, scenic wonders, and some historic sites, they become less willing to do so when the decisions directly affect their pocketbooks. They may be willing to pay slightly higher fees to use state or national parks, but they rebel when the choice is between preservation of a single species and putting food on their family's table. As a result, land use policies are more likely to take into account the economic rather than scientific impact of decisions.

Fourth, decisions about land use policies are often made in the cloistered setting of administrative hearing rooms, hearings poorly attended by those affected by the decision-making process and only marginally publicized. The language of resource management is esoteric, and the science often unsubstantiated. Thus, the debate over the future of public lands has historically been dominated by resource users, such as timber and mining companies. More recently, however, environmental groups have "learned the language" of land and forest management, often hiring former industry experts. Still, most Americans know little about what is happening to the millions of acres still under federal control, and only well-organized groups that closely monitor regulatory actions (most of them based in the West) are in a position to speak for the public interest.

Last, there is evidence of a growing rebellion against government intrusion, especially among small property owners who are fighting land-use restrictions, and by members of the wise use movement discussed previously. Sometimes the protesters can convince officials to soften their rules. For example, Elmyra Taylor's modern home in Hanover, Virginia, was lumped into a historic district in 1988 without her consent, limiting her ability to make any changes without approval from a local architectural board. In response, she and her neighbors decorated their homes with Christmas lights and pink flamingos. The board of supervisors later eased its restrictions.[29]

PRIVATE PROPERTY AND PUBLIC LANDS

One of the most controversial land use issues of the decade — regulatory takings — has galvanized private property owners through the United States who feel the government has unfairly appropriated their land without paying them for its value. The basis for their position is the Fifth Amendment to the Constitution, which states that private property may not be taken for public use without just compensation, and a 1922 U.S. Supreme Court case that affirmed the concept of a regulatory taking.[30] For years the courts have attempted to interpret the meaning of the amendment, especially in cases where privately owned land was needed for public use, such as the construction of a new freeway. Local governments routinely have condemned houses in the freeway path, paying the owners damages, usually the fair market value of the home.

In 1985, University of Chicago law professor Richard Epstein published a controversial book that placed the concept of takings in a regulatory context.[31] Epstein argued that all forms of government regulations are subject to scrutiny under the takings clause, leading private property rights advocates to demand that the government pay them for the loss of the right to use their land, regardless of the reason. They were joined in their efforts by conservative organizations like the Cato Institute and the Federalist Society, who used the takings and property rights issue to bolster their attempt to reduce government intervention. Since Epstein's book was published, the concept of takings has been applied to a broad range of environmental legislation, from wilderness and wetlands designations to the protection of endangered species.

Under the Endangered Species Act, for example, the federal government has the power to prevent landowners from altering their property in any way if it threatens a species or its habitat. From a legal perspective, the reasoning is that the protection of a species (the common good or public interest) must be weighed against the interest of an individual property owner. Proponents of property rights counter that view by arguing that the government should be prevented from imposing on individual landowners the cost of providing public goods. They cite regulations, such as those that restrict development that would adversely affect wetlands, as examples where individuals are unfairly being asked to give up the use of their land without compensation for their loss. Other cases have involved the expansion of national park boundaries and wilderness designations or instances where a private property owner's land is appropriated for a wildlife refuge or recreational area. In order to press their demands upon the political system, individuals with property grievances have joined grassroots organizations like the American Land Rights Association, Defenders of Property Rights, and Stewards of the Range. The groups have sought to gain media attention for their cause, and have sought remedies in both the judicial and legislative arenas.[32]

The Supreme Court has not provided clear guidelines for determining when a taking has occurred and when compensation is due. There is little question that, when the government actually takes possession of land, fair compensation must be awarded the previous owner; the problem comes when government regulation places some limit on how property owners can use their land. The decisions of the Court send mixed signals concerning the difference between a compensable taking and a regulation that must be complied with by property owners. In some cases, if the government requires a physical intrusion, the Court has required compensation. The Court assesses the economic impact of a regulation in determining whether it crosses the line to become a taking. But the justices have been unable to decide on enduring principles. They have devised some criteria for assessing government actions, but the weight given each factor varies from case to case. Many decisions appear to be the result of a judgment about whether the Court concludes that a regulation serves an important public purpose and is valid or whether it is unjustifiably meddling in the affairs of landowners and is a taking.[33] Property rights activists have also pursued their cause in the U.S. Court of Federal Claims, which hears claims against the U.S. Treasury involving $10,000 or more. In two 1990 cases heard in this venue, the court seemed to indicate its willingness to expand compensation to property owners when all, or virtually all, viable economic use of the land is removed through federal regulation, such as that of the Clean Water Act permit requirements.[34]

In the legislative arena, activists have sought to gain protection for private property in both state legislatures and in Congress. One type of proposal, called "look before you leap," requires governments to assess the takings implications of laws, regulations, and other governmental actions. The bills seek to deter governments from taking actions that would require compensation to property owners, thus saving the government money. However, since there is no widely accepted definition of what constitutes a taking, the standards to be used are unsettled. A second type of legislative proposal (introduced in both state legislatures and as a part of the Republican *Contract with America*) would trigger compensation when a property's value is diminished by a specific percentage as a result of government regulation. Supporters have also sought a "takings impact analysis" similar to that called for under the National Environmental Policy Act. The concept was advanced in an executive order during the administration of President Ronald Reagan, and calls for an evaluation of whether or not a government regulation would deprive a property owner of the use of the land. But the proposals have been criticized by environmental groups who warned that such legislation would slow down the wheels of government regulation and would bankrupt the government.[35]

When takings proposals have been placed before the voters in state referendums, they have largely failed. The opposition to such measures is mainly a result of their projected costs and the likelihood that they will result in higher taxes. Opponents fear that takings regulations will become a "nightmare of dueling appraisers and dueling lawyers" who will argue over every analysis and every assessment, becoming an expensive new entitlement program that would have a chilling effect on environmental regulation.[36]

Environmental organizations have somewhat belatedly realized the potential impact of the property rights movement as it relates to public land use. Their lethargy may have been because much of the debate was being carried out in the courts, where the judicial wheels move slowly and the justices seldom make sweeping new judicial interpretations. But highly publicized cases, a flurry of state initiatives, and the changeover to a Republican-controlled Congress have mobilized environmental groups to monitor state and federal legislation more closely. So far, they appear to have been successful in confining property rights issues to the judicial arena where policy making is more likely to be incremental and limited.

NOTES

1. Aldo Leopold, *A Sand County Almanac* (New York: Oxford University Press, 1949), 258.

2. Christopher McGrory Klyza, *Who Controls Public Lands? Mining, Forestry, and Grazing Policies, 1870–1990* (Chapel Hill: University of North Carolina Press, 1996), 28–29.

3. "Mining Reform," Natural Resources Defense Council, available at <http://198.240.72.81/mining-4.html>, March 18, 2000.

4. In 1970, Congress enacted the Mining and Minerals Policy Act (consisting of three short paragraphs), but rather than reform practices, it simply provided that the secretary of the interior provide a report on the domestic mining industry. The statute provided explicit support for domestic mineral production and has been termed "little more than a rhetorical device intended to placate the mining industry." See R. McGreggor Cawley, *Federal Land, Western Anger: The Sagebrush Rebellion and Environmental Politics* (Lawrence: University Press of Kansas, 1993), 57.

5. Denzel and Nancy Ferguson, *Sacred Cows at the Public Trough* (Bend, OR: Maverick Publications, 1983), 171–172.

6. Allan Freedman, "Long-Term Solutions Elusive for Stressed Park System," *Congressional Quarterly Weekly Report,* August 24, 1996, 2386–2389.

7. *The California Desert Protection Act of 1994,* P.L. 103-433.

8. John H. Cushman Jr., "Senate Approves Parks Bill after Deal on Alaskan Forest," *New York Times,* October 3, 1996, A1.

9. See Alison Mitchell, "President Designates a Monument across Utah," *New York Times,* September 17, 1996, A15; and "A New and Needed Monument," *New York Times,* September 18, 1996, A22.

10. "Resource Strategy Gains Ground," *National Parks,* November/December 1998, 12.

11. Tom Kenworthy, "Burn Now or Burn Later," *Washington Post National Weekly Edition,* September 9–15, 1996, 31.

12. *Federal Wildland Fire Policy: Executive Summary,* available at <http:///www.fs.fed.us/land/wdfire3.html>, March 18, 2000.

13. *Federal Wildland Fire Policy: Use of Wildland Fire,* available at <http://www.fs.fed.us/land/wdfire7a/html>, March 18, 2000.

14. See Dale Bumpers, "Profit from the Parks," *National Parks,* March/April 1992, 2386–2387.

15. *Documents and Processes That Implement the General Management Plan,* available at <http://www/nps.gov/planning/yosemite/vip/fact/f02.html>, March 18, 2000.

16. "A Good Plan for Yosemite," *San Francisco Chronicle,* July 29, 1998.

17. See Aurelio Rojas, "Rock Climbers Sue over New Yosemite Project," *San Francisco Chronicle,* May 28, 1998, A19.

18. Jeff Achey, "Access Denied," *Climbing,* November 1, 1998, 75–80, 140–145; "U.S. Forest Service Bans Use of Fixed Anchors for Climbing in Wilderness," news release, USDA Forest Service, Washington, DC, June 1, 1998, available October 1, 1998 at <http://www.outdoorlink.com:80/accessfund/usfsnews/html>.

19. "Climbers Alert," August 14, 1998, available October 1, 1998 at <http://www.outdoorlink.com:80/accessfund/usfsalert2/html>.

20. George Wuerthner, "How the West Was Eaten," *Wilderness, 54,* no. 192 (Spring 1991): 28–37.

21. See Wesley Calef, *Private Grazing and Public Lands* (Chicago: University of Chicago Press, 1960); Phillip O. Foss, *Politics and Grass* (Seattle: University of Washington Press, 1960); and Gary D. Libecap, *Locking Up the Range* (Cambridge, MA: Ballinger, 1981).

22. See William E. Riebsame, "Ending the Range Wars?" *Environment, 38,* no. 4 (May 1996): 4–9, 27–29; and J. M. Feller, "What Is Wrong with the BLM's Management of Livestock Grazing on the Public Lands?" *Idaho Law Review, 30,* no. 3 (1993–1994): 555–602.

23. Wuerthner, "How the West Was Eaten," 36. The ranching and livestock culture and its influence on grazing policies are noted in Paul F. Starrs, *Let the Cowboys Ride: Cattle Ranching in the American West* (Baltimore, MD: Johns Hopkins University Press, 1998).

24. William L. Graf, *Wilderness Protection and the Sagebrush Rebellions* (Savage, MD: Rowman and Littlefield, 1990), 229.

25. Paul Rauber, "National Yard Sale," *Sierra,* September–October 1995, 28–33.

26. 104th Congress, H.R. 643.

27. 104th Congress, H.R. 1713, S. 852.

28. 104th Congress, S. 1459.

29. Lisa J. Moore, "When Landowners Clash with the Law," *U.S. News and World Report,* April 6, 1992, 80–81.

30. *Pennsylvania Coal Co. v. Mahon,* 260 U.S. 393 (1922).

31. Richard Epstein, *Takings: Private Property and the Power of Eminent Domain* (Cambridge, MA: Harvard University Press, 1985).

32. For a discussion of the strategies used by property rights groups, see Bruce Yandle, ed., *Land Rights: The 1990s' Property Rights Rebellion* (Lanham, MD: Rowman and Littlefield, 1995); John D. Echeverria and Raymond Booth Eby, eds. *Let the People Judge: Wise Use and the Private Property Rights Movement* (Washington, DC: Island Press, 1995); David Helvarg, *The War against the Greens: The "Wise Use" Movement, the New Right, and Anti-Environmental Violence* (San Francisco: Sierra Club Books, 1994); and Jacqueline Vaughn Switzer, *Green Backlash: The History and Politics of Environmental Opposition in the U.S.* (Boulder, CO: Lynne Rienner, 1997).

33. The development of takings cases is summarized in Vicki R. Patton-Hulce, *Environment and the Law: A Dictionary* (Santa Barbara, CA: ABC-CLIO, 1995), 291–296.

34. See Karol J. Ceplo, "Land Rights Conflicts in the Regulation of Wetlands," in *Land Rights: The 1990s Property Rights Rebellion,* ed. Bruce Yandle (Lanham, MD: Rowman and Littlefield, 1995), 106.

35. See Patricia Byrnes, "Are We Being Taken By Takings?" *Wilderness, 58,* no. 208 (Spring 1995): 4–5; and Neal R. Peirce, "Takings — The Comings and Goings," *National Journal,* 28 (January 6, 1996): 37.

36. See Barbara Moulton, "Takings Legislation: Protection of Property Rights or Threat to the Public Interest?" *Environment,* 37, no. 2 (March 1995): 44–45; Nancie G. Marzulla, *Property Rights: Understanding Government Takings and Environmental Regulations* (Rockville, MD: Government Institutions, 1997); and George Skouras, *Takings Law and the Supreme Court: Judicial Oversight of the Regulatory State's Acquisition, Use, and Control of Private Property* (New York: P. Lang, 1998).

FOR FURTHER READING

Katria Brandon, Kent H. Redford, and Steven S. Sanderson, eds. *Parks in Peril: People, Politics, and Protected Areas*. Covelo, CA: Island Press, 1998.

Gary C. Bryner. *U.S. Land and Natural Resources Policy: A Public Issues Handbook*. Westport, CT: Greenwood Press, 1998.

Charles Davis, ed. *Western Public Lands and Environmental Politics*. Boulder, CO: Westview, 1997.

Larry M. Dilsaver. *America's National Park System*. Lanham, MD: Rowman and Littlefield, 1997.

Eric T. Freyfogle. *Bounded People, Boundless Lands: Envisioning a New Land Ethic*. Covelo, CA: Island Press, 1999.

Robert B. Keiter, Sarah B. George, and Joro Walker, eds. *Visions of the Grand Staircase-Escalante: Examining Utah's Newest National Monument*. Salt Lake City: University of Utah Press, 1998.

Francis N. Lovett. *National Parks: Rights and the Common Good.* Lanham, MD: Rowman and Littlefield, 1998.
Robert Meltz et al. *The Takings Issue: Constitutional Limits on Land Use Control and Environmental Regulation.* Covelo, CA: Island Press, 1999.
Bob R. O'Brien. *Our National Parks and the Search for Sustainability.* Austin: University of Texas Press, 1999.

CHAPTER 5

Waste Management and the Global Toxics Legacy

We better understand all of this before we start putting waste in there.
— Brian Wernicke, California Institute of Technology geologist, on the suitability of a proposed nuclear waste repository in Nevada.[1]

In 1995, the Massachusetts Department of Environmental Protection gave the city of Brockton, Massachusetts, a grade of "D" on its recycling scorecard because only 6 percent of the city's residents were recycling their trash. By 1998, although nearly a quarter of the city was involved in recycling efforts, it was clear that Brockton was falling far short of the state's goal of 46 percent recycling by the year 2000.

To improve participation, the city, working with Waste Management, Inc., implemented the Green Bin-Instant Win sweepstakes. The city mailed information about the incentive program to nineteen thousand eligible households, along with a sweepstakes sticker that was to be affixed to their recycling bin. Each day, one household was randomly selected for a one-hundred-dollar prize, and five other households were entered into a thousand-dollar grand prize drawing, to be held at the conclusion of the eight-week program. After the contest was announced, Brockton's public works department distributed more than two thousand recycling bins, and the drivers of the recycling trucks found themselves the recipients of smiles, waves, and even soft drinks. One program official noted, "Some people thought the recycling driver selected the winner, and he had never been treated so kindly." In actuality, an independent auditing firm made the selections every day at 7 AM based on households that had properly separated recyclable items from their household trash.[2]

Policymakers have been reluctant to deal with the issue of municipal waste management, which is often viewed as an annoyance rather than as a serious environmental problem.

Brockton's action is only one of the inventive methods cities around the United States have attempted to reduce the amount of trash that must be hauled away by increasing the percentage of households that recycle. By far the most effective strategy appears to be one where residents are given a disincentive; that is, they are charged trash collection fees on the basis of how much trash they generate.

The job of cleaning up humanity's mess, whether it be household garbage or radioactive material produced from nuclear power plants, has become a more visible and acute problem on the environmental policy agenda. In years past, the issue has literally and figuratively been buried at the bottom of the pile of environmental problems facing policymakers. Historically, we have simply covered up the refuse of life with dirt or dumped it where it was out of sight (and out of mind). Now, old habits are coming back to haunt us as we produce more waste than ever before and run out of places to put it.

This chapter explores the management of waste and the strategies that are being developed to try to deal with this ongoing, and highly politicized, problem. The discussion begins by identifying the various types of waste produced and the attempts that have been made to deal with it. The main focus of the chapter is an analysis of the regulatory framework of waste management and the role of different levels of government that are grappling with a growing problem that has fewer resources for its solution. A separate section deals with the policy issue of nuclear waste resulting from civilian use and from the military's attempt to dispose of nuclear weapons. The chapter concludes with an overview of the global toxics legacy and the creation of international regimes to control hazardous waste trade.

THE NATURE OF WASTE: GENERATION AND DISPOSAL

Historians who have studied human development note that there has not always been a refuse problem, at least of the magnitude of modern times. Refuse is primarily an urban problem, exacerbated by limited space and dense populations. It must also be perceived to *be* a problem — understood to have a negative effect on human life — or else it will be viewed as an annoyance rather than as a health or environmental problem. That transition of perception occurred in the United States between 1880 and 1920, when the "garbage nuisance" was first recognized. City dwellers could no longer ignore the piles of garbage and the manure from horsecars that covered sidewalks and streets and polluted local waterways. A sense of community responsibility evolved as citizens developed an awareness of doing something about the problem. Garbage was seen not only as a health issue, but also as an aesthetic one, as it detracted from the overall attractiveness of city living. Gradually, municipal governments developed street cleaning and disposal programs (controlled by health officials and representatives of civic organizations) to begin to deal with the massive wastes generated by a growing industrial society.[3]

Just before the turn of the century, the United States imported one of the most common European methods of waste disposal, the "destructor," or garbage furnace. The British, with insufficient cheap land or water as dumping areas, had turned to incineration, which was hailed as a waste panacea. Cities throughout the United States quickly installed incinerators, while researchers continued to experiment with other European technologies such as extracting oil and other by-products through the compression of city garbage. During the first quarter of the twentieth century, the emphasis was on waste elimination, with little thought given to controlling the generation of waste. After World War I, however, the growth of the American economy changed the refuse situation with a dramatic increase in the manufacture of packaging materials — plastics, paper, and synthetics — which became a part of the waste stream. This not only increased the amount of waste, but posed new collection and disposal problems for local governments. One researcher estimates that solid waste increased about five times as rapidly as population increased after World War I. The most dramatic change in the composition of waste was the massive increase in the proportion of paper, which by 1975 accounted for nearly half of all municipal refuse. This increase is attributed to rampant consumerism during the 1970s, which fostered a boom in the packaging industry.[4] An even more pervasive waste problem emerged after World Wars I and II with the tremendous increase in chemical products, which were being discharged into the air, water, and/or land.

The Universe of Wastes

Waste is a generic term used to describe material that has no obvious or significant economic or other benefit to humans. Waste includes five major categories of materials that differ in their physical properties and origins.[5]

The largest component of the waste stream is industrial waste, which is nonhazardous and is generated by activities such as manufacturing, mining, coal combustion, and oil and gas production. It makes up nearly 94 percent of the waste universe. The second largest segment — about 5 percent — is hazardous waste, which is primarily generated by industry and which meets a specific legal definition. It comes under federal regulations because it poses a serious threat to human health or the environment if not handled properly. Sometimes the terms *toxic waste* and *hazardous waste* are used interchangeably, but this is not technically correct. *Toxicity* refers to a substance's ability to cause harm, and thus all waste could conceivably come under that definition. Since some wastes present only a minimal amount of harm if stored or disposed of properly, they are not considered hazardous. To be considered hazardous, waste must meet four criteria: the potential to ignite or cause a fire; the potential to corrode; the potential to explode or generate poisonous gases; and the capability to be sufficiently toxic to health. Federal regulations also classify as hazardous any other wastes mixed with hazardous waste, as well as by-products of the treatment of hazardous waste.

The problem of handling hazardous waste has become acute because waste-generating industries in the past were often unaware or unconcerned about the potential toxic effects of hazardous waste. Dangerous chemicals may percolate from holding ponds into underlying ground water or wash over the ground into surface water and wetlands. Some hazardous waste evaporates into the air or explodes, other types soak into the soil and contaminate the ground, and some forms bioaccumulate in plants and animals that might be consumed later by humans. Typical hazardous wastes include dioxin, petroleum, lead, and asbestos.

The third element of waste, composing about 1 percent, is municipal solid waste (MSW), the garbage and trash generated by households, offices, and similar facilities. Americans deserve their reputation for being a "throwaway society" since they produce more than twice the consumer trash of any other industrialized nation. Much of our waste comes from the packaging of products that we use daily such as aluminum cans, cardboard boxes, cellophane, plastic jugs, and glass bottles, but it also includes less obvious waste such as abandoned appliances, junked automobiles, and used tires.

The EPA's estimates of the amount of municipal solid waste likely to be generated in the future are staggering. Without source reduction (reducing the volume of waste material before it enters the waste stream initially), the amount of waste generated by the year 2000 will be 216 million tons, or 4.4 pounds per person per day. By 2010, the figure jumps to 250 million tons, or 4.9 pounds per person per day.[6]

The last two types of waste are medical and radioactive wastes, each of which make up less than one-tenth of one percent of the waste stream. Hospitals and other medical and dental facilities generate more than a half million tons per year of waste that must be specially managed. This type of waste gained considerable attention in the late 1980s when miles of beaches in New Jersey and New York had to be closed when improperly handled syringes and vials of blood began washing ashore. There was considerable media attention on the problem because it became linked to fear about the spread of the acquired immunodeficiency syndrome (AIDS).

Radioactive waste includes fuel used in nuclear reactors, spent fuel from weapons production, and mill tailings from the processing of uranium ore. This category also includes substances that have become contaminated by radiation, either directly or accidentally.

Disposing of the Problem

Primitive cultures had an easy answer to disposal — they simply left what needed to be disposed where they had created it. Leftover or spoiled food and excrement were allowed to rot on the ground, where they naturally decomposed and returned to the earth as fertilizing compost, completing the naturally occurring ecological cycle. Aside from odors and foraging wildlife, waste did not pose much of a problem until it got in the way of other human activities. As the population grew, people began to burn their waste or bury it in the ground — practices that have remained unchanged throughout most of our history. The method of disposal now used depends in large part on what type of waste is being managed, as the following overview indicates.

Burial and Landfills Dumping and burial have been among the most common ways of disposing of municipal waste, although communities have developed sanitary landfills as a way of avoiding the environmental problems caused by burial. The number of landfills declined as the federal government began regulating waste disposal in the 1960s and dropped further in 1979 when the EPA issued minimum criteria for landfill management. One of the biggest concerns over landfill operation has been pollution; since most landfills accept whatever household garbage is collected by waste haulers, there is often little screening of what gets dumped. As a result, landfills may contain a variety of substances, including paints, solvents, and toxic chemicals, that residents routinely put into their curbside trash. In older landfills, leachate (formed when water from rain or the waste itself percolates through the landfill) sometimes seeps into the ground, polluting the surrounding groundwater. Today's sanitary landfills, in contrast, are located on land where the risk of seepage is minimal, and most facilities are lined with layers of clay and plastic. A complex series of pipes and pumping equipment collects and distills the leachate and vents flammable methane gas, which is formed by the decomposition of waste. Many landfills now recover the gas and distribute it to customers or use it to generate electricity.

In the 1980s, there was considerable attention focused on the problem of landfill capacity. Projections warned that only 20 percent of the landfills in operation in 1986 would be open in the year 2008, despite increasing amounts of waste. As a result of this shortage of landfill space, the cost of disposal rose astronomically. The shortage occurred because the criteria for what becomes an acceptable disposal site changed, making it difficult to increase either the number or capacity of burial facilities. Historically, the key criterion for landfill operation was accessibility, but that gradually changed to a goal of minimizing health risks. By the 1930s, the United States switched from open dumping to sanitary landfills, which involves the compaction and burying of waste. Most cities established their landfills in the most inexpensive and accessible land available, which typically was a gravel pit, or wetland, with little attention given to environmental considerations. With the advent of the environmental movement in the 1960s and 1970s, planners began to consider whether a proposed site was near a residential area, was susceptible to natural phenomena such as earthquakes or flooding, or was a potential threat to water quality; they also considered the hauling distance from where the refuse was collected. Disposal costs today increase by as much as a dollar per ton for every mile the garbage is transported. Today's landfill operations are tightly regulated by federal restrictions that govern the location, design, operating and closure requirements, and cleanup standards for existing contamination. It is important to note that many of those restrictions were added only because of the political pressure of environmental organizations.

Incineration Many European nations have been successful at instituting waste incineration programs to deal with municipal waste. Their modern facilities produce minimal levels of visible emissions and have the added advantage of generating electricity as a by-product. The United States, in contrast, since the first garbage furnace was installed in 1885 on Governor's Island, New York, has been unsuccessful in convincing either policymakers or its citizens of the acceptability of incineration as a disposal method.

Incineration was initially accepted as a disposal method because it was considered the most sanitary and economical method available. Modifications of the European technology proved ineffective, however, for U.S. needs. Sanitation engineers became critical of the facilities, which often produced gas and smoke emissions because the waste was not completely burned when furnace temperatures were lowered to save on fuel consumption. Beyond design and operational problems, many of the incinerators were built by unscrupulous or inexperienced companies, and by 1909, 102 of the 180 furnaces erected between 1885 and 1908 had been abandoned or dismantled. Later adaptations of English technology produced a second generation of incinerators, and the facilities flourished until the 1960s. At that point, concerns about air pollution surfaced, and cities such as Los Angeles began to legislate against incinerators, setting standards so high that they virtually outlawed the plants. Although the technology was available to increase efficiency and reduce polluting emissions, the cost of upgrading equipment was high in comparison to disposal in sanitary landfills.[7]

There is still some support for incineration as a concept, especially among those who note the advantage of reducing the volume of waste or view the capacity of the incinerator as an energy generator. Critics argue that, even with improved technology, many facilities have suffered from mechanical breakdowns and costly repairs, and attempts to transfer European incineration technology to the United States have often been unsuccessful because American trash contains considerably more plastic that, when burned, produces toxic gases and leads to corrosion of equipment. Even plants that run efficiently are being closely scrutinized for adverse health effects. Environmental groups have raised questions about the toxicity of both the gases and the ash produced by the combustion process.

Despite these objections and problems, officials are taking a second look at waste-to-energy plants for MSW. Most of the plants are called "mass burn" facilities because they use unsegregated waste as a fuel, producing electricity that can then be sold to customers. Refuse-derived fuel plants remove materials that can be recycled from the waste stream, such as plastics and glass, and shred the remaining components, which are then burned in boilers. They have several advantages over other municipal disposal options because they require no change in waste collection patterns, their management can be turned over to a private owner if desired, low-cost financing mechanisms are available, and the market for the electricity they produce is guaranteed under the 1978 Public Utilities Regulatory Policies Act.[8]

Public opposition to incineration has proved to be the most formidable barrier to siting any new facilities, ending projects throughout the United States, from the LANCER facility in Los Angeles to the Brooklyn Navy Yard, where opponents promised to block a proposed incinerator with their bodies. New Jersey residents even rejected a referendum on the state's ballot over an incinerator that had been planned and approved for a decade. Political leaders have found the topic so volatile that it has created an acronym of its own — NIMTOO — for "Not In My Term of Office." The phrase refers to the virtual paralysis over waste management decision making that keeps municipal officials from approving incineration projects in favor of more expensive disposal solutions. The situation is different from that of Europe, where incineration has been more widely accepted. The difference lies perhaps in the contrast of political systems. Nations such as Denmark and Germany have a strong history of centralized decision making, which precludes the kinds of public participation and access to the legal system that allows citizens in the United States to have such an impact on decisions such as siting of hazardous waste facilities.

Ocean Dumping The dumping of wastes into the ocean is one of the few disposal methods that has received almost universal condemnation. The initial objections to the practice were not necessarily environmental — too much of the garbage dumped off the New York coast in the early 1900s floated back to shore. The practice was also considered too costly, since barges had to tow the garbage to deep water to keep it from floating back to the surface and washing up on local beaches. As downstream cities filed lawsuits against upstream cities, the legal ramifications of dumping municipal waste into waterways limited the practice as well. Burial of waste seemed much more attractive and inexpensive to early sanitation engineers by the 1920s. In 1933, New Jersey coastal cities went to court to force New York City to halt ocean dumping. A ruling was affirmed by the U.S. Supreme Court in 1934, when the practice of ocean dumping of MSW ceased as a major means of disposal.

The Supreme Court ruling applied only to municipal waste, and the ocean dumping of industrial and commercial waste continued unabated. Over the course of the 1960s, an estimated fifty million tons of waste were dumped into the ocean, most of it off the East Coast, where the rate doubled between 1959 and 1968. In the mid-1970s, there were nearly 120 ocean sites for waste disposal supervised by the U.S. Coast Guard. Of particular concern has been the use of ocean dumping for toxic wastes. Not until passage of the Marine Protection, Research, and Sanctuaries Act in 1972 was there a federal effort to stop the practice, followed by the Ocean Dumping Ban Act in 1988, which restricted offshore dumping of sewage sludge and other wastes.

The ocean depths have also been considered as sites for the burial of radioactive waste, and for more than a dozen years, the United States was part of an eight-nation, $100 million research effort that had considerable scientific support. But the issue was so politically sensitive that the research program was cut off as Congress focused on geological storage instead.[9]

Recycling The terms *recycling* and *recovery* refer to the reuse of materials, and most waste management analysts believe recycling represents one of the most underused yet promising strategies for waste disposal. There are two aspects of recycling: primary recycling, in which the original material is made back into the same material and is also recyclable (such as newspapers back into newspapers); and secondary recycling, in which products are made into other products that may or may not be recyclable (such as cereal boxes made out of waste paper). Recycling gained acceptance in the early 1970s as the public became more aware of the garbage crisis, the need to conserve natural resources, and the shortage of landfill space. About 7 percent of the MSW was recovered in the 1960s and 1970s; the amount then increased gradually during the 1980s and 1990s to about 20 percent today, although the rate varies from one community to another.

Recycling is actually less an environmental issue than it is an extremely volatile economic supply and demand issue. A shortage of markets for recycled goods represents the biggest obstacle to this waste management approach. During the early 1970s, recycling gained acceptance not only in the public's mind but economically as well. Rising costs of land disposal and incineration made recycling a booming business. Junked autos, worthless a few years before, were bringing up to $50 each, and prices for copper scrap rose 100 percent. Lead batteries became profitable recycling targets when the price of battery lead rose fourfold. Under President Richard Nixon, the federal government considered providing tax credits and direct cash subsidies to encourage the sale of recycled materials, but a 1974 EPA report recommended that such incentives were unnecessary because demand for recycling was high and prices were rising. Some states sought their own forms of monetary incentives, for example, Oregon, which pioneered a bottle-deposit law in 1972. The federal subsidy and incentive concepts never gained acceptance in Congress, however, and were not revived by President Gerald Ford when he assumed office after Nixon's resignation. Unfortunately for the future of recycling, prices collapsed in 1974 as quickly as they had risen, with waste paper prices dropping from $60 per ton in March 1974 to $5 by mid-1975.[10]

During the late 1980s and early 1990s, supplies of newspapers, cans, plastic, and glass began to pile up when communities and individuals believed they might be able to squeeze cash from trash, even when there were few markets for recycled goods. As demand for recycled goods increased, in some communities "recycling bandits" were taking newspapers out of curbside containers in the middle of the night or yanking it out of landfills. By 1995, 43 percent of all the paper consumed in the United States that was suitable for recycling made its way back to paper mills for reuse. The recycling of plastics, however, has not been nearly as successful. Usually, the plastic must be shredded and used in other products. When a drought in China and India severely reduced cotton production, waste companies found a market for plastic fiber because overseas firms and American clothing manufacturers liked the fiber and continued to use it, causing the price of used plastic bottles to rise.[11] One clothing manufacturer, Patagonia, manufactured a polyester sweater completely made from used soda bottles, and Deja Shoe makes casual footwear from used tire rubber and plastic soda bottles.

Some analysts believe that there may be a link between recycling and the economy, termed the recycling-bin index. In 1995, for example, prices for scrap paper soared, peaking at $240 a ton as a result of confidence about the economy and a strong market for finished paper products. But by 1996, the price was about $35 per ton, with many paper makers cutting back production.[12] The problem is compounded further by consumer reluctance to absorb the higher cost of recycled materials and fears about a slumping economy, which reduces paper sales and makes manufacturers reluctant to build new mills capable of processing used paper and cardboard.

There are several ways in which recycling can be made more attractive to both consumers and recyclers. The most obvious is to boost the demand to create an appetite for the swollen supply of materials, or apply sanctions against those who use virgin material. In 1992, for example, the Bush administration took the incentive route by directing all federal agencies to purchase environmentally sound supplies, including those made of recycled materials, and several states have enacted similar legislation. Other approaches have included providing tax incentives for new recycling operations, mandating commercial recycling, recycling organic waste. Nearly every state requires newspaper publishers to use some recycled fiber in their paper. Others have invested money into facilities that turn old newspapers into usable pulp in a process called de-inking, so publishers have pushed their suppliers to increase demand.

Is recycling a viable waste disposal alternative in the United States? Recycling programs in America have not been nearly as successful as programs in other parts of the world. Even though other countries do not produce nearly the amounts of waste as does the United States, recycling is much more commonly used in other countries. Deposits on beverage containers are almost universally used, and more reverse vending machines (where returned containers are accepted) are common in Europe. Source separation programs are in place throughout Western Europe and Japan, and even in developing nations like Egypt and Thailand, institutionalized scavenging and recycling programs are fully operational. The effectiveness of recycling in the United States appears to be largely dependent upon the way in which the programs are implemented. A national survey of 450 municipal recycling programs found several characteristics common to successful recycling efforts. The most successful voluntary efforts were in cities with clear, challenging goals for recycling a specific proportion of their waste stream, curbside pickup, free bins, private collection services, and compost programs. Mandatory recycling programs were most successful when they included the ability to issue sanctions or warnings for improper separation. In both types of programs, the highest participation was in cities that employed experienced recycling coordinators.[13] What all this means is that there are still a number of obstacles to be overcome before recycling — despite its inherent attractiveness — can be considered more than a supplemental answer to the solid waste dilemma.

Source Reduction The reduction of the amount of toxicity of garbage, more commonly known as source reduction, is now viewed as the most likely contribution to the solution of the global waste problem. Source reduction's benefits are twofold. It decreases the amount of waste that must be managed and preserves natural resources and reduces pollution generated during the manufacturing and packaging process. The Pollution Prevention Act of 1990 required the EPA to develop and implement a strategy to promote source reduction. Source reduction relies largely on behavioral changes, and some corporations have begun to reduce the amount of waste they generate, as models for residential consumers. AT&T, for example, reduces office paper waste by promoting double-sided copying; the Seattle-based Rainier Brewing Company began buying back and refilling its beer bottles in 1990; Toyota Motor Manufacturing switched to standardized reusable shipping containers, which save the company millions of dollars each year.[14] While business works actively to promote source reduction, consumers are gradually showing retailers that they are interested in purchasing products with reduced packaging. (See "Another View, Another Voice: The Divine Miss M: Environmentalist.")

THE POLITICAL RESPONSE

Unlike some environmental protection issues where the federal government has assumed primary responsibility, waste management regulations are usually locally enacted and implemented. The issue is complicated by the fact that neither policymakers nor the public initially considered waste to be a serious problem, especially hazardous waste, making it difficult to push the issue onto the policy agenda. Some observers believe that the problem is not garbage per se, but improper management of hazardous waste, litter, and uncontrolled dumping.

There are three major pieces of federal legislation that underscore the government's "hands off" policy toward waste that has dumped the problem in the hands of local government. Initially, the focus of regulation was on the problem considered the most visible — solid waste. In 1965, Congress passed the Solid Waste Disposal Act (SWDA), designed to offer financial and technical assistance to local governments rather than for regulatory purposes. The federal Bureau of Solid Waste Management, housed in the Department of Health, Education and Welfare, had jurisdiction over solid waste, but shared responsibility with the Bureau of Mines in the Department of the Interior. The agencies were underfunded and suffered from heavy personnel turnover, with the Bureau of Solid Waste Management moving its headquarters three times in five years. Creation of the Environmental Protection Agency in 1970 led to a consolidation of

Another View, Another Voice

THE DIVINE MISS M
Environmentalist

Bette Midler is known for her carefree style, her musical and acting talents, and her sometimes outrageous commentary. Her motto as a singer in Manhattan was "trash with flash." Few people are as aware, however, of her environmental reputation, as exemplified by the New York Restoration Project, which she founded in 1994.

Midler was born in 1945 in Aiea, Hawaii, and lived in Hawaii until she moved to pursue her musical career. When she moved to New York City, Midler was appalled at the amount of trash and litter that had accumulated around some of the Big Apple's most celebrated public spaces — its parklands. The New York Restoration Project was Midler's solution — a way of involving the community in cleaning, creating, restoring, and maintaining hundreds of acres of parkland, natural areas, and water systems. Midler wanted to target the areas that no other agency or group wanted to bother with.

One of the bigger projects involved the cleanup of Highbridge Park in Harlem. With a crew of volunteers, Midler's group lugged seventy-five hundred discarded tires out of the park, along with dozens of stripped-down, stolen cars. After removing tons of debris, the group discovered a stone staircase that had been buried in trash and waste for decades. At nearby Sherman Creek, the group's project is to open an access route to the waterfront. "Our goal is to bring life back to the Harlem River, where we'll be constructing the river's first boathouse — designed by architect Robert A. M. Stern — in over 100 years." Midler does not believe that one boathouse will make a dent in the area's environment, which has been blighted for years. Consequently, she has devised a series of other projects that rely heavily on education and community involvement. "We're running a boat-building program for neighborhood kids. We want to change the curriculum, start at the kindergarten level and teach respect for the land. Ultimately, the environment is personal."

AmeriCorps volunteers have added the New York Restoration Project to their list of community worksites, expanding the group's goals to include the development of outdoor science learning facilities for over a thousand students and of a volunteer database. The addition of AmeriCorps workers has also strengthened community outreach and led to a new project, sponsored and paid for in part by Midler. This time, Miss M set her sights on 112 Manhattan community gardens that were about to be auctioned off to developers. The New York Restoration Project, armed with $2.2 million (including $250,000 of Midler's own donation) helped purchase the plots.

Bette Midler is not a checkbook environmentalist. She joins Project members in cleanup efforts and monitors the progress being made at each

(continued)

site. One crew member praises Midler for her hands-on approach to community environmentalism, saying, "Anything that Bette gets involved with gets done."

For More Information

For more information on the New York Restoration Project, see its website at <www.nyrp.org> or e-mail the organization at <restore@nyrp.org>.

agency responsibilities, coinciding with the passage of amendments to the SWDA — the Resource Recovery Act of 1970. The legislation authorized a fourteenfold increase in funding, from $17 million to $239 million, for demonstration grants for recycling systems and for studies of methods to encourage resource recovery. The 1970 legislation also provided the foundation for the development of state waste management programs, and by 1975, forty-eight states had developed some form of program, with budgets ranging from zero to $1.2 million. Most of the state waste management programs were minimal, structuring themselves around the federal support programs rather than using federal assistance to help them develop a more comprehensive effort, and the statute remained essentially nonregulatory.[15]

With the passage of the Resource Conservation and Recovery Act (RCRA) in 1976, Congress intruded into what had been essentially local and state jurisdiction.[16] The required states to develop solid waste management plans and mandated the closing of all open dumps. The only disposal methods allowed under the legislation were sanitary landfills or recycling, with little attention paid to other potentially effective options such as bottle deposit or waste recovery facilities. Another portion of the RCRA dealt with hazardous waste management, but gave the EPA the responsibility of determining what waste was solid and what part was hazardous — a task that is not as easy as it might have seemed to Congress at the time the legislation was enacted.

One of the problems faced by some local officials is that there simply is not enough landfill space available in their area to dispose of wastes properly, and despite the RCRA legislation, many states were slow to develop alternatives. In other states, there is a surplus of landfill capacity. As a result, communities turned to exporting their waste to other states. In a 1978 case involving Philadelphia and New Jersey, the U.S. Supreme Court ruled that attempts by the states to restrict interstate transfers of waste violated the Commerce Clause of the Constitution.[17] The Supreme Court reiterated that position in two cases in 1992 and two more in 1994, and as a result, there was little that states with plenty of landfill space — such as Indiana and New Mexico — could do to stop other states' dumping. Under the court's ruling, state and local governments cannot ban, impose restrictions on, or place surcharges on solid waste simply on the basis of its origin. Publicly owned facilities, however, can restrict the solid waste that they accept to waste generated within the state.[18]

In the 1980s, Congress seemed to have difficulty developing hazardous waste legislation that was acceptable to both the industries that produced the waste and environmental group supporters who believed the issue was not receiving appropriate attention from federal and state regulators. The 1980 amendments to the RCRA allowed for broad exemptions to what was considered hazardous waste, and another set of amendments in 1984 still failed to remedy earlier deficiencies in the law. The RCRA expired in 1988, with several states still unable to complete the solid waste management plans required by the 1976 law. Congress chose to rely upon the EPA to "regulate solutions" to hazardous waste while Congress itself seemed more interested in dealing with MSW problems.[19]

Congressional attempts to pass a sweeping reauthorization of RCRA have been unsuccessful, as the continuing legislative gridlock over solid waste demonstrates. Congress has repeatedly rejected a national bottle deposit system, avoided the issue of industrial wastes from manufacturing and mining, and rolled back industry-wide recycling rates for paper and plastic. Both business and environmental groups have opposed most reauthorization efforts thus far because proposed legislation neither promotes enough recycling nor creates markets for recycled materials.

Policymaking is often triggered when specific events capture the attention to both the media and the public, and this is especially true of hazardous waste. As discussed in Chapter 1, disclosure of massive contamination at Love Canal in New York and at a site near Louisville, Kentucky, was the catalyst for a change in the regulatory focus. Citizens began contacting their representatives in Congress, demanding that some form of action be taken, and Congress turned toward the EPA for guidance on what type of legislative remedies might be available. Both Congress and the EPA did an environmental policy about-face by shifting their attention from solid to hazardous and toxic waste. Shortly after the RCRA's passage in 1976, the EPA's Office of Solid Waste, facing political pressures from citizens' groups and public concerns for immediate action, abruptly changed focus, and with the election of Ronald Reagan, the federal solid waste effort was completely eclipsed by hazardous waste concerns. The EPA's solid waste budget was reduced from $29 million in 1979 to $16 million in 1981 to $320,000 in 1982, while staff was reduced from 128 to 74 in 1981, with 73 of those 74 positions eliminated in 1982.[20] The RCRA's hazardous waste provisions require permits for companies storing, treating, or disposing of hazardous waste and gives EPA the authority to levy fines or hold individuals criminally liable for improperly disposed waste. This created a "cradle to grave" program by which EPA regulates hazardous wastes from the time they are generated to the time of disposal.

Abandoned waste sites became an extremely visible problem that forced Congress to revamp the regulatory provisions of the RCRA with the enactment in 1980 of the Comprehensive Environmental Response, Compensation, and Liability Act (CERCLA), more commonly known as Superfund. The CERCLA legislation initially included a $1.6 billion appropriation to clean up abandoned toxic and hazardous waste sites throughout the United States. But further research indicated that the number and magnitude of site cleanups was much larger than originally estimated. Realizing the long-term nature of waste cleanup, Congress reauthorized the program for another five years under the 1986 Superfund Amendments and Reauthorization Act (SARA). Legislators were dissatisfied with the slow pace of cleanup (only six sites had been cleaned up since 1980), so the SARA added $8.5 billion to the fund, and in 1990, Congress voted to continue the program an additional five years with another $5.1 billion. Oil and chemical companies were also taxed to augment the congressional appropriation, but that provision of the law was allowed to expire at the end of 1995, further reducing the program's operating budget. Members of Congress were unable to decide the thorny issue of how to finance the program, with debate over how much of a site's cleanup costs should be paid for by government and how much should be paid for by private companies.

Under Superfund, the EPA established a National Priorities List (NPL) of targeted sites, a relatively small subset of a larger inventory of tens of thousands of potential hazardous waste sites. Cleanup projects vary considerably from site to site, ranging from an abandoned steel mill to small parcels of land where toxic waste was once stored and leaked into the ground. The majority of sites are landfills, industrial lagoons, and manufacturing sites. Most of the nation's hazardous waste is treated or disposed of on-site with only a small percentage transported off-site for treatment, storage, or disposal. This avoids the problems associated with transporting waste and trying to find a place to take it once it has been removed. Congress also dealt with the cleanup problem under the corrective action program of the RCRA amendments. The legislation requires companies who are permitted to operate a hazardous waste treatment, storage, or disposal facility to also be responsible for the cleanup of that facility. Unlike Superfund, where the federal government must find the responsible party, RCRA permittees must themselves submit a cleanup plan.

Underground storage tanks (USTs) present an additional hazardous waste problem because they may leak and contaminate drinking water supplies. The United States is estimated to have over two million underground tanks that store petroleum and other chemicals, and the EPA estimates that 20 percent of the regulated tanks are leaking or have the potential to leak. Many of the tanks were installed during the 1950s, and the average lifetime use is only fifteen to twenty years. The EPA began regulating the tanks in 1984 under the RCRA amendments, requiring owners and operators to meet strict requirements for design, construction, and installation, including repair or closure of systems that do not meet federal guidelines. When the deadline for repairs and replacement of USTs arrived in December 1998, thousands of gas stations and other facilities across the United States were forced to close down. Some owners hurriedly tried to replace aging tanks, while others simply closed down.

The Superfund program has come under tremendous criticism ever since its inception, giving Congress ample reason to avoid or delay reauthorization and providing justification for cutting the program's budget. The implementation of the law has been much slower than originally anticipated as a result of budget cuts, so fewer sites have been cleaned up than the EPA had planned. In 1995 there were about 1,300 sites on the NPL, based on the quantity and toxicity of the wastes involved, the number of people potentially or actually exposed, the likely pathways of exposure, and the importance and vulnerability of the underlying supply of groundwater, with about 100 sites added to the NPL each year. Only about 350 of the sites had actually been cleaned up, although remediation was under way at more than 90 percent of the NPL locations. The remediation cost per site has soared, with an average of $30 million spent on each one in recent years. No one really knows how much the program will eventually cost, with estimates ranging from a half billion dollars to as much as one trillion dollars over the next fifty years.[21]

Another criticism relates to who ought to be responsible for paying for the cleanup. Congress has been divided on the issue of whether to revise the "polluter pays" concept, which involves extensive research and often costly litigation as to who originally created the waste. Industry has balked at one of the key components of the legislation, known as joint and several retroactive liability, which makes polluting companies responsible for the entire cost of cleaning up sites where wastes were dumped decades ago, even if they were responsible for only a portion of the contamination or before dumping was made illegal. Some legislators have sought to exempt small businesses from cleanup liability, arguing that Superfund regulations place an unfair burden on those firms that are least able to afford cleanup costs.[22]

Compensation for individuals seeking to recover damage claims has been equally contentious. Congress continues to be heavily lobbied — a lobbying effort led by the Chemical Manufacturers' Association (CMA) — to make it difficult for an individual to bring legal action against a company believed to be responsible for the improper storage or handling of hazardous waste. Proving that a site caused health problems leads to a complex legal maze from which few plaintiffs successfully emerge. A number of obstacles face those victims seeking compensation because of toxic waste problems, including that many chemical-caused illnesses have a long latency period (perhaps twenty to thirty years), making the assessment of the effects of exposure difficult. Some state laws provide that the statute of limitations begins with the first date of exposure, limiting claims by those exposed over a long period of time. In addition, hazardous waste injuries require potential claimants to submit to (and pay for) sophisticated and expensive medical and toxicological testing and to pay legal fees that may extend for years. Class-action suits are difficult to pursue because, even if a group of workers were exposed to a chemical hazard, the effects on one worker, a forty-year-old male, is likely to be considerably different from the effect on a twenty-four-year-old female of childbearing age. Not surprisingly, potential industrial defendants have opposed attempts to legislate ways of easing the compensation process.

In response to the criticism of the cost of the Superfund program, the Clinton administration prepared House and Senate bills that were introduced early in 1994. The administration's bills would have set uniform standards for site cleanups; encouraged proportional distribution of costs; used arbitration rather than litigation in settling disputes; used federal funds to pay for cleanups when responsible parties could not be held liable, rather than making other parties pay the balance; and established a new fund to pay environmental insurance fund costs. The bills had been fashioned in consultation with representatives from industry, environmental and community groups, and local governments under the National Commission on Superfund. Environmentalists pressured Congress to include groundwater decontamination requirements in the law. Advocates of cost:benefit analysis insisted that provisions be added to the law as well. The Senate failed to take action, preferring to wait and see if the House would be able to pass a bill. The House stopped work on the bill a few days before adjournment in October 1994.

Superfund was a major target of reform by Republicans in the 104th Congress. Senate Republicans proposed repealing liability for dumping of hazardous wastes before 1987, modifying the liability system, limiting natural resource damages, capping the number of new sites added to the NPL, requiring cost:benefit and least cost tests for remediation standards, and delegating to states responsibility for cleanup of Superfund sites including those located on federal land. House Republicans had a similar set of proposals; none were approved by both houses. Some progress was made in the 105th Congress to fashion a bipartisan bill, but members were unable to resolve many of the contentious issues that had plagued Superfund reform for years.

NUCLEAR AND MILITARY WASTE

Among the more politicized waste management problems that have found their way to the policy agenda involve the back end of the nuclear fuel cycle and the disposal of nuclear waste from military bases and nuclear weapons facilities. Back-end waste refers to solids, liquids, gases, and sludge, which must be treated to remove contaminants or diluted to reduce their toxicity and then stored. Radioactive waste decays at varying rates, so different types of disposal are needed for different types. Although low-level radioactive waste can safely be stored in containers that are buried in shallow trenches, researches have had to look at alternatives for high-level radioactive waste. Under the provisions of the 1982 Nuclear Waste Policy Act, the Department of Energy (DOE) was required to assume ownership of these wastes in 1998 and to store them. The initial plan was to store the waste in a temporary above-ground site, to be used only until a permanent site was ready.

After years of bitter congressional debate over where the repository would be located, in 1987 Congress directed that DOE focus on one site, Yucca Mountain, Nevada, located about ninety miles northeast of Las Vegas. State officials and the Nevada congressional delegation have protested the siting ever since, and they have been joined by environmental organizations and some scientists who believe the location is unsafe. In 1998, the Senate Energy and Natural Resources Committee refused to consider a bill that would have created an interim high-level nuclear waste facility next to the Yucca Mountain site. The Clinton administration and Nevada senators opposed the legislation, which was supported by the utility industry. Their lobbyists argued that almost forty thousand tons of nuclear waste — consisting primarily of used reactor fuel rods — are piling up at power plants in thirty-four states while the government fails to provide the centralized storage promised under the 1982 law. Table 5.1 indicates the amount of spent nuclear fuel stored at commercial power plants throughout the United States.

The dispute has been controversial for decades, and it is now mired in several different political venues. Using the judicial arena, California, for example, attempted to obtain title to one thousand acres of Interior Department desert land in 1998 to use as an interstate radioactive waste dump that would accept nuclear

Table 5.1 Spent Nuclear Fuel Stored at U.S. Commercial Power Plants by State, in Metric Tons (1999)

Alabama	1,827	Mississippi	392
Arizona	834	Missouri	342
Arkansas	690	Nebraska	421
California	1,603	New Hampshire	176
Colorado	16	New Jersey	1,369
Connecticut	1,505	New York	2,192
Florida	1,669	North Carolina	1,779
Georgia	1,182	Ohio	518
Illinois	5,215	Oregon	424
Iowa	257	Pennsylvania	2,920
Kansas	271	South Carolina	2,241
Louisiana	567	Tennessee	661
Maine	477	Texas	735
Maryland	781	Vermont	411
Massachusetts	495	Virginia	1,358
Michigan	1,500	Washington	292
Minnesota	789	Wisconsin	967
		Total	36,876

Source: "Nuclear Fuel Waste Nationwide," *USA Today,* December 31, 1998, 6A.

waste from research labs, hospitals, nuclear power plants, and other facilities in Arizona, North Dakota, South Dakota, and California. The federal government filed suit against the state; it was joined by environmental organizations, officials of nearby counties, and Native American groups.

The issue also reached the bureaucratic agenda of the Nuclear Regulatory Commission through the Nuclear Waste Technical Review Board, which was established by Congress to review the DOE's work. The board is caught between dueling scientists and studies that have discovered various flaws in the design and siting of the Yucca Mountain facility. One 1997 DOE study found that rainwater, which could dissolve nuclear waste, has seeped from the top of the mountain, down nearly eight hundred feet, at a rate much faster than scientists had expected. The finding led Nevada officials to claim that the site should be disqualified, although hydrologists and officials of the Nuclear Energy Institute (a trade association for nuclear utilities) disagreed. The flow is not like that of a household faucet with water running at forty-five gallons per minute. Only miniscule amounts are dripping through the cracks.[23]

The EPA had originally sought a site that would be stable for ten thousand years. However, a 1998 study by the California Institute of Technology and the Harvard-Smithsonian Center for Astrophysics in Cambridge, Massachusetts, warned that the ground around the site could be considered stable only over the next one thousand years. Using Department of Defense satellites, researchers found that the region was seismically active, and therefore could stretch more than three feet in the one-thousand-year period. The movement could crush any canisters of nuclear waste buried there, potentially exposing a wide area of the Southwest to radiation. The report was sufficient evidence to prompt the states governor to urge Congress and the DOE to start looking for other locations. Governor Bob Miller noted: "It seems like there is a never-ending trail of evidence that Yucca Mountain is unsuitable for permanently storing nuclear waste. There was an earthquake at the site a few years ago and there was substantial damage done, but no matter what the realities are, politics seem to take higher precedence."[24]

The DOE, which has spent more than $2.2 billion on the project thus far, turned to another study in late 1998 that found reasonable assurance that Yucca Mountain would meet long-term safety standards for many thousands of years. After fifteen years of research on the site's hydrology and geology, scientists reported that the performance of a geological repository over such long time periods cannot be proven beyond all doubt, adding that uncertainties can be reduced but never completely eliminated. The eighty thousand tons of used reactor fuel, which would be placed one thousand feet below the surface, will remain deadly for an estimated three hundred thousand years. But the DOE agreed that no final decision would be made before further research and a formal environmental impact review were conducted — expected sometime in 2001. Even if the site were found suitable, it would not be expected to be used until at least 2010, twenty-eight years after the passage of the Nuclear Waste Policy Act.

At the same time Yucca Mountain's fate was being debated, the federal government approved a plan to store five million cubic feet of transuranic waste (tools, rags, clothing, and other materials contaminated with uranium or plutonium isotopes during nuclear weapons production). The Waste Isolation Pilot Project (WIPP) complex near Carlsbad, New Mexico, took nearly twenty years to plan, develop, and build, at a cost of nearly $2 billion. The mile-square maze of tunnels in a geological salt formation a half mile underground was further delayed by legal challenges until 1998, when it was formally certified by the EPA. Environmental groups opposed the project because of concerns about the health risks of shipping nuclear waste by truck to the site and fears that the location was geologically unstable.[25]

Nonetheless, on March 26, 1999, the first shipment, consisting of six hundred pounds of nuclear debris from the Los Alamos National Laboratory, was trucked to the site, with only a handful of protestors as witness. Energy secretary Bill Richardson claimed that the WIPP's opening was part of the cleanup of the legacy of the Cold War and its waste. "The opening of this facility is a step to meeting this obligation," he said.[26]

Still unresolved, however, are the prospects for the long-term environmental cleanup of military bases. For decades, the Department of Defense (DOD) held itself exempt from environmental legislation under the guise of national security. Environmental groups accused the agency of disposing of solvents, dead batteries, dirty oil, and unexploded shells and bombs by dumping them on-site and thereby contaminating the underlying water or soil. In the 1980s, the DOD was estimated to be generating five hundred thousand tons of toxic waste per year, more than the top five U.S. chemical companies combined. One agency report identified nearly twenty thousand sites at eighteen hundred military installations that showed varying levels of contamination, nearly a hundred of which warranted placement on the NPL.[27]

In 1984, the courts directed the DOE to accept responsibility for the cleanup resulting from decades of military weapons production at over one hundred sites in thirty states around the country. Since 1989, DOE has spent over $20 billion on cleanup tasks, with the end nowhere in sight. Many researchers believe it will take decades before cleanup at all weapons sites are completed, at a total cost of almost $150 billion, while others believe the sites may be too contaminated to ever be cleaned up.[28]

To facilitate public oversight and monitoring, in 1998 a coalition of thirty-nine environmental groups reached agreement over a 1989 lawsuit that requires the DOE to provide greater access to information about the cleanup process. Now the agency must create a publicly accessible database on contaminated facilities and provide $6.25 million to help citizens groups and Indian tribes conduct technical and scientific reviews of cleanup activities.[29]

Internationally, the United States is being called on to clean up its military waste mess in Panama. For decades, areas along the Panama Canal were used as testing grounds for conventional, chemical, and biological weapons, some as late as 1993. Now the federal government must deal with a 1903 agreement requiring it to close all military bases by December 31, 1999; moreover, the 1977 Panama Canal Treaties require payment for any environmental cleanup. However, the two nations continue to be locked in disputes over the extent of the problem and whether there is adequate technology to do the job safely without damaging the tropical environment.[30]

Part of the difficulty involved in nuclear and military waste cleanup relates to jurisdictional disputes, which are not uncommon in environmental politics. The EPA does not control or manage contaminated facilities; its role is regulation and enforcement. The intent of Congress was to make the agency independent so that compliance could be assured. At the same time, the DOD operates under its own political agenda and direction; thus, environmental remediation is not always its highest priority. While staffers talk of a partnership arrangement between the two agencies, the reality is that there has been more study and discussion than actual cleanup.[31]

THE GLOBAL DIMENSION

While most nations have dealt with their waste problems independent of one another, the issue has now become globalized as a result of various developments in the way waste is managed, especially when developed countries attempt to ship their waste abroad. The issue gained international prominence in 1988 when three thousand tons of a flaky black material was dumped on a Haitian beach. A barge carrying the substance had entered the port with a permit to unload "fertilizer," which later turned out to be Philadelphia municipal incinerator ash laced with toxic residue. The United States is a key stakeholder in global waste policy because of an agreement (which lapsed in 1988) that it would accept spent nuclear fuel from research reactors in twenty-eight other countries in order to deter nuclear proliferation. Added to the list of concerns is what to do about improperly handled waste produced by the nations of the former Soviet Union.

Most of the import and export of waste is between industrialized nations with restrictive (and costly) regulations on hazardous waste disposal and developing cash-poor countries in the Pacific, Latin America, the Caribbean, and Africa. Although they often lack adequate facilities or technology for accepting or disposing of hazardous waste, the financial incentives (often extralegal) for developing countries are often too tempting to pass up. The EPA estimates the cost of disposing of a ton of hazardous wastes in the United States at $250–$300 per ton; some developing countries charged as little as $40 to accept waste. For years there was an extensive waste trade arrangement among the members of the European Community (EC), and some experts believe that as much as 10 percent of the thirty million tons of hazardous waste generated each year passed between European countries, with a smaller amount of domestic refuse and recyclable materials traded.[32]

At the 1972 UN Conference on the Human Environment, delegates made a commitment to regulate waste trading, although it was not until 1984–1985 that a UN Environment Programme committee developed the Cairo Guidelines, implementing that pledge. The guidelines included notification procedures, prior consent by receiving nations, and verification that the receiving nation has requirements for disposal at least as stringent as those of the exporter. Despite those restrictions, a coalition of African nations argued that the agreement was tantamount to exploitation or "waste colonialism." In 1987, the United Nations attempted to devise an agreement that would satisfy the African nations (who sought an outright ban on exports) and exporters (still seeking inexpensive ways of disposing of their wastes). In 1989, two attempts were made to further restrict the international trade in wastes. A group of sixty-eight less-industrialized nations from Africa, the Caribbean, and the Pacific, collectively known as the ACP countries, joined with EC officials in signing the Lome Convention, which banned all radioactive and hazardous waste shipments from the EC and ACP countries. A second agreement, the Basel Convention on the Control of Transboundary Movements of Hazardous Wastes and Their Disposal, which took effect in 1992, did not ban waste trade but allowed hazardous wastes to be exported as long as there is "informed consent" or full notification and acceptance of any shipments. Even though members of the EC and other nations have pledged not to export their hazardous wastes regardless of the Basel Convention, twelve African states subsequently signed the Bamako Convention in 1991, banning the import of hazardous wastes from any country — a move that further emphasized their determination not to become a dumping ground for other countries.[33] The Clinton administration initially called for a ban on all hazardous waste exports to developing countries, even though the shipping of hazardous wastes is not a commonly accepted practice in the United States. The United States also supported a ban on exports to any country by 1999, with only a few exemptions granted for items that can be recycled, such as scrap metal and paper. But at a 1994 meeting of the parties in Geneva, which the United States attended only as an observer, there was a consensus agreement reached that banned all hazardous waste exports, including recyclables, by December 31, 1997.[34]

The development of such a strong regime without full U.S. support came about as a result of the efforts of not only the developing nations seeking to ban waste trade, but also because of the pressure exerted by major environmental groups such as Greenpeace and its international affiliates. The organization made the issue one of the keystones of its activism, especially in developing countries. Calling efforts to ship waste abroad "toxic terrorism," Greenpeace members helped publicize the lack of monitoring and regulations over what materials were being transported, often under the guise of recycling.[35]

Waste management has also gained a more global focus as the nations of the former Soviet Union have appealed to the industrialized world for assistance in dealing with the phenomenal amount of toxic waste and radioactive materials produced from decades of military activity and inattention to environmental contamination. For decades, billions of gallons of liquid radioactive waste were secretly pumped underground near major rivers in Russia, and scientists have little information about the potential risk the practice now poses. Cleaning up nuclear power plants like Chernobyl is estimated to take as long as one hundred years and will cost billions more in assistance. Although the Clinton administration, its allies, and international financial institutions offered some support, the amount of money needed for cleanup in that region alone is virtually incalculable.[36] Although the area of the former Soviet Union continues to suffer from massive pollution of its water and air from manufacturing and other industrial processes, radioactive contamination is by far its most pressing, and most expensive, challenge. Existing international institutions are simply not prepared to deal with either the cost or the coordination of the legacy of the communist regime.

In 1998, the topic of toxic waste returned to the global environmental agenda as over one hundred governments met in Montreal, Canada, for the first round of talks on an international agreement to minimize emissions and releases of twelve persistent organic pollutants, such as dichlorodiphenyltrichloroethane (DDT) and polychlorinated biphenyls (PCBs), into the environment. The issue returned to the UN Environment Programme because there is growing scientific evidence that exposure to even very low doses of certain pollutants can lead to a number of diseases like cancer, immune and reproductive system disorders, and interference with infant and child development.

The globalized nature of the problem stems from two factors: decaying and leaching chemicals from dump sites and toxic drums first used from 1950 to 1980, which circulate through a process called the "grasshopper effect." Pollutants released in one part of the world can, through a repeated, and often seasonal, process of evaporation and deposit, be transported through the atmosphere to regions far away from the original source. Through bioaccumulation, the pollutants are also absorbed in the fatty tissue of living organisms, where concentrations can become magnified by up to seventy thousands times the background levels. The result is that persistent organic pollutants can be found in humans and other animals in regions thousands of miles away, such as the Arctic.[37] The negotiations are scheduled to continue until sometime in the first decade of the new millennium, when it is hoped a new international regime will be formed. However, the process shows how difficult and time-consuming it can be to attempt to reach agreement on international treaties, even when the health risks are well known.

POLICY STALLED: TOO LITTLE TOO LATE

Various agencies and analysts are exploring a number of waste management strategies from technological solutions, such as soil washing, chemical dechlorination, underground vacuum extraction, and bioremediation (the use of microbes to break down organic contaminants), to the use of price incentives and cost-based disposal fees. Despite these proposals, the waste management issue has been called an environmental policy paradox. Even though officials have been aware of the shortage of landfill space for decades and could have anticipated the need for alternatives, they have been unable to develop a viable long-term policy to deal with the problem. Observers point to the lack of a publicly perceived crisis, the incentives that have caused policymakers to choose short-term, low-cost options, and the incremental nature of the policy process. With regard to hazardous waste, officials at the federal level have failed to follow through on policy development with an appropriate level of resources to clean up the thousands of identified sites in the United States. In addition, the involvement of organized crime in the disposal industry has been connected to illegal disposal, or "midnight dumping" of hazardous wastes — a problem not yet solved by government officials at any level.[38]

It is equally accurate to characterize America's waste management practices as the policy of deferral. The inability of policymakers now to plan for future disposal needs (whether the waste be solid, hazardous, or radioactive) simply means that they are putting off until tomorrow an inevitable, and growing, environmental protection problem. Future generations will be forced to deal with the mounting heaps of trash, barrels of toxic waste, and radioactive refuse that is already piling up in our cities, at chemical companies, and at utilities all around the country. Other analysts note that there is a lack of information about the full costs of various disposal alternatives. Without sufficient research into the "true" costs of waste management strategies, it is impossible for the most efficient systems to be developed.

Meanwhile, it appears as if the future of American waste management will involve a combination of disposal methods, rather than any single strategy. Technological strategies and price incentives are of little value, however, until the legislative gridlock is broken and policymakers get serious about finding a solution, rather than just passing stopgap measures for short-term fixes. We know the problem is there, but no one seems willing to get down and dirty to tackle it.

NOTES

1. Mary Manning, "Nuke Study: Yucca Ground Stretching," *Las Vegas Sun,* March 27, 1998.

2. Eryn Gable, "Sweepstakes Spurs Interest in Recycling," *Governing,* December 1998, 48.

3. Martin V. Melosi, *Garbage in the Cities: Refuse, Reform and the Environment, 1880–1980* (College Station: Texas A&M University Press, 1981), 3.

4. Ibid., 189–192. In fairness to industry, however, it should be noted that the development of packaging has many beneficial consequences. Packaging has extended the shelf life of many goods (especially produce and dairy products) that otherwise might rot or spoil. Packaging also allows products to be stored and shipped in bulk and often results in lower prices.

5. For an expanded explanation of the typology of wastes and their disposal, see Travis Wagner, *In Our Backyard: A Guide to Understanding Pollution and Its Effects* (New York: Van Nostrand Reinhold, 1994), 126–183.

6. U.S. Environmental Protection Agency, *Characterization of Municipal Solid Waste in the United States: 1990 Update,* EPA/530-SW-90-042 (Washington, DC: Government Printing Office, June 1990), ES-3.

7. Melosi, *Garbage in the Cities,* 171–176, 217–218.
8. See Howard E. Hesketh, *Incineration for Site Cleanup and Destruction of Hazardous Waste* (Lancaster, PA: Technomic, 1990).
9. Michael J. Satchell, "Lethal Garbage: Nuclear Waste," *U.S. News and World Report,* November 7, 1994, 64–66.
10. See U.S. Environmental Protection Agency, *Measuring Recycling: A Guide for State and Local Governments* (Washington, DC: Environmental Protection Agency, 1997); and Richard A. Denison, ed., *Recycling and Incineration: Evaluating the Choices* (Washington, DC: Island Press, 1990).
11. Margaret Webb Pressler, "The Recycling Boom Is More Than Just Trash Talk," *Washington Post National Weekly Edition,* February 20–26, 1995, 33.
12. Timothy Aepppel, "Recycler Woes May Signal Soft Economy," *Wall Street Journal,* April 26, 1996, A9A.
13. David H. Folz and Joseph M. Hazlett, "Public Participation and Recycling Performance: Explaining Program Success," *Public Administration Review, 51,* no. 6 (November–December 1991): 526–532. See also David H. Folz, "Recycling Program Design, Management, and Participation: A National Survey of Municipal Expertise," *Public Administration Review, 52,* no. 3 (May–June 1991): 222–231.
14. Bette Fishbein and David Saphire, "Slowing the Waste Behemoth," *EPA Journal, 16,* no. 3 (July–August 1992): 46–49.
15. Louis Blumberg and Gottlieb, *War on Waste: Can America Win Its Battle With Garbage?* (Washington, DC: Island Press, 1989), 63.
16. See William L. Kovacs and John F. Klusik, "The New Federal Role in Solid Waste Management: The Resource Recovery and Conservation Act of 1976," *Columbia Journal of Environmental Law, 3* (March 1977): 205.
17. *City of Philadelphia v. New Jersey,* 437 U.S. 617 (1978)
18. See Rosemary O'Leary, "Trash Talk: The Supreme Court and the Interstate Transportation of Waste," *Public Administration Review, 57,* no. 4 (July–August 1997): 281–284.
19. See, "Recent Developments, Federal Regulation of Solid Waste Reduction and Recycling," *Harvard Journal on Legislation, 29* (1992): 251–254. For a more comprehensive analysis of the policy process as it relates to both the RCRA and Superfund, see Charles E. Davis, *The Politics of Hazardous Waste* (Englewood Cliffs, NJ: Prentice-Hall, 1993).
20. Blumberg and Gottleib, *War on Waste,* 66–67.
21. For more on the process of Superfund cleanup, see Daniel Mazmanian and David Morell, *Beyond Superfailure: America's Toxics Policy for the 1990s* (Boulder, CO: Westview, 1992); and John A. Hird, *Superfund: The Political Economy of Risk* (Baltimore, MD: Johns Hopkins University Press, 1994).
22. See Katherine N. Probst et al., *Footing the Bill for Superfund Cleanups: Who Pays and How?* (Washington, DC: Brookings, 1995).
23. Matthew J. Wald, "Study Aids Opponents of Nevada Burial," *New York Times,* June 20, 1997.
24. Manning, "Nuke Study: Yucca Ground Stretching."
25. "Nuclear Storage Receives A Boost," Associated Press syndicated column, December 19, 1998.
26. See Tony Davis, "Nuclear Waste Dump Opens," *High Country News,* April 12, 1999, 5; and James Brooke, "Deep Desert Grave Awaits First Load of Nuclear Waste," *New York Times,* March 26, 1999, A17.
27. See Michael Renner, "Military Mop-Up," *WorldWatch, 7,* no. 5 (September–October 1994), 23–29; and Seth Shulman, *The Threat at Home: Confronting the Toxic Legacy of the U.S. Military* (Boston, MA: Beacon, 1992).
28. Katherine N. Probst, "Long Term Stewardship and the Nuclear Weapons Complex," *Resources,* Spring 1998, 14–16.
29. Michael Cabanatuan, "Settlement to Ease Public Monitoring of Nuclear Weapons Cleanup Sites," *San Francisco Chronicle,* December 15, 1998, A22.

30. Larry Rohter, "Panama Wants U.S. Military to Remove Its Hazardous Debris," *San Francisco Chronicle,* October 15, 1998, C5.

31. For one government official's view, see Steven A. Herman, "Environmental Cleanup and Compliance at Federal Facilities: An EPA Perspective," *Environmental Law, 24* (July 1994): 1097–1109.

32. Duncan Lawrence and Brian Wynne, "Transporting Waste in the European Community: A Free Market? *Environment, 31,* no. 6 (July–August 1989): 14.

33. See C. Russell Shearer, "Comparative Analysis of the Basel and Bamako Conventions on Hazardous Waste," *Environmental Law,* 23, no. 1 (1993): 141.

34. Gareth Porter and Janet Welsh Brown, *Global Environmental Politics,* 2nd ed. (Boulder, CO: Westview Press, 1996), 84–88.

35. For a summary of the Greenpeace view, see the statement of James Vallette, coordinator of the Greenpeace International Hazardous Exports-Imports Prevention Project, in U.S. Congress, House, Committee on Energy and Commerce, Subcommittee on Transportation and Hazardous Materials, *Basel Convention on the Export of Waste,* hearing, 102nd Cong., 1st sess., October 19, 1991 (Washington, DC: Government Printing Office, 1991), 185–198.

36. For an overview of the problems involved, see Murray Feshbach, *Ecological Disaster: Cleaning Up the Hidden Legacy of the Soviet Regime* (Washington, DC: Brookings, 1995); James Stewart, "The Cloud over Chernobyl," *Washington Post National Weekly Edition,* June 26–July 2, 1995, 6–7; Margaret Shapiro and Curt Suplee, "Russia's Buried Monster," *Washington Post National Weekly Edition,* December 5–11, 1994, 18; Michael Dobbs, "Sacrificed to the Superpower," *Washington Post National Weekly Edition,* September 20–26, 1993, 13; and John Massey Stewart, ed., *The Soviet Environment: Problems, Policies, and Politics* (New York: Cambridge University Press, 1992).

37. "Treaty Talks Start on Persistent Organic Pollutants," UNEP Press Release 31, June 22, 1998.

38. See Zachary A. Smith, *The Environmental Policy Paradox,* 3rd ed. (Englewood Cliffs, N.J.: Prentice-Hall, 2000), 176–203.

FOR FURTHER READING

Peter Hough. *The Global Politics of Pesticides: Forging Consensus from Conflicting Interests.* London: Earthscan, 1999.

Herbert Inhaber. *Slaying the NIMBY Dragon.* Somerset, NJ: Transaction Publishers, 1998.

Allan Mazur. *A Hazardous Inquiry: The Rashomon Effect at Love Canal.* Cambridge, MA: Harvard University Press, 1999.

Steven Murdock, Richard S. Krannich, and F. Larry Leistritz. *Hazardous Wastes in Rural America.* Lanham, MD: Rowman and Littlefield, 1999.

Nelson L. Nemerow. *Strategies of Industrial and Hazardous Waste Management.* New York: Van Nostrand and Reinhold, 1998.

Katherine Probst and Thomas C. Bierle. *The Evolution of Hazardous Waste Programs.* Washington, DC: Resources for the Future, 1999.

Katherine Probst and Michael H. McGovern. *Long-Term Stewardship and the Nuclear Weapons Complex: The Challenge Ahead.* Washington, DC: Resources for the Future, 1998.

Travis Wagner. *The Complete Guide to Hazardous Waste Regulation.* New York: John Wiley and Sons, 1999.

CHAPTER 6

The Politics of Energy

It is no exaggeration to say that the way we manage the transition to a more competitive electricity industry will help determine the competitiveness of U.S. firms in international markets. Clearly, the stakes are large.

— Paul Portnoy, President, Resources for the Future[1]

On March 31, 1998, residents of California became the first in the nation to "shop" for their electric power in an open market. Previously, retail customers were limited to purchasing electricity from one of the three major investor-owned utilities that provided about 80 percent of electric service to the state. These three utilities (along with four other power companies) had been granted franchise areas in which they were given the exclusive right to provide electric service, but in exchange, they were heavily regulated by the California Public Utilities Commission (CPUC).

Under legislation signed by California governor Pete Wilson in 1996, the deregulation of the state's electricity industry inaugurated a four-year transition period that includes the development of a power exchange auction (PX) for buying and selling electricity and a restructured market that provides for customer choice. According to an official of the California Energy Commission: "Consumers will have access to many electricity suppliers. They will no longer be restricted to just one supplier, on a 'take it or leave it' basis. Prices are negotiable. This will create the opportunity for competition to occur with the likely outcome of falling electricity prices for all consumers."[2] During the transition period, which is expected to last until sometime in 2002, customers are expected to pay for costs that represent the power companies' unrecovered prior investments and costs incurred as a direct result of the move to a competitive market. Estimates of these costs range from several billion dollars to nearly $30 billion, with the CPUC charged with defining what items will be considered transition costs and what portion may be recovered by utility companies.

Emissions from power plants not only damage the local environment, they also contribute to transboundary pollution, which harms regions hundreds of miles away.

Consumer groups believe that California's deregulation policy is doing almost nothing to help the environment. An October 1998 study released by Public Citizen, a group founded by Ralph Nader, said that the "green electricity" being purchased by California consumers comes largely from renewable energy sources controlled by utilities, whose customers are already paying for it. In addition, the report noted, a consumer's purchase of green electricity can, in some cases, lead to the extended operation of fossil fuel plants and greater pollution. By year's end, about thirty-five thousand California households had chosen to buy power outside of their traditional utility — to buy "green" power.[3]

The new entrants into the electricity market disagree. Green Mountain Resources, a subsidiary of Vermont-based Green Mountain Power, believes that the free market offers the best opportunity for new investment in renewable energy. One Green Mountain official noted that the company's California marketing efforts are "unleashing consumer demand for renewable energy projects" and spurring investment in new plants. The company announced it was building two new 700-kilowatt wind-power turbines built in response to demand from California customers as part of its Wind for the Future energy package.[4]

There are several reasons why attempts to restructure the electricity industry are more difficult than other competitive arenas. Researchers at Resources for the Future believe that unlike other network industries, the flows of electricity across the network of interconnected power lines cannot be directed. As a result, additions to the transmission system of one utility will decrease power flows at neighboring utilities. In addition, electricity is a unique commodity in that it must be produced largely upon demand so that blackouts do not occur.[5] This explains why, in California, state regulators established a power exchange that provides more flexibility to traders by allowing them to bid for electricity on an hourly basis. The state's traders can estimate demand more accurately because the electricity is purchased closer to the time when it is delivered. The process also stabilizes prices because it allows participants to buy and sell orders as demand changes during the day. California's system represents about 90 percent of all the power transmitted through the state to commercial and residential users, making the volume second only to that in the United Kingdom, which sells power only to commercial customers.

The restructuring process has a number of policy outcomes, which must be balanced against one another. These impacts are termed *externalities;* they occur when a cost or benefit can be identified and yet a pricetag cannot be placed on the effect until the policy has been implemented. Externalities can be positive or negative, depending upon whether the market is affected positively or negatively. The lowering of electricity prices, for example, is expected to lead to higher levels of consumption, which in turn leads to higher levels of emissions — a negative effect. Several studies have attempted to determine the environmental impact of potential increases in emissions once greater access to the transmission system is allowed. Two Harvard researchers predicted that the use of existing coal-fired generators (especially in the Midwest) will increase, leading to substantial increases in emissions of nitrogen oxides.[6]

However, because customers can select the type of power source that provides them with electricity, it may be possible that, in the longer term, there will be a reduction in the less efficient and more polluting forms of energy — a positive externality. Some utilities may use newer, combined-gas cycle turbines rather than older, coal-fired plants, especially after access to transmission grids is improved. As a result of competition, restructuring may increase the number and type of electricity generators in each state's market, although new entrants may not withstand the transition and may be unable to bear the financial cost of operations as the market grows and consumers become accustomed to free choice in the marketplace.

Will restructuring have a positive impact on energy use in the United States? There is no easy answer to that question — and no easy solution. The politics of energy involve a wide range of stakeholders, technical expertise, regional differences, and emerging technologies.

Energy has been called a "transparent" sector of society because no one buys or uses it as an end in itself. All demand for energy is indirect and derived only from the benefits it provides. People do not buy gasoline because they *want* gasoline, but because they need it for their cars to take them where they want to go. Similarly, a manufacturing plant has a need for electricity only to run the machines that make the products the company sells.[7]

Our growing electricity needs make the debate both timely and controversial. Although energy is an issue of global concern, a stable, affordable supply is acutely important to the United States, which has just 5 percent of the world's population, but consumes nearly one-third of the world's energy. Over the next twenty years, energy consumption is expected to increase by 20 percent.[8] This increased demand comes when the nation is responding to environmental regulations that call for reducing power plant emissions from fossil-fueled plants, a virtual halt to building any new facilities, and political controversy over siting and the perceived dangers of nuclear power. Coupled with that opposition is that the average lead time for building new power plants is ten years. If consumption continues to increase at current rates, the United States could soon face an energy shortage.

This chapter examines the politics of energy, focusing on the United States. It reviews the various energy sources and looks at the political environment and regulatory aspects of energy policy. Last, the chapter concludes with an overview of global energy trends and projections for changes in energy use and conservation.

THE ENERGY PIE

Energy is needed to produce goods and services in four basic economic sectors: residential (heat for rooms and hot water, lighting, appliances), commercial (including air conditioners in commercial buildings), industrial (especially steel, paper, and chemicals), and transportation (of both people and goods). The crux of the energy debate has been to find efficient, environmentally safe, economical and stable sources of supply to meet those needs. Historically speaking, the United States has endured three global energy transitions, each separated by a sixty-year interval. In 1850, the United States derived nearly 90 percent of its energy needs from wood, which remained the dominant fuel into the late nineteenth century. In 1910, coal replaced wood as the dominant fuel, capturing 70 percent of all energy produced and consumed. Along with the transition from wood to coal came the migration from rural areas to the cities, the development of an industrial base, and the railroad era. In 1970, the third phase began when oil and gas reached the 70 percent level. Although there is no evidence that oil production will follow the same pattern as wood and coal, it is likely that there will be more changes in the relative percentages of each energy source.[9]

Edward Teller, the "father of the atomic bomb," once commented: "No single prescription exists for a solution to the energy problem. Energy conservation is not enough. Petroleum is not enough. Nuclear energy is not enough. Solar energy and geothermal energy are not enough. New ideas and developments will not be enough. Only the proper combination of all these will suffice."[10] Like a recipe for an "energy pie," which is essentially the situation in the United States today, Teller suggests that the answer to our global energy needs must be found in a blend of energy sources and strategies, rather than in a single fuel. This concept seems relatively reasonable were the costs and benefits of various forms of energy equal, but that is far from the case. Some forms of energy are relatively inexpensive to produce but are not in abundant supply. Other sources are expensive but less polluting. Still others are considered unsafe but could be made available to consumers around the world for pennies a day, improving the standard of living for millions of people in developing nations.

For thousands of years, humanity's primary sources of power were draft animals, water, and wind. Industrialization and the introduction of fossil fuels for power followed the invention of machines that could harness natural power sources. Oil, coal, and natural gas became the elements of what has been called the fossil fuel revolution — the expansion of power sources and, subsequently, the rise of the United States as a superpower in the global economy. While developing nations are still largely dependent upon biomass energy (primarily fuelwood), industrialized countries have expanded their fuel mix through petroleum exports and an increasing reliance upon nuclear power.

Initially, the United States depended on "Old King Coal" as its primary fuel source. Demand came from the transportation industry as railroads moved westward, and from metal industries (iron and steel) that forged the new tracks. Coal, found in thirty-eight states, was a relatively inexpensive and reliable energy source, and by the end of World War I, it accounted for about 75 percent of total U.S. energy use. Between then and World War II, automobiles began to be mass-produced; moreover, trucks and diesel locomotives requiring petroleum reduced the country's dependence on coal, while natural gas replaced coal in household furnaces and heaters. After World War II, new household appliances appeared — electric dishwashers, clothes dryers, and washing machines — that further expanded the demand for electricity.[11] While coal still accounts for about one-third of the energy pie, the average age of coal-burning plants is twenty-five years; consequently, facilities are quickly becoming outdated and closed down, partially in response to the air quality concerns outlined in Chapter 8.

The United States has huge reserves of natural gas, which makes up another third of the energy pie. Initially heralded as a clean, virtually pollution-free source of energy, the expansion of natural gas production has been heavily criticized by environmental organizations. A proposal for a pipeline from Wyoming to California was derailed when researchers found that the planned route passed through habitats of the endangered desert tortoise. Other plans to open up the outer continental shelf, including areas off the East Coast from central New Jersey to southern Georgia, along the eastern part of the Gulf of Mexico, and the California coast near Santa Barbara have been stalled due to intense opposition. Groups like the Sierra Club and the Natural Resources Defense Council also lobbied against plans by congressional Republicans to open up natural gas drilling within the Arctic National Wildlife Refuge.

About 20 percent of the U.S. energy pie is made up of crude oil, most of it imported from the Persian Gulf. In October 1973, the nations of the Organization of Petroleum Exporting Countries (OPEC) sharply increased the price of a barrel of oil from $3 a barrel to nearly $12, leading to a fuel crisis that, at least momentarily, focused the political agenda on energy. But as quickly as they had surfaced, concerns about the country's energy policies faded, and even a second energy crisis in 1979–1980 failed to ignite public interest. Americans assumed that there was an unlimited supply of fuel available — it was simply a matter of turning on the spigot. In August 1990, when Iraq's leader, Saddam Hussein, ordered his troops into Kuwait, thus once again threatening the world's oil supplies, few Americans showed much evidence of concern about whether or not their local gasoline pumps would go dry. When President George Bush signed the Energy Policy Act of 1992 — the first major legislative attempt to curb U.S. oil dependence in more than a decade — his action failed to generate more than a single day's media headlines. Even repeated bombings of Iraq by the United States and its allies in 1998 and intense political unrest in the Middle East throughout the decade did not seem to resonate with the American public as having a potential impact on petroleum supplies.

Renewable energy sources, which could conceivably serve as an alternative to our existing reliance on fossil fuels, have been used extensively in other countries but, with the exception of hydropower, not in the United States. Currently, these sources make up less than 10 percent of the energy pie. Supporters of renewable energy point out that they produce no waste to be disposed of and no greenhouse gases. They generally are safe for workers, and facilities can be constructed more quickly than plants using fossil fuels or nuclear power. Their biggest drawbacks are their unreliability as a fuel source and the higher cost of producing and distributing electricity from them.[12]

The political process has greatly affected U.S. attention to alternative fuel sources and the federal government's support for renewable energy research can be tied to both electoral cycles and to the cost of oil. The passage of the 1978 Public Utilities Regulatory Policies Act (PURPA), for example, requires utilities to purchase power from nonutilities at an "avoided cost" rate (the rate of expense the utility would have incurred had it generated the energy itself). PURPA became an incentive for alternative sources like cogenerators (large, industrial power users produce steam and electricity for their own needs and sell the excess to local utilities) and small hydroelectric plants that were guaranteed a market for the electricity they generated. Although hydroelectric power is among the cheapest sources of energy available, its use is becoming more limited as environmental groups have lobbied against the siting of new dams along waterways. A 1997 report to the Western Water Policy Review Advisory Commission noted that existing dams alter water temperature and the timing and magnitude of river flows; block fish migration and spawning; entrap nutrients and sediment, which harm the riparian habitat; and change the chemical makeup of downstream flows.[13] (See "Another View, Another Voice: Orlo Stitt: Supplenergy.")

Other forms of renewable energy — solar, wind, and geothermal power — were hailed as promising energy sources during the 1970s, when the newly created Energy Research and Development Administration funded proposals for "soft" energy. But by the mid-1980s, political support had faded and research dollars disappeared. Under the Reagan administration, budget cuts forced the Colorado-based Solar Energy Research Institute (SERI), headed by 1970's Earth Day organizer Denis Hayes, to halve its workforce, from one thousand to five hundred, in only a few months. Wind-power companies, which numbered over two hundred in the 1980s, were reduced to just a handful by the end of the century. The lack of tax incentives and government support coupled with a dying grassroots movement favoring alternative power, suppressed or delayed the adoption of non–fossil fuel applications throughout the United States.[14]

THE NUCLEAR POWER DEBATE

In contrast, support for nuclear power expanded, beginning in 1960 when Southern California Edison announced plans to build a huge facility at San Onofre, California, with a similar announcement by Pacific Gas and Electric to build a privately funded plant at Bodega Bay, California.[15] The companies were encouraged by the Atomic Energy Commission (AEC), the federal agency charged with regulating the new facilities, which announced its objective of making nuclear power economically competitive by 1968 in those parts of the country dependent upon high-cost fossil fuels. In 1962, as an incentive to encourage the building of large-capacity nuclear plants, the AEC offered to pay part of the design costs, and the rush to build began.[16] As seen in Figure 6.1, orders for new plants grew steadily between 1966 and 1974 and then dropped off

Another View, Another Voice

ORLO STITT
Supplenergy

In 1978, when the energy crisis had focused attention on the need for the world to consider non–fossil fuel energy sources, Orlo Stitt and his brother John started a residential construction company in the small town of Rogers, Arkansas. Stitt Energy Systems, Incorporated, had in its mission statement a goal of building energy-efficient homes that were enjoyable and comfortable "without the pain and sacrifice that is sometimes associated with energy conservation. These homes are attractive, livable, and affordable," Stitt says. "They don't look like the 'space-age' homes of the 1970s."[1]

He coined the term "supplenergy" to describe the combination of the concepts of supplemental supply, plenty, and energy. Stitt believes that the world's energy supplies will be provided by many sources of energy, each supplementing the other. His philosophy has gained credibility among homebuilders in the more than twenty years his company has been in business, winning five EnergyValue Housing Awards from the National Association of Home Builders in a three-year period and designation as an Energy Star Home by the EPA.

His major supplenergy project is South Sun Estates on the Lake, a solar energy, planned housing development in northwest Arkansas that juts out into Beaver Lake. The passive solar development — the first in the state — has covenants that call for all twenty-nine homes to be energy efficient. Stitt designs his homes based on three energy-efficient building options: passive solar siting, good construction practices, and the use of appropriate technology.

Among the beneficiaries of the approach are Kyle and Christine Sarratt, the owners of a three-thousand-foot, award-winning home in the subdivision. Stitt built the home for about $186,000 — comparable to the price of conventionally built homes in the area. Using supplenergy construction was estimated to add only about $2,000 to the cost of the house, which is offset by the nearly $75 per month the couple saves in energy costs. The high energy efficiency rating of the home had another advantage for the couple — it allowed them to get financing by stretching their debt-to-income ratio, a factor that made the home affordable.

Stitt believes in using a combination of passive solar heating and cooling strategies to get the kind of energy performance exemplified by the Sarratt home. For example, he had the builder excavate the site to allow as much south-facing window area as possible (nearly three hundred feet). He also used hollow insulating foam blocks filled with concrete, part of a design component called insulating concrete forms (ICFs). The hollow blocks are stacked to form

(continued)

a wall, then reinforced with steel rebar and filled with concrete. The forms act as insulation, and the wall is then covered with standard building materials so the home looks like an ordinary house. In addition, Stitt designed the home with an "ice house roof" design that dramatically reduces the cooling load by more than half, compared to conventional designs. More traditional features, such as a high-efficiency, cast-iron, wood-burning stove and ceiling fans in every room, are built in, along with a solar domestic hot water system. The sun, however, is the Sarratts's primary source of heat.

Solar energy design virtually disappeared from home-building projects after many Americans perceived that the energy crisis was "over" and federal support for research into solar power was almost eliminated. But Stitt believes that supplenergy is an affordable, attractive solution to rising home prices. He says that most of his customers are usually families thinking about the future. "Most people building these homes are concerned with sustainability for generations," he says. "We want resources for our children and our children's children to enjoy."[2]

For More Information

For more information on the supplenergy approach, contact Orlo Stitt at (800) 367-7374.

Notes

1. "Energy-Efficient Builder Tries for $0 Energy Bills on Research Home," Portland Cement Association, Press Release, September 22, 1997, available at <http://www.concrete-homes.cm/prstitt>.
2. Ibid.

Figure 6.1 Construction of Nuclear Generating Facilities, 1953–1997

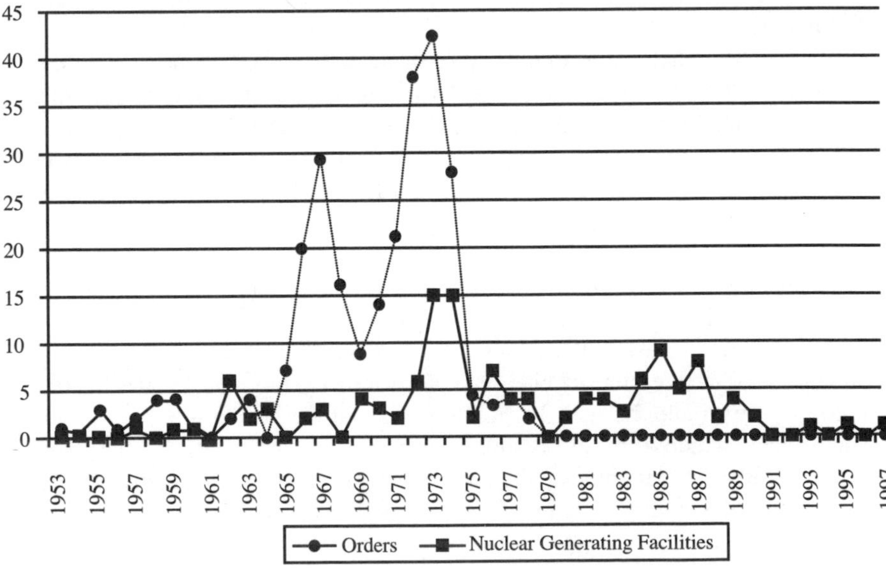

sharply between 1975 and 1978. No orders for nuclear-generating units have been placed by a utility or government agency since 1978, and no new facility has been issued a full-power operating license since 1996.

What happened to shorten the promising beginnings of nuclear power? First, the growth of the environmental movement in the early 1970s, combined with zealous antiwar sentiment, led to a strong sense of public opposition to anything associated with nuclear weapons, including nuclear power as an energy source. Second, that same public pressure led to increased government sensitivity about the impacts of new projects, as seen in the history of legislation outlined in Chapter 1. In 1971, the U.S. Court of Appeals ruled that the AEC had failed to follow the provisions of the National Environmental Policy Act in licensing the Calvert Cliffs facility near Baltimore, Maryland, followed by a similar ruling on the Quad Cities nuclear power station on the Mississippi River in Illinois. Both decisions focused attention on the environmental impacts of nuclear facilities and led to increased scrutiny of license applications.

Third, media coverage of a malfunctioning cooling system at Three Mile Island in 1979 and the explosion of a nuclear reactor at Chernobyl in 1986 made utilities still considering nuclear power think twice about the effects of widespread public opposition to such projects. These attitudes are still prevalent today and account for the general reluctance of policymakers to even consider this power source as an option.[17] Fourth, economics played a key role in scuttling the building of new facilities. Government estimates on the growth in demand for electricity in the 1970s turned out to be overly optimistic, and as demand for energy decreased, the cost of building new plants rose, making them non–cost-effective. In 1971, the estimated cost of building a typical facility was $345 million, but by 1980 the figure had climbed to $3.2 billion. The federal government had spent nearly $18 billion in subsidizing the commercial development of nuclear power by 1980, and smaller utilities could not afford to build on their own.

In addition, construction and licensing of new plants were taking as long as ten years — delaying the point at which utilities could begin passing the costs on to consumers and recouping their investments. Financial horror stories began to proliferate. Of five nuclear reactors started in the 1970s by the Washington Public Power Supply System, only one has been completed, and the utility ultimately defaulted on $2.25 billion in bonds in 1983.[18] When the Long Island Lighting Company began building its Shoreham plant in April 1973, the cost was estimated at $300 million. Delayed by protests from nearby residents and federally mandated design changes, the cost escalated to $5.5 billion by the time it was completed in December 1984.[19] Suddenly plans for *all* types of power plants — not just nuclear — were being shelved as too costly.

Although the United States has come to a halt in its construction of nuclear power plants, four other nations have pushed forward, with more than two-thirds of the world's facilities operating in France, Japan, the United Kingdom, and the republics of the former Soviet Union. The United States is still the leader in the amount of commercial nuclear power generation, followed by France, Japan, Germany, and Russia. Some regions have become almost totally dependent upon nuclear power, while others have been untouched by nuclear technology, including Australasia, Africa (except for South Africa), the Arab states of the Middle East, Southeast Asia, and most of Latin America (except Mexico, Argentina, and Brazil). For the most part, these nations have only traditional "poor country" energy sources — fuel wood, charcoal, and forage for animals — and there is almost a complete absence of nuclear power. Although the United States began to provide fissile material and millions of dollars in grants for research reactors in 1953, very few Third World countries have reached the point of having commercial nuclear power plants connected to their electricity supply networks.

There are several reasons why nuclear power has been limited to the most-industrialized nations. Prior to 1973, world oil prices were low enough to make nuclear power seem less attractive as an energy source than fossil fuels. In addition, most developing nations were too poor or too much in debt to develop nuclear plants, which are extremely capital-intensive. To do so would have meant sacrificing other priorities that were deemed more important. Last, concerns about the proliferation of nuclear weapons preoccupied those nations with the capacity for producing plutonium and uranium, limiting their desires to share the necessary raw materials.

Will nuclear power ever be reconsidered as a major source of energy? The answer to that question has little to do with science or technology and much to do with politics. Some industry officials believe such a change can take place only if the regulatory framework for licensing facilities is streamlined by Congress. Other analysts feel that utilities would be more likely to gain public acceptance for new nuclear facilities if they were sited or expanded near existing plants rather than in new areas. Public opposition to nuclear facilities, although still strong, appears to have leveled off. Attempts to close down facilities or ban nuclear power altogether have not been successful in a number of states, suggesting that Americans may not be so disenchanted with nuclear power to close down the industry completely. But most observers believe that, unless Congress moves forward with a plan to store nuclear waste (see Chapter 5) and dismantles aging reactors, the nuclear energy debate will remain at a standstill.

THE HISTORY OF POLICY PARALYSIS

Historically, U.S. energy policy has been separated by type of fuel, with different institutional associations and interests for each type and few attempts at coalition building. Coal interests from the Northeast have dealt with the Bureau of Mines, while states with uranium were more likely to converse with the Atomic Energy committees in Congress and the Nuclear Regulatory Commission. Seldom did jurisdictional boundaries cross over from one fuel to another, and as a result, terms like *disarray, turmoil,* and *inertia* are often used to describe

U.S. energy policy. Those terms are in part applicable because of the maze of legislative and regulatory obstacles that have developed, along with a profusion of competing interests. The result is an energy policy that is highly segmented and neither comprehensive nor effective. While many analysts have attempted to explain why U.S. energy policy has been so ineffective, the consensus appears to be that the government has intervened unnecessarily rather than allowing market forces to allocate scarce energy resources.[20] How did such a policy develop?

Before 1900, the U.S. government had an ad hoc approach to what was perceived to be an unlimited supply of energy resources. A sense of abundance and virtual giveaways of public lands resulted in many valuable resources coming under private ownership. Although there were early rumblings of competition among interests representing the various fuels, it was not until after the turn of the century that the government began to intervene. To assure a stable and competitive oil market, the government relied upon the Sherman Anti-Trust Act in 1911 to break up the Standard Oil monopoly, and during World War I, President Woodrow Wilson established the Petroleum Advisory Committee to allocate American supplies. After the 1921 Teapot Dome scandal, in which officials were convicted of leasing federal lands to oil companies in exchange for bribes, the Federal Oil Conservation Board was created to oversee the oil industry. By the 1930s, the federal government's role had changed to one of consumer protection, expanding its jurisdiction with the Natural Gas Act of 1938 and the creation of the Tennessee Valley Authority. There was never an attempt made to coordinate policy across fuel and use areas. Each area of energy supply — coal, gas, hydropower, oil, and nuclear power — was handled separately, as was each consumption sector — utilities, transportation, industrial, and residential. During the 1950s, as Congress approved a massive interstate highway system and transportation network, the Supreme Court ratified the Federal Power Commission's power to regulate natural gas prices, which held prices artificially low as gas consumption skyrocketed.[21]

As the environmental movement developed in the late 1960s and early 1970s, the process of developing energy policy became increasingly complex as more interests demanded to be included in the decision-making process. At the same time, the importance of energy as a political issue brought in congressional leaders who sought to respond to their constituents' demands that something be done about the long lines at the gas pumps and rising prices for fuels. One study of energy policy found eight distinct groups active in national energy politics.[22]

Between 1969 and 1973, a confluence of negative factors and events changed the history of American energy policy forever. First, predictions by a few officials about a dependence on foreign oil came true. Although the United States first began importing oil as early as 1947, oil from Arab sources reached over a million barrels a day by 1973, more than double the amount imported eighteen months earlier and 30 percent of total U.S. demand. Second, domestic oil production decreased because of price disparities over foreign oil and increasing costs for exploration and recovery. Third, new environmental legislation discouraged production of coal and nuclear power and brought a delay in completion of the trans-Alaska pipeline at the same time that Americans were driving more miles than ever before. Finally, the highly publicized Santa Barbara oil spill in 1969 had led to a five-year moratorium on offshore drilling, further restricting American oil production. The result was a nation made vulnerable to the vagaries of Middle Eastern politics.

The Nixon administration's approach to energy policy in the 1970s was marked by a series of failed attempts to do something about the impending crisis. Initially, the government imposed an Economic Stabilization Program, which froze prices on crude oil and petroleum products for ninety days, and froze wages and prices nationwide. In early 1973, Nixon restructured the country's mandatory oil import quota plan, which had limited foreign oil imports and allowed an unlimited purchase of home heating oil and diesel fuel for a four-month period. This action was followed by the creation of a hand-picked Special Committee on Energy comprised of key Nixon advisers, who recommended steps be taken to cope with price increase and fuel shortages. The strategy was to increase energy supplies, with little concern for modifying demand or conserving energy. By midyear, the administration's mandatory fuel allocation program had led to the closure of hundreds of independent gasoline stations. Then the administration shifted its policies once again by proposing that $100 million be spent on research and development for new energy technology and creation of a Federal Energy Administration to coordinate policy.

In October 1973, OPEC members, resentful of U.S. aid to Israel, voted to cut their oil production and to end all petroleum exports to the United States, resulting in a sharp increase in world oil prices and forcing the Nixon administration to drastically revise its approach. Nixon responded with Project Independence to eliminate foreign oil imports by 1980, and Congress enacted the Emergency Petroleum Allocation Act to distribute fuel supplies evenly.

Analyses of the politics of energy during this period point out a number of lessons learned from the 1973 crisis. For example, a "cry-wolf syndrome" arose when the first warnings appeared about dependence on foreign oil. One survey had even found that the majority of Americans were unaware that the United States imported any oil and were unable to understand how the most technically advanced nation in the world was simply unable to produce enough oil to meet demand. As a result, the concerns were often ignored or disbelieved. Decisions were often based on misleading or poor quality information, and confused and often contradictory policies resulted. A turnover in leadership (four different people held the position of White House energy policy coordinator in 1973) exacerbated the problem. From 1971 to 1973, the role of "energy czar" passed through the hands of seven men, each of whom had a different concept of what U.S. energy policy should be. Some, such as Secretary of Agriculture Earl Butz, were given new titles and responsibilities, while others, such as George Lincoln, were made heads of agencies that were then abruptly abolished (Office of Emergency Planning).[23] Last, by treating each fuel source separately and allowing the disparate interest groups to be so deeply involved in the decision-making process, the government never really took control of the crisis.

As a result of the 1973 crisis, a host of agencies took turns formulating energy policy. The Federal Energy Administration was created in May 1974, but the agency lacked direction and suffered from a lack of a clear sense of mission. It was designed to bring together smaller agencies that had historically been in conflict with one another and was caught between the competing objectives of regulating prices and expediting domestic resource development. After Nixon's resignation, Congress attempted to pick up the pieces by enacting the Energy Policy and Conservation Act of 1975, which levied a windfall profits tax on oil to control imports and gave the president the power to ration gas in an emergency. Other provisions included appliance standards, improved auto mileage standards, and authorized petroleum stockpiling.

The politics of energy took a different turn during the administration of President Jimmy Carter. The creation of a separate, cabinet-level Department of Energy in 1977 underscored the nation's crisis mentality, and Carter's campaign promise to reorganize government. The agency was charged with regulating fuel consumption, providing incentives for energy conservation, and conducting research and development into alternative energy sources. In 1977, an acute natural gas shortage led Carter to propose his National Energy Plan (NEP), as he characterized the energy situation as "the moral equivalent of war." The NEP differed from the Nixon administration's strategies because it called for greater fuel efficiency and conservation rather than increased production. In 1977, Congress also replaced the Federal Power Commission, which had been created in 1920, with the Federal Energy Regulatory Commission (FERC), giving the agency responsibility for oversight of the electric power and natural gas industries.

By the time Congress passed the National Energy Act in October 1978, Carter's NEP had been gutted. In retrospect, it has been argued that the Carter proposal was doomed from the beginning. Members of Congress found that their constituents were unwilling to make sacrifices (like reducing the number of miles they drove yearly) because they didn't feel there really was an energy shortage. Voters made it clear that they believed the entire energy crisis was concocted by the big oil companies to force prices upward and generate bigger profits. In addition, the Carter administration was guilty of taking its case directly to the people, rather than developing a program in consultation with Congress.

The Reagan administration, in contrast, marks an eight-year period of amicable cooperation between the petroleum and coal industries and the administration and a dramatic shift in energy research and development.[24] Reagan's strategy, outlined in his 1981 National Energy Plan, was to limit governmental intervention as much as possible, especially with regard to regulatory agencies, while supporting nuclear power and cutting research funds for alternative energy sources. Renouncing the Carter administration's goal of meeting 20 percent of the nation's energy needs through solar power by the year 2000,

Reagan even symbolically had his staff remove the solar panels Carter had installed at the White House. He was unsuccessful in dissolving the Department of Energy, which he viewed as indicative of Carter's "big government" approach, although his appointment of former South Carolina governor James Edwards signaled his intentions. The Reagan presidency was marked by a return to the strategies of the 1960s — including reliance on the free market to control prices, dependence on fossil fuels, tax benefits for oil producers, and little support for conservation.

George Bush continued the policies initiated by his predecessor. His 1991 national energy strategy sought to achieve roughly equal measures of new energy production and conservation. One of the cornerstones of that policy was to open up 1.5 million acres of the 19-million-acre Arctic National Wildlife Refuge in northeast Alaska for oil and gas exploration. After the Persian Gulf War in 1991, Congress seemed more inclined to move forward on energy policy, finally enacting the comprehensive Energy Policy Act of 1992 just prior to the November election. The new law restructures the electric utility industry to promote more competition, provide tax relief to independent oil and gas drillers, encourage energy conservation and efficiency, promote renewable energy and cars that run on alternative fuels, make it easier to build nuclear power plants, authorize billions of dollars for energy-related research and development, and create a climate protection office within the Energy Department. Critics point out that the bill does not address the issue of automobile fuel efficiency (one of the planks in Bill Clinton's environmental platform) and does not significantly reduce U.S. dependence on foreign oil, but rather caps existing levels of use. Still, it marks the first time in a decade that Congress has been able to compromise on the most contentious provisions — those dealing with alternative fuels and energy-related tax provisions.[25]

Early in his presidency, Bill Clinton proposed a broad tax on all forms of energy in order to raise federal revenue to reduce the budget deficit. The proposed tax, called a BTU tax because it was based on the heating ability of different fuels, as measured by British thermal units, would have raised the prices of gasoline, electricity, and other energy sources. Environmentalists supported the measure as a way to promote conservation and to begin to move away from fossil fuel consumption. The tax would have raised only approximately $22 billion per year, only a tiny fraction of the $6 trillion U.S. economy, but opposition from Democratic and Republican senators representing energy-producing states killed the idea.[26] The administration was successful in raising gasoline taxes by 4.3 cents per gallon in 1993 as part of its deficit reduction plan. During the 1996 campaign, when gas prices jumped 17 percent during the summer, Republican candidate Bob Dole called for a repeal of the gas tax, and President Clinton called for an investigation of the oil companies and ordered the release of 12 million barrels of oil from the nation's Strategic Oil Reserve to soften the price increase.[27] Increasing energy taxes sufficiently for significant conservation or revenue purposes requires more political skill than recent presidents and their congressional allies have been able to muster.

Clinton's record on energy policy did improve in 1998 when he announced a twelve-year extension of the federal ban on new oil and gas drilling off the East and West Coasts. The drilling moratorium had been imposed by President Bush in 1990 and was scheduled to expire in 2000. Although environmental organizations had hoped the president would make the federal ban permanent, the extension until 2012 was considered a reasonable compromise between environmental protection and the interests of oil and gas firms, which had argued that improved technology is making drilling safer.

The president extended the drilling moratorium (which is permanent in marine sanctuaries), by executive order in June 1998. Two months later, California Senator Barbara Boxer urged Interior Secretary Bruce Babbitt to ban drilling on forty existing, yet undeveloped, leases off the coast of California.[28] The leases, owned by several different oil companies, were not made a part of Clinton's drilling moratorium and include portions of the Santa Maria Basin, termed "the Saudi Arabia of California." The area is a vast reservoir of more than 500 million barrels of petroleum and still undetermined billions of cubic feet of natural gas. To lease owners, the oil and gas resources could mean a reduction of the nation's dependence on imported oil. Any interference in their legal right to develop the leases would constitute an illegal taking, although some observers believe that some kind of plan could be arranged to compensate the oil companies for the billions of dollars already spent on buying up leases. To environmental groups like the League for Coastal Protection and the Environmental Defense Center in San Luis Obispo, California, a potential leak not only poses environmental hazards, it also threatens the region's economy, which is largely dependent on tourism. But as one representative of the Western States Petroleum Association (the state's main oil industry trade group) put it, "There are a lot of [oil] resources off this coast. When it comes down to it, it's hard for me to believe that the Congress and the secretary of the interior are willing to walk away from them."[29]

However, regional, state, and local influences also affect energy policy. In Arizona in August 1998, the state's Corporation Commission agreed to expand a "solar portfolio" that would have required all utilities to provide a portion of their power from solar-electric sources. The four-year program would eventually provide consumers of the state's energy with at least 1 percent of it from the sun. But just three months later, the plan was dashed with the election of a new member to the three-member commission, who supported the dismantling of the solar portfolio. Two of the three members wanted an analysis showing that solar power not only benefits the environment but is also cost-effective. Because solar power is actually more expensive than sources like coal, gas, hydropower, or nuclear energy, the election of this single individual changed the state's entire energy policy. It is doubtful that most Arizona residents realized the impact of their vote in the election for the commission position. But the situation is typical of how many environmental policies are developed — they are shaped outside the legislative arena or by other forces unrelated to whether a policy is beneficial.

THE GLOBAL DIMENSION

Energy is considered to be a global issue for a number of reasons. It transcends the traditional boundaries of the nation-state and cannot be resolved by a single country. It is an issue that possesses a present imperative that forces nations to press for resolution. For example, oil is a finite commodity and thus it is crucial that alternative energy sources be found. The resolution of energy scarcity requires policy action — it will not resolve itself. Finally, energy is a global issue because of its persistence on the policy agenda — there is no consensus about how to solve the problems of supply and demand that have been identified.

The societal impact of energy use varies considerably from one region of the world to the next. In 1999, the richest fifth of humanity consumed 58 percent of the world's energy while the poorest fifth used less than 4 percent, according to the Worldwatch Institute. The United States, with 5 percent of the world's six billion population, uses nearly one quarter of global energy supplies; on a per capita basis, it consumes twice as much energy as Japan and twelve times as much as China. On a historical level, U.S. energy consumption has increased ten-fold since 1900 and has quadrupled since 1950.[30]

Energy consumption is closely tied to economic development, and throughout the 1990s, forecasters believed that as we entered the next century, in addition to increasing demand, there would be a changing profile of fuel use. But there are many factors that determine the world's demand for energy, and in 1998, expectations for economic growth and energy market performance in many areas of the world changed dramatically. An economic crisis in Asia proved to be deeper and more persistent than originally anticipated; oil prices crashed; Russia's economy collapsed; and economic and social problems intensified in energy-exporting countries and in emerging economies of Asia and Latin America. A deepening recession in Japan made recovery more difficult and increased the prospects for slower economic growth in Europe and North America. Overall, the rate of worldwide economic expansion fell by one-third relative to that achieved through most of the 1990s, despite efforts by the International Monetary Fund and the World Bank to counter the Asian recession.[31]

A second factor that has changed the forecasts for global energy consumption has been the signing of the Kyoto Protocol of the Framework Convention on Climate Change, described more fully in Chapter 9. The agreement requires developed countries to meet stringent targets for reducing greenhouse gas emissions. However, the protocol has not yet been ratified, and there is great uncertainty over what kind of technological advances will need to be made to meet the agreed-upon reductions.

Third, long-term global energy trends are affected by energy intensities — how much energy requirements increase in relation to growing income levels. In developed nations in North America and western Europe, for example, energy requirements have grown slowly in relation to increasing levels of economic activity, with energy use rising at about half the rate of economic expansion. But in developing countries, energy and economic growth have been more parallel. Rising living standards in Asia and Latin America, for instance, have resulted in greater access to electricity and motor vehicles, increasing energy demand, as have energy-intensive industries such as cement and steel. However, the U.S. Department of Energy forecasts that although global per capita energy consumption is expected to rise over the next two decades, the projected levels of energy intensity will remain low relative to those currently prevailing in developed countries. This would reduce the demand for energy in the developing countries, where more than two-thirds of the world's population resides. Still, energy consumption in 2020 is projected to increase by about 65 percent relative to 1996 levels, with more than half the increment expected in developing countries.[32]

The source of energy is also expected to change somewhat in the next two decades. In 1990, the world's primary energy sources were oil and gas, although oil was the slowest growing of all the major energy sources and natural gas the fastest growing. China and India are expected to account for more than 90 percent of the worldwide increment in coal consumption through 2020, while coal use in Eastern Europe and the former Soviet Union is forecast to decline as natural gas use increases. Nuclear energy is the only source expected to decline by 2020 after peaking in 2010, which is attributed to the retirement of nuclear facilities in industrialized countries such as the former Soviet Union and a vocal antinuclear lobby in Europe.[33]

One final global strategy to meet the world's energy needs is the so-called conservation alternative — a dramatic change in consumption patterns worldwide. Proponents believe that we must all go on an "energy diet," and that rather than looking for new sources of power, we should be conserving what is available and getting more out of it. Advocates of this approach point to the fact that Western Europeans use only half as much energy as Americans to maintain their lifestyle — evidence that energy conservation does not mean a starvation diet.

Thus far, however, while there has been support for conservation as a key element of future energy planning, international rhetoric has failed to result in any substantial changes, evidence of the kind of institutional immobilism characteristic of the stage of the policy process when governments fail to see a "problem" that requires them to take action. In the case of energy, most Americans do not have a sense that anything is "wrong." Although gasoline prices increased substantially in some parts of the United States in 1999, most other drivers were experiencing historically low prices at the pump. The energy supply appeared to be limitless, and no one seemed worried whether the light would come on at the flick of a switch. Policymakers reevaluated their estimates of the need for new power plants, and the lack of growth in the nuclear power industry reflected a change in attitude toward the source and need for alternative energy sources.

James Anderson notes that this scenario is the kind of situation where policymakers seldom are willing to move forward. The conditions associated with energy use have not produced sufficient anxiety, discontent, or dissatisfaction that would cause the public to seek a remedy. In order for this to happen, Anderson says, people would have to have some criterion or standard by which the troubling condition is judged to be both unreasonable or unacceptable and also appropriate for government to handle. He notes that "conditions do not become public problems unless they are defined as such, articulated by someone, and then brought to the attention of government."[34] As the century ended, the world's primary consumers of energy simply did not sense that a problem existed; they continued to purchase fuel-guzzling vehicles and increased their residential use of power at a rate that signaled complacency and inattentiveness rather than awareness of a global environmental problem.

NOTES

1. Timothy J. Brennan et al., *A Shock to the System: Restructuring America's Electricity Industry* (Washington, DC: Resources for the Future, 1996), xi.
2. Daniel Nix, "Electricity Industry Deregulation: What Is It and Will It Affect Me?" March 27, 1998, available at <http://www.energy.ca.gov/restructuring/restructure_FAQ.html>.
3. "Nader Group Questions Worth of Green Power Offers," October 23, 1998, available at <http://biz.yahoo.com/rf/981023/u6.html>.
4. Ibid.
5. Brennan et al., *A Shock to the System,* 10–11.
6. Henry Lee and Negeen Darani, "Restructuring and the Environment," CSIA Discussion Paper 95-13, Harvard University, Kennedy School of Government, December 1995.
7. This view of energy is presented in Thomas H. Lee, Ben C. Bell Jr., and Richard D. Tabors, *Energy Aftermath* (Boston, MA: Harvard Business School Press, 1990), 1.
8. U.S. Bureau of the Census, *Statistical Abstract of the United States 1996* (Washington, DC: Government Printing Office, 1996), 578–579.
9. Barry B. Hughes et al., *Energy in the Global Arena: Actors, Values, Policies and Futures* (Durham, NC: Duke University Press, 1985), 10–11.
10. Edward Teller, *Energy from Heaven and Earth* (San Francisco, CA: W. H. Freeman, 1979), 2.
11. There are numerous accounts of the development of American energy resources. See, for example, Robert J. Kalter and William A. Vogely, eds., *Energy Supply and Government Policy* (Ithaca, NY: Cornell University Press, 1976); Daniel Yergin, *The Prize: The Epic Quest for Oil, Money, and Power* (New York: Simon and Schuster, 1991); Richard Rudolph and Scott Ridley, *Power Struggle: The Hundred-Year War over Electricity* (New York: Harper and Row, 1986); and Walter Rosenbaum, *Energy Politics and Public Policy,* 2nd ed. (Washington, DC: Congressional Quarterly Press, 1987).
12. Keith Lee Kozloff, "Renewable Energy Technology: An Urgent Need, a Hard Sell," *Environment, 36,* no. 9 (November 1994): 4–9, 25.
13. Bruce C. Driver and Gregg Eisenberg, *Western Hydropower: Changing Values/New Visions* (Boulder, CO: Western Water Policy Review Advisory Commission, August 1997), 15.
14. See Daniel M. Berman and John T. O'Connor, *Who Owns the Sun? People, Politics, and the Struggle for a Solar Economy* (White River Junction, VT: Chelsea Green, 1996).
15. The company later canceled the Bodega Bay project.
16. For a comprehensive history of the development of atomic and nuclear power, see Margaret Gowing, *Reflection on Atomic Energy History* (New York: Cambridge University Press, 1978); and Peter R. Mounfield, *World Nuclear Power* (New York: Routledge, 1991).
17. See Paul Slovick, Mark Layman, and James H. Flynn, "Risk Perception, Trust, and Nuclear Waste: Lessons From Yucca Mountain," *Environment, 33,* no. 32 (April 1991): 6.
18. See Paul Loeb, *Nuclear Culture: Living and Working in the World's Largest Atomic Complex* (Philadelphia: New Society Publishers, 1986).

19. For perspectives on what happened at WPPSS and Shoreham, see Howard Gleckman, *WPSS: From Dream to Default* (New York: The Bond Buyer, 1983); and Karl Grossman, *Power Crazy* (New York: Grove Press, 1986).

20. See, for example, Walter J. Mead, *Energy and the Environment: Conflict in Public Policy* (Washington, DC: American Enterprise Institute, 1978).

21. James Everett Katz, *Congress and National Energy Policy* (New Brunswick, NJ: Transaction Books, 1984), 5–7.

22. John E. Chubb, *Interest Groups and the Bureaucracy: The Politics of Energy* (Palo Alto, CA: Stanford University Press, 1983), 14–15.

23. See John C. Whitaker, *Striking a Balance: Environmental and Natural Resources Policy in the Nixon-Ford Years* (Washington, DC: American Enterprise Institute, 1976), 66–68.

24. See Claude E. Barfield, *Science Policy from Ford to Reagan: Change and Continuity* (Washington, DC: American Enterprise Institute, 1982); and Don E. Kash and Robert W. Rycroft, *U.S. Energy Policy: Crisis and Complacency* (Norman: University of Oklahoma Press, 1984).

25. Holly Idelson, "National Energy Strategy Provisions," *Congressional Quarterly,* November 28, 1992, 3722–3730.

26. Susan Dentzer, "RIP for the BTU Tax," *U.S. News and World Report,* June 21, 1993, 95.

27. Howard Gleckman, "Gas Pump Politics," *Business Week,* May 13, 1996, 40–41.

28. Marc Sandalow, "Boxer Calls for Total Ban on New Offshore Oil Drilling," *San Francisco Chronicle,* August 1, 1998, A1.

29. "Offshore Oil Rigs: More in California's Future?" *San Francisco Chronicle,* August 9, 1998, A1.

30. Christopher Flavin and Seth Dunn, "Reinventing the Energy System," in *State of the World 1999,* ed. Lester B. Brown et al. (New York: W. W. Norton, 1999).

31. U.S. Department of Energy. *International Energy Outlook 1999,* available at <http://www.eia.doc/oiaf/ico99/world>.

32. Ibid.

33. Ibid.

34. James E. Anderson, *Public Policymaking: An Introduction,* 4th ed. (Boston: Houghton Mifflin, 2000), 88.

FOR FURTHER READING

Paul A. Ballonoff. *Energy: Ending the Never-Ending Crisis*. Washington, DC: Cato Institute, 1997.

Peter Beck, Michael Grubb, and John V. Mitchell. *The New Geopolitics of Energy*. Washington, DC: Brookings, 1997.

John J. Berger and Lester C. Thurow. *Charging Ahead: The Business of Renewable Energy and What It Means for America*. Berkeley: University of California Press, 1998.

Jerry Brown and Rinaldo Brutoco. *Profiles in Power: The Anti-Nuclear Movement and the Dawn of the Solar Age*. New York: Twayne Publishers, 1997.

Robert J. Duffy. *Nuclear Politics in America: A History and Theory of Government Regulation*. Lawrence: University of Kansas Press, 1997.

Rick Eckstein. *Nuclear Power and Social Power*. Boston, MA: Northeastern University Press, 1997.

David Kauzlarich and Ronald C. Kramer. *Crimes of the American Nuclear State: At Home and Abroad*. Boston, MA: Northeastern University Press, 1999.

Yoichi Kaya and Keiichi Yokobara. *Environment, Energy, and Economy: Strategies for Sustainability*. Washington, DC: Brookings, 1998.

Paul Runci and Jack Riggs. *2020 Visions: The Energy World in the Next Quarter Century*. Washington, DC: Brookings, 1998.

Ed Smeloff and Peter Asmus. *Reinventing Electric Utilities: Competition, Citizen Action, and Clean Power*. Washington, DC: Island Press, 1997.

CHAPTER 7

Managing Water Resources

Water shortages in parts of the world in the next 25 years will pose the single greatest threat to food production and human health.

— Summary of a study by the Consultative Group of International Agricultural Research[1]

In the highly politicized realm of environmental policy, do campaign promises really mean anything?

During the 1996 presidential campaign, candidate Bill Clinton promised his support for the creation of a program to preserve the historical and cultural heritage of the nation's rivers. In his 1997 State of the Union address, President Bill Clinton repeated his pledge, and instructed his cabinet to work with communities to forge an American Heritage Rivers initiative to protect natural resources and spur economic revitalization. Over the next eighteen months, the administration established an advisory committee that reviewed 126 nominations from forty-six states and the District of Columbia, along with more than 1,700 public comments and 200 congressional responses to the program initiative. Using the presidential power of executive order, which does not require congressional approval, in July 1998 Clinton formally announced the designation of fourteen historic waterways in twenty-four states. In a ceremony held along the banks of the New River in North Carolina, the president promised that the country would see "a river renaissance." To some, the south Appalachia pronouncement was vintage Clinton — more style than substance. But for others, the river initiative was remarkable for its deference to the political forces that shape environmental policy.

Each nomination was assessed for its responsiveness to federal criteria on whether the river was distinctive or unique because of its natural, economic, historical, cultural, and/or recreational resources. More important, nominations had to be run past a gauntlet of elected officials. For instance, senators from a state with a portion of the river could request that the nomination be removed from consideration, as could a member of the U.S. House

The protection of free-flowing alpine streams, like this one in the Weminuche Wilderness of southwest Colorado, is critical to managing water resources for recreational and consumer use, as well as species' habitats.

of Representatives from that district. If the two senators disagreed or disagreed with the House member, their views went to the advisory committee for evaluation on merit. The highly structured process resulted in the complete elimination of nine rivers and portions of sixteen others from consideration, although Oregon's Willamette River was reinstated by the president along with three others — evidence of the importance of political clout in the decision-making process.[2]

The management of water resources involves two major issues: the availability of water and its quality. Water scarcity and water pollution are global issues and have become increasingly politicized worldwide. The basic issue is that there is a continual shortage of fresh water for 40 percent of the world's population, with 0.5 percent of the world's water supply easily and economically available for human use. The rest is "locked up" in oceans, polar ice caps, surface collectors such as lakes and rivers, in clouds, or under the earth's surface, yet too deep to be drilled in wells. Coupled with the problem of supply is the planet's expanding population and the basic human need for water, along with increased agricultural and industrial demand. In some areas of the world natural causes such as climate change, El Niño and La Niña, and drought have led to shortages.

Even when water is available, it is often contaminated and unfit for human use. The debate over how best to improve water quality focuses on two issues: first, the pollution of surface waters (rivers, streams, lakes, wetlands, and even drainage ditches), largely from discharges directly into waterways, and second, the pollution of groundwater, which flows beneath the earth's surface and serves as a primary source of drinking water.

This chapter examines the world's management of its water resources, beginning with an overview of the reasons behind water scarcity. This overview is followed by a discussion of the American water wars and proposals to increase the supply of available water throughout the world. The second half of the chapter focuses on water pollution and an analysis of how politics have affected (and, in many ways, led to congressional gridlock over) water quality. The chapter concludes with a summary of the global dimension to water resource management, reviewing the political factors that have led to a similar policy stalemate in both developing and industrialized nations.

WHY DON'T WE HAVE ENOUGH WATER?

Human use of water has increased more than thirty-five-fold over the past three centuries, with most of the increase in the developing nations worldwide. There are three basic reasons why, despite significant outlays of funds, there is a shortage of fresh water for almost half of the world's population. The first reason deals with personal water use and an increasing global population. Each individual consumes only about two quarts of water per day, but there are dozens of other daily uses, such as washing clothing, taking baths or showers, cooking meals, flushing toilets, and watering lawns, as seen in Table 7.1. For example, the average American's personal water use averages ninety gallons per day, and another six hundred gallons per day are used in the manufacturing, chemical, and industrial processes that create the goods and services we take for granted as a part of modern life. That includes water used, for example, by utility power plants, breweries, steel makers, and mining operations. Agricultural use accounts for an additional eight hundred gallons per person per day, for a total of almost fifteen hundred gallons per person per day.

How much water do we need, and how much do we have? That question is at the heart of the water management debate. Unfortunately, the United States does not have an up-to-date assessment of its existing water supply, so many of the political decisions that are being made are based largely on speculation rather than on science. A similar problem exists internationally. As a result, political decisions about water management are often made in a scientific vacuum, based largely on the claims of competing interest groups and users.

But personal water consumption is just part of the water management problem. The world's population is growing at such an alarming rate (see Chapter 11) that existing sources of fresh water are insufficient to meet the human demand. Researchers predict that over the next three decades, global population is expected to grow by nearly two-thirds, from about 5.5 billion to 8.5 billion. Even more important is the increasing urbanization of the world's population, and the demands placed on natural resources and the existing infrastructure. Currently, the population of the industrialized world is about three-fourths urban, compared with about one-third in the developing world, and there are complex regional differences. By the year 2005, half of the world's people will live in an urban area; by 2025, that number will be two of three. Many of those urban enclaves are in areas with minimal rainfall or severe shortages already, such as Los Angeles, New York, Mexico City, and Calcutta. In northern China, for example, where three hundred cities are already experiencing water shortages, finding new sources of water will be a difficult task. Although the government has considered massive water transfers and has encouraged water conservation, existing supplies are almost fully utilized by agricultural users.[3]

Table 7.1 How Much Water Does It Take . . .

to brush your teeth?	2 gallons
to flush a toilet?	5–7 gallons
to shave with water running?	10–15 gallons
to run a dishwasher?	12 gallons
to wash dishes by hand?	20 gallons
to take a shower?	25–50 gallons
to wash a load of clothes?	59 gallons
to wash a car with a hose?	150 gallons

The second cause of water scarcity is the increased demand for industrial, commercial, and agricultural use of water. Almost every industrialized nation is relying more and more on water for manufacturing, oil refineries, and utility power plants. There is also a considerable amount of water used in commercial settings, such as office air-conditioning systems, which use water to cool air for employee and customer comfort. These industrial and commercial needs are greatest in urban areas, where the population base already places its own demands on the water system.

Agricultural water use is also behind the scarcity issue. Irrigation is the answer to how to grow crops in areas where there is insufficient natural rainfall. Piping systems and wells transfer water from natural sources (lakes, streams, or aquifers) to fields, basically altering the natural hydrological cycle. It takes nearly one thousand gallons of water to grow each pound of food we consume, making agricultural irrigation a major water consumer, although consumption varies considerably from one country to another. In the Middle East, where high birthrates combine with a lack of rainfall, irrigation is a massive undertaking. Egypt, for example, irrigates 100 percent of its cropland, while Israel irrigates almost two-thirds. Jordan anticipates a 50 percent increase in its water needs by 2005, and several nations are considering the need to shift water usage away from agriculture in order to satisfy demands for drinking water.[4] In the years after World War II, especially the 1960s and 1970s, irrigated land tripled worldwide to 160 million hectares, mostly in China, India, and Pakistan. Currently, 250 million hectares of land are being irrigated. The least-irrigated acreage (less than five million hectares) is in the sub-Saharan region of Africa. Most of this increase came largely at the urging of international donors hoping to increase food production — a generally accepted justification. The UN Food and Agriculture Organization estimates that irrigation will have to increase by 40 percent over the next twenty years to meet expected food supply demands. The largest planned increase in irrigated acreage will come in India, Pakistan, China, Mexico, and Brazil.[5]

The pressure to grow more and more food to meet the needs of the growing population is faced globally. In the United States, there are signs that too many farms are trying to irrigate too much land with too little water. Of the 165 billion gallons of water used in states west of the one-hundredth meridian (a line stretching north to south from North Dakota through Texas), 145 billion gallons, or 88 percent, will go to irrigation. Areas to the west of the meridian generally receive less than twenty inches of rain per year, while those to the east have a problem of too much water in some states. Despite the political costs of doing so, a shift in water priorities from agriculture to other uses would help to alleviate the scarcity problem in this country.

There are, however, many political considerations that make irrigation controversial throughout much of the developing world. Critics of massive irrigation projects point out that such schemes often involve massive relocation efforts as new dams and reservoirs are built. The building of the Aswan Dam in Egypt, for example, involved the relocation of over one hundred thousand people,[6] and between 1979 and 1985, the World Bank approved financing for forty hydropower projects that resulted in the resettlement of at least six hundred thousand people in twenty-seven countries.[7] Critics of massive irrigation projects also argue that they benefit only wealthy farmers, not the population as a whole, and may lead to public health problems from waterborne diseases and parasites.

Last, natural causes are also responsible for water shortages. The United States has had several recent periods of severe drought that have made water management a critical political issue in almost every state. In 1977, Californians began using "gray water" — kitchen sink and bathtub drainage — on their lawns when a severe drought hit the state. Signs were posted in college and university bathrooms urging conservation ("Is this trip necessary?"), and one of the most popular bumper stickers seen throughout the state reminded drivers, "Save Water: Shower with a Friend." Severe drought conditions in New York in 1985 led to a ban on watering lawns, and in 1986, drought in the southeastern United States led to massive crop and livestock losses. California, Oregon, and Washington declared drought conditions from 1986 to 1992, with the impact of water shortages affecting everything from ski resorts to forest fire conditions. Several of California's endangered bird populations were considered at risk from the drought, as were winter-run Chinook salmon because of diversion of water for human use. The severe drought in western states had additional environmental impacts. Hydroelectric capacity in these regions has been greatly reduced, causing California utilities to rely more on fossil fuels, which have increased emissions of carbon dioxide by more than 25 percent. These increased emissions also affect air quality in urban areas where pollution is already severe.

The same situation is true internationally. Drought in north-central and western Africa from 1968 to 1973 had devastating consequences for a region that already suffered from growing population and diminishing resources. India faced a massive drought in the mid-1980s, even though the nation's monsoon rains produce significant amounts of water. The Indian government has attempted to capture the runoff in large dams, but deforestation has led to massive flooding and some streams and rivers now dry up for parts of the year.

THE AMERICAN WATER WARS

American water policy is among the most politicized in the world, colored by political appointments and powerful industry lobbies, as this overview indicates. It is a policy that has recently changed as political clout has shifted from the farm and agricultural lobby, which controlled policy at the turn of the century, to urban interests who now dominate Congress. Water management in the United States has primarily been the responsibility of two federal agencies, although that responsibility is shared with a large number of public and private entities ranging from local sewage companies and irrigation districts to state water boards. The Corps of Engineers was originally created in 1802 under the Department of the Army and became the main construction arm of the federal government. In 1824, Congress gave the corps authority over navigational operations, and the agency gained additional jurisdiction through the Flood Control Act of 1936. Just four years after Franklin Roosevelt began his New Deal, the corps was embarking upon a reservoir construction program that erected ten large dams a year, on average, for fifty years. The authority was expanded further in 1972 with passage of the Clean Water Act, which brought its jurisdiction into wetlands permits.

The Reclamation Service (later renamed the Bureau of Reclamation) was authorized by Congress in 1902 with responsibility for aiding western settlement in a seventeen-state area.[8] One of the factors that made the bureau popular among Western farmers is that it was chartered with a limitation that it serve only those landowners who held title to 160 acres or less; thus the agency rapidly came to be influenced by local interests. During its early years, the bureau constructed massive water development projects, canals, and public works programs, such as Washington's Grand Coulee Dam (the largest single-purpose peacetime appropriation in U.S. history) and California's Central Valley Project. Between them, the two federal agencies quickly established a reputation as the home of the pork barrel — congressionally approved water projects that benefited a single district. Projects such as dams and flood control channels brought a visible product (and jobs) to the home base of a member of Congress, paid for by liberal cost-sharing formulas and substantial federal financing. In 1920, the Federal Water Power Act created the Federal Power Commission, which was replaced in 1977 by the Federal Energy Regulatory Commission (FERC). The commission was initially responsible for regulating the nation's water resources, but its charter was eventually redirected to oversee the electric power and natural gas industries.

There has always been a closely knit relationship between the congressional committees that had oversight responsibility for the agencies, the two agencies, and local water interest lobbies. Decisions on which projects to fund, and at what level, were frequently made by those leaders with the most political clout, or because of pressure from campaign contributors, rather than on the merits of good water management. Around 1900, for example, the National Rivers Congress, comprised of powerful business figures, contractors, and members of Congress (who were honorary members of the group) began monitoring Corps of Engineers projects. They were extremely successful at convincing Congress to continue authorizing funds for projects that had long since been completed. The water lobby became so powerful that in its heyday in the early 1960s, the chair of the House Appropriations Committee would boast that "practically every Congressional district" was included in the omnibus public works bills and that "there is something here for everybody."[9]

For the most part, America's growth spurt continued unabated after World War II, and few questioned the advisability of the corps's and bureau's massive undertakings. New water technology, modern farming and cropping techniques, and widespread pesticide use made agricultural expansion a key element of the postwar boom, with cheap, government-subsidized water the key. Land irrigated with government-financed water grew from 2.7 million acres in 1930 to more than 4 million acres after the war and nearly 7 million acres by 1960. But during the late 1950s and mid-1960s, water resource planning changed from an emphasis on economic development to municipal, industrial, and recreational purposes. The water lobby was forced to make some concessions to environmental groups, outraged when projects began to infringe upon scenic or preserved areas, such as a proposal to build Echo Park Dam in Dinosaur National Monument.[10] The Sierra Club mobilized its members when a plan to build a hydroelectric plant in the Grand Canyon surfaced, and in so doing, lost its federal tax-exempt status. The bureau "compromised" by agreeing instead to expand the coal-fired power plant at Mojave, near the Four Corners area, and environmentalists believed that they had saved the Grand Canyon.

There is another clear pattern to U.S. water policy: the regional nature of the dispute. Growing urban development in California once led to a call by some members of Congress for the state to import water from its water-rich neighbors in the Pacific Northwest. Frostbelt state representatives bristled at the idea that all the federal money was going to their sunbelt colleagues. Moreover, although the tug-of-war over rights to the Colorado River between Arizona and California is essentially over, the dispute created more legal documents (by weight) than any other in the history of U.S. litigation, on any subject.

By the mid-1970s, environmental groups turned their attention to water issues, becoming a potent force in policy making. Groups such as the Sierra Club, the American Rivers Conservation Council, the National Wildlife Federation, and the Natural Resources Defense Council pressured Congress to follow the requirements of the National Environmental Policy Act and used litigation as a tool for forcing compliance with new legislative initiatives. Bolstered by environmental support during his campaign, President Jimmy Carter began his administration in 1977 by developing a "hit list" of nineteen water projects that were to be deleted from the federal budget, including the Central Arizona Project. Carter underestimated the powerful water industry lobby, however, which was able to convince Congress to restore all nineteen appropriations.

Water industry officials cheered the 1980 election of Ronald Reagan, believing his appointment of Robert Broadbent, a Nevada legislator, as head of the Bureau of Reclamation was a positive omen. It turned out to be a conflicting sign, however, as Reagan continued Carter's cost-sharing requirements on water projects (the portion of a water project to be borne by the federal government). As state and local governments began to realize that they might have to pay a larger share of the cost for many of the projects, they became less attractive, and in some cases, financially burdensome. Part of the shift in policy can be traced to the growing clout of urban political interests over those of agriculture, as city politicians began to question why farmers were getting all the cheap water.[11]

Equally important was the discovery of dead waterfowl at the Kesterson National Wildlife Refuge in California's San Joaquin Valley. Ducks and geese were dying of a mysterious sickness that not only killed them, but resulted in birth deformities in their chicks. The eventual cause was found to be selenium, a trace element that can be toxic in high concentrations. The selenium was carried by the San Luis Drain from the politically powerful Westlands Water District in Fresno and Tulare Counties. In 1985, Secretary of the Interior Donald Hodel called for a halt in the drainage by June 30, 1986, but the public had by then had just about enough of the Bureau of Reclamation's projects and its negligence.[12] By 1987, the policy change became clear when James Zigler, the Department of the Interior's assistant secretary for water and science, announced that the bureau was changing its mission from an agency based on federally supported construction to one based on resource management. The empire-building days of the corps and the bureau were over, replaced by an administration that was paying more attention to urban needs for a stable water supply than to agricultural interests seeking cheap water for their fields.

Pricing inequities continue to be at the heart of the battle over water management in the United States. The "real" cost of providing and distributing water is often impossible to determine, and historically, municipalities have been reluctant to try to pass those costs on to developers and commercial interests. City leaders often avoided charging a new business the true cost of water delivery for fear it would discourage economic growth. As a result, the rate structure has often allowed large users to benefit because of a system that charges the user less the more water is used. Favored customers often receive preferential pricing, and some cities served by the same water district often unknowingly subsidize the water costs of other cities in their area through complex pricing arrangements. Residential users tend to subsidize industrial users throughout most of the United States today.

Another new wrinkle has been the development of "water markets" — transactions ranging from transfers of water rights to the sale and lease of those rights or the land above the water source. Market transfers are dependent upon the concept of reallocating water supplies, rather than coming up with new sources of water. Part of the affection for the market concept was purely economic — new capital projects were becoming increasingly expensive and politically unpopular in much of the West. One group even began purchasing water rights in Colorado as an investment, with the expectation that, as supplies diminished, the rights could be sold for tidy profit. Cities such as Phoenix and Scottsdale have also been active in the water market, buying thousands of acres of farmland outside their city limits to have a water source as their population increases and water within city boundaries runs short. Reallocation is gradually being looked upon as an alternative to finding a new allocation as the primary mode of water development.[13]

One of the more recent battles in the water wars has involved the rights of Native Americans to water resources. In 1908, in a far-reaching U.S. Supreme

Court case,[14] the Winters Doctrine granted Native Americans the right to all waters that arise under, border, traverse, or underlie a reservation and required that these waters continue to be made available to serve the current and future needs of the reservation. Historically, Native American claims to water rights were ignored by the Bureau of Reclamation and the Army Corps of Engineers, but a 1963 Supreme Court case[15] reinforced Native American authority over their land and water. Several nations explored the possibility of marketing their water rights, but the issue leaves open the question of the real value of water.[16]

The American water wars have also touched our southern border with Mexico, where the Colorado River flows on its way to the Gulf of California. In 1922, Congress approved the Colorado River Compact, which divided up the river's resources, giving the three lower basin states (California, Arizona, and Nevada) and the four upper basin states (Wyoming, Colorado, New Mexico, and Utah) 7.5 million acre-feet for each region (an acre-foot is the volume of water that covers 1 acre to a depth of 1 foot, or 325,851 gallons). It should be noted, however, that the actual flow of the river is closer to fourteen rather than fifteen million acre-feet. Congress also authorized the building of Hoover Dam in 1928, giving the United States total control over the Colorado River — a situation that understandably made our Mexican neighbors nervous. Seeking to keep Mexico as a wartime ally, the United States signed a treaty in 1944 that assigned 1.5 million acre-feet to Mexico and created the International Boundary Water Commission to administer the treaty. In the early 1960s, a combination of population growth, the drilling of wells on the U.S. side, saline runoff from drainage projects, and construction of the Glen Canyon Dam in Utah began affecting both the quantity and quality of Mexico's water allocation. It took nearly ten years for the two sides to reach an agreement that in 1973 guaranteed Mexico a fair share of the Colorado in usable form — a turning point in the region's development. Years later, the treaty has still not been fully implemented, in part because the United States has not held up its end of the bargain to operate a desalination plant in Yuma, Arizona.

IMPACTS AND SOLUTIONS

The growing pressure to tap more and more of the Earth's water resources is having a number of negative impacts on a global scale. More urban communities are tapping into underground aquifers, drying them up as residential and agricultural demand increases. In cases such as Mexico City and Phoenix, water levels are dropping as a result of heavy pumping, leading to subsidence — literally, the sinking of the city. In addition to a reduction in the availability of a valuable commodity, it is unlikely that the water in the aquifers will ever be fully replaced.

Among the most important consequences of poor water management are soil erosion and desertification, which threaten nearly a third of the Earth's surface.

Desertification refers to the process by which the land gradually becomes less capable of supporting life and nonproductive. Desertification occurs as a result of four causes: overgrazing on rangelands, overcultivation of croplands, waterlogging and salting of irrigated lands, and deforestation.

According to meteorologists, a reduction in vegetative cover resulting from desertification may reduce rainfall because of an increase in the albedo, the share of sunlight reflected back from Earth. According to the hypothesis, developed by Jule Charney of the Massachusetts Institute of Technology, less of the sun's radiation is absorbed at Earth's surface as albedo increases, so surface temperatures drop, causing a sinking motion in the atmosphere. Since the sinking air is dry, rainfall declines, and a degraded, higher-albedo area begins to feed on itself and become more desertlike.[17]

Adding to the desertification process are increasing levels of salt in the water. An additional one hundred million acres, mostly in India and Pakistan, is estimated by the UN Environment Programme to suffer from salinization, which occurs in dry regions when evaporation near the soil surface leaves behind a thin salt residue. Salinity also affects water quality in Peru and Mexico, where the annual loss of output as a result of salinization is estimated at one million tons of food grains, or enough to provide basic rations to five million people.

Water diversion has also led to the destruction of valuable wildlife habitats, as is the case in California. In 1940, the state's Division of Water Resources granted the Department of Water and Power (DWP) of Los Angeles a permit to divert virtually all of the flow from four of the five streams that flow into Mono Lake, the second-largest lake in California. The diversion represents about 15 percent of Los Angeles's total city water supply. The lake is located at the base of the Sierra Nevada near Yosemite National Park, and although saline, its brine shrimp population is the food source for millions of migratory birds and 95 percent of the state's nesting gulls. As a result of DWP's diversion through its Owens Valley aqueduct, the level of the lake has dropped and increased salinity levels, which threaten the entire food chain. The lake's surface level has been diminished by one-third, exposing gull rookeries to predators, and future diversions are expected to reduce the lake even further. The receding lake waters have exposed a lake bed composed of an alkali silt, which when dry becomes airborne and becomes a health hazard.

In 1983, the National Audubon Society filed suit against Los Angeles to stop the diversions,[18] arguing that the state had an obligation to protect the public trust embodied by the lake. The California Supreme Court agreed and sent the case back to the state's water board to determine whether and to what extent DWP ought to reduce its diversions. Despite nearly a decade of environmental studies, reports, investigations, and litigation, a solution to Mono Lake's dwindling water level still is not forthcoming.

There are two basic solutions to the water scarcity and management problem: conservation and technology. The first is relatively straightforward —

convince users to use less. The second involves a wide range of options from ancient to modern technological solutions. Water conservation is being implemented in many regions, ranging from urban communities to irrigation improvements in an attempt to reduce residents' dependency upon existing sources. Some of the easiest conservation efforts have been accomplished by metropolitan water districts that have enacted consumption ordinances or made water-saving showerheads and low-flow toilets available. These efforts are not temporary responses to drought — studies indicate that by 2010 southern California will have enough water to fulfill only 70 percent of its needs, making demand management practices a more likely strategy for reducing consumption.[19]

Conservation is not limited to urban areas. One of the most obvious strategies used to reduce seepage from agricultural irrigation was the replacement of unlined ditches with piping. Thousands of miles of earth-wall feeder ditches have been replaced in the United States, saving as much as 25 percent of the water in each one thousand feet of ditch. Improvements in furrow irrigation have resulted in irrigation efficiency improvements of approximately 10 to 40 percent, and low-head sprinkler systems have reduced loss to evaporation to almost zero. Through such methodologies, farmers can achieve water savings from 25 to 40 percent, leading to a stabilization of the underlying groundwater table in many areas.[20]

There are also a number of innovative solutions designed to increase shrinking supplies. One of the oldest methods involves desalination, long considered as one way in which communities could attempt to keep up with the explosive growth common to coastal regions. There are two basic methods of desalination: distillation (heating ocean water and distilling the vapor) and filtering water through a membrane in a process called reverse osmosis. Distillation produces water that is more pure, but reverse osmosis is more energy efficient and the facilities are smaller and more compact. More than two-thirds of the thousands of desalination plants currently in operation worldwide use distillation, with more than half of all desalination facilities located in the Middle East. Israel, one of the pioneers in desalination technology, opened its first plant in 1965 for the new desert town of Eilat. The first U.S. facility opened in Key West, Florida, in 1967, and over one hundred plants have opened to serve other coastal cities. Although there was widespread interest in desalination during the 1960s, public and government interest (and federal funding for research) seemed to go on hiatus during the 1970s and 1980s. The worldwide drought of the late 1980s, however, rekindled interest, especially in California. In 1992, officials dedicated a plant on Catalina Island, twenty-six miles off the coast of Los Angeles, which can provide 130,000 gallons of water a day, enough for a third of the island's needs.

Cloud seeding is another strategy that has historically been used to increase rainfall. Airplanes release tiny crystals of silver iodide into clouds with the potential to release water by forming a base of ice crystals, which eventually fall as ice or snow. Cloud seeding, when successful, can lead to a 5 to 15 percent increase in rainfall. Researchers are also considering the use of dry ice, a type of bacterium, and ground-based seeding programs using propane to trigger precipitation.

There are also several "megaprojects" being considered to transfer resources from water-rich areas to those most in need. In China, the government began construction in 1994 on the Three Gorges Dam, a massive project that will cost from $17 billion to $30 billion by the time it is finished in 2009. The dam is anticipated to increase China's electrical generating output by 10 percent and protect millions of people downstream from flooding. But it will also require more than 1.1 million people to relocate before the 400-mile-long dam can be created and threatens to destroy a number of national cultural treasures.[21]

Restoring degraded land is a much more complex problem, however. Efforts are being concentrated on stabilizing soil, diversifying crops, and focusing agricultural production on regions that are the most fertile and least erodible. In China and Ethiopia, for example, researchers are experimenting with ways to trap soil in shallow dams or terrace crops to increase productivity and hasten land reclamation. Other projects include the planting of soil-trapping grasses that form vegetative barriers, and alley cropping, which involves the planting of food crops between hedgerows of trees — a strategy that has been extensively used in tropical regions. Other UN projects are aimed at reducing the harvest length of certain crops or improving species productivity so that the land can be double- or triple-cropped.

Many of the proposals seem far-fetched, if not downright silly, such as towing icebergs from the Arctic to California to provide fresh drinking water for thirsty Los Angeles residents. Others get serious consideration from policymakers desperate for innovation. For example, Canada's Medusa Corporation proposed solving California's scarcity problem with floating vinyl water balloons, each the size of twenty football fields. The storage bags (up to twenty-four hundred feet long, six hundred feet wide, and eighty feet deep) would cost $6 million each and would hold a million tons of water from Alaska. The idea would be to tow the balloons, which would be partially submerged like an iceberg, down the coast to water-short cities. The concept was eventually termed "not viable" by representatives of the Metropolitan Water District of Southern California, which estimated that the region would need at least five balloons a day.

Such fanciful solutions are evidence of the desperate straits many regions are in as they seek an answer to the question of where the water is coming from. Although it is obvious to most that water conservation is the most obvious choice among these strategies, it is also one of the most difficult to implement as long as residents (especially those in the United States) are used to simply turning on the tap. Only when drought conditions force cities to adopt restrictive measures does conservation finally hit home. In summer 1992, for example, the city of Portland, Oregon, banned all use of water for watering lawns and gardens and washing cars when its Bull Run reservoir began to dry up. The city's water bureau established a special late-night patrol to catch flagrant violators — those sprinkling their lawns while the rest of the city slept. A "snitch line" allowed residents to inform the patrols of alleged violations, and some neighbors even turned to vigilante tactics — one woman's new lawn was attacked by vandals who accused her of violating the city's conservation ordinance. She awoke one July morning to find rows of sod neatly rolled up on her porch.

THE WETLANDS ISSUE

While the water resource debate has focused primarily on the issue of supply, water quality is an equally enduring problem for policymakers. Historically, legislative efforts at reducing pollution at the source have been ineffective, as will be seen later in this chapter. More recently, scientists have looked at wetlands restoration as another strategy for improving water quality. Wetlands are sensitive ecological areas that serve as breeding grounds for migratory birds and as plant habitats. They also serve as natural flood and storm control systems, and some communities are experimenting with using wetlands as a way of treating wastewater. Wetlands have become an increasingly important topic on the environmental protection agenda as scientists monitor the numbers of acres of wetlands lost to development.[22]

In addition to concerns about wetlands losses from an ecological perspective, the issue has become highly politicized. The Clean Water Act of 1992 included provisions that required anyone seeking to build or otherwise conduct business that would alter the landscape of wetlands to first obtain a permit from the Army Corps of Engineers. Of particular interest in the act is Section 404, which makes it unlawful to put dredged or fill material into navigable waters — the term *wetlands* was never mentioned in the legislation. But in 1975, a Washington, D.C., Court of Appeals decision held that the Clean Water Act applied, not only to rivers, but also to wetlands that drain into rivers, and eventually, the statute was applied to isolated wetlands with no connection to rivers or waterways. Four agencies — the Department of Agriculture, the EPA, the Department of the Interior, and the Army Corps of Engineers — have developed regulations to implement the law and to designate which areas are defined as wetlands, with an estimated seventy-seven million acres of wetlands privately owned. Since each of the agencies has its own interpretation of the wetlands designation, the importance of wetlands preservation has collided with private property rights and become one of the most contentious water management issues in the United States.

At the height of his campaign for president in 1988, George Bush announced on the shores of Boston Harbor that there would be "no net loss" of the nation's remaining wetlands — a concept that was the brainchild of then–Conservation Foundation president William K. Reilly (later Bush's nominee to become administrator of the EPA). During the 1992 presidential campaign, the term came back to haunt Bush as one of the major failures of his administration, eliciting criticism from both environmental groups and property owners.[23]

Farmers have been among the most vocal critics of federal wetlands policies. Their concerns were brought to the attention of the president by a group called the National Wetlands Coalition led by farming, oil and gas, and housing industry representatives, which had formed in 1989 to oppose sections of the wetlands program implementation. The organization asked the White House Council on Competitiveness, chaired by Vice President Dan Quayle, to develop a less restrictive wetlands definition.[24] The result was the release of the *Federal Manual for Identifying and Delineating Jurisdictional Wetlands* in August 1991. Under the new directive, the definition of wetland was expanded and an additional fifty million acres of land came under federal protection.

More than eighty thousand formal comments, most of them highly critical of the proposed manual, were sent to the EPA. Critics of the proposed rules change argued that millions of acres of previously protected land would be open to development, and environmental groups called upon Congress to study the problem further.[25] In contrast to the president's policy, a December 1991 report by the National Research Council recommended that the United States embark upon a policy of wetlands restoration, with a goal of a net gain of ten million acres of wetlands by 2010, a program that went far beyond the Bush administration's policy of "no net loss." Failure to implement such a policy, the report warned, would lead to permanent ecological damage that would reduce the quality of American life.[26]

While Congress held hearings over the wetlands designations, each agency charged with implementing the Clean Water Act interpreted President Bush's proposals in a different way. The Army Corps of Engineers used a 1987 version of a wetlands manual, the EPA and Fish and Wildlife Service used another developed in 1989, the Soil Conservation Service had its own slightly different criteria, and some federal agencies adopted the 1991 manual's proposed rules.[27]

The Clinton administration reexamined federal wetlands policies almost immediately, in large part due to court rulings that questioned whether the government had the authority to place sanctions on those who failed to meet wetlands permit criteria. In 1993, both the EPA and the Army Corps of Engineers reverted back to the use of the 1987 manual, abandoning the proposed rewriting of the law spearheaded by President Bush. While environmental organizations believe loopholes in the Clinton administration policy would lead to the loss of designation of half of the nation's remaining wetlands, critics of federal involvement have argued that wetlands protection is best accomplished by private organizations like Ducks Unlimited.

In 1995, the debate resumed as the Republican-controlled Congress sought to rewrite a Clean Water Act that would have established another new classification scheme for wetlands. Under the proposal, the least valuable lands would no longer be protected by the federal government, and less protection would be given to the remaining wetlands. The measure would also have required government agencies to compensate landowners for any loss in property values of 20 percent or more resulting from wetlands regulations, but the proposals failed to obtain sufficient bipartisan support.

One of the most interesting aspects of the wetlands controversy, however, is the politicization of the entire designation process. During the Bush administration, it became clear to most observers that the development of a new wetlands criteria would deteriorate to a battle between developers and property rights activists against environmental groups. The scientific community, with years of detailed reports and field testing, was gradually squeezed out of the process, with the result being a policy that satisfied neither side. Opposition to wetlands regulations continues, fueled by enforcement actions taken against landowners that have been widely criticized by private property activists and by policies that are still being tested in federal courts.[28] (See "Another View, Another Voice: Marjory Stoneman Douglas: Friend of the Everglades.")

THE NATURE AND CAUSES OF WATER POLLUTION

In 1965, when he signed the Water Quality Act, President Lyndon B. Johnson (LBJ) predicted that Washington's Potomac River would be reopened for swimming by 1975.[29] Yet the Potomac's Tidal Basin, with its Japanese cherry trees, has been called "the best decorated sewer in the world," making LBJ's prediction premature and unrealistic, as is the case of most of the legislative attempts to improve the quality of America's water supply. A number of factors have contributed to make the nation's waterways and drinking water as polluted now as they were in the 1960s. The debate over how best to improve water quality focuses on two issues: first, pollution of surface waters (rivers, streams, lakes, wetlands, and even drainage ditches), largely from discharges directly into waterways, and second, the pollution of groundwater, which flows beneath Earth's surface and is the source of nearly half of the nation's drinking water. Sources of groundwater contamination include landfills, biocide applications on farmland and urban lawns, underground storage tanks, leakage of hazardous waste, and waste disposal wells.

The current level of water pollution is largely a result of massive industrialization and inadequate waste disposal strategies that took place in the United States during the mid- to late nineteenth century. At that time, local officials were generally reluctant to antagonize industry and to try to stop the widespread practice of simply dumping industrial wastes into the closest waterway. Most of the early government concerns dealt with navigational hazards rather than health. In 1886, Congress prohibited the dumping of waste into New York harbor,

Another View, Another Voice

MARJORY STONEMAN DOUGLAS
Friend of the Everglades

"They call me a nice old woman, but I'm not." Although Marjory Stoneman Douglas is best known for her work in preserving the Florida Everglades, the woman called "the Willy Mays of the environmental movement," who died in 1998 at age 108, had a long history of political and social activism. Born in 1890 in Minneapolis, Douglas made her first visit to Florida with her parents in 1894. After a tumultuous childhood, graduation from Wellesley College in 1912, and marriage to an alcoholic husband who was later imprisoned for bank fraud, she returned to Florida in 1915. She joined other prominent Florida women to fight for women's suffrage in the conservative, male-dominated state, which became the last state to ratify the Nineteenth Amendment. She was a feminist well before gender issues assumed a prominent place on the political agenda.

Douglas started her writing career as a society columnist for the *Miami Herald,* and during World War I, she traveled to Europe to do public relations for the American Red Cross. She returned to Miami in 1920 and from 1926 until the early 1940s wrote for magazines like the *Saturday Evening Post.* When a friend asked Douglas to write a book on the Miami River, she countered with an offer to write what became *The Everglades: River of Grass* in 1947. At the time, the nation's largest subtropical wilderness was considered a dumping ground and swamp, and few except hunters and American Indians were aware of its vastness. Over the next forty years she wrote several environmentally themed books and a prize-winning play, *The Gallows Gate.*

Douglas's involvement with the Everglades went far beyond her writing, however. In 1927, she was a member of a group seeking the creation of the Everglades National Park, a goal finally reached in 1947. She founded the nonprofit group Friends of the Everglades in 1970 and was at the forefront of efforts to block construction of an airport in the fragile wetlands. In 1983, state officials began a major Everglades restoration project, while she continued to campaign for the cleanup of Lake Okeechobee and fought to restore the habitat and population of the endangered Florida panther. Her work won her numerous awards, including the Presidential Medal of Freedom, followed by initiatives from the Clinton administration in 1996 to spend more than $1.5 billion on the restoration of the South Florida ecosystem. A year later, at the Everglades National Park Fiftieth Anniversary Rededication Ceremony, Vice President Al Gore announced an agreement to acquire 50,000 additional acres, and in late 1997, President Clinton signed legislation designating 1.3 million acres as the Marjory Stoneman Douglas Wilderness Area in her honor. Six months later, the 108-year-old crusader died at the home in which she had lived since 1926.

"I know I've got my enemies, and I feel fine about it, thank you," she once said. "The developers don't like me. The farmers don't like me. But I'm a dedicated environmentalist, and I want everyone to become aware of what is going on because that's the only way we'll stop all this terrible destruction. People need to realize that this is all there is."[1]

For More Information

For more information about the Friends of the Everglades, visit its website at <www.everglades.org>.

Notes

1. Ray Lynch, "Marjory Stoneman Douglas, Protector of the Everglades, Dies at 108," *South Florida Sun-Sentinel,* May 14, 1998, Internet edition, 1.

followed by the 1899 Refuse Act, which prohibited the dumping of solid waste into commercial waterways. Not until the U.S. Public Health Service was formed in 1912 was there serious consideration given to monitoring pollution levels. Today, much of what is known about trends in surface water quality comes from the U.S. Geological Survey, which monitors waterways through its National Ambient Stream Quality Accounting Network, or NASQUAN, which began collecting information in 1974. Groundwater quality, in contrast, must be monitored from wells, or at the tap.

Basically, water contaminants can be divided into the following categories:

Organisms: Biological contaminants including bacteria, parasites, and viruses are included in this category. These occur in most water sources, although there are usually fewer in groundwater than in surface water. Human and animal wastes carry fecal coliform and fecal streptococcus bacteria, which may enter the water source from improper sewage treatment, cattle feedlots, or through failing, leaching septic tanks.

Suspended and Totally Dissolved Solids: Soil particles, inorganic salts, and other substances may make water brown or turbid (cloudy) and may carry bacteria and other harmful substances that pollute water. The problem is particularly acute in areas with significant erosion, including logged watersheds, construction sites, and abused rangelands. Agricultural practices are thought to be the largest single source of unregulated water pollution.

Nutrients: Some contaminants, such as phosphorous, iron, and boron, can be harmful when ingested in excess quantities. Nitrates, which are not harmful in limited concentrations, occur naturally in some vegetables such as beets and cabbage, and are used in the meat-curing process.

Metals and Toxics: A wide spectrum of heavy metals are commonly found in drinking water, among the most dangerous of which is lead. In 1991, the EPA issued new regulations requiring municipal water suppliers to monitor lead levels, focusing on households at high risk (those with lead service pipes) and at the location where lead content is likely to be the highest — at the consumer's faucet. In areas where water quality standards are not met, suppliers must add bicarbonate and lime to lower the water's acidity chemically. Other contaminants include radioactive minerals and gases. Toxic concentrations usually come from sources such as pesticides and chemical solvents used in a variety of manufacturing processes.

Municipal Wastewater Discharges: Domestic sewage accounts for a large percentage of the materials handled by municipal wastewater treatment plants, but other substances also routinely enter the wastewater stream, including hazardous chemicals dumped down drains and sewers by individuals, industries, and businesses.

THE POLITICS OF WATER QUALITY

Like many environmental issues, the politics of water quality is not linked to a single act of legislation. One of the factors that makes water policy somewhat difficult to understand is that Congress has given regulatory responsibility for water quality to EPA under a number of legislative mandates. The Resource Conservation and Recovery Act (RCRA), for example, gives the EPA the authority to regulate the treatment, transport, and storage of both hazardous and nonhazardous waste. The Comprehensive Environmental Response, Compensation, and Liability Act (CERCLA), more commonly known as Superfund, gives the EPA responsibility when groundwater is contaminated by inactive waste sites or accidental chemical releases. The Toxic Substances Control Act (TSCA) gives the EPA regulatory authority over the manufacture, use, and disposal of toxic chemicals, and the Federal Insecticide, Fungicide, and Rodenticide Act (FIFRA) regulates certain pesticides, which can also enter groundwater. Despite the overlap of these regulatory mandates, Congress has also enacted legislation specifically targeting surface and groundwater pollution.

Surface Water

The process of placing surface water on the political agenda has been a long one. Before World War II, only a few environmental organizations seemed interested in the deteriorating condition of America's lakes, rivers, and streams. The Izaak Walton League was among the first to draw attention to the contamination problem, noting in a report published in the late 1920s that 85 percent of the nation's waterways were polluted and that only 30 percent of all municipalities treated their wastes, many of them inadequately. Industrial interests like the American Petroleum Institute, the American Iron and Steel Institute, and the Manufacturing Chemists Association insisted that "streams were nature's sewers" and convinced key legislators that industrial dumping posed no environmental threat.[30]

The initial attempts to regulate surface water pollution were weak and ineffective. In 1948, Congress passed the first Water Pollution Control Act, which established the federal government's limited role in regulating interstate water pollution. The law also provided for studies and research and limited funding for sewage treatment. It also authorized the surgeon general to prepare or adopt programs for eliminating or reducing pollution in cooperation with other agencies and the industries involved. The emphasis on a cooperative approach, coupled with provisions that were both cumbersome and often unworkable, gave the law little impact. In 1952, a report to Congress indicated not a single enforcement action had been taken, and Congress began to hold hearings on a revision to the legislation. The 1956 amendments to the act eliminated many of the difficulties of the 1948 law, but still limited Congress's role to interstate waters and allowed Congress to delegate much of its authority to implement the law to the states. It did, however, condition federal funding of sewage treatment facilities on the submission of adequate water pollution plans by the states. This provided an incentive for states to write water quality standards to meet state goals for surface water pollution. Still, only one enforcement action was filed under this authority over the next fifteen years.

During the 1960s, Congress, led by Senator Edmund Muskie of Maine, became restless over the slow pace of water pollution control, since it was obvious that states were doing an inadequate job. In 1965, passage of the Water Quality Act established a June 1967 water quality standard for interstate waters and streamlined federal enforcement efforts. A year later, the Clean Water Restoration Act provided $3.5 billion in federal grants for the construction of sewage treatment plants and for research on advanced waste treatment. These early attempts at water quality legislation were weak and ineffective. They allowed the states to classify waterways within their jurisdiction, so a state could decide that a particular stream was best used for industrial use rather than for swimming. The use designation of the Cuyahoga River in Ohio, for example, was waste disposal — a fact that did not seem to bother most residents until the river caught fire in 1969. From an enforcement standpoint, the initial pollution laws were meaningless. For the two decades before 1972, only one case of alleged violation of federal water pollution control law reached the courts, and in that case over four years elapsed between the initial enforcement conference and the final consent decree.

President Richard Nixon's February 1970 message to Congress on the environment called for a new water pollution bill, which eventually became the 1972 Federal Water Pollution Control Act. The main emphasis of the legislation was on technological capability. In addition to establishing a regulatory framework for water quality, the bill gave the EPA six specific deadlines by which it was to grant permits to water pollution sources, issue effluent (wastewater) guidelines, require sources to install water pollution control technology, and eliminate discharges into the nation's waterways to make them fishable and swimmable.[31] A key component of the legislation was the establishment of the National Pollution Discharge Elimination System (NPDES), which made it illegal to discharge anything at all unless the source had a federal permit to do so. The NPDES had a historical basis in the 1899 Refuse Act, which had previously been thought to apply only to discharges that obstructed navigation. But the U.S. Supreme Court broadened the interpretation of the act in two cases that made it applicable to any industrial waste.[32]

Water quality continued to capture media interest when consumer advocate Ralph Nader publicized contamination along a 150-mile stretch of the Mississippi River between Baton Rouge and New Orleans known as the "petrochemical corridor." A public outcry after a February 1977 spill of carbon tetrachloride (a potential carcinogen) into the Ohio River contaminated Cincinnati's water supply further fueled the legislative fires, although Congress took no action to strengthen the 1972 law. Although the act was amended in 1977, it was not until the mid-1980s that there was general agreement among policymakers and environmental groups that the 1972 legislation had been overly optimistic in setting target dates for the standards to be met. Little progress had been made in improving the overall quality of the nation's waterways, although given the pace of the country's population growth and economic expansion, the argument could be made that at least the situation did not get much worse, or worse as fast. In 1987, Congress enacted a new legislative mandate — the Water Quality Act — over two vetoes by President Ronald Reagan. The new legislation expanded congressional authority to regulate water pollution from point sources — a confined conveyance, such as a pipe, tunnel, well, or floating vessel (such as a ship) that discharges pollutants — as well as from nonpoint sources, which is basically anything else. The Water Quality Act also required every state and territory to establish safe levels of toxic pollutants in fresh water by 1990.

Congress considered but failed to pass a new Clean Water Act in 1995 and 1996. Dubbed the "Dirty Water Act" by critics, the proposed legislation would have given states the option to develop their own runoff control programs and would have relieved some industrial polluters from having to pretreat wastes before discharging them into publicly owned treatment facilities. The 105th Congress also failed to pass any new water quality bills in its term, and leadership battles make action in the 106th and future sessions unlikely.

Groundwater and Drinking Water

The main groundwater source of drinking water is aquifers — layers of rock and earth that contain water or could contain water. For most of the twentieth century, groundwater was thought to be a virtually unlimited natural resource, constantly filtered and replenished and available for human use and consumption. Currently, about half of all drinking water is supplied through groundwater.[33]

As a policy issue, water quality has often suffered from differences of opinion over where the regulatory responsibility ought to lie, with regulatory authority divided between drinking water and groundwater. Federal authority to establish primary drinking water standards (those applying to materials that are human health standards) originated with the Interstate Quarantine Act of 1893, which allowed the surgeon general to make regulations covering only bacteriological contamination. But the first U.S. primary drinking water standard was not set until 1914 by the U.S. Public Health Service, whose main concern was the prevention of waterborne diseases. The federal standards were applicable only to systems that provided water to an interstate common carrier. From 1914 to 1974, the standards were revised four times — in 1925, 1942, 1946, and 1962 — and were gradually extended to cover all U.S. water supplies.

Groundwater regulatory authority was treated somewhat differently from the way drinking water regulatory authority was treated. There were those who felt that the federal government should not hold the responsibility for regulating and cleaning up groundwater. President Dwight Eisenhower, for example, believed water pollution was a "uniquely local blight" and felt that the primary obligation for providing a safe drinking water supply ought to rest with state and local officials, not with the federal government.[34] But with the creation of the EPA in 1970, the federal government reaffirmed its policy-making authority for water quality. With passage of the 1974 Safe Drinking Water Act, the EPA was authorized to identify which substances were contaminating the nation's water supply and set maximum contaminant levels, promulgated as the National Primary Drinking Water Regulations. The act was amended in 1986 to accelerate the EPA's regulation of toxic contaminants, and included a ban on lead pipe and lead solder in public water systems. It mandated greater protection of groundwater sources, and set a three-year timetable for regulation of eighty-three specific chemical contaminants that may have an adverse health effect known or anticipated to occur in public water systems.

During the summer of 1996, Congress and the Clinton administration, anxious to provide some evidence to voters that they were able to address pressing national issues, enacted amendments to the Safe Drinking Water Act. The amendments gave more discretion to states and local governments to determine what contaminants pose a threat to human health. The new law emphasized controlling the greatest risks for the most benefit at the least cost. It required local water agencies to issue annual reports disclosing the chemicals and bacteria in tap water. The reports must be written in simple, accessible language and sent to residents enclosed with their utility bills. Agencies must notify the public when water contaminants pose a serious threat. The law also authorized a $7.6 billion revolving fund to loan money to local water agencies for construction of new facilities. Small water systems can get waivers from compliance with the federal regulations. The measure was criticized by some Democrats for including water-related projects in states where Republicans were in tight reelection campaigns and by environmental groups for weakening national water quality standards.[35]

But passage of the 1996 amendments did not eliminate concern over water quality. One organization, the Environmental Working Group, released a report in 1996 analyzing EPA data that concluded that one in six Americans — 45 million people — receive water from a utility that has had recent pollution problems, including fecal matter, parasites, disease-causing microbes, radiation, toxic chemicals, and lead. More than 18,500 public water suppliers reported at least one violation of a federal drinking water standard in 1994 and 1995. The report urged water providers to supply more information to consumers about water quality. Representatives of the American Water Works Association subsequently criticized the study as an exaggeration of sporadic incidents that were unfairly described in the study as chronic problems.[36] By 1999, some 55,000 water systems serving 240 million Americans began producing "consumer confidence" reports at least once a year — evidence that some progress toward public participation and notification had finally begun.[37]

TOXIC CONTAMINATION

Until the early 1960s and the publication of Rachel Carson's *Silent Spring,* Americans paid little attention to the millions of gallons of toxic chemicals that were routinely being poured into waterways, dumped onto remote sites, or even stored on private property. The dangers posed by the storage and handling of toxic chemicals were either unknown or ignored. Only a series of highly publicized incidents and disclosures moved the toxics legacy onto the political agenda as a water quality issue.

In 1999, Touchstone Pictures released a film that rekindled Americans' interest in toxic pollution. *A Civil Action,* starring John Travolta as an attorney representing eight Boston-area families in which members developed leukemia, presented the true story of a four-year court battle against the W.R. Grace and Beatrice Food companies. Based on the 1995 award-winning book by Jonathan Harr,[38] the film recreated the controversy that erupted when the families sued the companies for drinking water contamination. The families alleged that Grace, a specialty chemicals company, had dumped solvents on the ground, but an EPA study later showed the chemicals, including trichloroethylene (TCE), could not have entered the families' drinking water. Nonetheless, the companies settled the suit out of court for $8 million, while never admitting guilt in the case.

Prior to the film's release, the Grace Company attempted to tell its side of the story, noting what it believed were inaccuracies in the book and evidence collected after the settlement. To reach consumers (and potential filmgoers), the company established a special website, and it prepared a public relations strategy to confront future criticism once the film started being discussed more widely. But the most glaring impact was that *A Civil Action* returned toxic pollution to the environmental policy agenda — sixteen years after the lawsuit was initially filed.

Groundwater can be contaminated from a variety of human sources, from dumping to runoff from agriculture use. Homeowners, for example, may unknowingly pour products down their kitchen drains or toilets, that contaminate the sewage stream. Some toxic contamination has been deliberate, while in other cases the groundwater was accidentally polluted long before researchers and officials even knew contamination was possible, or the extent to which it could be cleaned up. In Los Angeles, for example, California's Department of Health Services requested that all major water providers conduct tests for two hazardous substances, TCE and perchloroethylene (PCE), both routinely used in dry cleaning, metal plating, and machinery degreasing. The survey found hazardous levels of the two substances in several water production wells and traced them to the period between 1940 and 1967 when disposal of large quantities of chemical wastes was unregulated.

Other forms of toxic contamination are legal and permitted by officials. The nation's pulp and paper mills have been targeted by environmental groups as among the biggest polluters of U.S. waterways, with bleaching plants the source of millions of pounds of chlorinated compounds annually. Among the compounds identified in bleach effluent are dioxins (a generic term applied to a group of suspected carcinogens that are the by-products of other substances or processes), which have been shown to cause reproductive disorders in animals and immune system suppression and impaired liver function in humans.

The pace at which toxic contamination has been regulated and enforced, both at the federal and state levels, has been uneven and decidedly sluggish. The Clean Water Act of 1972 required the EPA to impose the best available pollution control technology standards on industries that discharge toxic waste into rivers, lakes and estuaries, or sewage treatment facilities. The agency did not take action to implement the law until 1976, when a lawsuit forced it to agree to regulate twenty-four of more than fifty industrial categories, including organic chemicals, pharmaceuticals, and pulp and paper industries. In 1987, Congress amended the legislation and ordered the EPA to update the old standards and to begin regulating additional categories by February 1991. When the congressional deadline passed, the Natural Resources Defense Council (NRDC) filed suit in U.S. District Court to force the agency to comply with the 1987 law. In its suit, the NRDC noted that the EPA had not developed rules for four of five, or fifty thousand of the seventy-five thousand, industrial plants that dump toxic substances directly into surface waters. In 1992, the EPA agreed to settle the lawsuit and extend federal standards to sixteen additional industry categories between 1996 and 2002, including industrial laundries, pesticide manufacturers, and hazardous waste facilities and incinerators.

Similarly, the states have failed to comply with the 1987 Water Quality Act provisions, which required them to impose limits on toxic pollution in their waters by 1990. In 1991, the EPA announced that it would impose federal rules on the twenty-two states and territories that had not set their own standards to reduce levels of 105 toxic compounds, including pesticides, solvents, and heavy metals.

Why has water pollution taken so long to gain policymakers' attention, and why has the EPA been so reluctant to move forward on the legislative mandates? There are several reasons that may explain the current status of water pollution control. One, EPA officials cite staff and budgetary constraints that virtually crippled the agency during the 1980s, especially under President Reagan, that put many water quality initiatives on hold. Two, the federal government had delegated much of its responsibility to the states, which are required to issue permits to industries that discharge pollution onto surface water. The permit limits vary from state to state and have generally been much more lenient than federal controls. Three, water quality issues have tended to take a back seat to air quality issues when it comes to the political arena. Congressional committees have focused on the more politically visible issues of smog and auto emissions rather than water quality. Although the 1972 law eliminated the gross pollution that causes rivers and lakes to look or smell bad, the more invisible but nevertheless hazardous toxic pollutants have been largely ignored until recently. Four, the overlapping of jurisdictions and responsibilities between the federal and state governments has led to a competition among agencies. Five, both environmental groups and public officials reluctantly admit that the compliance deadlines of the 1972 legislation were extremely unrealistic, forcing the EPA to scramble to come up with new rules that even the agency leadership knew were not attainable. Last, despite attempts at innovative conservation strategies and protection of existing sources, one of the compelling factors in water quality policy today is cost. Many of the new federal requirements place a severe burden on small communities that cannot afford expensive water treatment plants on budgets that are already stretched thin. The EPA is thus exploring more affordable and innovative technologies, although the cost of bringing public water systems into full compliance is estimated at $1–2 billion per year. Small communities may not be able to take advantage of some treatment technologies, for example, and may not have access to alternative water supplies. Thus, many of the proposed solutions may benefit large urban areas, leaving smaller, rural communities with few alternatives.

THE GLOBAL DIMENSION

As one of the world's most industrialized countries, the United States has the advantage of technology and monetary resources to make attempts to preserve water resources and to ensure a safe supply of drinking water. To most Americans, water quality is as much a matter of aesthetics as of health — a view shared among developed countries. But from a global perspective, the concerns and attention paid to the issue of managing water resources are quite different.

First, in most developing countries water policy has been almost totally health-based, with little attention paid to the recreational or scenic value of waterways — values considered luxuries in economies struggling to fund any type of environmental program at all. Although all nations respond to the problem of water scarcity through the strategies outlined earlier in this chapter, what minimal environmental resources developing countries have must be spread thinly between air and water pollution, with groundwater contamination receiving the bulk of funds.[39]

Second, some water resource policy is made on an ad hoc basis, with little or no centralized planning or decision making. Such is the case of the Aral Sea, which straddles the borders of Kazakstan and Uzbekistan in Central Asia. The demise of this important body of water is considered one of the world's worst environmental catastrophes among environmental groups. For three decades, local officials and international NGOs watched the dessication of the region as Soviet engineers diverted water for agricultural use from two rivers that feed the Aral Sea. Now the sea is split into two parts by a small patch of desert, and officials in the north have begun construction on a dam that would permanently block off water to the south — a proposal that will mean irreparable damage to the sparsely populated region.

In this instance, the problem is multifaceted. Scientists have repeatedly warned that more water is evaporating from the surface of the Aral Sea than flows in from one river in the north — the Syr Darya — and one in the south — the Amu Darya. The result is a plan to reduce the surface area of the southern portion in order to raise water levels in the north, where the formerly busy port of Aralsk is now separated from the sea by about ten miles of desert. Aralsk's mayor began construction on the new dam because the city's economy was dependent upon fishing. Without a dam, researchers at the Kazak Academy of Science predict that the entire Aral Sea will disappear by 2010. Already, the shrinking sea is only one-half its former size and one-quarter its volume, leading to the extinction of at least twenty species of wildlife and vegetation and creation of thirteen thousand square miles of saline wasteland.

Despite the awarding of over $600 million in international aid, mostly designated for research, there are few tangible signs that the problem is bring solved. A 1996 attempt to build a dam failed when water washed over the top; now the mayor pays workers about $15 a day to pile more sand on the dam's base because the Kazak government is unable to contribute more than a token amount to the project. The mayor hopes to build a forty-foot-high dam so that water levels in the north will return to 1960s levels. The result will be a dry, chalky dust seabed of fertilizer and pesticide residue in the south from upstream wheat and rice production. The salt fog already causes respiratory illnesses and cancer among those who live near Aralsk. Environmental groups appear to have moved on to other ecological disasters that are the legacy of the Soviet regime. And as one United Nations official put it, the dam will simply "change the geographic distribution of environmental damage."[40]

Third, despite the fact that the United Nations designated the decade of the 1980s as the International Drinking Water Supply and Sanitation Decade, millions of Africans still do not have access to the water resources considered a necessity in the industrialized world. Two of the most painful and debilitating parasitic diseases, guinea worm and schistosomiasis, which affect millions of residents in sub-Saharan Africa, are caused by poor sanitation and unsafe water supplies.

Fourth, many countries have only marginal enforcement operations to handle water pollution, and legislation to control and punish polluters is weak where it exists at all. There is a shortage of lawyers with expertise in environmental law, and even fewer judges who are informed or sympathetic. Enforcement of water quality regimes is made more difficult by the fact that water pollution ignores international boundaries, with many nations often sharing the same waterways. In Europe, for example, the problem was first recognized as early as 1868, when nations along the Rhine River agreed to a treaty that required vessels transporting toxic substances on the river to bear the word poison in French and German. The 1963 Berne Convention and the 1977 Rhine Chemical Convention dealt with deliberate discharge of pollutants, but neither document had effective enforcement mechanisms.

Finally, environmental organizations in the United States have been much more successful than their counterparts in other countries in raising the public's awareness about water quality. In many developing nations, polluted waters have always been a way of life, and there is little knowledge of the care and advantages of clean water. As a result, there have been fewer grassroots efforts to demand stronger enforcement and less media attention to gross violations and health risks.

Although efforts are being made to transfer American technology to both developed and developing nations to improve water quality, most observers believe the best that can be done for now is to buy time. Early efforts at providing assistance in the former Soviet Union were often poorly thought out or were abandoned before fulfillment, leading some governments to rethink their aid plans. As one researcher notes: "What the West needs at this point is not a detailed blueprint for future action, but a new intellectual framework for approaching the problem: patience is necessary. More importantly, policymakers must think in terms of multiyear time frames, collective action, mechanisms for developing joint strategies, and coordination."[41]

NOTES

1. Randolph E. Schmid, "Water Shortages Called Biggest Threat," Associated Press syndicated article, November 11, 1998.

2. "River Program Keeps Clinton Busy," *San Francisco Chronicle,* July 31, 1998, A2; "American Heritage Rivers Initiative," Council on Environmental Quality, Washington, DC, May 8, 1998, available at <http://www.epa.gov/rivers/veto.html>.

3. World Resources Institute, *World Resources 1994–95* (New York: Oxford University Press, 1994), 2, 73.

4. Sandra Postel, "Emerging Water Scarcities," in *The WorldWatch Reader on Global Environmental Issues,* ed. Lester R. Brown (New York: Norton, 1991), 127–143.

5. Montague Yudelman, "Sustainable and Equitable Development in Irrigated Environments," in *Environment and the Poor: Development Strategies for a Common Agenda,* ed. H. Jeffrey Leonard et al. (New Brunswick, NJ: Transaction Books, 1989), 61–85.

6. See Gilbert White, "The Environmental Effect of the High Dam at Aswan," *Environment, 30,* no. 7 (September 1988): 5–28.

7. Yudelman, "Sustainable and Equitable Development," 71.

8. See George Wharton James, *Reclaiming the Arid West: The Story of the United States Reclamation Service* (New York: Dodd, Mead, 1917).

9. Robert Gottlieb, *A Life of Its Own: The Politics and Power of Water* (New York: Harcourt Brace Jovanovich, 1988), 48.

10. See Wallace Stegner, *This Is Dinosaur* (New York: Knopf, 1955). At that time, the Bureau of Reclamation also had the proposed Glen Canyon Dam near the Arizona-Utah border on the drawing boards; the project was eventually built after the Echo Park controversy. Even though the Glen Canyon project provides hydroelectric power to 400,000 people in seven states, its original purpose was to store water in Lake Powell, which holds 26.7 million acre feet of water when full. Environmentalists are now seeking to see Lake Powell drained to restore Glen Canyon to its original beauty. For more information on this controversy, see the Glen Canyon Institute homepage at <http://www.glencanyon.org>.

11. See Constance Elizabeth Hunt, *Down by the River* (Washington, DC: Island Press, 1988), 11–14.

12. See Tom Harris, *Death in the Marsh* (Washington, DC: Island Press, 1991).

13. Gottlieb, *Life of Its Own,* 270–271.

14. *Winters v. United States,* 207 U.S. 564 (1908).

15. *Arizona v. California,* 373 U.S. 546 (1963).

16. See Marc Reisner and Sarah Bates, *Overtapped Oasis: Reform or Revolution for Western Water* (Washington, DC: Island Press, 1990), 92–98. See also Lloyd Burton, *American Indian Water Rights and the Limits of Law* (Lawrence: University of Kansas Press, 1991).

17. Postel, "Emerging Water Scarcities," 32.

18. *National Audubon Society v. Superior Court (Mono Lake),* 33 Cal.3d 419 (1983).

19. See Benedykt Dziegielewski and Duane D. Baumann, "Tapping Alternatives: The Benefits of Managing Urban Water Demands," *Environment, 34,* no. 9 (November 1992): 6–11.

20. Reisner and Bates, *Overtapped Oasis,* 111–122.

21. Patrick E. Taylor, "Dam's Inexorable Future Spells Doom for Yangtze Valley's Rich Past," *New York Times* (October 6, 1996): A12.

22. Responsibility for mapping wetlands rests with the U.S. Fish and Wildlife Service, which requires the agency to provide Congress with a collection of information on the status and trends in wetlands management, called the National Wetlands Inventory (NWI), every ten years. Future national updates are scheduled for publication in 2000, 2010, and 2020. For more information, visit the NWI website at <http://www.nwi.fws.gov>.

23. See Frank Graham, Jr., "Of Broccoli and Marshes," *Audubon, 7* (July 1990): 102.

24. Keith Schneider, "Administration Proposes Opening Vast Protected Areas to Builders," *New York Times,* August 3, 1991, 1.

25. Warren E. Leary, "In Wetlands Debate, Acres and Dollars Hinge on Definitions," *New York Times,* October 15, 1991, C4.

26. William K. Stevens, "Panel Urges Big Wetlands Restoration Project," *New York Times,* December 12, 1991, A16.

27. Jon Kusler, "Wetlands Delineation: An Issue of Science or Politics?" *Environment, 34,* no. 2 (March 1992): 7–11, 29–37.

28. See, for example, Karol J. Ceplo, "Land Rights Conflicts in the Regulation of Wetlands," in *Land Rights: The 1990s Property Rights Rebellion,* ed. Bruce Yandle (Lanham, MD: Rowman and Littlefield, 1995), 106; Todd Shields, "Judge Fines Developers $4 Million," *Washington Post* (June 18, 1996): D1; and "EPA's Most Wanted," *Wall Street Journal* (November 18, 1992), A20.

29. "Remarks at the Signing of the Water Quality Act of 1965, October 2, 1965," *Public Papers of the President: Lyndon B. Johnson* (Washington, DC: Government Printing Office, 1966), 1035.

30. Gottlieb, *A Life of Its Own,* 163.

31. See Alfred A. Marcus, *Promise and Performance: Choosing and Implementing an Environmental Policy* (Westport, CT: Greenwood Press, 1980), 141–149.

32. The Court's interpretation is outlined in *United States v. Republic Steel Corporation,* 362 U.S. 482 (1960) and *United States v. Standard Oil Company,* 384 U.S. 224 (1966).

33. Stormwater runoff is becoming an increasingly important issue in urban water policy. See Tom Arrandale, "Pollution in the Gutter," *Governing,* December 1998, 51–60. For an overview of drinking water issues, see Colin Ingram, *The Drinking Water Book* (Berkeley, CA: Ten Speed Press, 1996).

34. James Ridgeway, *The Politics of Ecology* (New York: Dutton, 1970), 51.

35. David Hosansky, "Drinking Water Bill Clears, Clinton Expected to Sign," *Congressional Quarterly Weekly Report* (August 3, 1996): 2179.

36. *U.S. Water News Online,* June 1996.

37. "Safe Drinking Water for America's Families," Washington, DC: Office of the President press release, August 11, 1998, available at <http://www.whitehouse.gov/CEQ/081198.html>. However, a 1998 EPA report cited agriculture as the biggest polluter of America's rivers and streams and as fouling 173,000 miles of waterways with chemicals, erosion, and animal waste runoff. The emphasis on farming as the source of groundwater pollution raised the ire of the owners of large corporate farms who sought congressional relief from any new regulations. See "EPA Calls Farming, Livestock the Biggest Polluters of Waterways," *San Francisco Chronicle,* May 14, 1998, A5.

38. Jonathan Harr, *A Civil Action* (New York: Random House, 1995). See also Susan Spencer-Wendel, "Chemical Firms Girds for 'Action,'" *San Francisco Chronicle,* January 2, 1999, E6.

39. The difficulties in funding pollution control problems are outlined by Philip R. Pryde, ed., *Environmental Resources and Constraints in the Former Soviet Union Republics* (Boulder, CO: Westview, 1995); and by Robert Mendelsohn, ed., *The Economics of Pollution Control in the Asia Pacific* (Brookfield, VT: Edward Elgar, 1996).

40. Andrew Kramer, "Bringing the Sea Back to Aralsk," *San Francisco Chronicle,* November 30, 1998, A11.

41. Murray Feshbach, *Ecological Disaster: Cleaning Up the Hidden Legacy of the Soviet Regime* (New York: Twentieth Century Press, 1995), 106.

FOR FURTHER READING

Hussein A. Amery and Aaron T. Wolf. *Water in the Middle East: A Geography of Peace.* Austin: University of Texas Press, 2000.

Maude Barlow. *Blue Gold: The Global Water Crisis and the Commodification of the World's Water Supply.* San Francisco, CA: International Forum on Globalization, 1999.

John M. Donahue and Barbara Rose Johnson, eds. *Water, Culture, and Power: Local Struggles in a Global Context.* Covelo, CA: Island Press, 1998.

Wendy Nelson Espeland. *The Struggle for Water: Politics, Rationality, and Identity in the American Southwest.* Chicago: University of Chicago Press, 1998.

Mark Fiege. *Irrigated Eden.* Seattle: University of Washington Press, 1999.

James R. Karr and Ellen W. Chu. *Restoring Life in Running Waters.* Covelo, CA: Island Press, 1999.

Jeffrey J. Pierce, Ruth F. Weiner, and P. Aarne Vesilund. *Environmental Pollution and Control*. Boston: Butterworth-Heinemann, 1998.
Sandra Postel. *Pillar of Sand: Can the Irrigation Miracle Last?* New York: W. W. Norton, 1999.
Paul Simon. *Tapped Out: The Coming World Crisis in Water and What We Can Do about It*. New York: Angle Publishing, 1999.
Julie Stauffer. *The Water Crisis: Constructing Solutions to Freshwater Pollution*. London: Earthscan, 1999.

CHAPTER 8

Air Quality: Pollution and Solutions

Los Angeles Mayor Fletcher E. Bowron announces at a press conference that the city's smog will be entirely eliminated within four months.
— August 14, 1943[1]

Think of San Francisco — the Golden Gate Bridge, the scenic Marin Headlands, the trolley cars going half way to the stars — and dirty air.

In 1998, the EPA redesignated the Bay Area's air quality status because the region exceeded federal air quality standards for ozone in two of the last three years in the agency's three-year cycles, from 1995 to 1997. Officials registered seventeen summer days when readings violated federal standards, even though emission levels had been below EPA compliance levels for twenty-two consecutive months. The action meant that the region would have to revise its clean air plan to show what additional measures would be taken to bring the Bay Area back into compliance.

Federal and state air quality regulations are extremely complex and involve dozens of stakeholders. The EPA, in enforcing the statute, argued that "the Clean Air Act sets certain rules that apply to everyone. When a region slips, it needs to do more. The Bay Area had a hell of a slip for a couple of years. And now the challenge is to get them back over the line." Business organizations, like the Bay Area Council, which represents major employers in the nine-county area, argued that the EPA's ruling "flies in the face of common sense. The record for the last twenty-two months has been total compliance — no violations. The redesignation will send the wrong message — that the air is dirty here."[2]

That is exactly the message that a coalition of San Joaquin business, environmental, and political leaders wanted to send, and why they petitioned the EPA to enforce its own regulations. "This is a very important decision for the health of future generations of children living here in the Bay Area," remarked Denny Larson, a spokesperson for Communities for a Better Environment, one of the groups that petitioned the EPA. "The

◁ ***Nearly three hundred thousand people breathe the noxious fumes from metal smelters first built by political prisoners in the Siberian city of Norilsk, considered one of the most polluted cities in the world.***

air district has been soft on the big polluters like power plants and oil refineries since the 1980s. Once they had clean air status, there was no hammer to force them to clean up. That's how we got unhealthy air."[3]

Most areas in California fail to meet the EPA's air quality standards. For that reason, policymakers continue to look for innovative strategies that go beyond the measures they have previously taken. For example, in 1998, the state's Air Resources Board (ARB) revised its policies for measuring exhaust from diesel trucks and buses after a five-year controversy. The California Trucking Association had argued that smog check devices used from 1991 to 1993 were inaccurate, challenging roadside inspections, leading several groups to file class-action suits.[4] The ARB, working with the Society of Automotive Engineers, developed a new test that the trucking industry says it can live with. But state air regulators delayed a decision on a proposal to list diesel exhaust as a "toxic air contaminant," bowing to oil companies, the trucking industry, farm groups, and engine manufacturers who accused the ARB of using "junk science" to justify the listing. Environmental organizations and independent scientists, in turn, accused the industry of mounting a massive disinformation campaign to delay the implementation of new ways to further reduce public exposure.[5]

What made the issue even more controversial was a 1998 EPA study that found that the catalytic converter, a mechanism that has significantly reduced smog from automobiles, is now a large and growing cause of global warming. The study estimated that nitrous oxide, a compound produced by the device that is three hundred times more powerful than carbon dioxide, now makes up 7.2 percent of the gases that cause global warming. Increases in cars with the device and in the number of vehicle miles traveled has meant the creation of more nitrous oxide, half of which is created by automobiles and trucks. An EPA official who worked on the study noted, "You've got people trying to solve one problem, and as is not uncommon, they've created another."[6] Attempting to deal with the conflicting strategies, the EPA admitted that "there are still major scientific uncertainties" about the effect of catalytic converters on nitrous oxide emissions. EPA agreed that the current data are incomplete and added that technicians will continue to study nitrous oxide emissions from current automobile models.[7]

While this issue illustrates the difficulties of dealing with conflicting studies, science, and economics, air quality was a problem long before the mayor of Los Angeles made his optimistic prediction.

There are references to the fumes produced at the asphalt mining town of Hit, about one hundred miles west of Babylon in the writings of King Tukulti around 900 B.C.E. In 61 C.E. the philosopher Seneca reported on the "heavy air of Rome" and its "pestilential vapors and soot." Marco Polo refused to use coal as a fuel because of its smoky odors. Foreigners traveling to Elizabethan England were astonished and revolted at the filthy smoke produced by domestic fires and workshops.[8] In the United States, concerns about air pollution increased in almost direct proportion to the nation's growing industrialization. In 1881, the Chicago City Council adopted an ordinance that prohibited dense smoke emissions, and in 1905, Los Angeles enacted a similar measure aimed at emissions of dense smoke from flues, chimneys, and smokestacks in the city.[9] The history of cleaning up urban air pollution is marked by small successes on what has proven to be a much longer road than most early municipal officials ever anticipated.

There are three characteristics that can be used to describe global attempts to improve air quality: one, in the United States, local government historically has been given most of the responsibility for pollution control; two, policy efforts have been split between those wishing improvement because of impaired visibility and those who recognize the health effects of pollution; and three, in most other parts of the world, the national government, rather than municipalities, has taken the initiative for improving air quality, with varying degrees of success. This chapter reviews these characteristics and the challenge of developing policies to control urban air pollution both in the United States and in other countries and explores the ways in which the problem has been expanded to other concerns such as toxic air pollution and visibility.

WHAT IS AIR POLLUTION?

Until well into the twentieth century, the components of pollution were thought to be primarily smoke and soot (suspended particulate matter) and sulfur dioxide — waste products from home heating, industrial facilities, and utility power plants. With industrialization and the advent of the automobile, that list has expanded to include a broad range of emissions.

As Table 8.1 indicates, today the term is usually applied internationally to the six conventional pollutants identified and measured by the EPA: carbon monoxide, lead, nitrogen oxides, ozone, particulate matter, and sulfur oxides. Of more recent scientific study are air toxics, such as lead and benzene, regional and global pollutants, such as acid rain and carbon dioxide, and atmospherically reactive gases, such as chlorofluorocarbons. The conventional, or "criteria," pollutants are found in the atmosphere, and although most are human-made, some, like particulate matter, include the fine particles of dust and vegetation that are natural in origin and small enough to penetrate the most sensitive regions of the respiratory tract. There are three primary categories of sources for conventional pollutants: stationary or point sources, such as factories and power plants, mobile sources, including cars, trucks, and aircraft, and domestic sources, such as home heating or consumer products.

The EPA sets standards of pollution exposure, and federal legislation sets a target date by which regions must meet those standards. The federal government has a variety of sanctions, ranging from fines to shutting down facilities, which can be levied for noncompliance. During the past two decades, U.S. levels of sulfur dioxide, carbon monoxide, particulate matter, and lead have all been reduced, in some cases sharply. When the Clean Air Act Amendments were passed in 1990, 274 areas were designated as nonattainment for at least one of the criteria

Table 8.1 Components of Air Pollution

Criteria Pollutant	*Sources*	*Health Effects*
Carbon monoxide (CO)	Motor vehicles	Interferes with ability of the blood to absorb oxygen; impairs reflexes
Lead (Pb)	Motor vehicles, lead smelters	Affects kidneys, reproductive and nervous systems; accumulates in bones; hyperactivity in children
Nitrogen oxides (NOx)	Electric utility boilers, motor vehicles	Causes increased susceptibility to viral infections, lung irritation
Ozone	Formed by a chemical reaction of NO_2 and hydrocarbons	Irritates respiratory system; impairment of lung function; aggravates asthma
Particulate matter (PM10)	Combustion from industry, forest fires, windblown dust, vehicles	Organic carcinogenic compounds can migrate into lungs, increasing respiratory distress
Sulfur oxides (SO_2)	Utility plant boilers, oil and chemical refineries	Aggravates symptoms of heart/lung disease; increases respiratory illnesses and colds

pollutants. By 1999, only 129 areas were not in attainment. Improving air quality is one of the great environmental policy success stories. However, despite the progress, the EPA found that in 1999, nearly 100 million Americans lived in areas that exceeded the ozone standard.[10]

THE RESPONSIBILITY DILEMMA

For most of the twentieth century, air pollution has been considered a local problem, and as a result, most of the efforts to do something about it have been accomplished by municipal governments. By 1912, industrial smoke, the hallmark of urban growth after the turn of the century, was regulated in twenty-eight U.S. cities with populations of two hundred thousand or more. Smoke was the prime target of most ordinances because it was visible, but there was little attention paid to controlling the problem.[11]

The federal government up until the passage of the Clean Air Act in 1963, took only passing interest in the problem. The Bureau of Mines conducted research on smoke control (which at the time was considered to be the only form of pollution) in 1912, and in 1925, the Public Health Service began to study carbon monoxide in automotive exhaust, but for the most part, the federal role was minor. A six-day smog siege in Donora, Pennsylvania, in 1948, which resulted in the deaths of twenty persons and illness for six thousand residents, focused national attention on a problem that up until then had been considered to be limited to Los Angeles. The Donora incident was followed in December 1952 by a similar sulfurous smog episode in London, and in 1953 in New York, resulting in two hundred deaths.[12] All three events lent some urgency to the problem. As city officials began to realize the irrelevance of political boundaries to pollution control, they began to coordinate their regulatory efforts.

The discovery in 1949 that automobiles were a prime source of pollution forestalled statewide controls on industrial sources, and local government stepped in to fill the void left by federal inaction. In 1955, Los Angeles officials began to coordinate their efforts with the nation's top automakers, and Congress appropriated $5 million for research into motor vehicle emissions — the beginning of federal intervention in urban air pollution regulation. Research in the early 1960s debunked the idea that pollution was a problem only in the area immediately adjacent to the source or in urban areas. Studies began to show that pollution was being transported over long distances, causing environmental damage in regions far removed from the actual source. Long-range transport of sulfur and nitrogen compounds across international boundaries — a phenomenon known as acid rain — made air pollution a global problem (see Chapter 9).[13] These findings made air quality much more than a simple local question and focused problem solving on Congress.

During the 1960s, four members of Congress did attempt to bring the federal government back into the air pollution policy debate: Edmund Muskie, senator from Maine; Abraham Ribicoff, former secretary of the Department of Health, Education, and Welfare (HEW); Kennedy Roberts, member of Congress from Alabama; and Paul Schenck, member of Congress from Ohio. Their efforts were largely responsible for the passage of the pioneering 1963 Clean Air Act, which expanded research and technical assistance programs, gave the federal government investigative and abatement authority, and encouraged the automobile and petroleum industries to develop exhaust control devices. In November 1967, President Lyndon Johnson signed a second air quality bill, which left the primary responsibility for air pollution control with the state and local governments, suggesting that the federal agencies study, but not establish, national automobile emission standards.

Meanwhile, environmental groups were pressuring Muskie to produce a new federal bill, and the senator, an early contender for the 1972 Democratic presidential nomination, felt the sting of their criticism. A 1970 report by consumer activist Ralph Nader referred to "the collapse of the federal air pollution effort" and laid the blame squarely on Muskie's shoulder.[14] Muskie and the members of his Public Works Committee staff, relying on estimates provided by the National Air Pollution Control Administration (a part of HEW), proposed tough new federal standards for air quality and a timetable by which the standards had to be met through the filing of state implementation plans (SIPs). The 1970 Clean Air Act required the newly created Environmental Protection Agency to (1) develop national air quality standards; (2) establish emission standards for motor vehicles, effective with fiscal 1975; and (3) develop emission standards and hazardous emission levels for new stationary sources. The legislation went further than ever before by giving the EPA responsibility for regulating fuels and fuel additives, for certifying and subsidizing on-the-road inspections and assembly-line testing of auto emission control systems.[15] States faced a formidable task when the 1970 act gave them responsibility for preparing emission reduction plans. In addition to facing tight deadlines for plan preparation, neither the states nor the newly created EPA knew very much about translating federal standards into emission limits on sources. Therefore, relatively crude rules — like requiring all sources to diminish emissions by some specified percentage — were often employed.[16]

Critics charge that the 1970 law had several major faults. First, there was some ambiguity over the intent of the act with regard to the setting of auto emission levels. The legislation provided automakers with a one-year extension if they made a good-faith effort to comply but found technology was not available to meet the new standards. Second, Congress appropriated only minimal amounts for research for development of control devices that were in some cases required but that did not yet exist. Third, stationary sources such as steel mills and utility power plants faced serious problems because control devices were either prohibitively expensive or technologically unfeasible.[17]

Five major automakers (Chrysler, Ford, General Motors, International Harvester, and Volvo) responded in early 1972 by filing for an extension of the requirement that they meet emission standards by 1975, arguing that they needed additional time to comply with the law. Their request for an extension was denied by EPA administrator William Ruckelshaus, so the automakers appealed to the federal court, which ordered Ruckelshaus to review his original denial.[18] The automobile manufacturers argued that the necessary catalyst technology would not be available in time to meet the federal deadline, and Chrysler and American Motors testified that, even if the vehicles could be mass-produced in time, they would break down.[19] Ruckelshaus redenied the request for an extension, then reconsidered and granted the automakers what they were seeking, setting interim standards that the automobile companies did not appeal.

Implementation of the 1970 law was further hampered by what one observer has called "the enduring reluctance of the public to make significant sacrifices for the sake of healthy air."[20] The nation was locked into a pattern of rapid inflation and high unemployment, which was coupled with the imposition of an oil embargo by the Organization of Petroleum Exporting Countries (OPEC) in October 1973. With rising concern over energy supplies, in March 1974, President Nixon proposed a package of thirteen amendments to the 1970 Clean Air Act, which froze the interim 1975 auto emission standards for two more years. In 1975, the automakers applied for another one-year extension, which was granted by new EPA administrator Russell Train, largely as a result of claims that the catalysts produced a sulfuric acid mist.[21]

In 1977, industry pressure to relax the emission standards on automobiles resulted in the passage of new Clean Air Act amendments. The legislation suspended the deadlines for automakers and extended the deadlines by which states were to have attained federal standards to 1982. If a state's implementation plan made all reasonable attempts to meet the standards but was unable to do so, the state had to submit a second plan, which would bring the area into compliance no later than December 1987, an issue that primarily affected California. A key element of the 1977 law was a provision, shepherded through Congress by the Sierra Club, that states be required to show that any new sources of pollution would not worsen existing pollution conditions. This complex concept, known as prevention of significant deterioration (PSD), required businesses to install the best available control technology (BACT) to ensure that any potential pollution was minimized.

The concept had first been outlined in a 1972 Sierra Club suit again EPA administrator William Ruckelshaus[22] in which the organization argued that the EPA's guidelines under the 1970 Clean Air Act would permit significant deterioration of the nation's clean air, violating congressional intent. The federal district court agreed, ruling that the EPA could not approve state implementation plans that degraded existing air quality even if the region still met national air quality standards. The EPA appealed, but the U.S. Supreme Court's 1973 4-4 ruling upheld the district court. The EPA proposed new regulations to implement the Court's ruling in 1974.

The EPA showed more flexibility toward industry with the introduction in 1979 of a "bubble" policy, which allowed businesses to find the least expensive method of reducing pollution from an entire plant or series of plants, rather than from an individual source (as if the entire facility were under a regulatory "bubble"). The policy allowed companies to choose how to reduce emissions and to use more innovative strategies than was previously required.[23]

The Clean Air Act was scheduled for reauthorization in 1981, but a change in policy direction came with the Reagan administration, and as a result, the 1970 legislation remained virtually unchanged until 1990.[24] Chief among the congressional barriers to a new law were Representative John Dingell, a Democrat from Michigan, chairman of the House Energy and Commerce Committee, who stalled efforts to enact legislation that would impose new standards on automakers, and Senate Majority Leader Robert Byrd, a Democrat from West Virginia, who protected the interests and jobs of coal miners in his region affected by acid rain proposals.

Clean air legislation regained its place on the policy agenda in the late 1980s partly as a result of changes taking place in Congress. Restless Democrats in the House were openly expressing their hostility to Dingell and Henry Waxman of California, members of the House Energy and Commerce Committee, whose personal battles were perceived as holding up the reauthorization. The result was the formation of the Group of Nine — moderate Democrats hoping to break the legislative logjam over urban smog. In the Senate, Byrd was replaced as majority leader by George Mitchell of Maine, who promised an end to the deadlock. Both houses had the opportunity to end the deadlock when the Bush administration unveiled its own clean air proposal, forcing the key players to resolve their differences.[25]

The resulting legislation, signed by President Bush in 1990, contained several far-reaching proposals that went far beyond the 1970 and 1977 acts. The bill established five categories of cities, termed nonattainment areas (marginal, moderate, serious, severe, or extreme), and set new deadlines by which they must meet federal ozone standards. Only one region, the Los Angeles/South Coast Air Basin, was classified as extreme by the EPA and was given twenty years to meet federal standards. In contrast, severe nonattainment areas have fifteen years from November 1990 (the date of the enactment of the amendments), serious areas have nine years to comply, moderate areas have six years, and marginal areas have three years. Plants emitting any of 189 toxic air pollutants are required to cut emissions and would be forced to shut down by 2003 if these emissions posed more than a one in ten thousand risk of cancer to nearby residents. Chemicals that harm Earth's protective ozone layer are to be phased out more rapidly than under the Montreal Protocol, to which the United States is a signator. One of the most contentious portions of the bill dealt with acid rain, requiring an annual reduction of sulfur dioxide emissions by 10 million tons by the year 2000 and annual nitrogen dioxide emission reductions of 2.7 million tons by that same date. The cost of the legislation was hotly debated, ranging from $25 to $35 billion dollars. Much of that burden falls on coal-fired utility power plants, many of them in the East and Midwest, which are required to reduce SO_2 emissions. Automakers estimate the costs of compliance will add hundreds of dollars to the price of new cars, and small businesses will also feel the pinch with controls on dry cleaners, gasoline service stations, and other sources.[26]

President Bush called passage of the 1990 Clean Air Act "the cornerstone of our environmental agenda." But the battle was far from over. The implementation of the 1990 act has been just as controversial as its development. Congressman Waxman charged, "We'll never see clean air in large parts of the country."[27] There are a number of factors that make implementation difficult. Among the most difficult hurdles that the EPA faces is the regulatory time frame of the seven-hundred-page legislation. The law ordered the EPA to complete 150 regulatory activities, including 100 rule makings, in only two years.

Second, the implementing regulations are among the most complex that the agency has ever issued. While the issue of nitrogen oxide emissions (one of two acid-rain-causing chemicals) took only two pages of the 1990 act, the regulations crafted by the EPA took hundreds of pages. Because of the large volume and complexity of the rules, the EPA has been forced to rely upon outside consultants for many of its rule makings and on its advisory committees for assistance in prioritizing what rules to tackle first. Many of those advisory groups, such as the

Acid Rain Advisory Committee, with forty-four members, were packed with industry members and few representatives of environmental groups.[28] Among the most complex provisions of the law are those dealing with air toxics, an area in which EPA staff members are notoriously short on expertise.

Within a year of passage of the 1990 law, Congress began to step back from the thrust of the 1990 amendments. One portion of the legislation, for example, was designed to require state and local planners to adhere to air quality goals when formulating transportation projects. Theoretically, the intent was to force municipalities to look for alternatives to increased use of single-occupancy vehicles. But in 1991 President Bush proposed, and Congress accepted, plans for a 185,000-mile national highway system that would increase auto use — at odds with the intent of the air quality act — by giving the most funds under the program to those with the highest gasoline use.[29]

President Bush's 1992 State of the Union message stalled the implementation process when the president announced a ninety-day freeze on all federal regulations, and then extended it another 120 days after that. The freeze affected several clean air regulations, including the Pollution Prevention Act, which required polluters to report on the amount of toxic chemicals they generate before they were released. Later that year, the president overruled an EPA regulation that required industries to obtain permits that include limits on the pollution emitted by each plant. Industry had originally sought the right to exceed the limits after minor changes in plant operations, without going through the costly and time-consuming process of obtaining a new permit. Citizen groups considered the permit process an important opportunity for public participation, and the EPA, which drafted the regulation, agreed. Bush then overturned the regulation as a part of his emphasis on deregulation.

In November 1993, the Senate Environment and Public Works Committee issued a "report card" on the implementation of the Pollution Prevention Act. It gave the EPA A grades for its acid rain and stratospheric ozone programs, a B– for its small business assistance program, a C for its management of the state implementation plan process, and a D both for development of air toxic standards and for the implementation of the California Low Emission Vehicle Program.[30] The Senate study trumpeted the success of the acid rain program in devising a market-based approach to environmental regulation and emphasized the importance of environmental quality-based performance standards that create incentives for the development of new technologies.

These shortcomings in implementation were serious, but seemed manageable, until the dynamics of implementation underwent a fundamental change with the election of Republicans in statehouses and Republicans as the new majority party in Congress in November 1994. During the first years of implementation, regulations focused on industrial polluters. But when the focus shifted to people's driving habits, opposition to clean air action skyrocketed. Disgruntled citizens generated considerable opposition to state implementation plans, joined by industry groups who saw a political opening to gain some regulatory relief. Governors, in response, began challenging the EPA. As long as Congress was there to back up the EPA and reopening the act to weaken its provisions was not an option, the EPA could hold firm. Once the new Congress took office in 1995, however, and amending the act was a real possibility, the EPA had to scramble to accommodate state demands. Much of the criticism of the Clean Air Act in the states focused on the enhanced inspection and maintenance system, developed to replace the traditional tail-pipe test required under the Clean Air Act. The system was to be implemented through centralized locations to ensure quality control and to separate clearly the testing and repairing of motor vehicles. The EPA required that states with ozone nonattainment areas include the enhanced program as part of their effort to reduce pollution, but in the fall of 1994, several states balked. Groups representing service station owners who could perform the original testing and motorists began criticizing the enhanced inspection and maintenance program; California was the first state to be permitted to develop an alternative system of testing at both centralized locations and traditional service stations. Additional states then began pressing the EPA for exemptions.[31] Other programs aimed at reducing vehicle emissions have been just as controversial. Illinois officials complained in early 1995 that the EPA had failed to provide guidance on how states were to require carpooling in companies with more than 100 employees. Pennsylvania officials excused employers in the Philadelphia area from complying with the car pool requirement.

Some two dozen bills were introduced during the first months of the 104th Congress to amend the Clean Air Act. One House bill would have repealed the entire 1990 Clean Air Act; two House bills provided that the employer commuting program be optional; a Senate bill would have made carpooling voluntary options for states; and two Senate bills called for making auto inspections voluntary. While Congress made no major changes in the Clean Air Act between 1995 and 1998, it passed several laws that made significant changes. A 1995 budget bill that cut fiscal year 1995 spending prohibited the EPA from spending any money to force states to comply with vehicle inspection and maintenance and commuter vehicle trip-reduction programs. In November 1995, Congress passed a highway bill that included some clean air provisions: it ordered the EPA to give states full credit in determining their compliance with the law for noncentralized inspection and maintenance programs and abolished federal regulation of speed limits, which the EPA estimated would increase nitrogen oxide emissions by about 5 percent per year, as vehicles traveled faster and burned more fuel. The following month, Congress passed a bill making the commuter vehicle trip-reduction program optional, so states with highly polluted areas would not be forced to require employers to require employee carpooling. Throughout the budget process in 1995, Congress included additional riders to appropriations and balanced budget bills that would have restricted EPA's implementation of the Clean Air and other acts, but President Clinton's vetoes blocked those measures, and Congress abandoned them in 1996.

The Clean Air Act has contributed to great reductions in air pollution. But the health effects associated with current levels of pollution are serious. Even

EPA officials admit that Americans will wait years to see cleaner air as a result of the 1990 legislation. Full implementation of the law will not take place until 2005, at the earliest.[32]

ASSESSING THE IMPACT OF POLLUTION

Why has there been such a concern over the impact of pollution? There are five types of environmental damage attributable to air pollution: (1) damage to vegetation, including crops and forests; (2) damage to animals, birds, and insects; (3) damage to synthetic materials, including painted surfaces, rubber, nylon, and metals; (4) soiling of materials, such as clothing and buildings; and (5) weather and climatic changes, including visibility deterioration, surface temperature increases, and reduced solar radiation. But the most serious impact that concerns policymakers is one of health. It is difficult to pinpoint exactly when concerns about health effects of air pollution made their way to the policy agenda. Smoky chimneys and smokestacks were considered part of the price urban dwellers paid for living in an industrialized society, and most people were probably unaware of any damage to their health.

One factor that made it difficult for policymakers to reach consensus on what to do about air pollution was the lack of a consensus about its sources. States had primary responsibility for regulating air pollution, and their responses were as varied as the sources of the problem. Eventually, air pollution disasters in Pennsylvania, New York, and London focused public attention on the hazards.

The emphasis on the health effects of pollution was largely a result of the role of the U.S. Public Health Service, which was given responsibility for air pollution legislation from 1959 until the passage of the Clean Air Act in 1963. Although there was little policy initiation before 1963, the surgeon general did convene the First National Conference on Air Pollution in 1958. Since 1970, research has shown that many Americans are affected by air pollution. One study found that asthmatics are especially sensitive to sulfur dioxide, and EPA researchers have discovered that otherwise healthy, exercising individuals show significant effects after six to eight hours of breathing ozone at levels even below the threshold of the current health standard. Still remaining to be answered are the long-term effects of repeated exposures to smog. The American Lung Association, one of the leading organizations to call for more regulation to reduce the health impacts of air pollution, estimates the annual health cost of air pollution at $50 billion.[33] Cost estimates include days lost from work as a result of pollution-related illnesses, as well as the actual cost of care.

More than one hundred studies have been published that have identified the health effects of urban ozone pollution (see Table 8.2). People breathing ozone, even at concentrations below the national standards, appear to be susceptible to increased respiratory hospital admissions, frequent and severe asthma attacks, inflammation of the upper airways (in healthy children), coughing and breathing pains, reaction to irritants, sensitivity to allergens, and decreased lung function much like smokers suffer from. Epidemiological studies show a strong correlation between increased mortality and ozone pollution. Research published in the 1990s also focused attention on the health effects of particulate pollution, and many scientists became convinced that fine particles were the most serious public health threat from air pollution. The health effects of particulate matter at levels below the national air quality standards (as well as when air quality exceeds the standards) include increased respiratory hospital admissions, increased frequency and severity of asthma attacks, increased school absences, increased respiratory symptoms such as wheezing and coughing, increased hospitalization for cardiovascular problems, and increased mortality. In two major studies of particulate pollution, the risk of early death was estimated to be from 17 to 26 percent higher in areas with high levels of PM10. A study by the Natural Resources Defense Council estimated that 64,000 people may die prematurely from cardiopulmonary causes linked to particulate air pollution. The research focused on the health effects of fine particles, released during combustion, that were not easily expelled by the respiratory system's normal safeguards when breathed by humans.[34] (See "Another View, Another Voice: Renee Morrison: Chester Street Activist.)

The goal of air quality standards, as Congress provided in the Clean Air Act, was to "protect the public health" with an "adequate margin of safety."[35] In the face of compelling research in peer-reviewed scientific publications concerning

Table 8.2 U.S. Air Quality Nonattainment Areas for Ozone (1 hour standard) 1999, by State

Birmingham, AL	Springfield, MA
Phoenix, AZ	Baltimore, MD
Los Angeles/South Coast Air Basin, CA	Kent/Queen Anne Counties, MD
Sacramento, Metro, CA	St. Louis, MO/IL
San Diego, CA	Sunland Park, NM
San Francisco/Oakland/San Jose, CA	New York/North NJ/Long Island NY/NJ
San Joaquin Valley, CA	Cincinnati-Hamilton, OH/KY
Santa Barbara/Santa Maria/Lompoc, CA	Lancaster, PA
Southeast Desert, CA	Pittsburgh/Beaver Valley, PA
Ventura County, CA	Philadelphia/Wilmington/Trenton PA/DE
Greater Connecticut	Beaumont/Port Arthur, TX
Washington, D.C.	Dallas/Ft. Worth, TX
Atlanta, GA	El Paso, TX
Chicago/Gary/Lake County, IL/IN	Houston/Galveston/Brazoria, TX
Louisville, KY	Manitowoc County, WI
Baton Rouge, LA	Milwaukee/Racine, WI

Source: U.S. Environmental Protection Agency, Office of Air Quality Planning and Standards, "USA Air Quality Nonattainment Areas," October 25, 1999.

Another View, Another Voice

RENEE MORRISON
Chester Street Activist

While the EPA can point with some pride to the successes it has had in reducing ambient air pollution, the record on toxic air emissions is poor, at best. Even though the government requires industrial polluters to submit detailed reports about toxic chemicals they release, in a 1998 study, two environmental organizations charged that the reports are seriously flawed. The nation's Toxics Release Inventory was designed to provide citizens with the "right to know" what emissions are polluting their neighborhoods. But the Environmental Working Group and Communities for a Better Environment found that the pollution database was so inaccurate that one refinery's address would have placed it in the middle of a bay and another company's location was inventoried as fifty miles east of its actual location.

Renee Morrison, a fifty-ish mother of four sons, is aware of the need for environmental action at the community level to protect her family. She lives in a low-income neighborhood in Oakland, California, unofficially called Lower Bottom. Morrison's activism comes by way of her mother, who dragged her daughter to meetings of the Chester Street Block Club and reminded her, "You have to fight for everything." By educating themselves on toxic emissions, Morrison and more than three hundred neighbors successfully forced the EPA to shut down an incinerator located in a scrap yard not more than twenty yards from homes where their families live.

The incinerator, which spewed emissions into the air from a twenty-foot-tall stack, began operating in February 1997; it was designed to burn vinyl chloride that had saturated soil and groundwater at a nearby industrial site a decade earlier. At the time, EPA officials told the community that the twenty-four-hour-a-day operation would emit only salt and steam and posed no health risk. Residents grew suspicious of the incinerator's emissions, however, and they began asking questions of local and federal officials, also seeking guidance from a local environmental group, Green Action.

After pressure from Morrison and her neighbors, the EPA belatedly admitted that there was more to the air pollution issue than what they had told residents initially. Confronting an EPA official at a community meeting, Morrison's approach was in stark contrast to her angry neighbors. Speaking in a low-key voice, she chided federal officials for lying. "We know you guys screwed up big time, and you've apologized and we accept it but. . . ." Officials said later that they appreciated Morrison's control and leadership. "She gave us the opportunity to respond without disrupting the meeting, and she let us know she was angry," one EPA official said. Morrison, who had asked the EPA to send someone "who could speak in practical terms instead of scientific

(continued)

language a lay person [could] not understand," was also praised by the executive director of Green Action. "She is an everyday person who has her hands full raising her family and doing her job, and yet she has found the time to get informed about the toxic threat to her community and educate and inspire her community. As I see it, Renee Morrison is a hero."[1]

For More Information

To find out about toxic air emissions in your neighborhood, check out the Toxics Release Inventory at <http://www.epa.gov/opptintr/tri>.

Notes

1. Chip Johnson, "Activist Smokes Out Stack Smell," *San Francisco Chronicle,* August 1, 1998, A15.

the health effects of particulates and ozone, in November 1996 the EPA proposed new, tighter standards for ozone and proposed a new PM2.5 standard to regulate fine particles. The agency argued that the new particulate standards would result in 60,000 fewer bronchitis cases, 9,000 fewer hospitalizations for respiratory problems, fewer visits to doctors, less use of medication, less suffering by those with respiratory disease, improved visibility in national parks and wilderness areas, and prevention of as many as 20,000 premature deaths a year. The proposed ozone standards would result in 1.5 million fewer cases of breathing problems where lung function declines by at least 20 percent, fewer hospitalizations and visits to emergency rooms, less school and work absenteeism, and reduction of crop damage by $1 billion. The EPA also argued that every dollar spent on emissions reductions from 1970 to 1990 resulted in $15 to $20 worth of reduced health care cost. Critics, like the U.S. Conference of Mayors and the Air Quality Standards Coalition, comprised of industry executives, testified in congressional hearings that the proposed standards were too expensive and urged the EPA to do more research before finalizing the regulations. But in June 1997, President Clinton endorsed a compromise proposal and promised the EPA would be flexible in implementing the regulations.

The government's concern over public health has also focused on the control of toxic air contaminants. Five metals found in air — beryllium, cadmium, lead, mercury, and nickel — are known to pose various hazards to human health. With the exception of lead, most of these substances pose a risk primarily to those living adjacent to the source, such as a waste dump or factory. Lead, however, is much more widely dispersed as a component of vehicle fuels and paints. Lead poisoning is characterized by anemia and may lead to brain dysfunction and neurological damage, especially in children. The elimination of lead from automobile fuels in the United States, Japan, and Canada has reduced emissions significantly, but few developing countries have made an attempt to phase out lead in gasoline. The problem is compounded by a lack of emission controls on lead smelters, battery manufacturing plants, and paint production facilities.

Little is known about the health risk posed by the tens of thousands of synthetic chemicals available today. Although research is ongoing, many of the effects of toxic contamination, such as cancer, are not apparent until decades after exposure. Although many of these substances are produced by factories and industrial processes, such as pulp and paper processors, smaller sites, such as municipal waste dumps, dry cleaners, and print shops are also responsible for toxic emission releases. Pesticides and herbicides used in agricultural application also are released into the atmosphere.

As is often the case in policy development, government regulation of toxics has typically come on the heels of crisis, and in this case, events outside the United States. In July 1976, an explosion at a herbicide manufacturing facility in Sevesco, Italy, released a toxic cloud of dioxin and other chemicals that spread downwind. Dioxin is a generic term applied to a group of suspected cancer-causing substances that are known to cause severe reproductive disorders as well as immune system problems and impaired liver function. Although no deaths were directly attributed to the incident, within two weeks plants and animals were dying and residents were admitted to local hospitals with skin lesions. More than seven hundred persons living near the plant were evacuated, and five thousand others in the surrounding areas were told not to garden or let their children play outside. It took two weeks for local authorities to discover that a toxic chemical had been involved and to implement effective safeguards.[36] The incident resulted in the Sevesco Directive in 1984 — an agreement by members of the European Community that plants using hazardous chemicals must inform residents of the nature and quantity of the toxics they use and the risks they pose. Later that year, the accidental release of forty tons of isocyanate at a Union Carbide facility in Bhopal, India, refocused attention on the need to require safeguards in developing nations as well. The incident resulted in death or injury to hundreds of thousands of residents near the plant.

Two landmark pieces of U.S. legislation, the Federal Insecticide, Fungicide, and Rodenticide Act (FIFRA) of 1972 and the 1976 Toxic Substances Control Act (TSCA), which regulates how toxic chemicals are to be used, were a result of such incidents. The laws allow the EPA to regulate chemicals that pose an unacceptable health risk, such as polychlorinated biphenyls (PCBs), which were first regulated in 1978. In addition, the Emergency Planning and Community Right-to-Know Act of 1986 now provides communities with access to information about toxic chemicals in their region. The law calls for extensive data collection and for the creation of state emergency response commissions to plan for chemical release emergencies. The federal government also conducts the Toxics Release Inventory, an annual inventory of toxic releases and transfers of about three hundred toxic chemicals from over twenty thousand manufacturing facilities nationwide. As information about the health effects of each substance is gathered, chemicals of little or no toxic concern are removed from the list, while others are added. Before a new pesticide may be marketed or used in the United

States, it must first be registered with the EPA after a series of health, economic, and cost:benefit studies. If the studies indicate that the risks outweigh the benefits, the EPA can refuse to register the product or regulate the frequency or level of application. This process was used to ban the pesticide DDT in 1972 and to cancel registrations for thirty-four other potentially hazardous pesticides.[37] In 1996, Congress passed a new pesticides law that created a single standard for regulating pesticides in food, rather than having different rules for raw and processed food. Only pesticides that pose a "reasonable certainty of no harm," understood to mean resulting in a risk of no more than one-in-one million lifetime risk of cancer, are permitted.[38]

Yet some observers believe that the United States's progress toward controlling toxic air pollutants has been glacially slow. Before the passage of the 1990 Clean Air Act, the EPA had completed regulations for only seven toxic chemicals, and no information was available on the toxic effects of nearly 80 percent of the chemicals used in commerce.[39] Information generated from the Superfund Right-to-Know rule indicates that more than 2.7 billion pounds of toxic air pollutants are emitted annually in the United States. EPA studies indicate that exposure to such quantities of air toxics may result in one thousand to three thousand cancer deaths each year.[40] The 1990 legislation, however, does offer a comprehensive plan for reducing hazardous air pollutants from major sources and includes a list of 188 toxic air pollutants for which emissions must be reduced. In addition to publishing a list of source categories that emit certain levels of these pollutants, the EPA must develop standards for pollution control equipment to reduce the risk from the contaminants. Based on information from the Toxics Release Inventory as well as additional estimates of emissions from mobile sources and dispersed or area sources such as residential wood-burning stoves, the EPA reported in 1995 that 4.4 million tons of toxics are released into the air each year. The mobile and area sources account for 70 percent of hazardous air pollutant emissions. (Motor vehicle and wood-burning stoves alone account for 47 percent of all toxic emissions.) Efforts to reduce air toxic emissions may also reduce levels of PM and ozone, since many sources emit several different kinds of pollutants.[41]

The Clinton administration proposed in 1996 expanding the requirements of the Toxics Release Inventory to get better data on what pollutants were being released into the environment. The new requirements would increase the number of facilities required to report their emissions to 30,000, up from the 23,000 required to report under the old system. The EPA also won in 1996 an important court victory that permitted it to add 286 new chemicals to the inventory of those that must be reported.[42] It is difficult to know whether air toxic emissions are increasing or decreasing because of the numerous problems that have plagued monitoring and reporting efforts. But some sectors of the economy, such as the chemical industry, have committed to reducing dramatically their emissions through pollution prevention programs. Publication of toxic emissions inventories appears to have created a powerful incentive for companies to reduce emissions; companies have also frequently found that reducing emissions also reduces production costs and increases profits.[43]

Reductions in the EPA's budget and costly and time-consuming studies of the health effects of toxics are still barriers to effective regulation of hazardous air pollutants. Some toxics, such as mercury and lead, last a long time in the atmosphere before they are deposited in bodies of water where they are ingested by fish or plants, later harvested for human consumption. The Clean Air Act calls for studies by the National Academy of Sciences and the EPA that will review and recommend improvements to current techniques for estimating risks to public exposure to air toxics. The Council of Economic Advisers estimated the cost to industry of the air toxics program would be as much as $6 to $7 billion in 2005. It is impossible to quantify, however, the potential health benefit costs, since the results of reducing the damage may not be seen for many years.[44]

VISIBILITY

While contemporary air quality concerns have focused primarily on the health effects of pollutants, it is important to remember that one of the reasons why public officials in Los Angeles first viewed air pollution was in the context of visibility. Complaints from the public about the haze over the city and the inability to see the mountains that ring the South Coast Air Basin drew attention to the problem long before health issues were studied and the impacts exposed. Now the controversy over visibility is centered in the Southwest, and at the heart of the issue is the Grand Canyon.

Although visibility began to be reduced in the 1940s as the West began to become more populated, public interest did not coalesce until 1975, when the National Parks and Conservation Association alerted its members to the growing clouds of sulfur dioxide, nitrogen oxide, and fine particulates that had begun to build up in the atmosphere, often obscuring the vistas in the Grand Canyon and in Utah's Bryce Canyon. The primary sources of the brownish haze were believed to be fossil fuel–fired power plants, copper smelters, industrial boilers, chemicals production, and mobile sources like cars and trucks. The origination of the pollutants can be hundreds of miles away in urban areas, transported on the desert winds.

By 1977, the problem was widespread enough to warrant a special section in the Clean Air Act Amendments, with visibility regulations promulgated in 1980. It is at this point that the National Park Service (NPS) took on the role of leader in visibility research. One controversial 1985 NPS study found that visible plumes from stationary sources were not the most important source of visibility impairment. Rather, regional haze, including soil-related materials, seemed to be the cause. Through the remainder of the decade, disputes focused on whether or not human-caused sources were responsible for the visibility problems, with the 1987 Winter Haze Intensive Tracer Experiment (WHITEX) tests and other studies determining that emissions from the coal-fired Navajo Generating Plant at Page, Arizona, as the largest contributor. Interior Secretary Manuel Lujan, Jr. promptly called for a new study, no doubt influenced by the fact that a quarter of the Navajo plant was owned by the federal government.

From a political standpoint, the NPS studies filled a void left by the EPA. The EPA had moved on to other air quality issues and focused its regulatory efforts on ozone. The NPS, however, was faced with the daily barrage of questions from park visitors who wondered why such a national treasure in this part of the largely uninhabited West could become despoiled by urban centers and consumer needs for electric power.

In 1996, the congressionally created Visibility Transport Commission, made up of eight governors, four tribal leaders, and other advisors, made sweeping and unprecedented recommendations that were designed to gradually improve visibility from sixteen national parks and wilderness areas in the Colorado Plateau. This time, the blame for the veil of haze was shared by fires and dust, along with the everyday actions of residents driving cars, operating refineries, and chimney emissions in eleven states and northwest Mexico. The commission's recommendations, including a slow, voluntary reduction in emissions that would reduce pollution by 70 percent by 2040, were widely criticized because they failed to address the visibility problem in a timely manner and did not comprehensively identify what some felt was a single source.

Subsequently, the visibility issue was picked up by other environmental organizations. In 1998, the Sierra Club and the Grand Canyon Trust filed lawsuits against the owners of the last coal-fired plant without standard pollution control devices in the West — the Mojave Generating Station near Laughlin, Nevada, just seventy-five miles from the Grand Canyon. The suit charged that the plant's operators were guilty of years of violating Clean Air Act emissions standards — regulations unenforced by the EPA. Mojave releases 40,000 tons of sulfur dioxide and 10,000 tons of particulates into the air annually.

But the controversy over Mojave was much more than a battle between environmental groups and a corporation (Southern California Edison is the majority owner and operator of the plant). Caught in between were the Hopi and Navajo employees, who had come to depend on the plant for jobs. A threatened closure of the plant would have significant economic impacts throughout the region; Native American leaders called on the company to install the necessary technology rather than shut down the plant.

In October 1999, following a court settlement, Southern California Edison agreed to spend $300 million on filters and scrubbers to reduce sulfur dioxide emissions by 85 percent and particulates by 99 percent by 2006. In addition to avoiding years of potential litigation, the agreement improves the utility's competitive position in a deregulated market, accelerating the installation of pollution control equipment the company said it had already planned to purchase. But environmental organizers disagreed, arguing that the cleanup plan was announced only after the two groups had filed the lawsuit.

The Mojave plant had been a "problem" for years, but environmental groups had never been able to move it from the systemic agenda to the institutional agenda. Even after passage of the Clean Air Act Amendments in 1990, the plant continued to operate in violation of the law's provisions. The heavy competition for a place on the policy agenda kept Mojave out of the majority of the public's attention, with the exception of members of organizations like the Grand Canyon Trust. Rather than attempting to put pressure on federal legislators (many of whom were more sympathetic to the utility's interests) the groups chose to utilize the judicial arena as the best venue for pleading their case. As a result, the visibility at the Grand Canyon is expected to improve, the plant remains open as an important regional employer, and the issue moves to the policy implementation stage.

THE GLOBAL DIMENSION

The air quality issue has been approached differently between developed and less developed nations throughout the world, although the United States is considered to be at the vanguard of pollution control.[45] Great Britain has been at the forefront of European regulatory programs, enacting the Alkali Acts in 1863, which required that 95 percent of the emissions from industrial alkali facilities be controlled. In 1956, the Clean Air Act granted local authorities power to regulate "smoke control areas" and a 1968 law expanded those powers. Pollution episodes in London in 1972 and 1974, caused largely by fuel oil emissions, resulted in legislation in 1974 that reduced the sulfur content of fuel.[46] In other developed regions, environmental deterioration emerged as a political issue more or less simultaneously in the late 1960s, when many countries introduced similar protective legislation, although success has varied from one nation to another. Japan, for example, which has traditionally been a pioneer in requiring industrial pollution controls, has made progress, but it is being countered by emissions of pollutants from household energy consumption and the transportation sector. A study by Japan's Environment Agency found that, although industrial emissions had dropped considerably over the past twenty-five years, increased electricity use (from air conditioning and household appliances) and diesel truck emissions (which are not controlled by Japan's strict automotive exhaust regulations) increased dramatically.[47]

In eastern Europe and the republics of the former Soviet Union, industrialization that went unchecked for decades has led to a continuing air quality nightmare. Strict Soviet emission standards established in the 1950s were virtually ignored, and figures on emissions were kept secret during the Communist regime. Local leaders often had no idea how much pollution was being emitted by factories in their area, and in Poland, the electrostatic precipitators installed on factory chimneys to control dust were often switched off at night to save electricity.[48]

Even though air pollution is almost as serious in the urban areas of less developed countries — Mexico City, São Paulo, Cairo, Beijing, Bangkok — the problem has taken a backseat to efforts to increase economic development. Attempts by international organizations such as the United Nations to encourage more restrictive air pollution controls are often met by skepticism in Third and Fourth World countries, where leaders have a less global view. They argue that attention to environmental matters should follow the attainment of a higher standard of living for their people.

Private cars and geography are the primary culprits in Mexico City, where twenty million residents are crammed into a valley of nearly ten thousand square kilometers ringed by mountains — the same conditions responsible for Los Angeles's notorious smog. Vehicles at the high altitude (2,240 meters above sea level) burn fuel inefficiently, releasing unburnt hydrocarbons, which are then trapped at street level, especially during the winter. In 1990, the city suffered from the most polluted conditions ever, and the nation's ecology ministry twice declared an emergency, requiring industries temporarily to cut their operations by half. In response, Mexico's president announced a five-year, $4.6 billion program to clean up dirty industries or move them out of the city entirely. In addition, the city enacted a mandatory program restricting automobile use and forced the government-owned petroleum company to reduce the lead content in gasoline and shut down its city refinery, the largest single source of industrial pollution. Hundreds of trees were also planted in a companion effort to create a green belt.[49]

Air pollution in developing countries is approached differently than in industrialized nations for a number of other reasons. In China, pollution was long considered a problem of capitalist societies that exploited workers and resources. But the expansion of the Chinese population has outgrown China's attempts at environmental management, and most of its air pollution control policies have had only limited success. China's reliance upon coal as a fuel source, for example, has resulted in high levels of suspended particulates and tremendous visibility impairment. Although China has relatively few privately owned vehicles, cars there are considerably more polluting (estimates indicate that they produce from fifteen to fifty-five times the amount of hydrocarbon emissions as comparable Japanese models), so any increase in vehicles within the cities will sharply affect pollution levels. In his 1998 visit to China, President Clinton warned against pursuing economic growth at the expense of the environment. Ten of the world's most polluted cities are in China, and as foreign investors develop new factories, pollution is likely to increase even more.[50]

While the United States can accurately claim credit for major reductions in air pollution over the last five decades, the international perspective is one of mixed success. Industrialized nations in western Europe come close to matching the U.S. record in curbing pollutants, while the problems facing eastern Europe are still being identified. In developing nations, attempts to control emissions are often thwarted by policies that encourage economic growth at the expense of the environment. Like many other environmental protection policies, there is no "one-size-fits-all" solution for this problem and only very limited resources to use for policy implementation.

NOTES

1. Ed Ainsworth, "Fight to Banish Smog, Bring Sun Back to City Pressed," *Los Angeles Times,* October 13, 1946, 7.
2. Alex Barnum, "EPA Revokes Bay Area's Clean-Air Designation," *San Francisco Chronicle,* June 26, 1998, A1.
3. Vince Beiser, "Area's Air Becomes Dirty Word," *San Mateo Times,* June 26, 1998, 1.
4. Charlie Goodyear, "Smog Check for Big Rigs, Buses Finally Ready to Roll, *San Francisco Chronicle,* June 3, 1998, A28.
5. Alex Barnum, "Truck Industry Fights Diesel Plan," *San Francisco Chronicle,* July 31, 1998, A23.
6. Matthew L. Wald, "Autos' Converters Increase Warming as They Cut Smog: A Split over Solutions," *New York Times,* May 29, 1998, A1, A13.
7. "Catalytic Converter Role in Greenhouse Gas Emissions to Be Studied Further by EPA," *Daily Environment Report,* June 1, 1998, A8.
8. For examples of the earliest awareness of air pollution, see Donald E. Carr, *The Breath of Life* (New York: Norton, 1965), 28–34; and Arthur C. Stern et al., *Fundamentals of Air Pollution* (New York: Academic Press, 1973), 53–59.
9. For a chronology of the early air pollution efforts, see James E. Krier and Edmund Ursin, *Pollution and Policy* (Berkeley: University of California Press, 1977), 46–47.
10. "USA Air Quality Nonattainment Areas," U.S. Environmental Protection Agency, Office of Air Quality Planning and Standards, October 19, 1998, available at <http://www.epa.gov/airs/nonattn.html>.
11. Krier and Ursin, *Pollution and Policy,* 47.
12. For a description of the London episode, see Peter Brimblecombe, *The Big Smoke* (London: Methuen, 1987), and Fred Pearce, "Back to the Days of Deadly Smogs," *New Scientist,* December 5, 1992, 25–28.
13. Derek Elsom, *Atmospheric Pollution* (New York: Basil Blackwell, 1987), 4–5.
14. John C. Esposito, *Vanishing Air: The Ralph Nader Study Group Report on Air Pollution* (New York: Grossman, 1970), vii.
15. John C. Whitaker, *Striking a Balance: Environment and Natural Resources Policy in the Nixon-Ford Years* (Washington, DC: American Enterprise Institute, 1976), 94.
16. See Marc K. Landy, Marc J. Roberts, and Stephen R. Thomas, *The EPA: Asking the Wrong Questions: From Nixon to Clinton,* expanded ed. (New York: Oxford University Press, 1994.
17. See Alfred Marcus, "EPA," in *The Politics of Regulation,* ed. James Q. Wilson (New York: Basic Books, 1980), 267–303.
18. *International Harvester v. Ruckelshaus,* District of Columbia Court of Appeals, 155 U.S. App. DC 411 (February 10, 1973).
19. Whitaker, *Striking a Balance,* 104.
20. Alfred A. Marcus, *Promise and Performance: Choosing and Implementing an Environmental Policy* (Westport, CT: Greenwood Press, 1980), 123.
21. Whitaker, *Striking a Balance,* 104.
22. *Sierra Club v. Ruckelshaus,* 344 F.Supp. 256 (1972). For an analysis of the case, see Thomas M. Disselhorst, "Sierra Club v. Ruckelshaus: On a Clear Day . . ." *Ecology Law Quarterly,* 4 (1975): 739–780.
23. For examples of how the "bubble" policy has affected industry, see Elsom, *Atmospheric Pollution,* 176–177.
24. See Arnold W. Reitze Jr., "A Century of Air Pollution Law: What's Worked, What's Failed, What Might Work," *Environmental Law, 21,* no. 4:2 (1991): 1549–1646.
25. For a detailed chronology of these events, see Richard E. Cohen, *Washington at Work: Back Rooms and Clean Air* (New York: Macmillan, 1992).

26. See Norman W. Fichthorn, "Command and Control vs. the Market: The Potential Effects of Other Clean Air Act Requirements on Acid Rain Compliance," *International Law, 21,* no. 4:2 (1991): 2069–2084; and Alyson Pytte, "A Decade's Acrimony Lifted in the Glow of Clean Air," *Congressional Quarterly Weekly Report,* October 27, 1990, 3587–3592.

27. Michael Weisskopf, "Writing Laws Is One Thing — Writing Rules Is Something Else," *Washington Post National Weekly Edition,* September 30–October 6, 1991, 31; see also Henry Waxman, "An Overview of the Clean Air Act Amendments of 1990," *Environmental Law, 21,* no. 4:2 (1991): 1721–1816.

28. Henry V. Nickel, "Now, the Rush to Regulate," *The Environmental Forum, 8,* no. 1 (January–February 1991): 19.

29. Mark Mardon, "Last Gasp Next 185,000 Miles?" *Sierra, 76,* no. 5 (September–October 1991): 38–42.

30. See U.S. Senate Committee on Environment and Public Works, "Three Years Later: Report Card on the 1990 Clean Air Act Amendments," November 1993.

31. Alex Daniels, "Tempest in a Tailpipe," *Governing,* February 1995, 37–38.

32. "Questions and Answers: An Interview with William G. Rosenberg," *EPA Journal, 17,* no. 1 (January–February 1991): 5.

33. John R. Garrison, "Will the New Law Protect Public Health?" *EPA Journal, 17,* no. 1 (January–February 1991): 58.

34. See *Breath-Taking: Premature Mortality Due to Particulate Air Pollution in 239 American Cities* (New York: Natural Resources Defense Council, May 1996). See also Douglas W. Docker et al., "An Association between Air Pollution and Mortality in Six U.S. Cities," *The New England Journal of Medicine, 329,* no. 24 (December 9, 1993): 1753–1759; and C. Arden Pope III et al., "Particulate Air Pollution as a Predictor of Mortality in a Prospective Study of U.S. Adults," *American Journal of Respiratory Care Medicine,* 151 (1995): 669–674.

35. 42 U.S.C. 7409(b)(1)(1990).

36. Elsom, *Atmospheric Pollution,* 58. See also Angela Liberatore and Rudolph Lewanski, "Environmental Disasters and Shifts in Italian Public Opinion," *Environment, 32,* no. 5 (June 1990): 36.

37. The EPA set standards for arsenic, asbestos, benzene, beryllium, mercury, radionuclides, and vinyl chloride.

38. "Bipartisan Agreement Reached on Pesticides," *New York Times,* July 17, 1996, A16.

39. Walter A. Rosenbaum, *Environmental Politics and Policy,* 2nd ed. (Washington, DC: Congressional Quarterly Press, 1991), 149.

40. U.S. Environmental Protection Agency, *The Clean Air Act Amendments of 1990: Summary Materials* (Washington, DC: Government Printing Office, November 15, 1990), 4.

41. U.S. Environmental Protection Agency, *National Air Quality and Emissions Trends Report, 1995* (Research Triangle Park, NC: U.S. EPA, 1996): 49–58.

42. H. Joseph Heber, "Utilities, Incinerators, Mines to Make Reports," *Washington Post,* June 27, 1996, A13.

43. Stuart L. Hart, "Beyond Greening: Strategies for a Sustainable World," *Harvard Business Review,* January 1997, 66.

44. Lydia Wegman, "Air Toxics: The Strategy," *EPA Journal, 17,* no. 1 (January–February 1991): 32–33.

45. For an overview of global/urban air quality efforts, see, for example, Derek Elsom, *Smog Alert: Managing Urban Air Quality* (London: Earthscan, 1996); and Jorge E. Hardoy, Diana Mitlin, and David Satterwaite, *Environmental Problems in Third World Cities* (London: Earthscan, 1993).

46. Elsom, *Atmospheric Pollution,* 194–208.

47. See David Swinbanks, "Pollution on the Upswing," *Nature, 351* (May 2, 1991): 5.

48. See, for example, Philip R. Pryde, ed., *Environmental Resources and Constraints in the Former Soviet Republics* (Boulder, CO: Westview, 1995); and Joan De Bardeleben, *To*

Breathe Free: Eastern Europe's Environmental Crisis (Washington, DC: Woodrow Wilson Center Press, 1991).

49. Latin American urban issues have become an important segment of global environmental policy. See, for example, Alan Gilbert, *The Mega City in Latin America* (Washington, DC: Brookings, 1997); and Peter Ward, *Mexico City: The Production and Reproduction of an Urban Environment* (London: Belhaven Press, 1990). For a specific study of the Mexican government's efforts to regulation air quality, see Clifford J. Wirth, "The Governmental Response to Air Contamination in Mexico City," paper presented at the 1998 Annual Meeting of the American Political Science Association, Boston.

50. Joe McDonald, "Environmental Problems in Guilin Also Threaten to Ravage China," *San Francisco Chronicle,* July 2, 1998, A14; and Terence Hunt, "Clinton Plea for China's Environment," *San Francisco Chronicle,* July 2, 1998, A1.

FOR FURTHER READING

Christopher J. Bailey. *Congress and Air Pollution.* Manchester, UK: Manchester University Press, 1999.

Thad Godish. *Air Quality.* Boca Raton, FL: Lewis Publishers, 1997.

Wyn Grant, Anthony Perl, and Peter Knoepfel, Eds. *The Politics of Improving Urban Air Quality.* Northampton, MA: Edward Elgar, 1999.

Robert Jennings Heinsohn. *Sources and Control of Air Pollution.* Upper Saddle River, NJ: Prentice-Hall, 1999.

Frederick W. Lipfert. *Air Pollution and Community Health: A Critical Review and Data Sourcebook.* New York: John Wiley, 1998.

John McCormick. *Acid Earth: The Politics of Acid Pollution,* 3rd ed. London: Earthscan, 1997.

Marvin S. Soroos. *The Endangered Atmosphere: Preserving A Global Commons.* Columbia: University of South Carolina Press, 1997.

Cecil F. Warner, Wayne T. Davis, and Kenneth Wark Jr. *Air Pollution: Its Origins and Control.* Menlo Park, CA: Addison-Wesley, 1998.

CHAPTER 9

The Global Commons

Pollution doesn't carry a passport.
— Thomas McMillan, Canadian Environmental Minister[1]

In June 1998, the United States Department of Justice (DOJ) announced that it had reached a plea agreement for a $9 million criminal fine against Royal Caribbean Cruises, one of the world's largest passenger cruise lines. Noting that "Our oceans are not a dumping ground for polluters," a DOJ official underscored the fact that the company had pled guilty to eight felony counts, including two counts of obstruction of justice. The company admitted that it discharged oil-contaminated bilge waste including harmful quantities of oil from its cruise ships. The fine also penalized the company for maintaining and using false records it gave to the U.S. Coast Guard and for concealing and covering up its failure to use proper equipment to offload large quantities of bilge waste while in port.[2]

The cruise ship's actions were discovered in late 1994 as part of an ongoing operation by the DOJ and the U.S. Coast Guard, called the Vessel Pollution Initiative. An aircraft with sophisticated tracking equipment detected a seven-mile oily wake behind one of the cruise line's ships, and inspectors found evidence of witness tampering and misuse of pollution control equipment. "When a company pollutes, lies and obstructs justice, it is no better than a common criminal. Indeed, some may consider Royal Caribbean's actions worse, since the company had the vast financial resources needed to easily comply with environmental laws but ignored them for one simple reason — to save a few dollars," another DOJ prosecutor said.[3] Almost simultaneously, the cruise line announced that it was designing "the most environmentally sensitive cruise ships in the world" by replacing its diesel engines with aeroderivative gas turbines.[4] But the company's environmental record had clearly been tarnished by the fine — the largest ever for an environmental crimes case involving cruise ships.

◁ *Wind farms, as shown here, were first built in the 1970s as a source of renewable energy, but much of the public considers the large metal structures a visual blight on the rural landscape.*

The term "commons" or "common pool resource" was popularized by biologist Garrett Hardin in his 1968 essay, "The Tragedy of the Commons."[5] Using as an analogy the medieval practice of grazing cattle on an open pasture, Hardin theorized that each individual livestock herder would graze as many cattle on the pasture (the commons) as possible if acting purely from economic self-interest. The result, of course, would be overgrazing of the commons to the point where all the herds would starve.

Implicit in Hardin's metaphor is the idea of common-property resources, which share two characteristics. The first is that the physical nature of the resource is such that controlled access by potential users is costly, and in some cases, virtually impossible. The second characteristic is that each user is capable of subtracting from the welfare of other users.[6] This concept is especially applicable to the three topics which are covered in this chapter: transboundary pollution, the atmosphere, and the oceans. It also is exemplary of the way in which environmental politics has been globalized or transnationalized. This approach requires policymakers to consider how human activities affect the entire planet, rather than only what is happening in their own backyard.

TRANSBOUNDARY POLLUTION

There are several reasons why nations cooperate in addressing problems of transboundary pollution. It may be in their own self-interest to support cooperative pollution reduction agreements in order to protect the quality of life within their own boundaries. It is advantageous to them to help establish dispute resolution mechanisms so they can pressure their neighbors to comply with environmental accords. Nations may recognize that collective benefits such as a stable climate and healthy oceans are in everyone's interest and compel some sacrifice of the freedom to engage in polluting activities. International organizations, norms, and laws play an important role in reflecting that self-interest. Cooperative efforts are bolstered through scientific research that clearly and compellingly identifies collective threats and offers feasible solutions. As scientific consensus develops over an environmental problem, nations are encouraged to participate in solutions. Some countries seek to be leaders in the global community, while others simply wish to avoid the criticisms of others. Domestic politics plays a critical role, and environmental activists demand that their own governments comply with their global commitments and contribute to collective solutions. Political leaders may see global environmental leadership as central to their own political prospects or part of their personal policy agenda. Industries that must comply with domestic environmental regulations have a strong incentive to urge their governments to pressure other countries to enforce similar standards on their industries. In some cases, economic powerhouses like Japan and the United States can compel compliance by other nations who want to continue trade with them or otherwise benefit through cooperative relations.[7]

However, there are significant challenges to making effective international environmental agreements. International law recognizes the sovereignty of each nation, and countries guard that sovereignty jealously even as they participate in global environmental conventions and agreements. Environmental preservation is often a public, global good: the protection of clean air and water and the preservation of forests, lands, and biodiversity produce benefits that are available to others whether or not they help pay the costs of preservation. Countries, like individuals, are tempted to be free riders when others will provide benefits and bear the burdens. Environmental issues are intertwined with economic, national security, and other concerns that complicate agreement making. Negotiators seek to fashion international rules that are consistent with their own form of national regulation. Powerful domestic interests may also resist any kind of environmental regulation, global or domestic. Agreements are a complex product of scientific consensus, the relative power of participant nations, the costs of international transactions, and other variables that are difficult to balance.[8]

Given the inevitable domestic economic and political barriers, for example, the international community must create incentives to ensure that participating nations implement programs that achieve the goals given them in global agreements. If there is no means of encouraging and pressuring nations to implement the agreements, then implementation will constantly be threatened by calculations that some countries can avoid the compliance costs and perhaps gain competitive advantage for domestic industries. Some countries will comply with agreements as a means of demonstrating leadership or as a result of farsightedness on the part of their leaders. To bolster such motivations, agreements will need to include several kinds of provisions. They must provide for a global reporting system so that emission levels can be compared with limits included in the agreements. An international body will be required to monitor reporting data and to impose sanctions when compliance agreements are not satisfied. Economic sanctions must be imposed when implementation failures occur. They may range from cutoffs of foreign assistance to import barriers on goods produced in noncomplying countries. An international body will have to be empowered to decide disputes. As indicated above, financial and technological assistance must be provided to the poorer countries to encourage compliance and to make it even possible. These sanctions and incentives are of limited power, since they require unparalleled cooperation and unity on the part of the nations of the world. The process of formulating global agreements itself will be critical in building support for the measures agreed to by ensuring that all parties believe that their interests were considered and share a commitment to make the agreement work.

THE UNITED STATES, MEXICO, AND CANADA

In the 1970s, researchers began to develop a new understanding of the forces that lead to long-range transboundary air pollution and acid deposition while, at the same time, environmental crises focused attention on transnational water pollution. These issues are of interest to most Americans when they involve the nations along the U.S. borders — Canada and Mexico. All three countries have a common interest in combining their technological resources to solve problems that literally "drift" into their boundaries. Although the problems are global in scope and importance (with many new transboundary problems beginning to occur in Asia), they are also somewhat regionalized.

For the United States and Canada, the major border issue is acid rain, or acid deposition as it is also known. For many years, it had gone undetected because in its early stages there was little evidence of its impact. Today, no country on Earth receives as high a proportion of acidic deposition from another nation as Canada receives from the United States. Approximately one-half the total amount of acid deposition that falls on Canada comes from the United States, in comparison to the 20 percent Canadian sources deposit on the United States.

There are three primary components of acid rain: sulfur dioxide, nitrogen oxides, and volatile organic compounds (VOCs). The most common of the pollutants, sulfur dioxide, comes primarily from the combustion of coal, which reacts with oxygen in the air. The sulfur content of coal varies considerably with the geographic region in which it is mined, so not all areas experience acid deposition to the same degree. Coal from the western portion of the United States, for example, typically has a sulfur content of about 0.5 percent, which is considered to be very low. In contrast, coal mined in the northern region of Appalachia and some midwestern states has a sulfur concentration of 2 to 3 percent. Scientists measure acid deposition as wet (rain, snow, fog) and dry (particles and gases). Acidity is measured on a pH scale from 1 to 14, with lemon juice measured at 1, vinegar at 3, and distilled water at 7. Although there is no single threshold value below which precipitation is considered to be "acid rain," readings below 4.5 are generally considered highly acidic. The most widely accepted standard for unpolluted precipitation is 5.6, which is twenty-five times the acidity of pure water.[9]

Acid rain causes several types of environmental damage, and because its effects are not merely localized, it can cause increased acidity levels in bodies of water that are fed by rainfall. The impact can damage entire ecosystems and may show up along the entire food chain. Researchers have found reduced yields of crops attributable to acid rain, and studies show it also contributes to health problems. Soil nutrients are declining in Canada, and the long-term impact also includes damage to our cultural heritage, since there is evidence that acid rain has damaged some of the most beautiful historical artifacts in the world.

Canada and the United States have a long history of disputes as well as cooperative agreements related to transboundary pollution, the most famous of which is the Trail Smelter Arbitration of 1941. The case involved sulphur emissions from a smelter built in Canada in 1896 just a few miles north of the United States. Originally the claims against the smelter dealt with plumes of sulphur that traveled across the border and damaged the property of apple growers in Washington state, but the case later formed the basis for questions of jurisdiction in international environmental law that would be reflected in subsequent treaties.[10] In 1978, the two nations signed the Great Lakes Water Quality Agreement, and in 1980, a Memorandum of Intent Concerning Transboundary Air Pollution.[11]

Further negotiations on transboundary pollution issues between the United States and Canada were driven by Title IV of the 1990 Clean Air Act Amendments (discussed in more detail in Chapter 8). The primary goal of this portion of the statute was to reduce sulphur dioxide emissions in the United States by ten million tons below 1980 levels; another section called for a two-million-ton reduction in nitrous oxide emissions by the year 2000. The reductions were expected to come from a tightening of restrictions placed on fossil fuel–fired power plants, along with the promotion of pollution prevention and energy efficient strategies and technologies. The EPA's Acid Rain Program is responsible for implementing the legislation by employing both traditional and innovative market-based approaches such as the active trading of emissions allowances given to utilities based on historic fuel consumption.[12]

Subsequently, the two nations signed the 1991 U.S.–Canada Bilateral Air Quality Agreement,[13] which requires each nation to accept specific emission reduction goals and establishes procedural and institutional mechanisms for future cooperation. The United States agreed to reduce annual sulphur dioxide emissions, achieve a permanent national emissions cap, and to meet certain technology-based standards for the reduction of nitrogen oxides (NO_X) from both stationary and mobile sources. For its part, Canada agreed to reduce sulphur dioxide emissions in seven of its easternmost provinces and maintain that cap until 1999, until a permanent cap went into effect in 2000. The agreement also required Canadians to meet technological standards to reduce NO_X emissions from mobile sources and reduce stationary NO_X emissions. The treaty affirmed the use of notification and consultation agreements to facilitate bilateral cooperation, and charged the International Joint Commission (IJC) with oversight of the provisions. The IJC is a permanent bilateral commission of three members from each country, and was originally established to deal with water quality issues stemming from the 1909 Boundary Waters Treaty. It is considered one of the great success stories in Canadian–U.S. relations.[14]

Since the treaty went into force, significant progress has been made, as Canada surpassed both its international and domestic commitments to reduce emissions of sulphur dioxide and was on target to meet its reduction in nitrogen dioxides. The U.S. EPA's Acid Rain Program and controls on motor vehicle emissions are expected to meet and then exceed its commitment, largely due to the adoption of more stringent NO_X standards, with a second phase of SO_2 emission reductions beginning in 2000.[15] The two countries have now agreed to address the issues of ground-level ozone and particulate matter emissions. Cooperative studies and diplomatic negotiations are expected to lead to the formation of an addition, or annex, to the original 1991 agreement.

The U.S.–Canadian response to acid rain is considered by some U.S. officials to be a model for tackling emerging environmental issues because the agreements have incorporated input from stakeholders such as utilities, coal and gas companies, emissions control equipment vendors, labor leaders, academicians, and state and provincial pollution control agencies, along with environmental organizations. The use of continuous monitoring and reporting systems, excessive emissions penalties, and the use of market-based incentives, are said to create a program that will achieve cost-effective emissions reductions.[16] Even though Canada has met and exceeded its commitments, national leaders remain concerned about acid rain and are working towards a post-2000 strategy based on reports that additional emission reductions of up to 75 percent would be required in targeted regions of eastern Canada and the United States to prevent further damage to Canadian ecosystems.[17] The problem is far from being solved, but there is clear evidence of an intent to cooperate, form bilateral agreements, and conduct joint research to resolve border issues.

In contrast, the transboundary pollution issues between the United States and Mexico are perceived as being more complex and more difficult to solve than those with Canada. The severity of environmental problems is increasing dramatically, due in large part to the growth of industry and population along the Mexican side of the border. For instance, in 1950, the combined populations of the eleven largest border municipalities was slightly over one million. By 1980, the figure had jumped to 4.2 million; it had doubled by 1990.

The problems faced by the two countries are common to most nations facing transboundary pollution: drifting air pollutants, water pollution, illegal waste dumping, public health issues, and in the case of the United States and Mexico, congestion. The problems are best exemplified by the Maquiladora zone — a sixty-mile-wide free trade zone along the two-thousand-mile U.S.–Mexican border — which was established in 1965. Subsequently, more than 2,500 maquiladoras (factories jointly owned by U.S. and Mexican corporations operated on the Mexican side of the border) have led to increased dumping of hazardous waste and water and air pollution that has gone largely unregulated over the years. The New River between Mexicali, Mexico, and California's Coachella Valley has been contaminated by over one hundred toxic chemicals. In other areas, raw untreated sewage from the "colonias" (slums) has been responsible for numerous public health problems and outbreaks of disease.[18]

Why is there such difficulty in solving pollution problems among these three nations? The answer is a complex one that focuses on the difficulty of developing a regional cross-border perspective that allows the resolution of problems encountered by numerous stakeholders. One issue that is particularly applicable to the United States and Mexico stems from restrictions under the U.S. Constitution, which limits the role of state and local governments in foreign affairs. The Constitution grants exclusive jurisdiction to the federal government, including the development of treaties and the regulation of commerce, even when the agreements may take the form of compacts, alliances, or confederations. As a result, international agreements are often carried out as executive orders or as congressional-executive agreements, rather than as treaties, such as the case of the 1992 North American Free Trade Agreement (NAFTA), which will be discussed in greater detail later in this chapter.

Similarly, state laws both authorize and limit the scope of authority of local governments, agencies, and authorities, as well as the state government itself.

Texas, for example, established a Texas-Mexico authority "to study all Texas-Mexico issues and problems, including health and environment." It allows the state to "explore, develop, and negotiate interstate compacts relating to trade, infrastructure, and other matters with the appropriate officials of the united Mexican states or any of its political subdivisions or any other foreign trading partners."[19] Local governments are given some authority by the state to allow for some cross-border activities and cooperation, such as mutual fire protection agreements, the provision of health services, and operation of toll bridges.[20]

The problem of border congestion and the resulting air pollution problem is being addressed by the Western Governors' Association as a way of dealing with an issue that affects several states. In 1998, the organization began doing research at four of the most heavily-traveled border crossings: San Ysidro–Otay Mesa–Tijuana, El Paso–Cuidad Juarez, Nogales-Nogales, and Laredo–Nuevo Laredo. The research findings, along with the development of consensus solutions to the problems faced by border communities, are a small step towards finding a way of addressing transboundary pollution that can be replicated in other parts of the world.[21]

Some researchers believe that state and local governments on both sides of the border could become key stakeholders in the resolution of border environmental problems, especially if they choose to involve existing institutions such as the Border Environment Cooperation Commission, the North American Development Bank, and the International Boundary Water Commission. These bodies could apply their expertise, cross-border contacts, and desire to work cooperatively to solve environmental problems that are becoming more intense with increased border economic activity.[22] But much of the problem solving has instead been "fast-tracked" (subjected to rapid negotiation under fixed time limits) under NAFTA, making Congress and the executive branch the key players.

THE NORTH AMERICAN FREE TRADE AGREEMENT, THE GENERAL AGREEMENT ON TARIFFS AND TRADE, AND THE WORLD TRADE ORGANIZATION

NAFTA represents the first international trade agreement to address the environmental impacts of free trade, while substantially reducing tariffs and trade among the United States, Mexico, and Canada. The treaty included an environmental side agreement which was designed to promote bilateral environmental cooperation, especially with Mexico, which is known for its lax pollution laws and haphazard enforcement of the few regulations that do exist. Critics (including labor unions and human rights groups) feared that the $6 trillion free trade zone established by NAFTA would liberalize trade but would also threaten 365 million consumers who sought economic integration.[23] They feared the undermining of U.S. regulations that can be characterized as indirect ways of protecting domestic industries and may be rejected by international tribunals as trade restrictions. They point to the 1991 decision by a panel established by the General Agreement on Tariffs and Trade (GATT), which found that a U.S. embargo of Mexican tuna caught in drift nets that also trapped dolphins was a nontariff trade barrier. The 1972 U.S. Marine Mammal Protection Act (MMPA) authorized the federal government to embargo tuna from other nations caught by any means that results in the incidental killing of or injury to ocean mammals beyond what is permitted under U.S. standards.[24] Tuna fishing boats often follow dolphins to locate the tuna and then cast nets on the dolphins to harvest the fish. Amendments enacted in 1984 required nations from which the United States imports tuna to demonstrate that they have a dolphin conservation program comparable to the U.S. program.[25] Amendments in 1988 imposed a limit for foreign nations operating in the tropical Pacific Ocean to a dolphin take of no more than 125 percent of what U.S. vessels took. These amendments also required the federal government to impose an intermediary embargo on tuna from countries importing tuna from nations that are subject to a primary embargo by the United States.[26] The 1992 amendments (also called the International Dolphin Conservation Act) authorized the lifting of primary embargoes for countries that commit to a five-year moratorium on using nets on dolphins in catching tuna, and the amendments banned the sale of or importation into the United States of tuna that is not "dolphin safe" — requiring, among other things, that dolphin nets not be used in harvesting tuna.[27]

In September 1990 the U.S. Customs Service banned tuna imported from Mexico, Panama, and Equador. Mexico challenged the ban in 1991 and a GATT panel was convened to hear Mexico's claims. The United States acknowledged that the MMPA violated the GATT prohibition against quantitative limits on imports, but argued that it was a domestic standard that nevertheless satisfied GATT's standard that imported products not be treated less favorably than domestically produced ones. The panel found that the U.S. action violated GATT because: (1) it did not qualify as an internal regulation applying equally to imports or fall within any of the general exemptions, (2) it constituted a quantitative restriction, and (3) regulated land was a unilateral action on the part of the United States.[28] U.S. fishing companies complained bitterly that Mexican companies could harvest tuna much more cheaply than the Americans who complied with U.S. laws protecting dolphins. The Mexican government, however, responded to the public outcry by voluntarily adopting some measures to protect dolphins.

While the agreement encourages nations to improve food safety and technical standards and to not reduce environmental standards in order to attract investment, there is little recognition of the importance of internalizing environmental costs and the challenges for less developed countries in competing in global markets without further compromising environmental quality and natural resources.

Under NAFTA, parties can establish levels of protection of human health and ecology based on "legitimate" objectives.[29] The only trade regulations permitted are those that affect "product characteristics or their related processes and production methods."[30] But NAFTA does not expressly provide for that; environmental laws can be challenged as discriminatory and can be reviewed by dispute panels. One problem is that states may not be able to impose more stringent environmental standards than the federal government can, because only the participating nations can impose more stringent standards. If, for example, California had more stringent pesticide residue standards than the rest of the nation, Mexican exporters of food who failed to meet the California standards could challenge them as "arbitrary or unjustifiable distinctions." California itself could not appear before the NAFTA panel but would have to be represented by the federal government. Mexico could argue that the California standard is a "disguised restriction" on trade, aimed at protecting domestic producers, since no other state had felt compelled to provide that level of safety.[31] Another NAFTA provision, concerning energy, might conflict with environmental protection efforts. Parties are free to "allow existing or future incentives for oil and gas exploration, development, and related activities."[32] But such provisions could be used to restrict efforts to reduce fossil fuel combustion in response to the threat of global climate change.[33]

Opponents of NAFTA fear that stimulating the Mexican economy will increase pollution levels and resource damage; proponents believe that a healthier economy will translate into greater environmental protection. One of the most important provisions of NAFTA is that environmental standards should be "harmonized upward," that parties should use "international standards . . . without reducing the level of protection of human, animal, or plant life or health."[34] NAFTA requires that a party "should not waive or otherwise derogate" from environmental and health standards in order to encourage investors."[35] But the language is the hortatory "should" rather than the obligatory "shall." And trade agreements have been criticized for encouraging standards that satisfy the lowest common denominator.[36] In sum, the environmental provisions in NAFTA appear to be significantly greater than those of GATT: parties are more free to choose their own appropriate level of protection, the least-trade-restrictive test is eliminated, harmonization of standards is aimed upward, there is deference to the three major international environmental treaties, and the language discourages the relaxing of standards in order to entice investors. Despite these strengths, NAFTA does not list explicit environmental goals, it fails to recognize subnational governments, many provisions are vague, parties are not obligated to comply with environmental treaties, and no mechanism exists to develop regional environmental agreements or to establish common standards for protecting shared air and water. Perhaps the greatest test of NAFTA will be the possibility it provides for devising solutions to transboundary problems and solutions that are tailored to the environmental, social, and political contexts in which they occur.

In 1995, GATT was replaced by the World Trade Organization (WTO) to ensure the free flow of trade. But contentious negotiations and protests in 1999 in Seattle proved that environmental issues and trade are inextricably linked, a problem discussed in more depth in Chapter 12.

THE ATMOSPHERE

Ever since the 1860s, when British scientist John Tyndall first described a phenomena we now call the greenhouse effect, the public has learned how human activities have affected the atmosphere and climate. Unfortunately, researchers have been unable to agree whether our future is tied to an impending ice age that will result in continental glaciation or a warming trend that will melt the glaciers and send coastal cities into the sea. The debate flourished around the turn of the century when Nobel Prize–winning Swedish scientist Svante Arrhenius calculated that a doubling of the carbon dioxide in the atmosphere would raise the average surface temperature of Earth. His calculations were confirmed by American geologists Thomas Chamberlain and C. F. Tolman, who studied the role that the oceans play as a major reservoir of carbon dioxide. In the 1930s, after three decades of warming temperatures and the development of a massive dust bowl in the central United States, other scientists warned of the dangers of rising temperatures, which had already been tied to increasing levels of carbon dioxide in the atmosphere. But between the 1940s and 1970s, global temperatures fell, and many reputable scientists prophesied a new ice age rather than a warming trend.[37] The global warming forecast was resurrected again in June 1988 when Dr. James Hansen, director of the National Aeronautics and Space Administration's (NASA) Institute for Space Studies told a Senate Committee, "The greenhouse effect is here."

Humans' ability to cause changes in the atmosphere is a relatively recent phenomenon — primitive peoples did not have the technology to alter the environment as we do today. With the Industrial Revolution came technological devices such as the steam engine, electric generator, and internal combustion engine, which have forever altered the planet, the water we drink, and the air we breathe. That ability to alter the environment is threatening to some, but considered a natural part of the evolutionary process by others. Some believe that Earth exists as a living organism in which internal control mechanisms maintain the stability of life — a theory called the Gaia hypothesis.[38] According to this theory, environmental problems such as ozone depletion will be brought under control naturally by the environment itself, which will make the necessary adjustments to sustain life. Critics of the theory, however, refer to policies built on such optimism as "environmental brinksmanship" and warn that we cannot rely upon untried regulatory mechanisms to protect the planet from large-scale human interference. This section looks at two issues with obvious global dimensions: global warming and stratospheric ozone depletion. It provides an overview of the scientific controversy and identifies the ways in which the two issues differ politically.

Global Warming

Although global warming is ostensibly a subject for scientific debate, it reached the political agenda at full force between 1997 and 1999. Global warming refers to the process by which solar radiation passes through Earth's atmosphere and is absorbed by the surface or reradiated back into the atmosphere. The phenomenon is also called the "greenhouse effect" because some heat is trapped in the atmosphere, warming the earth like the panels of a greenhouse, but keeping some of the heat from going back out.

There are about twenty so-called greenhouse gases that make up Earth's atmosphere, with the five major sources identified in Table 9.1. Changes in the volume of these gases affect the rate at which energy is absorbed, which then affects Earth's temperature. Greenhouse gases are emitted or absorbed by virtually every form of human activity, as well as by oceans, terrestrial plants, and animals, which contribute to the carbon dioxide cycle. Scientists are primarily concerned about increases in levels of carbon dioxide, since it is difficult to quantify the exact cause and effect of other greenhouse gases. The more carbon dioxide builds up, the more heat is trapped near Earth.

Although researchers began studying the effect of carbon dioxide on climate in the early part of this century, the implications of such changes were not seriously considered until the early 1970s. A World Climate Conference in Geneva in 1979 was one of the first efforts at organizing international research, followed by a series of studies and conferences over the next ten years. One of the most respected reports was published in 1987 by the World Commission on Environment and Development, which recommended a global approach to a broad spectrum of environmental problems, including greenhouse warming.[39]

There is little controversy over the scientific evidence that the levels of carbon dioxide have increased by about 50 percent since the late 1700s, 25 percent over the past century, and are now increasing at the rate of 0.5 percent each year. Most of the studies agree that continued emissions of greenhouse gases will lead to a warming of Earth's temperature between 1.5 and 4.5 degrees Celsius (or 2.7 to 8.1 degrees Fahrenheit). So far this century, global average temperatures have risen between 0.5 and 1 degree Fahrenheit.

Why should we be concerned about what seems like relatively small changes in temperature? There are a number of possible scenarios attributed to global climate change. One of the most respected scientists who has studied the issue, Dr. Stephen H. Schneider of the National Center for Atmospheric Research, believes

Table 9.1 Major Greenhouse Gases

Gas	*Where It Comes From*
Carbon dioxide	Fossil fuel sources including utility power plants, refineries, automobiles
Chlorofluorocarbons (CFCs)	Solvents, foam insulation, fire extinguishers, air conditioners
Halons	Compounds used in fire extinguishers
Methane	Natural sources such as decaying vegetation, cattle, rice paddies, landfills, oil field operations
Nitrogen oxides	Fertilizers, bacteria

that the temperature increases will lead to a rise in sea levels through the heating of the oceans, and possibly higher levels from the melting of polar ice as well. Drought and prolonged heat would be expected to lead to a greater likelihood of fire damage, more severe air pollution and air stagnation, and increased energy use leading to a need for more power production. Some of the changes forecast to occur might not be as negative. Global warming might lengthen the growing season for grain in Siberia, allowing some nations to increase their food production. The flip side of the equation, however, would be a loss to U.S. farmers, who are currently the world's leading grain exporters, with an accompanying impact on our economy.

Are the models of doom correct? Despite human advances and technological breakthroughs, the atmosphere remains an element of the environment that is imperfectly understood and uncontrolled by humankind. The uncertainty over global warming comes from three sources: predicting future climate, predicting future impacts, and assessing costs and benefits of policy responses.[40] The polarization among the members of the scientific community has spilled over to the political arena, where policymakers are trying to decide which view is the most reliable. The debate is joined by industry representatives (primarily electric utilities) who argue that it is foolhardy to make costly changes in technology or lifestyle changes until all the evidence is in. They seek support and funding for further study and analysis until there is a general scientific consensus.

Nonetheless, there is a growing body of scientific evidence that, given the various scenarios, it is imperative that steps be taken immediately to avoid the devastating effects of climatic change being forecast, with general agreement of a need for a major reduction in carbon dioxide emissions. Such a strategy would require substantive (and costly) changes in the way we live, and not only in the United States. Although the burden of cost is likely to fall disproportionately on the industrialized nations of the North, developing countries in the South will be asked to make drastic changes in their current patterns of energy use. This raises a whole host of policy questions. Will industrialized nations share their technology and expertise with the less developed countries? If so, will they also give their financial support to those nations to help them reduce their dependence upon fossil fuels? Could developing countries, already facing massive foreign debt, afford to switch to alternative fuels without aid from the North? Is the United States willing to set an example with its policies and rely more on energy conservation and non-fossil fuel sources?

The answers to those questions are at the heart of the international debate over global warming. Though industrialized countries have been dealing with the issues for over a decade through bodies such as the Intergovernmental Panel on Climate Change (IPCC) and are aware of the ramifications of the problem, developing nations are less likely to perceive global warming as a potential risk. They are less represented on various international study boards and have devoted fewer resources to research on the potential impact of global climate change. As a result, they are understandably less concerned and less anxious about finding a solution.

Despite these uncertainties, one compelling argument is for an "insurance policy" approach to greenhouse warming. Such a strategy calls for reductions in energy consumption and enhanced conservation — policies that would benefit the United States by reducing the nation's dependence upon foreign oil. The energy savings would have spillover effects as well, such as reducing the need to drill for oil in environmentally sensitive areas and reducing the emissions that contribute to acid rain. Such policies would not solve global warming, advocates say, but would buy more time for additional research and the opportunity to find better solutions. Even though most scientists admit that additional research is needed to predict the timing and magnitude of global warming, there is a growing consensus that some initial steps such as those to reduce carbon dioxide emissions can be taken now without a major economic disruption.

Dealing with atmospheric change became an even more complex issue towards the end of the twentieth century, when scientific debate and political pressures escalated. New studies made scientific consensus more difficult as research funds decreased, especially in the United States. To complicate matters, in 1998 the EPA reported that the catalytic converter, developed by automakers to reduce nitrous oxide emissions that are a component of smog, is actually contributing to global warming. The EPA found that nitrous oxide emissions are increasing rapidly, due to more vehicles on the road and an increase in the number of miles traveled by cars that have catalytic converters. Still another study reported that some satellite data that showed a cooling of the Earth's atmosphere was flawed because of a "quirkiness" in satellite orbits. The finding, reported in 1998, seemed to reinforce data showing a gradual global warming, although other scientists downplayed the study.[41]

Other groups began to mobilize to force the issue back onto the political agenda. In 1999, the American Geophysical Union (AGU) issued a statement claiming that while there has been a "substantial increase" in atmospheric concentrations of carbon dioxide and other greenhouse gases and that current levels were expected to increase, there was still considerable uncertainty about the effects on earth. The group also noted that potential changes might be rapid and geographically unevenly distributed, causing more disruption. Still, the AGU recommended that "the present level of scientific uncertainty does not justify inaction in the mitigation of human-induced climate change and/or the adaptation to it."[42] The Global Coral Reef Alliance and the World Conservation Union also blamed the killing of the world's marine life and coral reefs on global warming and the subsequent increase in sea-surface temperatures.[43]

A similar debate erupted on the economic front, focusing on the costs of global warming. A 1998 study by the President's Council of Economic Advisers predicted that American households would pay only $70 to $110 a year more for energy. The study relied on an optimistic model that required only small emission reductions from U.S. companies, and it was heavily criticized by environmental organizations.[44]

While researchers argued among themselves, U.S. policymakers appeared hesitant to make decisions on how to proceed, perhaps due to lukewarm and sometimes conflicting responses on the part of their constituents. A 1997 Gallup

Poll found that most Americans believed automobile exhaust was a major cause of global warming but did not want policymakers to take steps that would incur high economic costs, such as great increases in energy rates or unemployment. The study also found most respondents were opposed to a global warming treaty that would hold the United States to stricter energy standards than other large nations.[45] Another 1997 poll, by the Survey Research Unit at Ohio State University, noted that substantial proportions of Americans said that they believed in the existence of global warming and 61 percent believed the results would be bad. Over three-quarters of the respondents said they would be willing to pay higher utility bills in order to reduce the amount of air pollution resulting from some electricity generation. They also advocated significant effort by the government and businesses to combat global warming, while voicing pessimism about how much was actually being done.[46]

Somewhat understandably, members of Congress and the Clinton administration argued about what direction U.S. policy should take. Vice President Al Gore, for instance, used a 1998 study by the Commerce Department's National Oceanic and Atmospheric Administration that showed that the first five months of the year set new global records for temperature, as did 1997. Gore noted that additional heat in the climate system can lead to more extreme weather — more floods, more drought, more fires, and more storms. He then chided Congress, saying "Congress' approach to global warming is: know nothing, do nothing, say nothing."[47] His criticisms were not unfounded. Earlier that year, members agreed to cut $200 million from appropriations for energy efficiency and research into renewable resources, and even attempted to eliminate funding for any program that even talked about climate change, whether in public forums or administration planning sessions. The result, some officials believed, would be to bar EPA and White House advisors from doing anything, even simply talking about it, to advance the climate change debate.[48]

Overall, progress toward achieving global consensus (among both scientists and policymakers) was slow until the late 1980s and mid-1990s. The creation of the IPCC in 1988 marked the beginning of contemporary efforts to bring science and policy together, after which they attended a series of conferences that included governments that had previously been working independently on the issue of atmospheric change. Prior to the 1992 Earth Summit in Rio de Janeiro, delegates to the International Negotiating Committee agreed to develop a framework convention: the United Nations Framework Convention on Climate Change (FCCC). At the Rio conference, 154 governments signed the document, after which they attended a series of Conferences of the Parties (COP). In March 1995, the first COP adopted the Berlin Mandate, putting all FCCC parties on a schedule to negotiate and develop a legal instrument at the next COP. A second COP, held in Berlin in July 1996, placed an emphasis on emission reductions from the more developed world, with timetables set for the next COP.

The parties who met in Kyoto for COP 3 in December 1997 had an ominous task — to gain the political support of the United States, which historically had refused to agree with the goal of reducing emissions to 1990 levels by the year 2000. When the Clinton administration entered the debate in 1993, policy changed abruptly when the president announced his support for the FCCC but said that the United States wanted the emissions deadline to be extended between 2008 and 2012. His position was heavily criticized by members of Congress, who were unconvinced that the purported threat of global warming was serious enough to force Americans to pay more for energy. When Vice President Al Gore addressed the Kyoto COP, he stressed that the U.S. position was that some developing countries should also be willing to reduce their emissions levels, as the industrialized countries agreed to do.

The resulting agreement, the Kyoto Protocol to the 1992 Climate Change Treaty, was designed to reduce emissions from six greenhouse gases to 1990 levels between 2008 and 2012 — the target date sought by the U.S. delegation. Countries unable to meet their own emissions targets could purchase emissions credits from other nations that met their targets, with developing countries such as China and India setting voluntary reduction targets. This was one of the more controversial issues at Kyoto, since the two nations are major emitters of greenhouse gases.[49] The agreement, however, marked only the beginning of what became a long process of negotiations and conferences, beginning with the November 1998 COP 4 in Buenos Aires and following with COP 5 in Amman, Jordan, in October 1999. The Kyoto Protocol was termed a limited success but an important first step by U.S. negotiators. Negotiations on the timetable for emissions reductions continued in Argentina, and after pressure from other developed nations, the U.S. delegation agreed to sign the treaty. However, most observers noted the talks were largely symbolic, and agreed it was unlikely the treaty would be ratified by the U.S. Senate during the final two years of the Clinton administration. COP 4 also continued the debate along north/south lines as rich and poor nations argued over how to share responsibility for reducing greenhouse gas emissions.[50]

The significance of what took place through this series of negotiations is that a majority of the world's governments recognized, and agreed to take action on, a problem that has clearly gained support from the scientific community. Unlike other environmental policies, which have been approached from a regional or subregional basis, the Kyoto Protocol was a significant, if limited, move toward true global policy making. It also is an example of what has been called "cross-cutting" issues — atmospheric climate change and stratospheric ozone depletion, two terms that are frequently used interchangeably but are distinct from a chemical perspective — from their impact on human health and the environment, and from their cause.

Stratospheric Ozone Depletion

Ozone is an element of Earth's atmosphere caused by a photochemical reaction of hydrocarbons (produced mainly from the burning of fossil fuels) and sunlight. In one sense, there is "bad" ozone and "good" ozone. At the surface of Earth, ozone is one of the major components of smog, but higher up in the stratosphere (between six and thirty miles above Earth's surface), the ozone layer provides a filtering layer of protection against the harmful effects of ultraviolet radiation. Without such protection against ultraviolent radiation, medical experts believe that there would be a substantial increase in skin cancers and genetic changes in some types of plants and animals.

In the early 1970s, scientists warned that the exhaust gases from high-flying supersonic transport planes could damage the ozone layer. Studying components of the high-altitude atmosphere, they discovered that CFCs, which are synthetic, reacted with ultraviolet light when released into the atmosphere, forming chlorine. Chlorine is known to attack ozone molecules, and the researchers warned that, unless steps were taken to reduce CFC production, between 7 and 13 percent of the Earth's protective ozone layer would be destroyed. CFCs are found in thousands of synthetic products and are used primarily in air conditioning and refrigeration, foam packaging, and insulation. They are also used in cleaning the sides of the space shuttles, in sterilizing whole blood, and as a solvent in cleaning computers. Congress responded in 1977 by including provisions in the Clean Air Act Amendments, which authorized the EPA administrator to regulate substances affecting the stratosphere, and in 1978, the EPA banned the use of CFCs in most aerosols. At the time, scientists were unable to measure the damage to the ozone layer, but on the strength of the theoretical evidence alone, Congress responded.[51]

With the election of Ronald Reagan in 1980, research into CFCs came to a standstill and the search for substitute compounds subsided. Even though the United States had banned CFCs in aerosols, the nonaerosol use grew to record levels with the United States producing about one-third of the world total. The issue gained new prominence in 1985 when a group of British scientists in Antarctica, who had been monitoring ozone levels for thirty years, found a "hole" in the ozone layer approximately the size of North America above the continent that lasted nearly three months each year.[52] The National Science Foundation sent its own team of researchers to Antarctica later that year, and, although they could not agree on an exact cause, they concluded that chlorine chemistry was somehow involved and that the hole was getting larger. In 1992, one study by the European Ozone Secretariat and another by NASA concluded that the ozone shield had also thinned markedly over the Northern Hemisphere. Although researchers were unable to discover a similar ozone hole over North America like that over the Antarctic, they warned that the increased levels of ozone-destroying chemicals were cause for alarm. As the scientific evidence of stratospheric ozone depletion mounted, the environmental protection wheels began to turn in the political arena. (See "Another View, Another Voice: Mario J. Molina: Discovering the Achilles Heel of the Universe.")

Balancing the Options

Even though the evidence that CFCs are responsible for ozone depletion is not irrefutable, there were a number of differences in the response of the govern-

Another View, Another Voice

MARIO J. MOLINA
Discovering the Achilles Heel of the Universe

In 1995, Professor Mario J. Molina of the Massachusetts Institute of Technology (MIT) shared the $1 million Nobel Prize in chemistry with two other atmospheric chemists, Paul Crutzen of the Max-Planck Institute for Chemistry in Mainz, Germany, and F. Sherwood Rowland of the University of California, Irvine. Molina and his colleagues, who were credited with the discovery of the depletion of the Earth's ozone layer, had worked for more than a decade researching what the Nobel committee called "the Achilles heel of the universe."

Molina grew up in Mexico City and recalls that he was fascinated by science even before going to high school there. "I still remember my excitement when I first glanced at paramecia and amoebae through a rather primitive toy microscope,"[1] he notes, later converting one of his family's bathrooms into a makeshift laboratory. A budding violinist, at one point he considered a career in music, but he eventually enrolled in the National University of Mexico in chemical engineering with a goal of becoming a research chemist.

From Mexico he went to the University of Freiburg in Germany, but he felt he was weak in the background subjects he needed for a Ph.D. in physical chemistry: mathematics and physics. He later decided to seek admission to a U.S. university and enrolled at the University of California, Berkeley, in 1968. While there, he was part of a research group studying molecular dynamics to investigate the distribution of internal energy in the products of chemical and photochemical reactions. He calls his Berkeley years as "some of the best of my life" because he was working in an intellectually and culturally stimulating environment, just after the free speech movement had converged on the campus.

After completing his Ph.D. and postdoctoral research on chemical dynamics, Molina moved to Irvine, California, in 1973 to study with F. Sherwood Rowland, who had been a pioneer in the field of "hot atom" chemistry. Only three months later, Molina and Rowland developed a new theory that the continuing release of chlorofluorocarbons (CFCs) would cause a significant depletion of the stratospheric ozone layer. Their work had been based on Crutzen's earlier study of chlorine atoms produced by the decomposition of CFCs. The research was published in the June 28, 1974, issue of the scientific journal *Nature,* setting off a flurry of news media coverage and scientific inquiry, which continues today.

Molina left Irvine for the Jet Propulsion Laboratory in Pasadena in 1982, expanding his work after the discovery of the seasonal depletion of ozone over Antarctica. His wife, Luisa, became his collaborator in experimenting with chlorine peroxide, a new compound that turned out to be important in understanding the rapid loss of ozone in the polar atmosphere. In 1989, the couple

(continued)

transferred to MIT, where Molina continues his research on the potential implications of changes in the chemical composition of the Earth's atmosphere.

Despite the fact that his CFC research resulted in the Nobel Prize and numerous other scientific awards, Molina says that the discovery was due to serendipity and credits colleagues and friends who have been researching atmospheric chemistry. "When I first chose the project to investigate the fate of chlorofluorocarbons in the atmosphere, it was simply out of scientific curiosity. I did not consider at that time the environmental consequences. I am heartened and humbled that I was able to do something that not only contributed to our understanding of atmospheric chemistry, but also had a profound impact on the global environment."[2]

Notes

1. Available at <http://www.nobel.se/laureates/chemistry>, July 21, 1998.
2. Ibid.

ment and industry from that of global warming. First, the issue of stratospheric ozone depletion was perceived as a more "manageable" problem than global warming, which is a much more complex and multifaceted problem than developing substitutes for CFCs. While industry officials called for more research into global warming before they were willing to accede to costly changes in production and technology, CFC manufacturers almost immediately agreed that CFC production should be reduced, even in the absence of proof that CFCs were damaging the ozone layer.

In 1988, the DuPont Company, the inventor and world's largest user of CFCs, announced that it was phasing out production of two types of CFCs altogether. Other manufacturers and users of CFCs followed suit, and competition began to find replacement products and processes. The significance of the CFC strategy, from a political standpoint at least, is that the United States and its industry leaders were willing to take action even before all of the scientific evidence was in. This "preventive action on a global scale" was a unique approach to environmental protection. Rather than bucking the trend and refusing to cooperate, companies such as DuPont immediately began researching alternatives and substitutes for CFCs. And rather than stalling for time, the U.S. government took a leadership role and sought the strongest action possible — a complete ban on CFCs. The cost of finding replacements for the estimated thirty-five hundred applications where CFCs are used could reach $36 billion between now and 2075, according to the EPA.[53] As a result, what might initially be seen as an unreasonable cost of compliance is now being viewed as a new marketplace by many in the chemical industry. Forced to find substitutes for products and processes, some companies anticipate higher profits, while others fear that substitute substances will have their own complications. For example, one substitute — hydrochlorofluorocarbons, or HCFCs — is being criticized by environmentalists because HCFCs still contain ozone-damaging chlorine. But they are less damaging than CFCs and may prove to be a valuable transitional substitute while industry research continues.

Second, the U.S. government accepted the premise that a unilateral phaseout of CFCs was not acceptable for solving such a global problem. The United States initiated an international agreement to phase out CFC production within ten years, a move that led to the signing in September 1987 of the Montreal Protocol on Substances That Deplete the Ozone Layer. The document set a strict timetable of step-by-step reductions in CFCs and other ozone-depleting substances, leading to a complete production ban by 2000. Developing nations were given a ten-year grace period before full compliance is required, but many have refused to sign the treaty because of the expense involved in switching to new technology.

After scientists warned that the 50 percent reduction was not adequate to reduce the destruction of the ozone layer, the United States enacted even more stringent domestic legislation with passage of Title VI of the Clean Air Act Amendments of 1990. The legislation required an accelerated phaseout of the compounds that pose the greatest threat to the ozone layer: CFCs, halons, carbon tetrachloride, and methyl chloroform, with elimination as soon as possible and no later than 2002. Under the terms of the amendments, the EPA now requires the mandatory nationwide recycling of CFCs in motor vehicle air conditioners, the biggest user of CFCs in the United States. The American efforts were not designed to replace a stronger version of the Montreal Protocol, but instead were expected to serve as a model for future international agreements. Subsequent negotiations among the parties to the protocol in London in 1990 and Copenhagen in 1992 led to a speeding up of the CFC phaseout. Delegates in Copenhagen also agreed to reduce HCFCs by 35 percent by 2004, by 99.5 percent by 2020, and to a total ban by 2030. The parties also added methyl bromide, which may be responsible for 10 percent of the ozone lost so far, as a "controlled substance," which means emissions would be frozen at 1991 levels. Methyl bromide is used to fumigate soils and crops in some less industrialized countries. The Copenhagen amendments are expected to reduce deaths resulting from the thinning of the ozone layer by forty thousand.[54]

In 1994, the protocol's scientific assessment panel concluded that the single largest action to reduce the threat to the ozone layer would be to phase out methyl bromide emissions; in a 1995 Vienna meeting, the parties agreed to phase out its use by 2010 in the developed nations and freeze its use in the developing world at 1995–1998 levels by the year 2002.

Ozone-depleting substances (ODS) are largely a problem emanating from the North, but the efforts to raise living standards in the South could have a tremendous impact on emissions levels. The participation of the developing countries is critical, since increased use of CFCs in China and India could largely negate reductions in emissions throughout the rest of the world. The Montreal Protocol gave developing countries an additional ten years to comply with the production bans and also included promises from the North to help fund the transition in the South to ODS alternatives: the developing countries agreed to freeze CFC use by

1999 and phase it out by 2010.[55] One of the most important elements of the ozone protection agreements was the creation of a multilateral fund to help developing countries finance their implementation of the international commitments. The budget during the three-year pilot phase of the fund, from 1991 to 1994, was $1.3 billion. Twenty-five countries contributed $860 million to the core fund, and $420 million came from individual countries for parallel funding or cofunding of specific projects. Thirty-four countries contributed to the replenishment of the fund in 1994, including thirteen recipient countries. In exchange for the new round of financial support, the eighty countries participating in the fund agreed on a restructuring of the governing process. Actions by the thirty-two member governing council now require support from 60 percent of the members; these members must also have contributed at least 60 percent of the funds.

Only a few countries have implemented laws and regulations to ensure reduction in the manufacturing or use of CFCs. Despite the consensus concerning the threat of ozone depletion, the relatively small number of CFC producers, and other factors that should have led to rapid effective international action, the Protocol was still slow in coming (the agreement was signed thirteen years after publication of the first article that suggested the ozone layer was threatened) and slow in being implemented. We may have acted too late to prevent widespread harm from a weakened ozone layer. Global consumption of CFCs has decreased from a peak in 1987, but ozone depletion is still proceeding twice as fast as expected over parts of the Northern Hemisphere; 200,000 additional deaths from skin cancer in the United States alone could occur during the next 50 years as a result.

The United States has not pursued a similar strategy with regard to greenhouse warming. While the United States took a leadership position with ozone depletion, the United Nations has been the vanguard for development of an international regime to address global climate change.

Third, media coverage of the ozone-depletion issue kept attention focused on the U.S. efforts to develop an international agreement and prevented the administration negotiators from weakening the proposed CFC controls. For example, on May 29, 1987, the media published reports that Secretary of the Interior Donald Hodel was attempting to revoke the authority of the U.S. delegation to negotiate significant reductions in ozone-destroying compounds. After newspaper headlines reading "Advice on Ozone May Be: 'Wear Hats and Stand in Shade'" and "Administration Ozone Policy May Favor Sunglasses, Hats; Support for Chemical Cutbacks Reconsidered," the public outcry over the apparent change in the U.S. position created a backlash that virtually guaranteed the imposition of stringent controls.[56] Media coverage of global warming, in contrast, has been colored by the lack of scientific consensus on the rate of onset and the potential magnitude of the problem. The attention given to global warming has not been as focused, if only because the potential impacts are more uncertain, less tangible, and less immediate than those of ozone depletion. Global warming lacks an equivalent to the ozone hole upon which the media and public can focus their attention.[57]

It is this lack of scientific consensus that is perhaps the most important difference in how the policy debate has developed. At least initially, concerns about global warming were dominated by scientists who debated the consequences of human interference in the environment. There were many more attempts to measure the nature of global climate change before taking action than had been the case with CFCs. Increased production of carbon dioxide and rising atmospheric turbidity were recognized as two important factors capable of causing climate change, but there was uncertainty whether the result would be a warming or a cooling of the atmosphere. There have been dozens of scientific congresses and meetings, but the task of building consensus among scientists has been formidable.

Equally difficult has been the task of agreeing on what should be done about greenhouse warming. For example, the National Academy of Science report made several recommendations to Congress, including a phase out of CFCs and other halocarbon emissions and the development of substitutes that minimize or eliminate greenhouse gas emissions; enhanced energy conservation and efficient development of a new generation of nuclear reactor technology that is designed to deal with safety, waste management, and public acceptability; and reduction of global deforestation, initiation of a domestic reforestation program, and support for international reforestation efforts to restore the cleansing capacity of forests.

Critics argue that, while several of these proposals may have some merit, others do not. For example, a UN Environment Programme study has noted that, while reforestation is probably a good idea on its own merits, it probably cannot do much to slow the accumulation of carbon dioxide in the atmosphere. A much larger area than France would have to be reforested annually to "mop up" the carbon dioxide released from the burning of fossil fuels.[58] The most likely option is to reduce source production of greenhouse gases through energy conservation and a switch to cleaner-burning fuels such as natural gas and nuclear energy (see Chapter 6). If the experts cannot agree on the nature and extent of the problem, it is unlikely that they will agree on solutions as well.

Last, the global warming issue lacks the support of major actors in the political arena, including the United States. In order for an international agreement to be effective, it must also have the support of the developing countries, which are becoming dependent upon fossil fuels. This was not the case with CFCs and the Montreal Protocol. In that instance, sufficient concessions could be made outside the fishbowl of media publicity to allow room for negotiation and compromise. Global warming does not have a similarly low profile. What that means is that the process of reconciling differences among developing and industrialized nations to produce a global warming agreement will be much more politicized and therefore much more difficult. Until there is sufficient scientific consensus on the problem itself, there is little foundation for future policy making.[59]

THE OCEANS

Nothing is more exemplary of the concept of a global commons than the Earth's oceans and seas. They are the source of all living things, a factor in our weather and climate, a source of food, a transportation network, and the home of valuable marine resources. Yet for most of human history, the oceans have also been a dumping ground, assimilating (to some degree) our wastes, receiving little attention from policymakers until the last forty years.

The two major ocean-related environmental policy issues are the protection of the world's marine resources and control of marine pollution. There are multiple facets to both these issues, but few international regimes have successfully attempted to deal with oceanic policy. One reason for the lack of effective agreements is that we know very little about the oceans, and as a result, policymakers are perceived as hesitant and less inclined to sign treaties that might have a negative impact on their nation in the future. In addition, the oceans affect virtually every country — even landlocked ones — and a rogue state or major international stakeholder can thwart policy making simply by refusing to adhere to or sign a regime. These problems frame the issue of ocean politics, beginning with the protection of marine resources.

Overfishing is perhaps one of the most critical issues, since fish are an important renewable resource, serving as both a food source and as a source of income for much of the developing world. Once thought of as an inexhaustible bounty of food, marine resources are being quickly depleted because of technological advances and the world's increasing appetite for fish. Awareness of the problem began in 1936 after the publication of John Steinbeck's novel, *Cannery Row,* which chronicled the Pacific sardine fishery and the abundance of the sea. Less than thirty years later, the fishery collapsed, and small sardine fishing enterprises are only now beginning to open. A similar event occurred in Peru from the 1950s to the 1970s, when anchovy fishing made up about one-fifth of the world's entire fish take. In what has been called "the most spectacular collapse in the history of fisheries exploitation," annual landings plunged from ten million metric tons to less than one million metric tons in the next ten years. So far, there has been no recovery of the anchovy industry.[60]

The United States has faced similar losses as the decline of fish has dwindled over the last twenty-five years, especially in New England. The New England Fishery Management Council instituted a moratorium on new commercial entrants into the marketplace, restrictions on how many days companies could fish, closing of areas, and the requirement that net mesh sizes be increased. The Clinton administration attempted to help by issuing a $30 million aid package for the New England fishing industry to offset expected losses, and the president declared the collapse of the industry a national disaster. In late 1996, Congress passed legislation to revamp management of fisheries and move towards sustainable fishing of the nation's waters, one of the few environmental statutes passed during the 104th Congress.

Controversy exists over the use of drift nets — nets that hang vertically like curtains in the open ocean and stretch for twenty to forty miles — which sweep over an area of the ocean the size of Ohio. The nets are suspended by floats at the ocean's surface and catch fish by their gills as they attempt to swim through. In addition to being extremely efficient at catching fish, the drift nets also capture marine mammals, birds, and nontarget fish. The Sierra Club estimated that seven million dolphins were killed between the 1960s and 1980s, when drift nets were commonly used. They were also blamed for a 1988 crash in the Alaska pink salmon industry, when only twelve million fish, rather than an expected forty million, were taken by Alaskan trawlers.[61] The use of drift nets virtually ended in 1990 when American environmental organizations urged a boycott of any tuna that was caught in drift nets because of the damage done to the dolphin population. The action led to the labeling of cans as "dolphin safe" when several companies began to comply. In 1995, the United States and ten other fishing nations agreed that there would be a move towards dolphin-safe fishing practices so that their catch would be allowed into the U.S. market.

A year later, the Clinton administration proposed reversing the ban that allowed only dolphin-safe tuna into the U.S. market and allowing the use of the nets. In an unusual division among environmental organizations, groups such as Greenpeace, the World Wildlife Federation, the National Wildlife Federation, and the Environmental Defense Fund agreed with Vice President Al Gore's proposal to reinstitute drift net use. Their position was that the fishing industry had improved the methods by which tuna are caught and that there has been a 90 percent drop in dolphin mortality since 1990, with only about four thousand dolphins killed each year. But the proposal was strongly opposed by the Sierra Club and the Earth Island Institute, which called Gore's plan "the dolphin death act."[62]

Equally controversial are the fish called straddling stocks — fish that, oblivious to national jurisdiction, move freely in and out of a country's fishing boundaries. Canada, for example, closed many of its fishing areas and restricted others to only Canadian boats, extending its enforcement jurisdiction and inspecting vessels to insure compliance with its laws. The actions led to the March 1995 boarding and seizure of the Spanish trawler *Estai,* on grounds the boat had fished in Canadian waters, used small mesh nets, and falsified its records. The incident created an international uproar as Spain denounced Canada for "piracy" and Canada announced that it was simply attempting to conserve international fish stocks. The event was not an isolated one. A 1998 report by the Worldwatch Institute noted that: "If the industry is to survive, fisheries management will need to make a fundamental shift away from managing fish supplies to managing the fishers and how they fish. The key is not deciding who takes how many fish, but to balance the need to supply food and jobs with the needs of the resource." The report concluded, "Until the requirements of fish and fishers are taken into consideration, there may be little to prevent blockades from turning into all-out gun battles."[63]

Equally serious is the impact of marine pollution, which ranges from floating debris like bottles and other nonbiodegradable items, to petroleum discharges, an overload of nutrients, dredged materials, and synthetic organic compounds that pose a threat when they are taken up through the food chain. They become a human health hazard when they accumulate in food fish, affecting coastal residents who depend upon fish as a primary food source. Pollution from oil tankers, like the *Exxon Valdez* in 1989 and the grounding of an oil tanker off the coast of Oregon in 1999, keep this problem in the cycle of public interest. The concern about oil spills has been significantly reduced by new tanker designs, even though each day, more than 3,200 tankers full of oil cross the world's oceans, dwarfing other vessels. One of the largest supertankers, the *Jahre Viking,* carries more than 600,000 tons of oil, enough to fill a line of fuel trucks two hundred miles long.[64]

Marine pollution poses a number of serious environmental policy issues that are complicated by the nature of the oceans themselves. First, there is much uncertainty about the short- and long-term effects of ocean pollution. Scientists are still not sure of the potential impact on human health or of the ability of the oceans to adapt to change. Evidence suggests that the marine food chain is easily disrupted and that any major changes could affect the chemical balance that exists between marine organisms and seawater. A study published in 1996 by the U.S. National Oceanic and Atmospheric Administration reported that fourteen elements and compounds had been found in mussels and oysters at 154 sites along the U.S. coastline in 1996. While contamination levels had declined overall, there were still many significant levels of many of the substances, such as DDT, polychlorinated biphenyls (PCBs), and lead, whose discharge into waterways is illegal. The study provides a sobering example of how difficult it is to rid the oceans of pollution.[65]

Second, many policymakers are grappling with the issue of what to do about waste generally. Is it better to dispose of human-made waste on land, which is expensive but where it can be confined, or dump it into the ocean, which is free but where the effects are unknown? Or is it better yet to minimize the generation of waste by changing industrial processes or recycling? As the volume of waste grows, and as land-based disposal becomes less acceptable and costly for urban residents, ocean dumping begins to look somewhat more attractive, although eventually it may become the most costly alternative.

Third, marine pollution is not only what is dumped into the oceans but also the effect it has on coastal zones and beaches and the thirty-five major seas of the world, some coastal and some enclosed by land. Millions of dollars of tourist business are estimated to be lost every time beaches are closed because of pollution when debris washes ashore. Six of these great bodies of water — the Baltic, Mediterranean, Black, Caspian, Yellow, and South China Seas — are suffering from ecosystem disasters to the point where they are on the verge of collapse.

The political system has approached the protection of the oceans and its resources in several ways, beginning in 1926 with an agreement by seven nations to control oil pollution. In the 1950s and 1960s, eight of nine multilateral agreements signed involved oil pollution; from 1970 to 1985, only thirteen of thirty-six dealt with oil.[66] In 1954, for example, in response to the growing transport industry, thirty-two nations met to draft the International Convention for the Prevention of Pollution of the Sea by Oil (OILPOL). Representing 95 percent of the world's shipping tonnage, the parties prohibited discharges of oil within fifty miles of the coast, with fines extended to ports that were unable to accommodate waste oil. The act was amended and strengthened several more times through 1969, when provisions were attached regulating any type of ship discharges.[67]

Recognizing the limitations of existing oil pollution regulations, several more agreements were signed over the next ten years: the London Dumping Convention (1972), which limited the disposal of many pollutants at sea, including high-level radioactive waste, and the MARPOL Convention (1973), otherwise known as the Convention of the Prevention of Pollution by Ships. In 1974, the UN Environment Programme prioritized oceans through the creation of the Regional Seas Programme. The program covers ten regions and involves more than 120 coastal states, one of the few regional approaches to solving common pool problems.

The United States has also attempted to deal with marine protection, using the power of the presidency. In 1998, President Clinton, attending the National Oceans Conference in Monterey, California, signed a directive to extend the nation's moratorium on off-shore oil leasing. He also signed an executive order to speed U.S. efforts to map and monitor coral reefs and announced several initiatives, including a plan to develop an advanced ocean-monitoring system.[68] By using the executive order, the president was able to bypass a slow-moving, and often critical, Congress and advance his own environmental agenda.

By far the most important of the marine regimes is the UN Convention on the Law of the Sea, considered by some to be one of the most notable achievements in international diplomacy of the twentieth century. The convention was completed in 1982 after fifteen years of negotiation and drafting that began in Geneva in 1958. What makes this agreement so important is its comprehensiveness, establishing more equitable relationships among the member states and distinct zones of sovereignty and jurisdiction for coastal nations. Its 320 articles and nine annexes include rules for the high seas and the rights and duties of members with respect to navigation, protection of the marine environment, and research. It lays down rules for drawing sea boundaries, transit passage for international navigation, and the establishment of a 200-nautical-mile exclusive economic zone (EEZ) over which coastal states have sovereign rights with respect to natural resources and economic activities.

The Law of the Sea agreement provides the legal framework to govern the oceans and their resources, and, for the first time, recognizes that the resources of the deep seabed are part of the world's common heritage. The convention did not enter into force until 1994, a year after it obtained the necessary sixty ratifications. A key feature of the convention is an elaborate system of dispute settlement mechanisms, including compulsory procedures entailing binding decisions by the International Tribunal for the Law of the Sea and the Commission on the Limits of the Continental Shelf. Land-locked and geographically disadvantaged nations have the opportunity, under the agreement, to participate in exploiting part of the zones' fisheries on an equitable basis, with special protection given to highly migratory species of fish and mammals.[69]

The United States refused to ratify the convention, and in 1994, Secretary of State Warren Christopher announced that the United States would accept changes that made the agreement more acceptable to business interests. One of the more controversial issues dealt with the mining rights to the seabed floor, which President Ronald Reagan had rejected in 1982, saying it clashed with free-enterprise principles by requiring mining companies to pay substantial royalties and to share sophisticated technology with developing countries.[70] American negotiators eventually developed an acceptable provision that allows the United States and other industrial countries to have an effective veto over the convention's administrative body, the International Seabed Authority. However, the U.S. Senate still refuses to ratify the agreement.

The treaty is typical of the kinds of disputes that are becoming increasingly more common between rich and poor countries in dealing with common pool resources. Wealthy nations such as the United States resent being asked (or forced) to share their more advanced technology with newly developing or poorer countries. There is additional antagonism when poorer countries demand some form of redistribution of wealth in the belief that the oceans and their resources should be more equitably shared. Although the Law of the Sea is now in force, there will undoubtedly be continuing ethical and economic disputes as the convention is fully implemented.[71]

NOTES

1. David R. Francis, "Canadian Calls for Global Action on Environment," *The Christian Science Monitor, 79,* no. 158 (July 10, 1987): 12.

2. U.S. Department of Justice, "Royal Caribbean to Plead Guilty to Conspiracy, Obstruction of Justice," press release 98-248, June 2, 1998.

3. "Cruise Line Fined $9 Million," *San Francisco Chronicle,* June 3, 1998, A6.

4. Michael Valenti, "Luxury Liners Go Green," *Mechanical Engineering, 120,* no.7 (July 1, 1998): 72.

5. Garrett Hardin, "The Tragedy of the Commons," *Science, 162* (December 13, 1968): 1243–1248.

6. See John A. Baden and Douglas S. Noonan, *Managing the Commons,* 2nd ed. (Bloomington: Indiana University Press, 1998); Susan J. Buck, *The Global Commons: An Introduction* (Covelo, CA: Island Press, 1998); and David Feeny et al., "The Tragedy of the Commons: Twenty-Two Years Later," in *Green Planet Blues,* ed. Ken Conca, Michael Alberty, and Geoffrey D. Dabelko (Boulder, CO: Westview Press, 1995), 54.

7. For an in-depth discussion of international cooperation, see Oran R. Young, *International Governance: Protecting the Environment in a Stateless Society* (Ithaca, NY: Cornell University Press, 1994).

8. For a helpful summary of these issues and an application to transboundary pollution, see Juliann Allison, "Following the Leader: The Role of Domestic Politics in U.S.-Canadian Air Quality Negotiations," paper prepared for the annual meeting of the Western Political Science Association, March 14–16, 1996.

9. Marvin S. Soroos. *The Endangered Atmosphere: Preserving the Global Commons* (Columbia: University of South Carolina Press, 1997), 31.

10. The Trail Smelter case can be found as *United States v. Canada*, Arbitral Tribunal, 1941, 3 UN Rep. Int'l Arb Awards (1941). It later became the genesis for Principle 21 of the Stockholm Declaration.

11. 20 I.L.M. 690 (1980).

12. For information on the EPA's Acid Rain Program, see the website at <http://www.epa.gov/acidrain.html>.

13. 30 I.L.M. 676 (1991).

14. "Prime Minister Jean Chretien and President Clinton Mark 90th Anniversary of IJC," press release, January 11, 1999, available at <http://www/ijc.org/news/bw1101999e.html>.

15. United States/Canada Air Quality Agreement, *1998 Progress Report,* International Joint Commission (1998). For another perspective, see Juliann Emmons Allison, "Fortuitous Consequences: The Domestic Politics of the 1991 Canada–United States Agreement on Air Quality," *Policy Studies Journal, 27,* no 2 (1999): 347–359.

16. "A Model Program," United States Environmental Protection Agency, Acid Rain Program, available at <http://www.epa.gov/acidrain/overview.html>, March 18, 2000.

17. Air Quality Agreement, *1998 Progress Report,* 2, citing the report of the Acidifying Emissions Task Group, *Towards a National Acid Rain Strategy* (1997).

18. Thomas Lundmark and John B. McNeese III, "State and Local Government Participation in Solving Environmental Problems at the U.S.-Mexican Border," *Journal of Environmental Law and Practice, 3,* no. 2 (September–October 1995): 37–38.

19. Tex. Govt. Code Section 481.0075(a) (1995).

20. Tex. Govt. Code Section 481.061(a) (1995).

21. For more information on the projects, see the Western Governors' Association website at <http://www.westgov.org>.

22. Lundmark and McNeece, "State and Local Government Participation," 42–43.

23. For an examination of the concerns surrounding NAFTA and GATT, see Pierre Marc Johnson and Andre Beaulieu, *The Environment and NAFTA* (Washington, DC: Island Press, 1996), and Daniel Esty, *Greening the GATT* (Washington, DC: Washington Institute for International Economics, 1994).

24. 16 U.S.C. sec. 1361–1421h, at sec. 1371 (1972).

25. 16 U.S.C. sec.1371 (1984).

26. 16 U.S.C. 1371(a)(2)(B)(II), 137(1)(2)(C)(1988).

27. 16 U.S.C. 1415 (1992).

28. Steve Charnovitz, "Dolphins and Tuna: An Analysis of the Second GATT Panel Report," *Environmental Law Reporter, 24* (October 1994): 10567–10587.

29. NAFTA, Art. 904.2.

30. NAFTA, Art. 915.

31. Steve Charnovitz, "NAFTA: An Analysis of Its Environmental Provisions," *Environmental Law Reporter, 23* (February 1993): 10069–10072.

32. NAFTA, Art. 608.1.

33. Charnovitz, "NAFTA: An Analysis of Its Environmental Provisions," 10071.

34. NAFTA, Arts. 713.1, 714.1. See Bartlett P. Miller, "The Effect of GATT and the NAFTA on Pesticide Regulation: A Hard Look at Harmonization," *Colorado Journal of International Environmental Law and Policy, 6,* no. 21 (1995): 203–205.

35. NAFTA, Art. 1114.2.

36. For an analysis of this issue, see Robert Housman, "The North American Free Trade Agreement's Lessons for Reconciling Trade and the Environment," *Stanford Journal of International Law, 30,* no. 379 (1994): 394–410.

37. See, for example, J. D. Hays, John Imbrie, and N. J. Shackleton, "Variations in the Earth's Orbit: Pacemakers of the Ice Ages," *Science, 194* (December 10, 1976): 1121–1131. The authors conclude, "A model of future climate change based on the observed orbital-climate relationships, but ignoring anthropogenic effects, predicts that the long-term trend over the next several thousand years is towards extensive Northern Hemisphere glaciation," 1131.

38. See James E. Lovelock, *Gaia* (Oxford: Oxford University Press, 1979).

39. World Commission on Environment and Development, *Our Common Future* (Oxford: Oxford University Press, 1987).

40. See, for example, James F. Kasting, "The Carbon Cycle, Climate, and the Long-Term Effects of Fossil Fuel Burning," *Consequences,* 4, no. 1 (1998): 15–27; Jonathan Patz, Paul R. Epstein, and Thomas A. Burke, "Global Climate Change and Emerging Infection Diseases," *Journal of the American Medical Association,* January 17, 1996; and John P. Holden et al., *Scientists' Statement on Global Climatic Disruption* (Washington, DC: Ozone Action, 1997), available at <http://www.ozone.org>.

41. Dian J. Gaffen, "Falling Satellites, Rising Temperatures?" *Nature, 394* (August 13, 1998): 615–616.

42. American Geophysical Union statement, January 29, 1999, available at <http://www.agu.org/sci_soc/policy/climate_change.html>.

43. "Coral Reefs Hurt by Warming," Reuters New Service, November 13, 1998.

44. H. Josef Hebert, "Global Warming Costs Analyzed by White House," *San Francisco Chronicle,* August 1, 1998, A8.

45. Alec Gallup and Lydia Sand, "Public Concerned, Not Alarmed about Global Warming," Gallup Poll, December 2, 1997, available at <http://www.gallup.com/POLL_ARCHIVES/971202.html>.

46. John A. Krosnick, Penny S. Visser, and Allyson L. Holbrook, "American Opinion on Global Warming," *Resources, 133* (Fall 1998): 5–9.

47. "Vice President Gore Announces New Data Showing Warmest June on Record," press release, July 14, 1998, available at <http://www.whitehouse.gov/CEQ/19980715-5125.html>.

48. Allan Freedman, "Clinton's Global Warming Plans Take Heat from Congress," *Congressional Quarterly Weekly Report,* October 25, 1997, 2598. Other criticisms came from American business interests. See "Big U.S. Industries Launch Attack on Warming Treaty," *Wall Street Journal,* December 12, 1997, A3.

49. See Bert Bolin, "The Kyoto Negotiations on Climate Change: A Science Perspective," *Science,* January 16, 1998, 330–331; and William K. Stevens, "Despite Pact, Gases Will Keep Rising," *New York Times,* December 12, 1997, A16.

50. See Joby Warrick, "Climate Talks Extended in Pursuit of an Accord," *Washington Post,* November 14, 1998, A3; United Nations, "Climate Change Meeting Adopts Buenos Aires Plan of Action," press release, October 14, 1998, available at <http://www.cop4/informed>; "Eisenstat Notes Progress: Climate Change Negotiations," available at <http://www.usia.gov/topical/global/environment/envcl>.

51. For a narrative description of the rise of the ozone depletion issue to the top of the environmental protection agenda, see John J. Nance, *What Goes Up: The Global Assault on Our Atmosphere* (New York: Morrow, 1991).

52. See Susan Solomon et al., "On Depletion of Antarctic Ozone," *Nature, 321* (June 19, 1986): 755–758.

53. Martha M. Hamilton, "The Challenge to Make Industry Ozone-Friendly," *Washington Post National Weekly Edition,* October 7–13, 1991, 21.

54. Debora MacKenzie, "Agreement Reduces Damage to Ozone Layer," *New Scientist,* December 5, 1992, 10.

55. "Data Point to Ultimate Closing of Ozone Hole," *New York Times,* May 31, 1996, A11; Amal Kumar Naj, "Chemicals Bad for Ozone Are Declining," *Wall Street Journal,* May 31, 1996, B8A.

56. Steven J. Shimburg, "Stratospheric Ozone and Climate Protection: Domestic Legislation and the International Process," *Environmental Law, 21,* no. 2175 (1991): 2188.

57. Peter M. Morrisette, "The Montreal Protocol: Lessons for Formulating Policies for Global Warming," *Policy Studies Journal,* 19, no. 2 (Spring 1991): 152–161.

58. Ibid., 158.

59. Many researchers believe that the next step in gaining compliance with international environmental agreements is through joint implementation. See, for example, Farhana Yamin, "The Use of Joint Implementation to Increase Compliance with the Climate Change Conven-

tion," in *Improving Compliance with International Environmental Law,* ed. James Cameron, Jacob Werksman, and Peter Roderick (London: Earthscan, 1996), 229–242; and Axel Michaelowa, "Joint Implementation — The Baseline Issue," *Global Environmental Change, 18,* no. 1 (April 1998): 81–92.

60. Merry Camhi, "Overfishing Threatens Sea's Bounty," *Forum for Applied Research and Public Policy,* Summer 1996.

61. Brian J. Rothchild, "How Bountiful Are Ocean Fisheries?" *Consequences,* 2 (1996): 15.

62. Gary Lee, "Tuna Fishing Bill Divides Environmental Activists," *Washington Post,* July 8, 1996, A7.

63. Anne Platt McGinn, "Rocking the Boat: Conserving Fisheries and Protecting Jobs," *Worldwatch Paper, 142* (June 1998), 10.

64. "Why Oil Spills Are Increasing," *Los Angeles Times,* March 26, 1993, A1.

65. William J. Broad, "Survey of 100 U.S. Coastal Sites Shows Pollution Is Declining," *New York Times,* January 21, 1997, B10.

66. David Hunter, James Salzman, and Durwood Zaelke, *International Environmental Law and Policy* (New York: Foundation Press, 1998), 773–734; and Peter M. Haas, *Saving the Mediterranean: The Politics of International Environmental Cooperation* (New York: Columbia University Press, 1990), 11.

67. Hunter, Salzman, and Zaelke, *International Environmental Law and Policy,* 734.

68. Remarks by the President to the National Oceans Conference, June 12, 1998, Monterey, CA, available at <www.whitehouse.gov/WH/New/html/19980615-1292>.

69. "Sea Law Convention Enters into Force," *UN Chronicle, 32* (March 1995), 8–12.

70. Steven Greenhouse, "U.S., Having Won Changes, Is Set to Sign the Law of the Sea," *New York Times,* July 1, 1994, A1.

71. See Ian Townsend-Gault and Michael D. Smith, "Environmental Ethics, International Law, and Deep Seabed Mining: The Search for a New Point of Departure," in *Freedom for the Seas in the 21st Century,* ed. Jon M. Van Dyke, Durwood Zaelke, and Grant Hewison (Washington, DC: Island Press, 1993), 392–403.

FOR FURTHER READING

John A. Baden and Douglas S. Noonan. *Managing the Commons*. 2nd ed. Bloomington: Indiana University Press, 1998.

J. Samuel Barkin and George E. Shambaugh, eds. *Anarchy and the Environment: The International Relations of Common Pool Resources*. Albany: State University of New York Press, 1999.

Richard Elliot Benedick. *Ozone Diplomacy: New Directions in Safeguarding the Planet*. 2nd ed. Cambridge, MA: Harvard University Press, 1999.

Elisabeth Mann Borgese. *The Oceanic Circle: Governing the Seas as a Global Resource*. New York: United Nations University Press, 1999.

Susan J. Buck. *The Global Commons: An Introduction*. Covelo, CA: Island Press, 1998.

Biliana Cecin-Sain and Robert W. Knecht. *The Future of U.S. Ocean Policy: Choices for the Next Century*. Covelo, CA: Island Press, 1999.

Ross Gelbspan. *The Heat Is On*. Boulder, CO: Perseus Books, 1999.

Suzanne Iudicello, Michael Weber, and Robert Wieland. *Fish, Markets, and Fishermen: The Economics of Overfishing*. Covelo, CA: Island Press, 1999.

Richard Kiy and John D. Worth, eds. *Environmental Management on North America's Borders*. College Station: Texas A&M University Press, 1999.

Boyce Thorne-Miller. *The Living Ocean: Understanding and Protecting Marine Biodiversity*. Covelo, CA: Island Press, 1999.

John D. Wirth. *Smelter Smoke in North America: The Politics of Transborder Pollution*. Lawrence: University Press of Kansas, 2000.

CHAPTER 10

Endangered Species, Biodiversity, and Forests

Conservation isn't just about protecting beautiful places or protecting our outdoor recreation opportunities. It's really come down to protecting the integrity of the diversity of life and the evolutionary process.
— Dave Foreman, environmental activist[1]

It was not until 1940 that divers off the coast of Southern California were able to delve deep enough into the marine ecosystem to discover the white abalone, one of eight species of once plentiful California abalone. The white species remained undetected for years because its habitat — 80 to 300 feet deep in the ocean — made them difficult to harvest. Even after their discovery, divers largely ignored them for two decades until improved technology and diving skills allowed them to be taken in by large commercial fishers. The white abalone became a delicacy because, although they were somewhat smaller than the more common red abalone, they were more tender and did not need to be pounded before cooking, making them a gourmet food item.

Like many species that originally seem to exist in limitless supply, the white abalone could be found in dense populations in the area from Santa Barbara to just south of the Mexican border. While only a few metric tons were harvested in the late 1960s, by 1972 the catch peaked at 65 million metric tons. It fell to less than 1 metric ton only seven years later — the species had been virtually wiped out. In one 1992 biological census, there were only 3 live abalone and 119 empty shells in an area of about 6.5 acres. Prior to the 1970s, there would have been about 12,000 abalone in the area.

One of the most contentious and visible forest management practices is the use of clearcut logging, where virtually every tree is cut down and the land left barren, as on this steep hillside in Washington State.

The white abalone is not yet considered extinct, but it may become the first mollusk to be added to the endangered species list as a result of human activity. To avert that listing, biologists are developing an abalone management policy to learn more about the species' reproduction habits and to potentially save some in a laboratory. One part of the effort will require divers to go to the area in small submarines, where they will anesthetize the animals, which live on rocks and have to be pried off. They hope to encourage the white abalone to spawn under laboratory conditions, although that has never been done before, and then reseed the ocean depths with young mollusks. The United States is also attempting to work with the government of Mexico, which continues to consider the white abalone as an exploitable resource and will not allow survey teams into the country's international waters.

But there is little that biologists can do about natural causes of depletion, such as sea otter depredation, the development of microorganic diseases that cause withering of the animals, or natural forces like El Niño and La Niña, which cumulatively impact white abalone stock. The best officials can hope for is that the damage done to the white abalone may provide information on how to save the black, pink, and green abalone stock, which have also experienced catastrophic decline. Many marine biologists believe it may already be too late.[2]

We have only the beginning of an understanding of the diversity and numbers of forms of life that currently exist on this planet. There may be as many as thirty million species currently in existence, primarily insects and marine invertebrates, with only about 5 percent of them named and identified. That number is thought to be only a tiny percentage of the species that have inhabited earth during its millions of years of history — perhaps less than 1 percent of as many as four billion. Some species have disappeared as a result of cataclysmic change, such as changes in the level of the seas or massive ice movements, while others disappearing can be attributed to the appearance (and often, the intervention) of humans.

Estimates of the current rate of species extinction vary considerably from one source to another and are largely dependent upon the period of time covered. From 1600 to 1980, for example, nearly two hundred vertebrate extinctions were documented, over half of them birds. But since 1980, habitat destruction, hunting, pesticide use, pollution, and other human-made causes have led to the extinction of as many as one thousand species per year, primarily in tropical regions. The *Global 2000 Report to the President* projected that between a half-million and two million species extinctions would occur by the turn of the century. Most of those losses were attributed to the clearing or degradation of tropical forests, although marine species are threatened by damming, siltation, and pollution.[3]

This chapter focuses on the politics and history of legislation, both in the United States and internationally, to protect wildlife, plants, and their habitats, the wildlife bureaucracy, and the role of nongovernmental organizations (NGOs) in species protection. The last section of the chapter provides an overview of the biodiversity and forests debate by examining the ways in which the United States and other nations are attempting to preserve these priceless lifeforms.

PROTECTIVE LEGISLATION

The development of laws protecting wildlife can be traced back to earliest legal history, but those laws have often differed in terms of what has been protected and why. Under Roman law, wild animals, or *ferae naturae,* were given the same status as the oceans and air — they belonged to no one. As Anglo-Saxon law developed, however, an exception was made: private landowners had the right to wildlife on their property. As land was parceled out to the nobility as "royal forests" around 450 C.E., hunting restrictions began to be imposed, and only the king was given sole right to pursue fish or game anywhere he claimed as his realm. As the English political system developed, there were very few changes in this theory except to perpetuate a system by which only the wealthy or nobles were qualified to take game. Those same restrictions found their way to American shores and flourished until the mid-nineteenth century, when a major policy shift occurred as the U.S. Supreme Court established the basis for a doctrine of state ownership of wildlife. The federal government's role in defining the legal status of wildlife was limited to an 1868 statute prohibiting the hunting of furbearing animals in Alaska and in 1894 a prohibition on hunting in Yellowstone National Park. The states began to regulate fishing within their waters just after the Civil War, a policy that was upheld by the Court using the commerce clause of Article 1, Section 8 of the Constitution. What is important about the decisions of this period, however, is that the states' regulatory authority was based on a fundamental nineteenth century conception of the purpose of wildlife law — the preservation of a food supply.[4]

Contemporary U.S. legislation protecting plants and animals can be divided into four categories: migratory and game birds, wild horses and burros, marine mammals, and endangered species. What is unique about these legislative provisions is that, in addition to offering protection for reasons of aesthetics or biological diversity, Congress has also sought to regulate the commerce and trade in these species. Generally, it is illegal to possess, offer for sale, sell, offer for barter, offer to purchase, purchase, deliver for shipment, ship, export, import, cause to be shipped, exported, or imported, deliver for transportation, transport or cause to be transported, carry or cause to be carried, or receive for shipment, transport, carriage, or export any of the protected plants and animals.

Three separate legislative efforts have been enacted — all within the last thirty-five or forty years — which indicates how recently American concern for endangered species has reached the political agenda. The first, the Endangered Species Preservation Act of 1966, mandated the secretary of the interior to develop a program to conserve, protect, restore, and propagate selected species of native fish and wildlife. Its provisions were primarily designed, however, to protect habitats through land acquisition, and little else. The species protected under the law were those "threatened with extinction" based on a finding by the secretary in consultation with interested persons, but the procedures for doing that went no further. It did not limit the taking of these species, or commerce in them, but it was an important first step in the development of the law.

The Endangered Species Conservation Act of 1969 attempted to remedy those limitations by further defining the types of protected wildlife, and more importantly, by including wildlife threatened with worldwide extinction and prohibiting their importation into the United States — an international aspect not included in the earlier legislation. Instead of using the broad term *fish and wildlife* (which was interpreted as only vertebrates), the 1969 law included any wild mammal, fish, wild bird, amphibian, reptile, mollusk, or crustacean. The list of species was to be developed using the best scientific and commercial data available, with procedures for designation pursuant to the rule making in the Administrative Procedure Act. This formalized a process that had been haphazard and highly discretionary under the 1966 act.

President Richard Nixon warned that the two laws did not provide sufficient management tools needed to act early enough to save a vanishing species and urged Congress to enact a more comprehensive law, which became the Endangered Species Act (ESA) of 1973. There are several notable features in the law that distinguish it from previous efforts. One, it required all federal agencies, not just the two departments identified in the 1966 and 1969 acts, to seek to conserve endangered species, broadening the base of protective efforts. Two, it expanded conservation measures that could be undertaken under the act to include all methods and procedures necessary to protect the species rather than emphasizing habitat protection only. Three, it broadened the definition of wildlife to include any member of the animal kingdom. Four, it created two classes of species: those "endangered" (in danger of extinction throughout all or a significant portion of its range) and those "threatened" (any species likely to become an endangered species within the foreseeable future).

From an administrative standpoint, the 1973 law was considerably more complex than were previous legislative efforts. It included a circuitous route by which a species was to be listed by the secretary of the interior, delisted when the species' population stabilized, and changed from threatened to endangered and vice versa. The secretaries of commerce and the interior have virtually unlimited discretion in deciding when to consider the status of a species, since the law did not establish any priorities or time limitations.

Generally, a species is considered for listing upon petition of an interested group that has developed scientific evidence regarding the specie's population. In 1992, for example, a single biologist working in Oregon's Willamette Valley discovered specimens of Fenders' blue butterfly, a one-inch-long species thought to be extinct. Researchers found ten spots where the butterfly was found and estimated that there were only 2,000 to 2,500 of the insects in existence. The biologist prepared a report on the butterfly's status for the U.S. Fish and Wildlife Service (USFWS) as the first step toward its possible designation as threatened. Reports are then considered by the secretary of the interior, although the time frame for consideration is totally discretionary. Some species have become extinct while waiting to be listed.

Listing, however, is but the first phase in a very lengthy process. Once a species is added to the list (which is made official by publishing a notice in the *Federal Register*), the federal government must decide how much of its habitat needs to be protected. The 1973 law is somewhat vague in indicating how "critical" habitat is to be determined and when that determination must be made. The law then requires the government to develop a recovery plan for the species. Recovery is defined by the law as the process by which the decline of an endangered or threatened species is arrested or reversed and threats to its survival are neutralized to ensure its long-term survival in the wild. The plan delineates, justifies, and schedules the research and management actions necessary to support the recovery of a species, including those that, if successful, will permit reclassification or delisting. Typical recovery plans involve extensive public participation and include the cost of each strategy.

One of the most controversial aspects of the planning process is the assignment of individual species recovery priorities, which signifies the imminence of extinction and the designation of those species to which a known threat or conflict exists (usually from development projects). About one-quarter of the listed species are in conflict with other activities and receive the designation. The law was amended in 1988 to make more specific the requirement that the secretaries of the interior and commerce develop and implement recovery plans and to require a status report every two years on the efforts to develop recovery plans for all listed species and on the status of all species for which recovery plans have been developed.

Plants are also protected under the ESA, with the first four plants (all found on San Clemente Island off the California coast) listed in 1977. Before the 1988 amendments, it was illegal only to "remove and reduce to possession" listed plants, and then, only those on lands under federal jurisdiction. Under the amended provisions, there is a prohibition against maliciously damaging or destroying plants on federal lands, and making it illegal to remove, destroy, or damage any listed plant on state or private land in knowing violation of state law.

INTERNATIONAL PROTECTION AGREEMENTS

The development of an international regime to protect endangered species has come largely from the leadership of the United States. The 1969 Endangered Species Conservation Act included a provision directing the secretaries of the interior and commerce to convene an international meeting before June 30, 1971, to develop an international agreement on the conservation of endangered species. Although it was a year and a half late, that meeting produced the Convention on Trade in Endangered Species of Wild Fauna and Flora, or CITES as it is better known. The United States was the first nation to ratify the convention in January 1974, and it became effective July 1, 1975.

It is important to note, however, that CITES is not strictly a conservation agreement; it focuses on matters of international trade rather than on preservation per se. One of the key aspects of the CITES treaty is that it creates three levels of species vulnerability: Appendix I (all species threatened with extinction that are or may be affected by trade), Appendix II (all species that are not now threatened with extinction but that may become so unless trade in specimens is strictly regulated), and Appendix III (species subject to regulation for the purpose of preventing exploitation). Within ninety days of the date when a species is added to an appendix, and upon a showing of an overriding economic interest, party nations may make a "reservation" to the convention. The reservation means that they do not accept the listing of a species in a particular appendix and, therefore, are not subject to the trade prohibitions.

CITES establishes an elaborate series of trade permits within each category and between importing and exporting authorities. Exempt from the trade restrictions are specimens acquired before the convention applied to that species, specimens that are personal or household effects, and specimens used in scientific research. The CITES agreement is supported by a secretariat, provided through the UN Environment Programme, and a Conference of the Parties (COP), which meets every two years for the purpose of regulating trade in each species.

When the CITES agreement was first ratified, it received the support of the majority of nations that are active in wildlife trading because it helps them to protect their resources from illegal traders and poachers. Several countries that are deeply involved in wildlife trading as importers and exporters of products chose not to sign on to CITES. The result is an active animal smuggling industry, much of it centered in Southeast Asia.[5] Japan, the world's biggest importer of illegally traded goods, initially made twelve reservations to the convention, including two species of endangered sea turtles, although it agreed to phase out its trade in those species. The sea turtle shells, primarily those of the hawksbill and olive ridley species, are made into eyeglass frames, cigarette lighters, combs, handbags, belts, and shoes.

Perhaps the most publicized and controversial listing under CITES is the African elephant. The elephant had already been listed by the United States as a threatened species in 1978, but in 1988 the World Wildlife Fund and Conservation International sponsored a scientific study of the African elephant population and recommended that it be listed under CITES Appendix I — threatened with extinction. The listing was supported by the United States and several other nations (including Kenya and Tanzania) at the October 1989 COP, along with a proposed ban on trade in ivory products, a position opposed by Botswana, Malawi, Mozambique, South Africa, Zambia, and Zimbabwe. Their opposition was a result of several of the nations managing to increase their elephant herds through nationally supported economic incentives. They felt that there was no need for their countries to suffer the loss of the lucrative ivory trade because herds in other African states were being diminished through poor wildlife management practices.

In the end, the United States–led position won, and the elephant achieved Appendix I status. Prices in African raw ivory dropped by as much as 90 percent, reducing any real incentives for poaching and smuggling, and it appeared that the problem was resolved. But the issue continued to be raised at the 1992 and 1994 COPs, as African representatives sought relief from CITES to sell ivory from culled elephants, arguing that they had managed their herds effectively to stabilize the population. They felt as if they were being penalized for their efforts, and denounced attempts by countries without elephants to dominate the discussion. Environmental organizations, who were actively monitoring the CITES meetings, pointed out that the elephant population still had declined, convincing members to keep the ivory trade ban in effect.[6]

In 1997, however, there was an abrupt shift of policy when environmental ministers representing 138 nations met in Zimbabwe. After years of rancorous debate, Botswana, Namibia, and Zimbabwe were given permission to sell previously stockpiled ivory tusks to Japan under an experimental program that included an international monitoring system and increased enforcement of antipoaching laws. Legal trading resumed in 1999 and will be a real test of international resolve to ensure a future for the elephant. The three countries agreed that ivory sales will go toward conservation and community programs for wildlife.[7]

One of the flaws in the CITES provisions is that CITES has little real power over the actions of individual nations and whether or not they choose to comply with the treaty. For example, the parties established a panel comprised of affected states and nongovernmental organization representatives to monitor elephant populations and whether or not the species should be downlisted on a case-by-case basis. But the panel's recommendations are only advisory, and no mechanism exists within the secretariat to prosecute noncompliance with the convention. Thus, any real efforts at species protection are voluntary and reliant upon the parties' recognition of the value of preserving biodiversity.[8]

A second major international species protection agreement is the Convention on Biological Diversity, which was negotiated both before and during the Earth Summit in Rio de Janeiro in June 1992. Unlike the dissension that marked the initial reservations to CITES, the biodiversity convention gained the support of virtually every member of the United Nations except the United States. President George Bush, who had threatened to boycott the conference, refused to sign the biodiversity treaty in an action that embarrassed the U.S. delegation in a highly publicized dispute. Under the terms of the agreement, the parties agree that a state has sovereignty over the genetic resources within its borders, including any valuable drugs and medicines that may be developed from endangered animals and plants. The convention is an important extension of CITES because it commits countries to draw up national strategies to conserve not only the plants and animals within their borders but also the habitats in which they live. Other provisions require countries to pass laws to protect endangered species, expand protected areas, restore damaged ones, and promote public awareness of the need for conservation and sustainable use of biological resources. When President Clinton assumed office, he signed the treaty, but because the Republican-controlled Congress refused to ratify it with a two-thirds vote, the United States was allowed only an observer role when the first COP was held in 1994.[9]

Before the Earth Summit, habitat protection found international support largely through organizations such as the International Union for Conservation of Nature and Natural Resources (IUCN) and by regimes such as the International Convention Concerning the Protection of World Cultural and Natural Heritage, which entered into force in 1972. More than 1,200 national parks have been established worldwide, covering nearly 2.7 million square kilometers — an area larger than Alaska, Texas, and California combined. One of the challenges facing global efforts to preserve wildlife habitats is basically one of economics: in times of declining budgets, many governments are finding it difficult to support parks and reserves over human needs. Countries such as New Zealand, for example, are reorganizing their parks to earn more revenue from them, and several African nations are using tourism as a way of financing wildlife refuges. But there are less obvious problems as well. Most national parks are outlined by some type of physical barrier, such as a fence or moat, but animals within do not always respect those limitations. Large mammals and birds of prey, for example, demand a large ecosystem for their habitat, which may cross national borders. This makes it unlikely that, even when strictly protected, national parks by themselves will be able to conserve all, or even most, species.

THE MAKING OF WILDLIFE POLICY

Federal authority for the regulation protection of wildlife is a case study in the growth of bureaucracy, characterized by name changes and power struggles within the agencies. Power is shared by a number of agencies, most of which have their counterparts at the state level. Until 1939, the Bureau of Biological Survey in the Department of Agriculture held regulatory authority for all wildlife, with the exception of marine fisheries, which were under the jurisdiction of the Bureau of Fisheries in the Department of Commerce. Both agencies were absorbed by the Department of the Interior and then consolidated into the U.S. Fish and Wildlife Service in 1940, but in 1956, the Fish and Wildlife Act divided authority into a Bureau of Sports Fisheries and Wildlife and a Bureau of Commercial Fisheries, much as had been the case prior to 1939. President Richard Nixon's federal reorganization of 1970 transferred the Bureau of Commercial Fisheries to the National Oceanic and Atmospheric Administration and the agency became the National Marine Fisheries Service, once again under the Department of Commerce. The Bureau of Sports Fisheries and Wildlife went back to its previous designation as the Fish and Wildlife Service in 1974, remaining in the Department of the Interior.

The structure of congressional committees also contributes to the fragmentation of policy making, since various committees and subcommittees have jurisdiction over different types of animals and their habitats. Political change can add to the confusion over which committee handles which species, as was the case in 1995 when the members of the 104th Congress eliminated entirely the Merchant Marine and Fisheries Committee, which had been in existence for 107 years. Its duties and staff were then parceled out to other committees, making the protection of the oceans and sealife more complex.

Congress, in the 1988 amendments to the ESA, directed federal agencies to more closely monitor those species facing substantial declines of their populations and to carry out emergency listing when necessary. Generally speaking, the longer a species has been listed, the better its chances for its population stabilizing or improving. For the most part, those species listed less than three years do not yet have final approved recovery plans, although they may have plans in some stage of development. Recovery outlines are developed within sixty days of publication of the final rule listing a species and are submitted to the director of the Fish and Wildlife Service to be used as a guide for activities until recovery plans are developed and approved.

In response to criticism from various interests about the way in which the ESA was being implemented, President Clinton established the National Biological Service within the Department of the Interior as a way of improving the existing bank of information on species and their habitat. The agency was given responsibility for developing an inventory of plant and animal populations, but some members of Congress viewed it as a base for advocates seeking to expand the scope of the ESA. Clinton's advisors believed that the new bureau was absolutely essential if the federal government hoped to speed up the process of listing and recovery, which had fallen far behind in the review process.

But the 1995 change from a Democrat controlled Congress, which generally supported the ESA in principle, to a Republican one, which sought major reforms, marked a major turnaround for the nation's wildlife policies. The Endangered Species Act officially expired on October 1, 1992, but Congress had still appropriated funds and could continue do so unless the act is totally repealed. As one of its initial actions, the Republican leadership declared a moratorium on the listing of any new species under the ESA, using the argument that there was uncertainty about how best to implement its provisions. The moratorium lasted until May 1996, creating an additional backlog of casework for agencies already besieged by budget cuts and an overall lack of resources. Republicans also targeted the National Biological Service, whose budget was included under the Department of the Interior. In a conference agreement, legislators agreed to eliminate the agency and shift most of its functions to the U.S. Geological Survey, whose budget was slashed along with its ability to implement much of its chartered responsibilities. President Clinton vetoed the interior appropriations bill, objecting to provisions that included a 10 percent spending reduction for the department, along with a laundry list of issues relating to grazing on federal lands, offshore oil drilling, and mining patents.[10]

Amending the ESA was one of the top priorities of congressional Republicans in the 104th and 105th Congresses, aiming at a major ESA reform proposal. Several bills sought to eliminate species recovery as the primary goal of the act, provided more opportunities for states and landowners to be more involved in decisions related to endangered species, created biodiversity reserves, gave more leeway to landowners, and would reimburse private property owners for loss in land value resulting from endangered species regulation. Conservatives and property rights activists kept the pressure on the leadership to pass reform legislation, but failed.

Both the Clinton administration and Congress agreed that the ESA was flawed, but one of the primary disagreements between the two branches was whether the law ought to be repealed so that policymakers could begin with a clean slate, or whether or not piecemeal, incremental changes could be made that would prove satisfactory to all the parties involved. Some reforms were made through the regulatory process, circumventing the legislature and therefore not requiring actual amendments to the law.

THE ROLE OF ORGANIZED INTERESTS

While government agencies are responsible for implementing the legislative aspects of wildlife protection, environmental organizations, industry trade associations, and grass-roots opposition groups have clashed over how the laws ought to be interpreted. Wildlife protection groups began to flourish in the late nineteenth century, and many of them survived to become the mainstays of the contemporary environmental movement, such as the National Aubudon Society, founded in 1905. Others, such as the Wilderness Society (1935) and the National Wildlife Federation (1936) were products of the surge of interest instigated by President Theodore Roosevelt. The vast majority of wildlife organizations, however, have a more recent origin, partly as a result of a spate of legislative activity just after Earth Day 1970. The National Wildlife Federation, which monitors environmental organizations, reported that, of the 108 national wildlife and humane organizations identified in its study, 14 percent had been founded before 1940, and 68 percent since 1966. The decade surrounding Earth Day (1965–1975) accounted for the founding of 38 percent of all groups with a species orientation.[11]

The tactics used by groups to influence the implementation of wildlife policy range from the traditional to the radical. Some organizations see their role within the context of legislation, such as the Wilderness Society's efforts at lobbying Congress to increase appropriations for habitat protection. Other groups focus on advocating for species by lobbying the implementing agency directly. In the mid-1990s, for example, the San Diego Biodiversity Project sought the listing of ten endangered plants and animals in southern California, while the Hawaii Aubudon Society wanted the government to designate critical habitat for seventeen species of Hawaiian forest birds.

Other groups have taken independent steps to preserve species, bypassing the federal bureaucracy. The Nature Conservancy, for instance, founded in 1951, buys up endangered habitats to save the species living on them from extinction. The organization has purchased or negotiated donations of more than five million acres worldwide, making the group the custodian of the largest private nature sanctuary in the world. Another notable accomplishment of the group is their Biological and Conservation Data System, a biogeographic database of more than four hundred thousand entries that can be used to assess species diversity on a region-by-region basis. It allows the group to establish protection priorities and is also used by public agencies and resource planners in preparing environmental impact studies.

Somewhat ironically, sport hunting organizations, such as Ducks Unlimited and the Boone and Crockett Club, organized by Teddy Roosevelt in 1887, have also been active in species preservation. Many of the national hunting organizations have dedicated their efforts to preserving wildlife habitat and the enforcement of game laws. They have been instrumental in advocating management policies for species such as the North American deer, wild turkey, pronghorn antelope, and migatory waterfowl. Equally active have been recreational fishing enthusiasts, who have joined environmental organizations in seeking a ban on gill and entangled nets. The American Sportsfishing Association and fishing equipment manufacturers contributed funds toward a successful ban on netting in Florida waters, with most of the donations coming from rank-and-file anglers.[12]

Environmental organizations have been joined in their efforts by a number of corporate interests seeking to capitalize on Americans' love of wildlife. Firms such as the DuPont Chemical Company and General Wine and Spirits, Inc. (bald eagle), Manhattan Life Insurance Company (peregrine falcon), Sony Corporation (California condor), and Lockheed Martin Corporation (bighorn sheep) have made significant financial contributions to species restoration. As one publicist suggested, "People simply love animals. If your company is associated with kindness to animals, some of that love will rub off on you."[13]

The ESA has also been the focus of some of the environmental opposition groups discussed earlier in Chapter 2. Typical is the organization, Grassroots ESA Coalition, an umbrella group headquartered in Battle Ground, Washington. It claims to represent more than 350 other organizations seeking to "reform the ESA in a way that benefits both wildlife and people, something the old law has failed to do."[14] Unlike industry groups with the financial resources to make campaign contributions, the Grassroots ESA Coalition has urged its members to contact members of Congress through telephone calls and letter-writing campaigns in support of reform legislation. Other organizations have called for an outright repeal of the ESA rather than for incremental reforms.

THE CONTINUING SAGA OF SPECIES PROTECTION

The passage of the ESA and CITES has not laid the issue of endangered species protection to rest; the debate over these animals' fate continues among scientists, policymakers, and a large number of nongovernmental organizations. All agree that the law is flawed — there is no agreement on what strategy to adopt to deal with conflicting values associated with species and their habitats.

President Clinton's efforts to defeat the Republican plans to gut the ESA were successful, and by the 106th Congress, it appeared that most representatives were prepared to move on to other issues. On Earth Day 1998, the president and Vice President Al Gore called on Congress to support, not thwart, their efforts.[15] Meanwhile, federal agencies and nongovernmental organizations were placing pressure on the administration to deal with the backlog of listings resulting from the 1995–1996 moratorium. When the moratorium was lifted and funding was restored, 243 species were awaiting final listing determinations. Under Clinton, approximately eighty-five species a year were added to the list.[16]

In 1998, the U.S. Fish and Wildlife Service adopted a new policy called Listing Priority Guidelines, which was designed to delist and reclassify twenty-nine birds, mammals, fish, and plants that have achieved, or are moving toward, recovery. The two-year project amounts to the most extensive delisting and reclassification since the ESA was adopted in 1973, since only sixteen species had been restored in more than twenty-five years. By removing recovered species from the list, the agency could redirect its resources to species with greater needs. Still, the overall numbers were small. Towards the end of 1999, nearly twelve hundred U.S. species were listed as endangered or threatened, with less than nine hundred species with recovery plans, as seen in Table 10.1.

A second controversial element of species protection are species recovery plans. Prior to the 1990s, the USFWS relied upon this strategy to save endangered species, a process that often took years and resulted in limited success. In 1985, for example, the USFWS decided to remove the last six California condors from the wild as a way of protecting the species. After a monumental tracking and trapping effort, and amidst considerable public opposition and an injunction by the National Audubon Society, staff from the San Diego Wild Animal Park captured the last of the known wild birds in 1987. The government allowed several nonprofit groups to begin captive breeding programs, and eventually they began to release young condors back into their natural habitat in southern California and northern Arizona and to track their activities. Critics believed the efforts were counterproductive since many of the rereleased birds later died.[17] In 1987, similar efforts to protect endangered sea otters by moving them to a protected habitat area off the coast of southern California also were largely unsuccessful.

Public policy is not static; it is responsive to factors such as changes in public opinion, electoral change, and the availability of resources. One of the most dramatic examples of the dynamics of politics and policy is the changing attitudes towards predator species such as the wolf. As early as 1630, the Massachusetts Bay Company paid trappers a one-cent bounty for killing wolves, a practice that continued with westward expansion. In 1705, the government took an even more aggressive role when the Pennsylvania colony hired the first predator control agent, who was paid to kill wolves using public funds. Throughout the 1800s, the public was uniformly supportive of policies such as strychnine poisoning and, eventually, the use of steel-jawed traps and rifles to kill unwanted predators. The U.S. Forest Service, responding to complaints by ranchers who

Table 10.1 Endangered Species Box Score (listings and recovery plans as of September 30, 1999)

Group	*Endangered*		*Threatened*		*Total Species*	*Species with Plans*
	U.S.	*Foreign*	*U.S.*	*Foreign*		
Mammals	61	248	8	16	333	48
Birds	74	178	15	6	273	76
Reptiles	14	65	22	14	115	30
Amphibians	9	8	8	1	26	12
Fishes	69	11	42	0	122	91
Clams	61	2	8	0	71	45
Snails	18	1	10	0	29	20
Insects	28	4	9	0	41	27
Arachnids	5	0	0	0	5	5
Crustaceans	17	0	3	0	20	12
Animal Subtotal	356	517	125	37	1,035	366
Flowering Plants	550	1	135	0	686	530
Conifers	2	0	1	2	5	2
Ferns and Others	26	0	2	0	28	28
Plant Subtotal	578	1	138	2	719	560
Grand Total	934	518	263	39	1,754	886

Total U.S. Endangered 934 (356 animals, 578 plants)
Total U.S. Threatened 263 (125 animals, 138 plants)
Total U.S. Species 1,197 (481 animals*, 716 plants)

*There are 1,775 listings (1,213 U.S.). A listing is an E or a T in the "status" column of 50 CFR 17.11 or 17.12 (the Lists of Endangered and Threatened Wildlife and Plants). The following types of listings are combined as single counts in the table: species listed both as threatened and endangered (dual status), and subunits of a single species listed as distinct population segments. The endangered population only is tallied for dual-status populations (except the olive ridley sea turtle, for which only the threatened U.S. population is tallied). The dual status species include Stellar sea lion, gray wolf, piping plover, roseate tern, green sea turtle, olive ridley sea turtle, bull trout, chinook salmon, sockeye salmon, and steelhead in the United States, and argali, chimpanzee, leopard, and saltwater crocodile elsewhere. Distinct population segments tallied as one include the coho salmon, chum salmon, bull trout (and the chinook salmon, sockeye salmon, and steelhead already mentioned). Several entries also represent entire genera or even families (including lemurs, gibbons, sifakas, uakaris, Achatinella tree snails, etc.).
Source: U.S. Fish and Wildlife Service, Division of Endangered Species <http://endangered.fws.gov/boxscore>.

were losing livestock to predators, began paying trappers to kill wolves on national forest grazing lands, and by 1915, a full-fledged wolf eradication program was underway. Eventually, local governments, livestock associations, and ranchers paid a tax to fund trapping operations. As a result, the wolf was virtually eradicated from the eastern United States by the 1880s, and by 1914, most wolves in the Western plains states had been killed, with only a few pockets persisting in the Southwest.

Federal policy changed with the passage of the 1973 Endangered Species Act, providing nominal protection for wolves because their numbers and habitat had been diminished. But there was a conflicting USFWS policy that permitted the killing of wolves that could be identified as predators. In 1978, a group of environmental organizations challenged the policy, and eventually, a U.S. Federal District Court judge ruled that wolves could be trapped only after a significant predation had occurred and that efforts must be directed at capture rather than killing.[18]

The court case did not resolve the wolf issue, however. State fish and game agencies had considerable discretion in determining how to implement the ESA and the court's ruling, with environmental organizations clamoring for a strict interpretation of the law's intention to conserve a threatened or endangered species. The USFWS responded with a new policy of attempting to reintroduce wolves to the same areas of Wyoming and central Idaho, where they had previously had a policy of killing them. In 1995, twenty-nine wolves from Canada were brought to Yellowstone National Park in an effort to build up the population, along with sixty wolves that had migrated on their own from Canada into Montana. The recovery program's goal is to remove the wolf from the endangered species list altogether by establishing breeding pairs — a project expected to cost $6.7 million by 2002. One federal judge ruled the government's wolf recovery program illegal in 1997, ordering wolves removed from Yellowstone — an action that pitted agricultural interests against the Earth Justice Legal Defense Fund and the National Audubon Society.[19] In March 2000 the 10th Circuit Court of Appeals overturned the 1997 ruling, allowing the wolf reintroduction in Yellowstone to continue.

But the wolf controversy did not stop with the Yellowstone program. A similar proposal to reintroduce wolves into New Mexico and Arizona as members of "experimental, nonessential" populations became equally controversial in 1997. Thousands of public comments on the proposal were received, and more than a dozen public hearings were held. Eventually, biologists released eleven Mexican gray wolves on the Arizona–New Mexico border, and initially the project appeared to be a success. The captive-reared wolves stayed away from cattle, gained weight, and reproduced within weeks of their release. But several wolves were later found shot to death, with environmental groups pointing the fingers at ranchers, and local officials in the area accusing the federal government of meddling in the local economy. The controversy over wolves stretched further in 1998 when the Interior Department announced a plan to remove about twenty-five hundred wolves in Minnesota, Michigan, and Wisconsin from the ESA because their populations were becoming safe from extinction. (See "Another View, Another Voice: Michael Finley: Superintendent, Yellowstone National Park.")

The wolf policy is a mixture of politics and symbolism, with one observer characterizing the program as "the line in the sand that divides the old West from the new. Both sides want us to see this as a distillation of all endangered species

Another View, Another Voice

MICHAEL FINLEY
Superintendent,
Yellowstone National Park

The reintroduction of the wolf into Yellowstone National Park has involved an untold number of participants, from ranchers convinced the animal is a predator unworthy of protection to environmental organizations who see the wolf's return as symbolic of the nation's commitment to endangered species. The conflict involves conservation biologists, officials from the twenty-two counties and three states surrounding Yellowstone, animal rights activists, and ordinary citizens. At the center of the controversy is Michael Finley, Superintendent of Yellowstone National Park.

Finley grew up in the West, and received a bachelor of science degree in biology from Southern Oregon State College (now Southern Oregon University) in 1970. He continued his studies there for another year in the environmental education program, focusing on outdoor education. But his degree did not take him into the schools; rather, he began a long career in public service that had made him one of the most experienced park service employees in the nation.

Initially, Finley worked part-time and as a seasonal employee with the U.S. Forest Service — a job typical of those intending to become a park ranger — his ultimate goal. "I had no idea that I would become an administrator," he says, "because all I really wanted was to work in a national park." Over the years, he began a slow and steady climb up through the National Park Service (NPS) hierarchy, learning the myriad aspects of park management, such as law enforcement, species conservation, human resources, road maintenance, concessions management, and public relations. By the time he was named Superintendent of Yellowstone in November 1994, he had already served as the superintendent of two of the park service's "big four:" Yosemite and Everglades National Park. He spent one year away from the day-to-day operations of the parks when he served in the legislative division of the NPS in Washington, D.C. There, he learned how difficult it was to coordinate what he calls "the political team" — the scores of agencies beside the NPS that affect park management. While working actively with members of Congress for support of NPS programs and budgets, his duties also brought him into contact with other bureaucracies within the Department of the Interior and the Department of Agriculture, providing him with the background and context in which park policy is made.

Finley has been a visible and outspoken advocate for the national parks, even filing a controversial suit against the state of Florida during the Bush administration to protect the Everglades. During the Clinton presidency, he considered the wolf reintroduction program as one of two major accomplishments while at Yellowstone. In 1994, prior to the species' protection controversy,

(continued)

he had strongly opposed the development of the New World gold mines in Montana. He joined with environmental groups in opposition to further mining near the park, emphasizing both the real and the potential damage to the greater Yellowstone ecosystem. Initially, Finley's position did not meet with the support of the president, whose interest was focused on a broad and eventually unsuccessful amendment to the 1872 General Mining Law. When Clinton learned of the mining project's impact, Finley would later be told by the secretary of the interior that "you have the longest leash in the world," enabling Finley to take his case to the media and the public. Congress eventually enacted legislation that provided a $62 million buyout of the mining property, including funds for reclamation of sites that had previously been damaged. Finley notes that this solution meant the mine owners received appropriate compensation for their private property and the federal government was able to salvage acreage that further protected Yellowstone's resources.

President Clinton also became a supporter of the wolf reintroduction program after Finley gave the president a tour of the park's wolf recovery facilities. Finley believes that through such one-on-one lobbying, he has been able to provide visitors, whether it be the president, members of Congress, or media representatives, an honest and reasoned view of the controversy. After all, he says, "politics is a competition of ideas."

conflicts, as a simple question of either/or."[20] The controversy is far from over and is notable because it so clearly indicates how policy is responsive to the political environment. Poisoning wolves was relaxed under one president's administration and totally lifted when another president took office. The public accepted predator control laws for centuries and then changed its mind as science began to play a more important role in the policy process. In some ways, policy "success" was even further politicized when the Clinton administration ordered the USFWS to prioritize the delisting and reclassification of certain species. Recovery efforts also became media events, as was the case in 1998 when Interior Secretary Bruce Babbitt announced that the peregrine falcon's numbers had increased sufficiently to be removed from the federal list of endangered species. In 1970, pesticide poisoning had reduced the bird's numbers to only thirty-nine pairs in the continental United States; by the time of Babbitt's announcement, an estimated sixteen hundred breeding pairs were thought to exist in North America. Babbitt used the occasion in Stone Mountain, Georgia, to release a small falcon from its cage, commenting, "The Endangered Species Act is working. It's a part of our American spirit and heritage."[21] While the peregrine's delisting was highly publicized and applauded, it also could be seen as a policy that favors high-profile species over those that are less attractive or well known. Similar extinction struggles are still faced by thousands of species, with only a few, such as the prairie dog and desert bighorn sheep, the beneficiaries of public support and media attention.[22]

Perhaps the most controversial of the contemporary elements of species recovery are habitat conservation plans (HCPs). The process of developing these plans stems from two sections in the ESA that provide the means for federal agencies to authorize, fund, or carry out development projects while insuring that such projects would not jeopardize the existence of the species. However, private and nonfederal developers were not covered by the statute, creating problems if a project might result in the killing, harming, or harassment of a threatened or endangered species. In 1982, Congress amended the ESA by allowing the creation of HCPs, which allow development to continue even if there is a threat to a species, as long as some form of conservation mitigation takes place. A landowner can be issued a permit to legally proceed with an activity that would otherwise be illegal and harmful to a species by enhancing or restoring a degraded or former habitat, creating new habitats, or establishing a buffer area around existing habitats. The compromise concept was designed to allow developers, environmental groups, and government agencies to come up with "creative partnerships" without halting development altogether or placing a burden on private property owners.

Initially, HCPs involved mostly small parcels of land of less than one thousand acres; by the end of the decade more than two hundred permits for HCPs had been issued with hundreds more in some stage in the permit process. Over time, the permits have often covered projects exceeding 500,000 acres — large-scale, regional developments that have been criticized by environmental groups as violating the spirit of the ESA.

Among the more noteworthy HCPs is the landmark 1993 agreement (renewed for another ten years in 1998) that created a partnership between the USFWS and a timber unit of Georgia-Pacific Corporation. Under the agreement, Georgia-Pacific agreed to conserve the habitat of the endangered red-cockaded woodpecker on its four million acres of timberlands in the Southeast. Under the plan, company foresters locate active clusters of the birds, which nest in living pine trees and live in family units called groups. The groups typically consist of a breeding pair and up to four helping birds. Once a group is located, the company maintains and protects buffer zones, prohibits new road building in the area, and provides adequate foraging habitat. There is also active cooperation among biologists from the public and private sectors who work with the USFWS officials to learn more about the bird's habitat and range needs. Meanwhile, the company is permitted to continue its logging activities.[23] Similar plans have been established for multispecies protection in other states, allowing companies to continue timber operations on private lands that disturb the habitat of more than a single animal.

Despite these proposals, the ESA is more likely to be the subject of debate in the judicial arena rather than in Congress, where amendments and repeal attempts have made little progress. Many of the disputes involve private property owners who have sued for compensation for economic losses they believe they are entitled to under the Constitution when the government "takes" their land by declaring it part of an endangered or threatened species' habitat.[24] In 1975, the USFWS had expanded its definition of "harm" to a species by including any action which caused the destruction of critical habitat, even if the species itself was not harmed. In a 6–3 decision in 1995, the U.S. Supreme Court upheld the federal government's definition of what constitutes "harm" under a policy developed under George Bush. The administration had agreed to allow logging in areas that had been declared critical habitat for the threatened Northern spotted owl. In *Babbitt v. Sweet Home Chapter of Communities for a Greater Oregon,*[25] the latter a timber-industry-sponsored group, the court ruled that the common meaning of the term "harm" is broad and in the context of the ESA would encompass habitat modification that injures or kills members of an endangered species. The majority of the court also noted that the statute had been reasonably interpreted, while the dissenters on the court argued that the definition was so broad that it had the effect of penalizing actions regardless of whether they were intended or foreseeable.[26]

Environmental organizations hailed the *Sweet Home* decision as precedent for protecting entire ecosystems rather than individual species and believe that it gives government agencies such as the Fish and Wildlife Service more discretion in implementing the law. But groups within the environmental opposition called upon Congress to take action to alter the ESA. One critic called the court ruling "one more step down the road to agency control" and said it gave administrative agencies much more power than the Constitution intended.[27]

There is a growing wave of opinion that the debate over the future of endangered species (and biodiversity in general) is becoming more political and less scientific in nature. Some observers of the process believe that the most important decisions about species survival are being made by political appointees who make policy only in response to the groups who provide financial support for their benefactors. This produces, they argue, a system in which there is a natural tension between politicians and scientists, and as the issue of conserving biodiversity become more important, it inevitably becomes more political.[28]

Environmental group leaders note that there are three factors that make it difficult to keep biodiversity on the public agenda: a lack of an easily identifiable opponent, a lack of any immediate impact on human life-styles, and a lack of cohesiveness by large groups around the widespread preservation of species. It is difficult, they say, to generate support or to motivate groups to mobilize to action even though species are becoming extinct because people's daily lives do not appear to be affected. The most difficult task seems to be convincing people, despite their concerns for endangered species, that there is a relationship between their own activities and the causes of endangerment. As a result, public attention begins to dissipate as policymakers realize the full costs of implementing protection measures.

One of the paradoxes of both the ESA and the CITES agreements is that a species is not protected until its population becomes so low that it is likely to become extinct. When that happens, recovery becomes both inefficient and costly. Recovery then begins to compromise the activities of other agencies (international, federal, state, and local), which must change their policies to accommodate the situation, increasing the probability of conflict. What this tells us about the future of endangered species and their habitats is that their protection requires the building of a much broader political constituency than currently exists. The actions of isolated organizations dedicated to the preservation of an individual species are unlikely to convince policymakers that there is a need for change. Instead, public policy is more likely to be politicized by groups whose economic prospects are influenced by what happens to their future.

THE FOREST DEBATE

While the protection of endangered species has been the center of the biodiversity controversy during the last three decades, an even longer running debate has continued over the world's forests, which cover almost one-third of the Earth's surface land. The issue is complicated by the fact that the planet is home to a variety of forest ecosystems, from the ancient forests of the United States, to the boreal forests of northern Canada and Russia, to the tropical forests circling the equator between the Tropic of Cancer and the Tropic of Capricorn. The management of forest resources has become an interest of global concern because in many instances, the conflicts that have erupted represent a duel between the "haves" and the "have nots." The issue has pitted environmental activists from urban areas against rural landowners, and representatives of industrialized nations against Third and Fourth World nations who have accused developed countries of "economic imperialism" in their attempts to control the fate of other countries' natural resources. The physical and biological diversity of forests, the large number of forest owners with often conflicting objectives, and increasing demands for wood for fuel, paper, shelter, and artistic uses have made forest management especially challenging for policymakers.

This section of the chapter examines the forest debate from two perspectives. First, it provides an overview of the United States' timber management policy and the agencies charged with protecting forest resources. Second, it examines the global dimension of the ways in which other nations have attempted to preserve boreal and tropical forest diversity.

THE U.S. TIMBER MANAGEMENT POLICY

About one-third, or approximately 730 million acres, of the U.S. land area is forested, two-thirds of which (about 480 million acres) is considered timberland, capable of growing commercial crops of trees. The federal government owns about 20 percent of those lands, with 7 percent owned by state and local governments, 1 percent by Native American nations, 58 percent by private nonindustrial owners, and 14 percent by the forest industry. American timber management is complex, and involves concerns about jobs, economic diversity, endangered species and their habitats, and global warming. At opposite ends in the policy debate are timber companies and environmental groups, with federal agencies caught squarely in the middle.

Federal stewardship of the nation's forest resources can be traced back to 1873, when the American Association for the Advancement of Science petitioned Congress to enact legislation to protect and properly manage U.S. forests. Despite the creation of a special bureau, the Division of Forestry, timber management practices were rife with scandal and exploitation. Forest policy was truncated by a division of responsibility between the Division of Forestry (in the Department of Agriculture) and the General Land Office (in the Department of the Interior). In 1901, the Division of Forestry changed its name, becoming the Bureau of Forestry, and four years later, became the Forest Service. From 1910 to 1928, the agency concerned itself primarily with fire prevention and control, and Congress had little power over forests on private lands.[29]

It was not until the Forest Service gradually began increasing the harvest of national forest land after World War II that the agency became the target of environmental interests. The need for timber that resulted from postwar economic growth was in conflict with public demand for recreational use of the nation's forests. Congress perceived the Forest Service as a commodity and income-producing agency, and timber harvests increased from 3.5 to 8.3 billion board feet during the decade of the 1950s.[30] In addition to competing public pressures, the development of a comprehensive federal forest policy was thwarted by the lack of congressional direction other than broad mandates.[31] As a result, the Forest Service operated under the dual traditions of planning — utilitarian and protective — that were the legacy of its first chief, Gifford Pinchot, who believed that wise use and preservation of forest resources were compatible goals. The resulting policy — multiple use — meant that the national forests were to serve competing interests: ranchers seeking land for grazing their livestock, recreational visitors seeking to spend their leisure time outdoors, and miners hoping to make their fortunes on as yet undiscovered lodes.

As a response to the fledgling environmental movement that advocated the setting aside of more wilderness areas, Congress enacted the Multiple-Use Sustained-Yield Act (MUSYA) of 1960, followed by the Forest and Rangeland Renewable Resources Planning Act (RPA) of 1974, and the National Forest Management Act (NFMA) of 1976. The MUSYA gave equal footing to the use of forests for recreation, grazing, and wildlife as well as timber and watershed uses, although there was little direction as to how the law was to be administered. Critics argued that the Forest Service was out of step with the emerging ethic of environmentalism, and the agency became perceived as an enemy of the people. Congressional leaders began to recognize the growing criticism over the federal government's lead of long-term planning, and the increasing polarization of forestry issues between the timber industry and environmental groups. Both the RPA and its amendments (the NFMA) provided the Forest Service with some direction, requiring inventories of forest resources and an assessment of the costs and benefits of meeting the nation's forest resource needs.

Although the legislation satisfied some critics, forest policy was far from complete, and the agency came under fire from its own employees, who alleged the Forest Service had been captured by timber interests and was inconsistent in its implementation of the law. In 1988, former staffer Jeff DeBonis founded a group called the Association of Forest Service Employees for Environmental Ethics (AFSEEE) as a way of encouraging its members to speak out against agency policies and abuses.[32] The organization began as an in-house protest against the Forest Service policy of clear-cutting — the logging of all trees within a given stand. The practice, in addition to being aesthetically unpleasing, often leads to erosion and has been widely criticized by environmental groups. DeBonis's organization marked one of the first times government employees had rallied against a particular cause, although some observers felt his actions were not constructive, given the Forest Service's history of institutional loyalty.[33] But DeBonis and his group believed the agency had forgotten its mission of serving the public and had become totally politicized.[34]

Today, the nonprofit organization includes not only Forest Service employees, but also other government resource managers, concerned citizens, and activists whose primary goal is to hold the agency accountable for responsible land stewardship. Program objectives include the redefinition of timber as an outcome of land management objectives, rather than as a commodity, with ecosystem integrity as the highest priority, keeping the public informed about resource management, protecting diversity and restoring resource productivity, and fostering and developing a land management ethic among citizens, agencies, and elected officials.[35]

Current forest policy has evolved from battles between environmental groups and timber companies during the 1980s, when the Reagan and Bush administrations supported massive logging in the Pacific Northwest. At one point, more than five million board-feet of timber were being cut per year in Washington and Oregon.[36] The most heavily logged areas were also home to several endangered or threatened species, including the Northern spotted owl. In 1991, a federal judge ordered a ban on logging until a species recovery plan for the bird was adopted. The controversy continued for two more years until 1993, when the Clinton administration brought the parties together in an attempt to work out a compromise. The result was the Northwest Forest Plan, an ecosystem management proposal that covered twenty-four million acres of forest in three states. Under the proposal, up to 1.1 million board-feet of timber could be harvested, allowing some mills to continue operation. The program has now entered into the policy implementation stage. The Forest Ecosystem Management Assessment Team, a group of more than one hundred scientists, has been given responsibility for coordinating the plan. Their efforts are complicated by the fact that over the last century, logging has been conducted in a haphazard manner that has created a quilt of heavily logged and reforested areas throughout the region. Full implementation means tying these patches of land together while balancing timber harvests and ecosystem protection.[37]

Many environmental organization leaders believe the plan has been a failure, charging that old growth forests far from urban political constituencies have been heavily logged. There is also criticism that at least initially, the program did not adequately protect key watersheds, approximately eight million acres of which are within the boundaries covered by the plan. Supporters, however, argue that the new timber regulations immediately reduced logging 80 to 85 percent below levels of the 1980s — a change few ever imagined would be possible. However, there is yet to be a systematic evaluation of the new forest program — the final stage in the policy process. Thus far, as implementation continues, much of the measure of success or failure of Clinton's policy is based upon conjecture and anecdotal evidence.

Symbolic of the debate over old growth is the Headwaters Forest Agreement, a plan to halt logging in the largest old-growth forest in private ownership in the world. The property, owned by Pacific Lumber, a unit of the Houston-based company MAXXAM, Inc., is also home to dozens of endangered species. After more than a dozen years of negotiations, the California legislature and Congress appropriated funds in late 1998 to purchase about 7,500 acres of land, including just over three thousand acres of uncut ancient forest. In addition, the agreement gives fifty-year protection for an additional eight thousand acres. The legislation also included economic assistance to timber-dependent areas and the development of a watershed analysis.

While state and federal officials applauded the long-sought agreement, it still did not meet with the approval of some environmental organizations because Pacific Lumber still can log its remaining 200,000 acres of forests. One group, the Environmental Protection Information Center, said the conservation plan was a "license to kill" endangered species.[38] But the land acquisition is exemplary of the all-or-nothing attitude of the less moderate environmental groups, who have called for an all-out ban on logging in old-growth areas. More likely is a reduction in the subsidies paid by the government for roads that allow timber companies to reach forested areas. One 1999 study conducted by the John Muir Project, an activist group associated with the Earth Island Institute, estimated that the federal program costs taxpayers more than $1.2 billion a year.[39]

Another shift in U.S. forest policy occurred in 1999 when U.S. Forest Service Chief Mike Dombeck announced that the agency would change its focus to more watershed protection, more wilderness, and less logging. In order to try and reshape the agency to reflect new forest performance standards, Dombeck said that the agency's employees would be evaluated chiefly by how well they improve soil erosion, stream purity, wildlife and fish abundance, watershed health, and other ecological features. This is an abrupt change from the traditional goal of board-feet targets for logging used previously. He called for "an invigorated land ethic" that would restore clear-cut lands and bring back endangered species — goals that many groups applauded, but to which they also expressed skepticism.[40] Whether or not the Forest Service is successful may well depend upon the policies of future presidents and Congress. In this instance, forest policy is greatly influenced by the tides of partisanship that are part of the electoral process.

THE GLOBAL DIMENSION

Deforestation is an equally volatile issue outside the United States. The boreal forests of the far North comprise nearly one-third of the world's timberland, serving as a major carbon sink as well as home to plants and animals and to a million indigenous people who have lived in the forests for centuries. Massive logging in Canada has disrupted ecosystems, displaced native peoples, polluted rivers with toxic chemicals used in the bleaching of pulp, and subsidized major multinational corporations. An estimated 90 percent of boreal logging is clear-cutting, and 25 percent of these areas do not regenerate as topsoil erodes away during and after logging, which also destroys permafrost, the layer below the topsoil that acts as a heat reservoir in the winter. As the permafrost retreats, risks to the forests from fires, pests, and species composition grows; the downward spiral contributes to the threat of global climate change as the carbon sink is lost and carbon from dead trees is increasingly released into the atmosphere.[41]

Logging of similar forests in Russia is occurring even faster in an effort to generate much-needed foreign currency. Clear-cutting, combined with emissions from smelters and radioactive pollution, poses a serious threat to forests throughout the former Soviet Union. Scandinavian forests, largely in private hands, are facing similar problems. Private landowners log old-growth forests next to lands where trees are protected. While reforestation is standard practice and a few companies have switched to chlorine-free production of paper, biodiversity has suffered. There are major challenges to boreal forests throughout the world: below-cost timber subsidies that waste resources, minimal environmental review of proposed logging efforts, disposal of timberlands that are home to indigenous peoples, and large-scale clearcutting that threatens the sustainability of forest production.[42]

Since almost all boreal forest policy is governed by sovereign nations rather than by international accord, individual countries have approached timber management in their own way. British Columbia, for example, has developed an ambitious program to replant forest lands that were heavily harvested in the nineteenth and early twentieth centuries. Little value had been assigned to forests, which were continuously cut so the land could be used for agriculture. By the 1940s, officials realized that the provincial forests were not limitless, and timber companies began replanting areas that had been clear-cut. The Forest Act of 1947 recognized the forests as economic resources and established the goal of ensuring a perpetual supply of timber under the principle of sustained yield forestry. By the early 1970s, provincial officials began to realize that logging rates were not sustainable, as timber cuts continued to climb as the promise of immediate jobs and profits overwhelmed a projected loss of sustainability. Modernization of logging technology resulted in job losses as timber harvests leveled off and increasing international competition impinged on profits. Preservationists lobbied successfully for the creation of parks that also reduced the potential supply of timber.[43] In 1993, the government, prompted by projections that forest harvests were likely to decline by 15–30 percent over the next fifty years, established a Forest Sector Strategy Committee to find ways to balance the competing values of forests and review policies that protect watersheds, wildlife, and the rights and concerns of indigenous peoples.[44]

British Columbia is an important case study in forest management because of its biological, cultural, and geographical diversity. Nearly two-thirds of the Canadian province is forested, providing over 60 percent of the province's export revenues (estimated at over $17 billion a year). Unlike the United States, where the federal government retains control of lands with public domain forests, in British Columbia, 94 percent of the land is publicly owned but managed by the provincial government. The provincial leaders make decisions as to whether or not the lands are best used for recreation, mining, or logging, or set aside as preserves and parks.

Timber policy in the province has been shaped by rapid population growth and accompanying development during the 1990s, along with the increasing clout of environmental organizations like the Forest Alliance of British Columbia and the Western Canada Wilderness Committee. Along with the Sierra Club and Greenpeace, these groups focused attention on the large temperate rainforest on the west coast of Vancouver Island near the Clayoquot Sound. The area is nearly pristine, with huge tracts of ecologically sensitive habitat and one of the largest protected old-growth forests in North America. While environmental groups sought to ban logging and to establish the area as a protected park, timber interests sought to log the area, supported by the indigenous Nuu-chah-nulth people, whose interests in the forest were primarily economic.

Although the Clayoquot controversy is far from over, the provincial government has established an extremely elaborate forest management program to protect the area in its present natural state. What makes this forest policy particularly noteworthy is that it was framed by environmental and timber groups based on scientific studies rather than simply rhetoric. Both sides brought in their own foresters and biologists, attempting to convince policymakers of the scientific validity of their claims. The result, as one observer notes, has been a debate imbued with scientific uncertainty crafted by knowledge brokers who continue to attempt to frame forest management policy in their own terms.[45]

Similar problems plague the world's tropical rainforests, four-fifths of which are concentrated in nine countries: Bolivia, Brazil (with one-third of the worldwide total), Columbia, Gabon, Indonesia (with another one-third), Malaysia, Peru, Venezuela, and the Democratic Republic of Congo. There are two major issues currently being addressed by global policymakers. One, although there is a lack of precise information about the rate of loss, there is consensus among scientists that tropical forests are disappearing at an alarming and ever-increasing rate. Two, there is also agreement that failure to effectively manage tropical forests can result in a number of negative impacts, including the loss of wood products for fuel and other uses, soil erosion, global warming, shrinking populations of plants in the wild, destruction of fish breeding areas, and loss of biological diversity and wildlife habitat.

Deforestation in tropical areas occurs primarily on lands not held by private citizens, especially in developing areas, where over four-fifths of closed forest areas is public land. In some countries, nearly 100 percent of all natural forest is government owned, giving officials total authority over the use and preservation of the land. Thus, the rates of deforestation vary considerably from one region of the world to another.

The logging of tropical forests and their products has been occurring for nearly five hundred years, beginning with the collection of rare and valuable spices such as pepper and cinnamon by Southeast Asian traders. However, early merchants tended to collect only what they wanted and did not destroy the forests in their search for spices. During most of the nineteenth century, Europeans sought African hardwood for furniture but left the rest of the forest intact. Latin American forests, in contrast, were often burned to the ground as Spanish settlers established colonial outposts and set up plantation agriculture, with the export of agricultural commodities quickly proving to be a lucrative enterprise for several nations. The United States entered the picture in the 1880s when U.S. investors edged out their Spanish competitors and built huge sugar processing facilities dependent upon crops in Cuba and in the Pacific islands of Hawaii and the Philippines. The sugar barons' quest for increased profits meant that increasingly more forest acreage was cleared and sugar cane became the primary vegetation in many areas, pushing out tropical woods. The logging of native forests for sugar cane was followed by devoting massive acreage to growing tropical fruits, such as bananas in Costa Rica and Nicaragua.[46]

In the 1920s and 1930s, international journals of forestry documented the rapid destruction of tropical forests, but there was little political attention to the problem at that time, as was the case between World War II and the advent of the international environmental movement in the early 1970s. The more highly publicized issues of pollution crowded the top of the environmental protection agenda, especially in industrialized nations. It was not until the early 1980s that international organizations, such as the UN's Food and Agriculture Organization (FAO), the UN Development Programme, and the World Bank began to systematically review scientific literature on deforestation.

Some of the forest protection issues are of relatively recent origin. In southern Chile, for example, widespread logging did not begin until the 1980s, when native trees were cut and ground into small chips that are shipped to Japan to be processed into paper. Although thirty million acres of Chilean forest are protected in reserves, the nineteen million acres estimated to be in private hands are often destructively cut by landowners seeking quick profits. The forestry industry has grown into one of Chile's main export earners. Attempts by groups such as the California-based Ancient Forests International and Chile's National Committee for the Defense of the Flora and Fauna have been largely unsuccessful in convincing the Chilean government to enforce existing regulations that limit cutting and provide for restoration. Few violators are prosecuted and even fewer are convicted by Chilean courts.

Now, as some countries' tropical forest resources are being depleted, international attention is being focused on regions where commercial logging was previously limited or inaccessible. Since the demand for tropical woods has not slowed, logging cartels are looking at areas of New Guinea, China, and New Caledonia, considered "hot-spot" regions of destruction. This means that more nations, by necessity, will become stakeholders and involved in the debate over forest diversity.

Efforts to protect tropical forests are much better funded and organized than attempts to preserve the Earth's ancient and boreal forest regions. Environmental organizations throughout the world have rallied against tropical deforestation, agreeing, for the most part, on the urgency of the problem. But there is also a gulf that separates the groups in their approaches to what should be done.

Globally, there is a division between the more radical groups seeking to ban trade in timber from virgin rainforests (such as the World Rainforest Movement), and more traditional groups, primarily in the United States, that believe the solution is to "green" the development process. Mainstream organizations such as the World Resources Institute and Friends of the Earth have supported the World Bank's efforts to improve economic conditions in developing countries. Other groups, such as Greenpeace, have established tropical forest units within their organization and attempted to lobby government officials to add more land to existing forest reserves, such as Costa Rica's Monteverde Cloud Forest. Indigenous peoples's groups, such as India's Chipko Andalan movement, have attempted to resist state encroachment upon their homelands. The groups are seeking to control not only forest practices, but also mining, the siting of dams, and other projects that affect natural resources and land management.

To slow the world demand for exotic woods, the more radical groups have proposed a ban on the sale of tropical timber. They want the International Tropical Timber Organization (ITTO) to severely restrict timber harvests and trade. The organization administers the 1984 International Tropical Timber Agreement, but critics argue that the group has the somewhat contradictory role of both protecting forests and regulating the timber trade upon which many of its member nations depend. Some attempts have been made to reduce trade in tropical wood under CITES, which covers both fauna and flora. In 1997, the United States worked out a compromise with Brazil to allow the United Nations to monitor trade in mahogany, although environmental groups had sought to have mahogany products included on a list that would have allowed only controlled trade. Developing nations have been critical of the United States and environmental groups for failing to recognize the desire of their people to overcome widespread poverty in areas dependent upon forest products and their allied jobs, including shipping and processing industries.

Other than an outright ban on timber, other solutions to tropical deforestation vary in their practicality and level of international support. The World Wildlife Fund and Friends of the Earth, for example, believe that the equipment and the types of forest management being used in these regions needs to be modernized. Current harvesting practices, they argue, are inefficient and waste much of the forest's resources. They have called for an end to existing logging practices and feel that technological advances could bring about extraction that is more compatible with sustainable management. Other observers believe that a complete restructuring of timber taxing and sales practices is needed, since governments in these areas receive only a fraction of the rents from logging. Virtually all tropical countries also provide generous tax incentives for timber processing and logging, with the benefits accruing to the wealthiest strata of the population. The most commonly voiced solution is the creation of forest reserves, which many researchers argue is the only way to save tropical forests at this point. They believe that destruction is proceeding too fast for restoration to be effective because a damaged tropical forest does not regenerate quickly. The idea is costly, even when coupled with the concept of debt-for-nature swaps that allow developing countries to repay outstanding loans to industrialized nations and lending institutions by establishing forest reserves as a way of paying off their foreign debt. But even the most optimistic estimates show that tropical deforestation is outpacing any current attempts to slow the rate of loss.

NOTES

1. B. J. Bergman, "Wild at Heart," *Sierra,* January–February 1998, 28.

2. Glen Martin, "State Experts in Race to Save White Abalone from Extinction," *San Francisco Chronicle,* July 7, 1998, A1.

3. U.S. Executive Office of the President, Council on Environmental Quality, *The Global 2000 Report to the President,* vol. 1 (Washington, DC: Government Printing Office, 1980), 37.

4. U.S. Executive Office of the President, U.S. Council on Environmental Quality, *The Evolution of National Wildlife Law* (Washington, DC: Government Printing Office, 1977), 17. One of the critical decisions of this period, *Geer v. Connecticut,* 161 U.S. 519 (1896), upheld a state law regulating the transportation of game birds outside Connecticut. Despite the narrow legal issue raised in the case, it is considered to be the bulwark of the state ownership doctrine even today.

5. One of the classic books on the issue of animal smuggling and poaching is John Nichol's *The Animal Smuggler* (New York: Facts on File, 1987). See also Susan Lieberman, "Japan Agrees to Phase Out Trade in Endangered Sea Turtles," *Endangered Species Technical Bulletin,* 16, nos. 7–8 (1991): 4–6. The issue has also involved illegal trade in ivory, due in part to political instability and diminished government support for antipoaching efforts in the Democratic Republic of Congo, which have allowed poaching to gradually creep back upward.

6. See "Elephant Skin and Bones," *The Economist,* February 29, 1992, 48; Peter Aldhous, "Critics Urge Reform of CITES Endangered List," *Nature,* 355 (February 27, 1992): 758–759; Peter Aldhouse, "African Rift in Kyoto," *Nature,* 354 (November 21, 1991): 175; and Steven R. Weisman, "Bluefin Tuna and African Elephants Win Some Help at a Global Meeting," *New York Times,* March 11, 1992, A8.

7. See Robin Sharpe, "The African Elephant: Conservation and CITES," *Oryx,* April 1997; Susan L. Crowley, "Saving Africa's Elephants: No Easy Answers," *African Wildlife News,* May–June 1997; and John Tuxill, "Losing Strands in the Web of Life: Vertebrate Declines and the Conservation of Biological Diversity," WorldWatch Paper 141, May 1998, 61–62.

8. See Nels Johnson, *Biodiversity in the Balance: Approaches to Setting Geographic Conservation Priorities* (Washington, DC: Biodiversity Support Program, 1995); Dana Clark and David Downes, "What Price Biodiversity?" *Center for International Environmental Law* (1995): 5–6; Lamont C. Hempel, *Environmental Governance: The Global Challenge* (Washington, DC: Island Press, 1996); and Lawrence E. Susskind, *Environmental Diplomacy: Negotiating More Effective Global Agreements* (New York: Oxford University Press, 1994), 102–103.

9. David E. Pitt, "A Biological Treaty to Save Species Becomes Law," *New York Times,* January 2, 1994, 1:4; Kal Raustiala and David G. Victor, "The Future of the Convention on Biological Diversity," *Environment, 38,* no. 4 (May 1996): 17–20, 37–45.

10. Bob Benenson, "Conferees' Interior Initiatives May Get Clinton's Veto," *Congressional Quarterly Weekly Report,* September 23, 1995, 2883–2884.

11. James A. Tober, *Wildlife and the Public Interest: Nonprofit Organizations and Federal Wildlife Policy* (New York: Praeger, 1989), 24.

12. For a perspective on the role of hunters in wildlife conservation, see Roger L. Disilivestro, *The Endangered Kingdom: The Struggle to Save America's Wildlife* (New York: Wiley, 1989). On the role of the recreational fishing industry, see George Reiger, "Good Vibes," *Field and Stream,* April 1995, 16–17, 22.

13. Tober, *Wildlife and the Public Interest,* 48.

14. Grassroots ESA Coalition *Mission Statement* (Battle Ground, WA: 1995).

15. "President Clinton: Saving America's Natural Treasures," press release, April 22, 1998, available at <http://www.pub.whitehouse.gov/uri-res/12R>.

16. "Back from the Brink," *People, Land, and Water,* June 1998, 20.

17. See Tober, *Wildlife and the Public Interest,* 59–83; Mark Crawford, "The Last Days of the Wild Condor?" *Science,* 229 (August 30, 1985): 845; David Phillips and Hugh Nash, *The Condor Question: Captive or Forever Free?* (San Francisco, CA: Friends of the Earth, 1981); and William W. Johnson, "California Condor: Embroiled in a Flap Not of Its Own Making," *Smithsonian,* December 1985, 73–80.

18. See *Fund for Animals v. Andrus,* 11 E.R.C. 2189 (D. Minn. 1978).

19. There are numerous viewpoints on the controversy. See, for example, Rick McIntyre, *A Society of Wolves* (Stillwater, MN: Voyageur Press, 1993); and Rocky Barker, *Saving All the Parts: Reconciling Economics and the Endangered Species Act* (Washington, DC: Island Press, 1993), 175–198.

20. Renee Askins, "Releasing Wolves from Symbolism," *Harpers,* 290 (April 1995): 16.

21. Pam Easton, "Peregrines Make a Comeback," August 25, 1998, available at <http: www.abcnews.com/sections/science/DailyNews/peregrine980825.html>.

22. See, for example, Rick Lyman, "Weighing Protections for Prairie Dogs," *New York Times,* January 12, 1999, A10; and Glen Martin, "Bighorns Get Special Status for Survival," *San Francisco Chronicle,* March 6, 1999, A18.

23. "Georgia-Pacific Unit, U.S. Fish and Wildlife Service Renew Landmark Agreement to Protect Endangered Red-Cockaded Woodpecker," press release, October 23, 1998.

24. See Lettie McSpadden, "Environmental Policy in the Courts," in *Environmental Policy in the Courts,* 3d ed., ed. Norman J. Vig and Michael E. Kraft (Washington, DC: Congressional Quarterly Press, 1997), 168–186.

25. 115 S. Ct. 2407 (1995).

26. See John H. Cushman, Jr., "Environmentalists Win Victory, But Action by Congress May Interrupt the Celebration," *New York Times,* June 30, 1995; and "Regulating Habitat Modification," *Congressional Digest,* March 1996, 72.

27. "Sweet Home v. Babbitt," *Update* (Stewards of the Range, Boise, ID, August 1995), 3.

28. Jeffrey A. McNeely, "Report on Reports," *Environment,* 34, no. 2 (March 1992): 25. See also Richard Tobin, *The Expendable Future: U.S. Politics and the Protection of Biological Diversity* (Durham, NC: Duke University Press, 1991).

29. For an overview of forest policy, see Frederick W. Cubbage, Jay O'Laughlin, and Charles S. Bullock III, *Forest Resource Policy* (New York: John Wiley and Sons, 1993); Christopher McGrory Klyza, *Who Controls Public Lands? Mining, Forestry, and Grazing Policies, 1970–1990* (Chapel Hill: University of North Carolina Press, 1996), 67–107; and Elizabeth May, *At the Cutting Edge* (San Francisco, CA: Sierra Club Books, 1998.

30. See Paul Culhane, *Public Lands Policies* (Baltimore, MD: Johns Hopkins University Press, 1981).

31. See Charles F. Wilkinson and H. Michael Anderson, *Land and Resource Planning in the National Forests* (Covelo, CA: Island Press, 1987).

32. See, for example, Paul Schneider, "When a Whistle Blows in the Forest," *Audubon,* 7 (July 1990): 42–49; and Jim Stiak, "Memos to the Chief," *Sierra 75,* no. 4 (July–August 1990): 26–29.

33. For perspectives on the U.S. Forest Service and its employees, see Herbert Kaufman, *The Forest Ranger: A Study in Administrative Behavior* (Baltimore, MD: Johns Hopkins University Press, 1960); and Harold K. Steen, *The U.S. Forest Service: A History* (Seattle: University of Washington Press, 1976).

34. See William Dietrich, *The Final Forest: The Battle for the Last Great Trees of the Pacific Northwest* (New York: Penguin Books, 1992): 161–168.

35. For more on AFSEEE, visit the website at <http://www.afseee.org>.

36. See Dietrich, *The Final Forest.*

37. Chris Carrel, "A Patchwork Peace Unravels," *High Country News,* November 23, 1998, 1.

38. Greg Frost, "Critics Call California Redwoods Plan 'Extortion,'" Reuters News Service, September 1, 1998. The Headwaters controversy can also be viewed from the perspective of the California Resources Agency at <http://ceres.ca.gov>, March 18, 2000.

39. "Logging Costs Taxpayers $1.2 Billion A Year," Environmental News Network, April 16, 1999.

40. Hal Bernton, "Forest Chief Asks Reduced Logging," *The Oregonian,* March 30, 1999; Paul Rogers, "New Ethic for Forests Unveiled," *San Jose Mercury News,* March 29, 1999.

41. Anjali Acharya, "Plundering the Boreal Forests," *WorldWatch* (May–June 1995): 21–29.

42. Ibid.

43. Western Canada Wilderness Committee, "How to Save Jobs in the B.C. Woods," *Educational Report, 12,* no. 8 (Winter 1993–1994).

44. See B. Willems-Braun, "Buried Epistemologies: The Politics of Nature in (Post) Colonial British Columbia," *Annals of the Association of American Geographers,* 87 (1997): 3–31; and Government of British Columbia, *British Columbia's Forest Renewal Plan* (Victoria, BC: Queen's Printer, 1994): 1–5.

45. For a general background on the Clayoquot Sound area, visit the website of the Forest Alliance of British Columbia at <http://forestalliance.org>. See also Ronald MacIssac, Anne Champagne, and Ron MacIssac, eds., *Clayoquot Mass Trials: Defending the Rainforest* (Philadelphia, PA, and Gabriola Island, BC: New Society Publishers, 1994); and Tzeporah Berman, *Clayoquot and Dissent* (Vancouver, BC: Ronsdale Press, 1994). The evolution of British Columbia's forest management policies is outlined by Sheldon Kamieniecki in "Testing Alternative Theories of Agenda Setting: Forest Policy Change in British Columbia, Canada," paper presented at the annual meeting of the American Political Science Association, Boston, 1998.

46. See Richard P. Tucker, "Five Hundred Years of Tropical Forest Exploitation," in *Lessons of the Rainforest,* eds. Suzanne Head and Robert Heinzmann (San Francisco, CA: Sierra Club Books, 1990), 39–52.

FOR FURTHER READING

Richard K. Baydack. *Practical Approaches to the Conservation of Biological Diversity.* Washington, DC: Island Press, 1999.

Anne Becher. *Biodiversity.* Santa Barbara, CA: ABC-CLIO, 1999.

Hanna J. Cortner and Margaret A. Moote. *The Politics of Ecosystem Management.* Washington, DC: Island Press, 1999.

Curtis H. Freese. *Wild Species as Commodities.* Washington, DC: Island Press, 1988.

Fred Gale. *The Tropical Timber Trade Regime.* Basingstoke, Hampshire: Macmillan Press, 1998.

Lakshman D. Guruswamy and Jeffrey A. McNeely, eds. *Protection of Global Biodiversity: Converging Strategies.* Durham, NC: Duke University Press, 1998.

Michael B. Jenkins and Emily T. Smith. *The Business of Sustainable Forestry.* Washington, DC: Island Press, 1999.

Elizabeth May. *At the Cutting Edge.* San Francisco, CA: Sierra Club Books, 1998.

Ralph Schmidt, Joyce K. Berry, and John C. Gordon, eds. *Forests to Fight Poverty: Creating National Strategies.* New Haven, CT: Yale University Press, 1999.

Beverly Peterson Stearns and Stephen C. Stearns. *Watching, from the Edge of Extinction.* New Haven, CT: Yale University Press, 1999.

Christopher Tollefson, ed. *The Wealth of Forests: Markets, Regulation, and Sustainable Forestry.* Vancouver: University of British Columbia Press, 1999.

CHAPTER 11

The Human Explosion: Managing Population Growth

While you are reading these words four people will have died from starvation. Most of them children.

— Dr. Paul R. Ehrlich, *The Population Bomb* (1968)[1]

In the six seconds it takes you to read this sentence, eighteen more people will be added [to the population.]

— Dr. Paul R. Ehrlich, *The Population Explosion* (1990)[2]

In 1968, when Paul Ehrlich's book, *The Population Bomb,* first appeared, most Americans were shocked. Ehrlich predicted a population explosion accompanied by massive famine and starvation — a prophecy that nevertheless did not come to pass. The reason? In the mid-1970s there was a slight decline in the global population growth rate, and it looked as though the population might stabilize at about 10.2 billion toward the end of the next century. Many demographers called Ehrlich an alarmist, while others argued that population growth was actually a positive force because it accelerated progress and development, forcing humanity to use more ingenuity and resourcefulness. Regardless of the timeliness of the prediction, Ehrlich was correct in pointing out that the Earth is a closed system, with limited resources. At the same time, the world's population is increasing at a current rate of three people every second — a quarter of a million new mouths to feed every day. Ehrlich's comments in his 1990 book brought into focus an issue that has profound economic, ethical, religious, and political implications. What will happen to the environment if steps are not taken to *manage* population growth?

Although the rate of human population growth has slowed over the last three decades, a population the size of Germany is being added to the world each year, primarily in developing regions like Africa. The result is depicted in the plight of these African refugees.

One of the key phrases often used to answer that question, and one that has appeared often in this book, is *sustainable development.* The term is used to describe policies that balance the needs of people today against the resources that will be needed in the future. It takes into consideration policies related to agriculture production, energy efficiency, health, reduction of poverty, and reduction in consumption. Individuals practice this concept when they recycle cans, bottles, newspapers, and plastics, carpool to work or bicycle instead of commuting alone in automobiles, turn their thermostats down to use less electricity, or install solar heating systems in their home. Each of these actions is taken in recognition that the Earth's resources are not unlimited and that we must restrict our consumption of those resources.

The possibility of sustainable development is built on the idea of carrying capacity. The carrying capacity of an ecosystem is the limit of resource consumption and pollution production that it can maintain without undergoing a significant transformation. If the carrying capacity is exceeded, then life cannot continue unless it adapts to a new level of consumption or receives external resources. Carrying capacity is affected by three main factors: the size of the human population, the per capita consumption of resources, and the pollution and environmental degradation resulting from consumption of each unit of resources. The task of residents of any ecosystem is to find what level of resource consumption and pollution production is sustainable. That may not be obvious until it is too late, but there are some intermediate indicators, such as the buildup of pollution and an increase in the resultant harms or a decline in a resource as it is depleted faster than it is replenished.

Population growth and consumption in the wealthy countries are the primary sources of global environmental threats. While population growth rates have stabilized in these nations, consumption of resources and generation of pollution and wastes continue to grow. But population growth in the developing world increases the pressure on the biosphere. The problems of environmental degradation and poverty are intricately intertwined. Many of the most pressing environmental problems are the by-products of modern, industrialized life. As one writer put it, "poverty can drive ecological deterioration when desperate people over exploit their resource base, sacrificing the future to salvage the present." Environmental decline "perpetuates poverty, as degraded ecosystems offer diminishing yields to their poor inhabitants. A self-feeding downward spiral of economic deprivation and ecological degradation takes hold."[3] People in the developing world depend immediately and directly on natural resources for their survival. In their struggle for survival, the poor of the world are likely to harm their environment and make their survival even more tenuous. Further, as resources are stretched for survival, poorer countries will have even less ability to mediate the effects of climate change and other problems, unlike residents of the developed world who will have the resources to protect themselves against at least some environmental threats.

The idea of sustainable development as used by the World Bank, United Nations, industry groups, and others is a very optimistic concept that assumes that economic growth will produce the wealth to pay for technological innovations that reduce environmental impacts. Free trade, neoliberal restructuring of national economies and policies, and economic growth and consumption are all compatible with environmental sustainability. But this view of sustainability clashes with the idea of carrying capacity and scarcity.[4] Studies by ecologists point to an inevitable crisis as exponential growth clashes with the finite resources of Earth. Developed by the Club of Rome, the Limits to Growth computer model, one of the earliest projections of the future of natural resources, technology, and pollution, concluded that by the year 2100 most nonrenewable resources would be exhausted, food supplies would dwindle, and massive famine and pollution would cause widespread deaths.[5] While there have been many critics of that study, few challenge the idea of limits; disagreements focus on when they will occur and how the variables interact.

Some optimists believe that pollution in the Western world "will end within our lifetime." They argue that the "most feared environmental catastrophes, such as runaway global warming," are unlikely. Environmentalism, "which binds nations to a common concern, will be the best thing that's ever happened to international relations." Nearly all technical trends are toward new devices and modes of production that are more efficient, use fewer resources, produce less waste, and cause less ecological disruption than technology of the past."[6] Others find that "just about every important measure of human welfare shows improvement over the decades and centuries" — life expectancy, price of raw materials, price of food, cleanliness of the environment, population growth, extinction of species, and the quality of farmland.[7] Some economists argue that we will never deplete resources — Earth's air, water, and crust will serve Earth dwellers for millions of years to come. The problem is not the existence of these resources, "but whether we are willing to pay the price to extract and use those resources."[8]

The optimists may be right in claiming that human ingenuity can respond to these problems and reverse these troubling trends. But the inexorable pressure from exponential growth threatens to overwhelm even the most optimistic projections. "We may be smart enough to devise environmentally friendly solutions to scarcity," one scholar has written, but we must emphasize "early detection and prevention of scarcity, not adaptation to it." But if we are not as smart and as proactive as optimists claim we are, "we will have burned our bridges: the soils, waters, and forests will be irreversibly damaged, and our societies, especially the poorest ones, will be so riven with discord that even heroic efforts at social renovation will fail."[9]

Population growth and the increased consumption and pollution accompanying it pose a profound challenge to the idea of ecological sustainability. This chapter explores the challenge of managing human population growth. It begins by presenting an overview of the scale of the global population boom and the factors that have caused the problems to be more acute in some areas than in others, placing U.S. population trends in perspective. It reviews the evidence for the assumption that there are not enough natural resources available, even with enhanced technology, to provide for the growing number of individuals born each year if present demographic trends continue into the new millennium. The chapter then outlines the political aspects of overpopulation and assesses the efforts by nongovernmental organizations (NGOs) and the UN to reduce birth rates and fertility through family planning programs. The chapter concludes with a brief summary of some of the challenges that population growth poses for policymakers.

TRENDS IN POPULATION AND PROJECTIONS

In 1798, Thomas Robert Malthus published "An Essay on the Principle of Population" in which he first argued that the "power of population" is indefinitely greater than the power of Earth to produce subsistence for humanity.[10] One of the ideas that has subsequently dominated the study of demography — the science of population — is demographic transition theory, a term used to describe a three-phase ecologic transition that leads to global overpopulation. In the first phase, human demands remain within limits that can be sustained by the environment, so there is enough food, water, and other resources for the needs of the population. In the second phase, human demands begin to exceed a sustainable limit and continue to grow. In the third phase, the ecosystem is unable to sustain the population, as there is little control over birth and death rates, and the system collapses.[11]

Although there has been criticism of the demographic transition theory,[12] there are many demographers who believe that Earth has already reached that third stage. The numbers of people already on the planet are staggering, and the projections for the future are considered even more alarming by some observers. The magnitude of growth in world population is disturbing, especially if we look closely at the last 150 years. Figure 11.1 provides a look at the milestone dates in world population growth from the year 1 C.E. through 1999 C.E.

As the growth curve indicates, while it took two hundred years (from 1650 to 1850) for the global population to double from five hundred million to one billion, it took only forty-five years (from 1930 to 1975) for it to double from two billion to four billion, and the trend continues. The UN Population Division projections through the year 2025 show an even greater increase, as seen in Figure 11.2. The world's total population is expected to grow from 5.6793 billion in 1995 to a projected 8.1771 billion by 2025.

One of the primary difficulties in making decisions about population policy is that, in the past, demographic data were often insufficient or contradictory, especially in developing nations. Since the 1970s, however, nearly every nation in the world has conducted some type of census or national population register. Studies of world population by various agencies and organizations have identified several critical trends in the growth figures.

First, there are differences in the ages of populations in the industrialized and developing worlds. At the beginning of the twenty-first century, about one of every three persons is a child; one of five, a person in the late teens or early

Figure 11.1 World Population Growth, 1 C.E. through 1999 C.E.

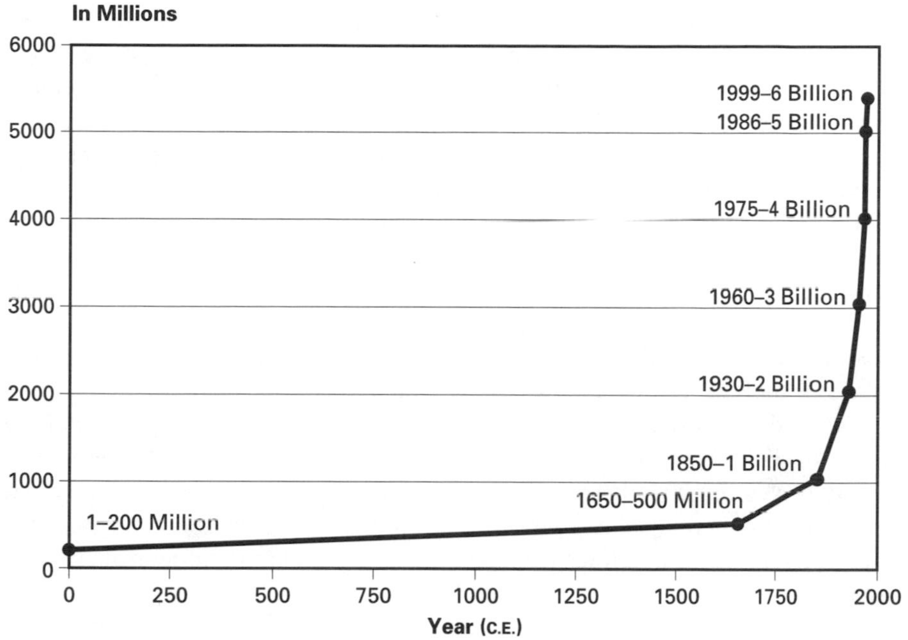

Figure 11.2 World Population Growth, 1995–2025

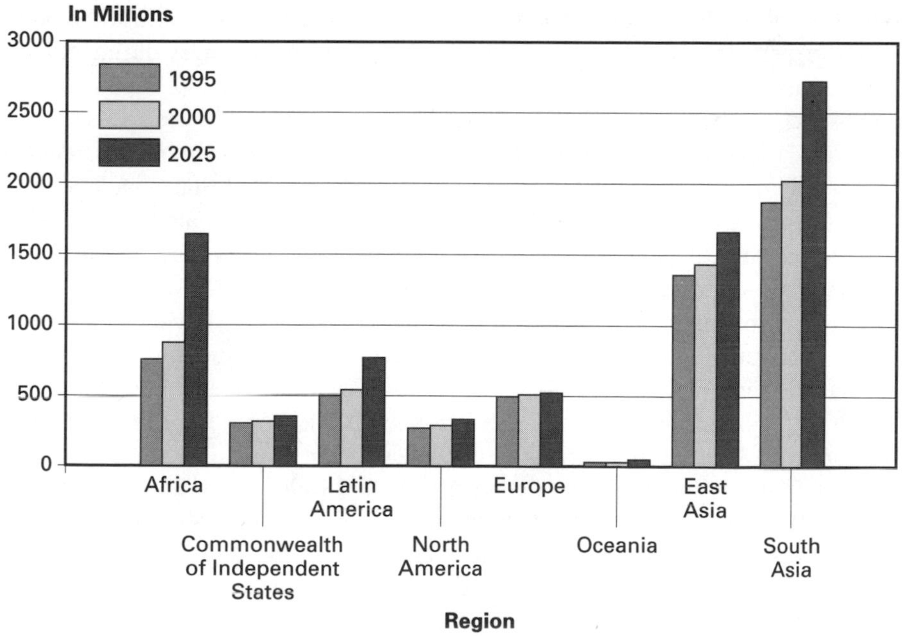

twenties, with the median global age being twenty-four. The most significant increase will be in the aged population; one of sixteen persons will be age sixty-five or older, with half of the world's elderly living in developing countries. The increasing number of older persons, when coupled with reductions in old-age mortality over the next four decades, will mean that there will be considerably greater demands upon the political system for social services and long-term care. Meeting the demands for the global aged will necessitate shifting resources from the young to the old.[13] At the same time, the majority of the population will be of childbearing age; although women are having fewer children today, there are more women giving birth. This is a critical demographic fact. Even if fertility rates decline, population growth will continue if the number of women of child-bearing age increases. More than a third of the world's population lives in countries where the mortality for young children is greater than one in ten, posing problems for health care, mobility, and productivity.

Second, the population is becoming more urbanized, with 45 percent of the world's peoples living in urban areas by mid-1990, 51 percent by the year 2000, and 65 percent by 2025.[14] Urban populations are growing at a much more rapid rate in the less developed regions of the world than they ever did in the industrialized nations, but that growth is less the result of people migrating from rural to urban areas than of high birth rates and low death rates in the cities.[15]

Third, the distribution of population varies considerably from continent to continent, which affects the population's economic well-being and impact on the environment. The four largest countries in the world account for virtually half the world's population but only 30 percent of the world's land surface. For example, the richest 15 percent of the world's population consumes more than one-third of Earth's fertilizer and more than half of its energy, while at the other extreme, perhaps one-quarter of the world's population go hungry during at least some seasons of the year. The vast majority of the world's peoples exist on per capita incomes below the official poverty level in the United States.[16]

Similar findings were reported in *The Global 2000 Report to the President,* a U.S. study of global population trends. The study reported that populations in sub-Saharan Africa and in the Himalayan hills of Asia have already exceeded their maximum carrying capacity — the number of people who can be sustained by the land — and the entire planet is approaching that level as well. The study goes on to document shortages in water supplies and food, as well as a loss of arable land, insufficient sources of energy, and massive extinctions of plant and animal species.[17]

Another important aspect of population growth is *where* it takes place. Population growth in the industrialized countries of the world has been relatively modest, rising about 15 percent between 1970 and 1990. In contrast, the population of developing countries grew by almost 55 percent during the same period, and the disparity is expected to grow even larger in the future. The executive director of the UN Population Fund (UNPF) notes that most of the increase in population growth will occur in Southern Asia, which now accounts for about a quarter of the world's population but will have nearly a third of the increase by the end of the century, and Africa, which has 12 percent of the population now but will account for nearly a quarter by 2000. These changes represent a radical shift in population, with areas such as Europe and North America growing very slowly and areas such as India, which will overtake China as the world's most populous country by 2030, experiencing rapid growth.[18]

Demographers have identified a number of factors to which population increases in some regions can be attributed. Some of those changes began to occur long ago, while others are more recent in origin. First, there have been dramatic changes in our way of life and ability to survive. Humans' transition from hunting and gathering to the agricultural revolution about eight thousand years ago removed much of the risk of dying from starvation, raising the world's overall standard of living, and high death rates kept the number of people in the world from growing rapidly until the mid-eighteenth century. Second, in the category of more contemporary change, the rapid acceleration in growth after 1750 was almost entirely the result of the declines in death rates, which occurred with the Industrial Revolution. Rapid advances in science lowered the death rate by finding cures for common diseases that had previously wiped out large segments of the population. The introduction of the pesticide DDT, for example, dramatically reduced deaths from malaria, which is transmitted by mosquitos, and similar victories reduced deaths resulting from yellow fever, smallpox, cholera, and other infectious disease. Similarly, the acknowledgment of the theory that germs were responsible for disease caused a gradual acceptance of basic sanitary practices such as washing hands and bathing, which further reduced the spread of disease. The impact of DDT and other health and technological advances can be seen clearly in Figure 11.1 where the growth curve begins its steep incline. Advances in medicine have also reduced infant mortality rates to the point where the birth rate continues to exceed the death rate — the bottom line in population growth. The result is that many fewer people die than are born each year.

Third, food production has increased, keeping up with population growth until the mid-1950s, when food became more scarce and prices began to rise in developing nations. By the mid-1960s, only ten nations grew more food than they consumed: Argentina, Australia, Burma, Canada, France, New Zealand, Romania, South Africa, Thailand, and the United States.[19] Now, demand for food outstrips availability in most of the undeveloped world. Food output per person declined 11 percent between 1984 and 1993. The fish catch per person has fallen by 7 percent. There are some indicators that human demands are approaching limits of natural resources to produce food because soil erosion, air pollution, aquifer depletion, and land degradation decrease agricultural productivity.[20]

Part of the problem are the barriers to food production resulting from public policies. As economic reforms have opened up the economies of some nations, food production has increased. But much of the arable land in the less developed countries is dedicated to the production of cash crops that are used to generate foreign capital to service debt or finance economic development. Consequently, food production for domestic use suffers. Commodity prices are unstable; when they are high, exporting nations benefit, as revenues exceed those that would result from growing food. However, as world commodity prices have fallen, less revenue is available for debt service and development, and countries have to import food to make up for the shortfall in food grown for local people. Trade agreements prohibit exporting countries from processing food, thereby increasing their profits; shippers, brokers, processors, and wholesalers all live in the most developed countries (MDCs) and capture the bulk of the profits from food sales. Foreign debt, assistance programs that promote cash crop production, pressures to generate foreign capital to pay for industrialization, inexorable pressure from population growth, and the increasing use of marginal lands for food production have combined to produce the food crisis in Africa and parts of Asia and Latin America.[21] The problem is not one of scarcity as much as it is of the economic system by which food is distributed. Foreign aid is also a problem: sending large shipments of food for distribution to poor nations sometimes disrupts domestic food production, drives down prices, and harms local farmers.

Fourth, climatic changes may affect the population problem even more. The effects of population growth may be exacerbated by global warming, according to a three-year report published by the Environmental Protection Agency. The study, which was conducted by fifty scientists in eighteen countries, used three computer models, which predicted a doubling, by the year 2060, of the greenhouse gases that may be responsible for a rise in Earth's temperature. If those increases continue, the result may be a decline in crop yields, especially in grain production in developing countries, and an increase in prices from 25 to 150 percent. The reduced supply, together with increased prices, is estimated to increase the numbers of those at risk from hunger in developing countries by between 60 million and 360 million and to increase the total of the world's hungry to 1 billion by 2060. Still unknown is the impact of the acquired immunodeficiency syndrome (AIDS) epidemic, which may have an even longer effect on population trends, especially in developing countries. Millions of people are thought to be infected with the human immunodeficiency virus (HIV), the majority of them in sub-Saharan Africa.

The pictures of starved and dehydrated children in Africa disguise a political reality, however. Although some of the problems associated with famine can be attributed to traditional food scarcity resulting from population increases and drought, some observers believe that the real issue is the radicalism of many African governments. One study of Ethiopia, for example, found that a long line of Marxist regimes and massive amounts of aid from the former Soviet Union exacerbated the traditional problems and resulted in persistent famine from 1983 to 1986. Despite $2 billion in worldwide aid, the Ethiopian government used its power to control food and water resources for purely political reasons.[22] In several African nations, millions of people have died because endless civil wars have made it impossible for other nations to safely bring in food and medical supplies. Even with a massive influx of aid in 1992, thousands of Somalis died each day because the country was in a state of virtual anarchy. Relief efforts were thwarted by roving bands of thugs who stole food and supplies as soon as they were brought in to refugee camps. Although the United States intervened alongside UN troops in 1992, many observers believe that Somalia's problems are exemplary of what is happening on much of the continent. (See "Another View, Another Voice: Stephen Moore: The Cato Institute.")

Not all of the forecasters have seen a vision of population doomsday, however. Others have a much more positive view of our ability to limit the desire to procreate or they point to errors in the population models that have been used to predict growth rates. One observer has termed the UN's projections as "so much statistical garbage," noting that the body has failed to accurately predict what is happening in major urban centers. In 1984, for example, the UN's World Population Conference demographers predicted that Mexico City's population would surge past seventeen million people, eventually overtaking Tokyo to become the world's biggest city, housing twenty-six million people by the year 2000. But in a 1996 study, the UN reported that Mexico City's population never did reach the seventeen million mark and was not likely to do so for another ten years. Most cities appear to reach a size beyond which urban problems such as pollution and congestion drive the population away in search of more liveable areas, as has been the case of cities such as London, New York, São Paulo, Rio de Janeiro, Cairo, and Calcutta.[23]

Critics have argued that the UN's population projections are "utterly unrealistic"; no allowance has been made for death rates rising as a result of problems connected with rapid population growth, including the need for an expanded food supply. New viruses and resistant strains of old viruses, along with general environmental deterioration, will likely bring about a population limitation resulting from a combination of plague, famine, or war.[24]

Last, there is more evidence that family planning efforts, discussed in more detail below, are beginning to pay off, especially in industrialized nations. If so, policy direction is likely to change somewhat to stabilize the world's population while focusing on women's rights, education, and children's health.

U.S. POPULATION TRENDS AND POLICIES

Although population growth management is a global issue, few Americans have much of an understanding of where the United States stands in relation to other countries. This is partly because historically population has been a nonissue and there have been few policies established to deal with either the composition or distribution of the nation's citizens. Most public officials have been reluctant to tackle the problem, mainly because of the sensitivity of the issues of birth control and abortion. Not until the 1960s did Congress begin to develop specific proposals to define the nature of the population problem, and it was not until the mid-1970s and the U.S. Supreme Court decision regarding abortion in

Another View, Another Voice

STEPHEN MOORE
The Cato Institute

The UNPF designated October 12, 1999, as "The Day of 6 Billion," marking, at least symbolically, the point at which the world's population passed another numerical threshold. The occasion was accompanied by worldwide reports on the significance of the six billion figure, since it indicates that population doubled in less than four decades. Once again, the alarms about the consequences of overpopulation and the resulting environmental crisis made headlines.

But for Stephen Moore, director of fiscal policy studies at the Cato Institute in Washington, D.C., the voices that call for population management and limitations on family size are just plain wrong. According to Moore, "There is no ethical, environmental or economic case for small families. For those of us who believe there is intrinsic value and dignity in every human life, we should celebrate, not decry, that there are now 6 billion human beings on the Earth."[1]

The Cato Institute, which was founded in 1977 as a nonpartisan public policy research foundation, is named after *Cato's Letters,* libertarian pamphlets that were part of the foundation for the American Revolution. Its staff members and researchers are considered by some to be among the country's leading advocates of free markets and limited government. The institute is ideologically aligned with several other conservative think tanks, including the Heritage Foundation and the American Enterprise Institute.

Moore joined the Cato Institute in 1990 after having served as a Fellow at the Heritage Foundation and as research coordinator for President Ronald Reagan's National Commission on Privatization. An economist who has written extensively on budgetary politics and fiscal policy, he also writes for *National Review* and served on *Time* magazine's board of economic advisors. His opinions on population frequently appear in the conservative *Washington Times*.

Moore denounces the predictions of most demographers, writing, "The population bomb propagandists have all the intellectual credibility of the Flat Earth Society." From his view, the key to understanding what the population increases mean stems from improved health and more wealth. He points to the increase in life expectancy (even in poor countries), decreases in infant mortality rates, declining birth rates in developing countries and a dramatic decline in famines in the last fifty years. He is especially critical of the UNPF and lobbied against congressional restoration of funding for the agency, saying, "It should be universally condemned for the evil acts in which it has participated." He refers to what he calls "population control fanatics in China" who have perpetuated "an ongoing genocide" and believes that the United Nations is promoting "a fundamentally anti-Christian philosophy." He also blames the world's hunger and environmental disasters on too much statism, perpetrated, he says, by the socialists behind the Iron Curtain.[2]

Moore and his colleagues represent a perspective on population that is not widely shared around the globe, especially among members of environmental organizations who fear the planet cannot absorb the estimated 2.9 billion people that will be born in the next fifty years. But his view also is indicative of the debate over ecology versus economy that has been raging since the 1960s.

For More Information

For more information on the Cato Institute, visit its website at <http://www.cato.org>.

Notes

1. Stephen Moore, "Defusing the Population Bomb," *Cato Today's Commentary,* October 15, 1999, 2–3.
2. Ibid., 1.

Roe v. Wade that the government was forced to address the issue directly.[25] Much of the U.S. population policy has subsequently focused on immigration and refugees and whether or not the government should lend support to international family planning efforts.

Several NGOs have been formed in the United States to try to bring attention to the problems of overpopulation. One of the first was the Washington, D.C.–based Zero Population Growth (ZPG), established in 1968 in response, at least in part, to Paul Ehrlich's book. ZPG advocates a sustainable balance of people that basically stays the same from year to year. In contrast, another organization, Negative Population Growth (NPG) which formed in 1972, seeks to slow, halt, and eventually reverse population growth through several extremely controversial measures, including a reduction in legal immigration to the United States to stabilize the population between 100 and 150 million rather than the current 250 million. NPF members seek to limit immigration to 100,000 persons annually, which they believe will encourage developing nations to solve their own environmental and population problems. They also advocate a massive increase in U.S. funding for population assistance programs for Third World countries and the use of noncoercive economic and social incentives for family planning. Their goals are similar to another U.S. organization, Population-Environment Balance, which was founded in 1973 and has lobbied extensively on the immigration issue. Other groups have focused on the direct provision of services rather than on policy making. In 1957, for example, the Pathfinder Fund began providing family planning services that include distribution of contraceptives, educational materials, medical kits, and training in developing countries.

The abortion issue has been raised for groups not directly associated with the UN programs or with population management. Prolife groups have also targeted environmental organizations such as the National Audubon Society, National Wildlife Federation, and Trout Unlimited, which had supported a moderate policy of voluntary family planning.[26] Threatened with boycotts of their advertisers and massive letter writing campaigns, the groups have personally witnessed the power and tenacity of the prolife movement.

Today, the United States has one of the higher population growth rates among developed nations in the world. Demographers predict that significant population growth is predicted to occur over the next fifty years, with the Census Bureau expecting a total U.S. population of 392 million by 2050, an increase of about 50 percent over the current population. About one-third of the growth will be attributable to immigration, specifically directed toward six states: California, New York, Texas, Florida, New Jersey, and Illinois. Immigration and births of those already living in this country will bring about dramatic changes in the ethnic population of the United States. In 1995, about one-fourth of the population was composed of racial minorities, which is defined as anyone who is not white and non-Hispanic. But demographers also predict that in the next fifty years that fraction will double, with nearly half the country composed of racial minorities. The Hispanic population, for example, is expected to rise from 22.5 million in 1990 to just less than ninety million by 2050, if immigration and high fertility rates continue. As a result, their share of the total population would increase from about 9 percent in 1990 to 22 percent in 2050.[27]

It is likely that the increase in the ethnic population will eventually be mirrored by changes in the political landscape, whether through an increase in the number of elected minority officials or by political backlash against immigrants. During the mid-1990s, several states, led by California, considered citizen initiatives or legislation to limit immigration, to reduce social services available to nonresidents, or to declare English the nation's "official" language.[28]

GLOBAL FAMILY PLANNING EFFORTS

While most nations have not adopted explicit policies to manage their population, there is implicit agreement that the key to balancing resources to people is by reducing fertility, especially in those countries where resources are scarce. Family planning efforts vary considerably in various parts of the world, and thus some countries have made more progress in reducing birth rates than have others. Information about birth control and access to contraception are known to be major causes of declining fertility, according to a World Bank study that reported that family planning programs account for 39 percent of the decline in population in developing countries.[29]

A historical review of the family planning policies shows that such programs have evolved relatively recently, considering that artificial birth control was illegal in most countries one hundred years ago. In the United States, birth control advocates first spread their doctrine of voluntary fertility in the late nineteenth century, based on the dual concerns of women's health and a rapidly growing poor population. Leaders such as Margaret Sanger, Marie Stopes, and Paul Robin were criticized for destroying the family structure, and opponents were successful in lobbying Congress to pass the Comstock Law in 1873, which outlawed advertisements or prescriptions of contraceptives. The federal statute was repealed in 1916, but similar state laws stayed on the books for another fifty years.[30]

Globally, the picture is different. Most of the countries that initially adopted family planning programs were Asian and included both large and small nations. India became the first country to adopt an official policy in 1951 to slow population growth, but no other nations followed suit until nearly a decade later, when Pakistan, the Republic of Korea, China, and Fiji adopted similar policies. In the early 1960s, when oral contraceptives and intrauterine devices were first becoming available, about sixty million women, or 18 percent of the women of childbearing age in the developing world, were practicing family planning. By the mid-1990s, about 55 percent of couples in developing countries were using contraception to control their fertility, with about 75 percent in the industrialized nations of the world.[31] Two factors have been identified as the causes behind this growth of an international family planning movement. First, there have been various cultural shifts, such as a growing sense of individualism and a corresponding decline in the perceived need to follow traditional ways. Second, people began to develop an awareness that rapid population growth represented a threat to their economic well-being.[32]

But there are a number of economic, social, and religious reasons why countries have shunned family planning as a way of bringing the birth rate down, especially in centrally planned countries such as China and Cuba. In many of these cultures, families simply *want* more children, even though more babies means more mouths to feed. It may also mean more hands at work in the field or more help in caring for aging parents. Population limitation is in direct opposition to the teachings of the Catholic Church, which has encouraged procreation and discouraged birth control and abortion, as is the case in most Islamic nations. When Pope John Paul II assumed office in 1978, the Vatican took a more active role than previously in opposing abortion and contraception. In 1984, the Pope sent a statement to the head of the UNPF in which he noted that contraception "increased sexual permissiveness and promoted irresponsible conduct," a view that continues to represent the Vatican's perspective.[33] Many couples refuse to use birth control devices because of rumors and myths about their effectiveness. In India, women refused to use a loop-shaped intrauterine device when word spread that it would swim through the blood stream and reach the brain or give the man a shock during intercourse. Vasectomy has been only marginally successful because of fears by men that it reduced their virility. As a result, the use of contraception varies considerably from one nation to another.

Contraception use is generally highest in the nations of Europe and lowest in Africa — a trend mirrored in population growth rates. Some countries that have recognized the problem have taken steps to make contraception more available and acceptable, while others have made only nominal efforts. Government-sponsored family planning programs have been the primary mechanism for population control in most developing countries. About a dozen nations have established a cabinet-level ministry for population, generally in developing countries where the issue is considered serious enough to require an official program. The commitment is often not very firm, however, in countries with an Islamic or Roman Catholic religious tradition. The more successful efforts have been in countries where indigenous NGOs have been the most active. Working at the grass-roots level, NGOs appear to develop a greater sense of trust with people than programs offered by the government or foreign donors. They are also more adaptable to local circumstance and have more flexibility in their operations than do more structured programs.[34]

Generally speaking, economic inequality is the best predictor of fertility rates. Residents of poorer nations want more babies because they are a source of labor, while those in midrange economies choose goods over babies. Citizens of rich nations (such as the United States) can afford to have both — babies and goods. For them, family planning is less of a priority and there is little incentive to limit family size.

THE ROLE OF THE UNITED STATES

The UN has now become the primary agent of worldwide family planning programs and has made a number of efforts to address the overpopulation issue. The UN Fund for Population Activities was established as a trust fund in 1967, financed by voluntary contributions from members. During its first fifteen years, it allocated over $1 billion in family planning assistance to member states. Following the 1968 UN Conference on Human Rights, the "Tehran Proclamation" identified the ability to control one's fertility and therefore access to birth control as a basic human right. The UN organization, renamed the UN Population Fund, has held five world conferences: in Rome (1954), Belgrade (1965), Bucharest (1974), Mexico City (1984), and Cairo (1994). At the Bucharest conference, the UN's World Population Plan of Action was established, led by the United States and other industrialized nations that urged developing countries to set targets for lowering their fertility rates. Many Third World nations and Eastern bloc nations rebelled, accusing the UN of supporting efforts by former colonial masters to suppress emerging nations and limit the strength of their armies.[35] Ten years later, at the Mexico City conference, those misconceptions vanished as leaders from 150 nations committed themselves to a voluntary reduction in population growth and a strong national family planning program. Although there was continuing concern about the continuation of high population growth rates in developing nations, fertility rates had declined modestly since the Bucharest meeting.[36]

In the intervening years between the population conferences, the UN's Conference on Environment and Development, held in 1992 in Rio de Janeiro, indicated how hesitant delegates were to tackle the population issue head on. For example, the term "appropriate demographic policies" was substituted in conference documents for the more traditional phrase "family planning," and many of the representatives of NGOs were critical of industrialized countries, which they perceived as failing to take responsibility for their own overconsumption of resources. But the meeting did produce, as part of its Agenda 21, a chapter on demographic dynamics and sustainability. Delegates agreed that the role of women should be strengthened and their rights fully recognized and noted that governments should ensure that women and men have the same right to decide freely and responsibly on the number and spacing of the children. But representatives of the Vatican and the Philippines were successful in weakening the exact language on family planning and in removing any remarks on contraceptives.[37]

At the 1994 Cairo conference, the issue of abortion overshadowed nearly every other agenda item. Delegates reached an uneasy compromise after what one observer termed "a Vatican-led handful of countries held the meeting hostage."[38] The final document provided that abortions "should be safe" where they are legal and that they should "in no case . . . be promoted as a method of family planning."[39] Vatican officials argued that economic reform should be the major focus of global leaders: "Demographic growth is the child of poverty. . . . Rather than reduce the numbers at the world's table, you need to increase the courses and distribute them better."[40] Other religious groups and foundations launched campaigns aimed at drawing attention to overconsumption in the United States and other wealthy nations, paralleling arguments of economists that the United States needs to save and invest more and consume less.[41]

The "Program of Action," a 113-page document approved in April 1994 by the UN committee responsible for the Cairo meeting, provides the basic outline for a twenty-year plan to promote women's rights and reduce population growth to 7.27 billion by 2015. A central theme embraced by nearly every one of the 150 delegates was the empowerment of women.[42] While few participants were completely happy with the results of the report, as one observer put it, "conferences and documents like these never get out ahead of where the people who agree to them are comfortable. What these conferences do is take an aerial snapshot of where we're at."[43]

One of the most promising products of the conference was the creation of "Partners in Population and Development: A South-South Initiative," announced by ten developing countries that came together to share their successes in reducing population growth. These successful strategies include offering a wide range of choices for family planning and careful integration with local cultural and political conditions.[44] The Women's Environment and Development Organization, formed in 1989, played a major role in shaping the agenda of the Cairo meeting and promised to maintain the pressure on governments and international bodies to include gender equality and empowerment of women in family planning and reproductive health efforts.[45]

Many challenges remain, however, in determining how to finance and deliver family planning and related services in ways that are consistent with local religious, cultural, social, and economic conditions. In many less developed countries, family planning services are still widely seen as a First World idea. Much of the focus will have to be on those countries that have the greatest population growth rates and the fewest resources to help empower women.[46] Some of the success stories touted at the Cairo meeting have been questioned by other experts. Bangledesh is often cited as an example of a model program, having reduced the average number of children from more than seven to fewer than four per women between 1975 and 1994, with contraception use increasing from 19 percent to 45 percent in a decade. The achievements came during a time when the country faced severe socioeconomic problems, floods, and storms, which placed extraordinary pressure on the country's political and economic resources. But one of the critics of the program believes that the decrease in Bangladesh's fertility rate has come at the expense of women who were pressured to undergo sterilization and through the diversion of funds needed to support the country's primary health care system.[47]

The United States's role in global population management has been somewhat contradictory. The U.S. Agency for International Development (AID) began promoting large-scale national family planning programs funded through international aid in the early 1960s, providing health care workers in many developing countries. Congress first earmarked foreign assistance appropriations in 1968, with nearly $4 billion in assistance allocated through AID over the next two decades. Initially, the United States also supported UN programs for education and family planning. But during the administration of President Ronald Reagan, the United States adopted what came to be known as the Mexico City Policy — an abrupt change in policy direction. The United States cut off its support (as the major donor) of the UN Fund for Population Activities and the International Planned Parenthood Federation, the largest multilateral agency and the largest private voluntary organization providing family planning services in developing countries.

The sudden policy about-face became tied to the issue of abortion, even though U.S. law (the 1973 Helms Amendment of the foreign assistance act) explicitly prohibits government funding for abortion programs overseas and even though legal abortions are permitted in only a few countries. In 1985, the Kemp-Kasten Amendment to the foreign assistance act banned any U.S. contribution to "any organization or program that supports or participates in the management of a program of coercive abortion or involuntary sterilization." The passage of the legislation effectively cut off U.S. support to China's family planning program, which was alleged to have forced women to have abortions, despite denials by the Chinese government. Congressional attempts to restore the UN funding by stipulating that the money not be spent in China were vetoed by President George Bush in November 1989.[48] The Bush administration's position puzzled those who pointed out that, by cutting back its aid to the UN program, the United States was actually encouraging the demand for abortion in those nations where there are no other alternatives.

The United States stood virtually alone in its refusal to contribute to the UN program, having previously been the primary donor, contributing $38 million of the $122 million program budget in 1984. But after the U.S. policy change, Germany, Canada, the United Kingdom, Japan, and the Scandinavian countries increased their donations, with Japan becoming the major donor and exceeding what the United States previously contributed.[49] After years of congressional debate, the result was that from 1986 to 1992 the United States eliminated all contributions to the UN program, with only a few bilateral assistance programs remaining intact.

In 1993, the Clinton administration reversed prior policies and began restoring U.S. aid to the UN program, with $430 million earmarked for international population assistance — the most ever contributed in the history of the program. In 1996, Congress agreed to appropriate $385 million for international family planning assistance and defeated a proposal by House Republicans to limit assistance to any international program that spent its own funds on any kind of abortion-related services (everyone agreed that U.S. funds could not be used to provide these services). The law required another vote by Congress before the funds could be released, and one of the few pieces of legislation enacted during the first few months of the new Congress in 1997 released the funds.[50]

However, as the UNPF marked its thirtieth anniversary in 1999, it was clear that the reduced participation of the United States had taken its toll on the organization's efforts to build integrative reproductive health programs. A four-year decline in donor contributions resulted in a $72 million shortfall in 1999; available resources covered only two-thirds of the fund's commitments to country programs. The result, UN officials said, would be an additional 1.4 million unwanted pregnancies, 570,000 induced abortions, and over 670,000 unwanted births.

Responding to an urgent appeal for funds, the government of the Netherlands pledged an additional 10 million Dutch guilders (about $4.7 million) to the fund for 1999, with another $4 million awarded by the United Nations Foundation, created by media mogul Ted Turner. His group's contribution allocated $2.3 million to improve adolescent reproductive health in the Pacific region; about $1.1 million to promote Jordanian adolescent girls' health and well-being; and $707,726 to enhance the reproductive health of adolescents in the Russian Federation.

In July 1999, the U.S. Congress voted to restore funding to the UNPF in fiscal year 2000, due to increasing criticism of the U.S. role. The action was tied to another brokered agreement under which the United States would pay about $1 billion in back dues to the United Nations to retain its voting rights, with a restriction that the funds not be used for any international family planning groups that support abortion. Women's groups and organizations like Planned Parenthood described the action as a compromise that made the women of the world the bargaining chip.

IMPLICATIONS FOR POLICYMAKERS

Because population growth management is inextricably linked to other types of public policy, social, cultural, and religious beliefs, economics, and political forces that are constantly changing, it has become one of the most critical, yet unresolved, issues facing policymakers today. The consequences of population growth, regardless of the exact magnitude and timing, have considerable repercussions for the resources of both developed and developing nations. The problem is exacerbated by the substantial disagreement among scientists as to the seriousness of the problem, making it difficult for policymakers to decide what kind of action, if any, to take. There are also opposing views on whether the population issue ought to be addressed by individual nations, allowing them to develop policies to control their own fertility rates and resource use or whether the problem should be dealt with on a global scale by organizations such as the United Nations.

There are a number of reasons why population management has slipped from the top of the political agenda, both in the United States and globally. Biologist and "population buff" Garrett Hardin, who was at the forefront of the ethical debate over population management, argued that a change in public attitude is to blame, among other factors. He noted that population is a chronic problem rather than a critical one, with the media preferring the latter to the former. As a result, there is much more media interest in covering "crises" such as the continuing conflict in the Middle East than the fact that a quarter of a million people were born on the day that Iraq invaded Kuwait. He also pointed out that many people fail to make the connection between population size and problems like air pollution from too many automobiles. Finally, Hardin believed that population questions raise issues that might be perceived as being selfish, bigoted, provincial, or even racist — criticisms that he himself had to bear.[51]

In the United States, members of Congress have not made population a high priority because there is little political incentive to do so. There are few interest groups to support a particular policy and a lack of a strong constituency for policy change in a system where institutional fragmentation is the norm.[52] Most environmental organizations have only tangentially addressed population growth management, preferring instead to focus on more specific resource issues.

But the most important policy implication relates to whether or not there will be sufficient natural resources to sustain the growth in population, wherever it may occur. One of the key indicators is the adequacy of the food supply, which has thus far kept pace with population growth in all regions of the world except Africa. But most studies of world population projections note that world food production potential is dependent upon increasing the amount of land under cultivation and increasing inputs of capital and fertilizers. Developing countries seeking to modernize their agricultural practices risk causing additional harm to the environment, whether it be by cutting timber in order to grow crops or adding more chemicals to the soil and water supply. Another important consideration is whether there will be sufficient energy resources for the growing population. Developing countries seeking to modernize and grow will place additional demands on natural resources to produce the power needed for everything from household appliances to factories.

Last, there is still suspicion among developing nations that countries such as the United States are more interested in curbing population growth in poorer countries as a way of protecting the environment rather than concentrating on reducing excess consumption in wealthier nations. This view has been expressed at numerous international conferences and exemplifies the continuing divisiveness between the industrialized nations of the world that already have the benefits of development and those countries that are still seeking to attain them. Some in the South also contend that the real population growth problem is in the North, since the environmental and natural resource impact of each person in the wealthy world is many times that of residents of the developing world. If population growth is to be curtailed in the South to reduce pollution and resource use, it should be combined with restraint on the consumptive patterns of the North.

NOTES

1. Paul R. Ehrlich, *The Population Bomb* (New York: Ballantine Books, 1968). The statement is conspicuously placed on the cover of Ehrlich's book.
2. Paul R. Ehrlich and Anne H. Ehrlich. *The Population Explosion* (New York: Simon and Schuster, 1990), 9.
3. Alan B. Durning, *Poverty and the Environment: Reversing the Downward Spiral,* Worldwatch Paper 92 (Washington, DC: Worldwatch Institute, 1989): 40–41.
4. For further discussion of these issues, see World Commission on Environment and Development, *Our Common Future* (New York: Oxford University Press, 1987), and Robert Repetto, "Agenda for Action," in *The Global Possible: Resources, Development, and the New Century,* ed. Robert Repetto (New Haven, CT: Yale University Press, 1985): 496–519.
5. Donella H. Meadows et al., *The Limits to Growth* (New York: Universe Books, 1972).
6. Gregg Easterbrook, *A Moment on the Earth: The Coming Age of Environmental Optimism* (New York: Viking Penguin, 1995), xvi.
7. Julian Simon, "Pre-Debate Statement," in *Scarcity or Abundance? A Debate on the Environment,* ed. Norman Myes and Julian L. Simon (New York: W. W. Norton, 1994), 5–22.
8. Tom Tietenberg, *Environmental and Natural Resource Economics,* 3rd ed. (New York: HarperCollins, 1992), 356–357.
9. Thomas F. Homer-Dixon, quoted in William K. Stevens, "Feeding a Booming Population without Destroying the Planet," *New York Times,* April 5, 1994.
10. See Philip Appleman, ed., *Thomas Robert Malthus: An Essay on the Principle of Population* (New York: W. W. Norton, 1976). For biographical material on Malthus and his theories, see Jane S. Nickerson, *Homage to Malthus* (Port Washington, NY: Kennikat Press, 1975); David V. Glass, *Introduction to Malthus* (New York: Wiley, 1953); William Petersen, *Malthus* (Cambridge, MA: Harvard University Press, 1979); and Donald Winch, *Malthus* (New York: Oxford University Press, 1987).
11. See Maurice King, "Health Is a Sustainable State," *The Lancet, 336,* no. 8716 (September 15, 1990): 664–667. For a historical perspective on demographic transition theory, see the work of Kingsley Davis, "The World Demographic Transition," *The Annals of the American Academy of Political and Social Science, 237* (January 1945): 1–11; and George Stolntiz, "The Demographic Transition: From High to Low Birth Rates and Death Rates," in *Population: The Vital Revolution,* ed. Ronald Freedman (Garden City, NY: Anchor Books, 1964).
12. See, for example, Ansley Coale, "The History of the Human Population," *Scientific American, 231* (1974): 40–51; and Kingsley Davis, "The Theory of Change and Response in Modern Demographic History," *Population Index, 29,* no. 4 (1963): 345–366.

13. William H. Frey, "Global Aging," *HD Focus, 1,* no. 1 (Winter 1994), 13.

14. "Population Conference Set for 1994," *UN Chronicle, 28,* no. 2 (June 1991): 74.

15. See, for example, Richard E. Stren and Rodney R. White, eds., *African Cities in Crisis: Managing Rapid Urban Growth* (Boulder, CO: Westview Press, 1989).

16. William C. Clark, "Managing Planet Earth," *Scientific American, 261* (September 1989): 48.

17. U.S. Executive Office of the President, Council on Environmental Quality, *The Global 2000 Report to the President* (Washington, DC: Government Printing Office, 1980). For a different view of the need for a new strategy for sustainable agriculture, see David Norse, "A New Strategy for Feeding a Crowded Planet," *Environment, 34,* no. 5 (June 1992): 6.

18. Nafis Sadik, "World Population Continues to Rise," *The Futurist,* March–April 1991, 9–14. See also World Resources Institute, *World Resources 1994–95* (New York: World Resources Institute, 1994), 27–42.

19. Ehrlich, *Population Bomb,* 38.

20. Lester R. Brown, et al., *State of the World 1994* (Washington, DC: Worldwatch Institute, 1994), 4–5, 177.

21. Norman Myers, *Gaia* (New York: Oxford University Press, 1988), 46–48.

22. See Steven L. Varnis, *Reluctant Aid or Aiding the Reluctant* (New Brunswick, NJ: Transaction, 1990), 3.

23. See, for example, Fred Pearce, "Where Have All the People Gone?" *New Scientist, 149* (March 9, 1996): 48.

24. Paul R. Ehrlich, Anne H. Ehrlich, and Gretchen C. Daily, "What It Will Take," *Mother Jones, 20* (September–October 1995): 52–56.

25. See P. T. Piotrow, *World Population Crisis: The United States Response* (New York: Praeger, 1973).

26. Frank Graham Jr., "Thoughts," *Audubon, 92* (January 1990): 8.

27. Carl Haub, "Global and U.S. National Population Trends," *Consequences,* Summer 1995, 10. See also Sam Roberts, "Hispanic Population Outnumbers Blacks in Four Major Cities as Demographics Shift," *New York Times,* October 9, 1994, A34.

28. On the bilingualism debate, see Gilbert Narro Garcia, *Bilingual Education: A Look to the Year 2000* (Washington, DC: National Clearinghouse for Bilingual Education, 1994); James Crawford, *Hold Your Tongue: Bilingualism and the Politics of English Only* (Reading, MA: Addiston-Wesley, 1992); and Kenji Hakuta, *Mirror of Language: The Debate over Bilingualism* (New York: Basic Books, 1986).

29. Nathan Keyfitz, "The Growing Human Population," *Scientific American, 261* (September 1989): 123.

30. See Peter Fryer, *The Birth Controllers* (New York: Stein and Day, 1965); and James Reed, *From Private Vice to Public Virtue: The Birth Control Movement and American Society since 1930* (New York: Basic Books, 1978).

31. Frances Fitzgerald, " A Manageable Crowd," *The New Yorker,* September 12, 1994, 7–8.

32. See Ronald Freedman, "Family Planning Programs in the Third World," *Annals of the American Academy of Political and Social Science,* 510 (July 1990): 33–43.

33. Barbara B. Crane, "International Population Institutions: Adaptation to a Changing World Order," in *Institutions for the Earth: Sources of Effective International Environmental Protection,* ed. Peter M. Haas, Robert O. Keohane, and Marc A. Levy (Cambridge, MA: MIT Press, 1993), 365–366.

34. See Julie Fisher, "Third World NGOs: A Missing Piece to the Population Puzzle," *Environment, 36,* no. 7 (September 1994): 6–11.

35. See Jason L. Finkle and Barbara B. Crane, "The Politics of Bucharest: Population, Development, and the New International Economic Order," *Population and Development Review, 2* (September–December 1976): 87–114.

36. Werner Fornos, "Population Politics," *Technology Review,* February–March 1991: 43–51. See also Jason L. Finkle and Barbara B. Crane, "Ideology and Politics at Mexico City: The United States at the 1984 International Conference on Population," *Population and*

Development Review, 11, no. 1 (March 1985): 1–28; and Michael E. Kraft, "Population Policy," in *Encyclopedia of Policy Studies,* 2nd ed., ed. Stuart A. Nagel (New York: Marcel Dekker, 1994), 631–633.

37. See Michael Grubb et al., *The Earth Summit Agreements: A Guide and Assessment* (London: Earthscan Publications, 1993), 106–108.

38. Emily MacFarquhar, "Unfinished Business," *U.S. News and World Report* (September 19, 1994): 57.

39. United Nations Conference on Population, "Plan of Action," September 1994, Paragraph 8.25.

40. Alan Cowell, "Is This Abortion? *New York Times,* August 11, 1994.

41. Wade Greene, "Overconspicuous Overconsumption," *New York Times,* August 28, 1994.

42. Barbara Crossette, "Population Meeting Opens with Challenge to the Right," *New York Times,* September 6, 1994.

43. Barbara Crossette, "U.N. Meeting Facing Angry Debate on Population," *New York Times,* September 4, 1994.

44. Barbara Crossette, "A Third-World Effort on Family Planning," *New York Times,* September 7, 1994.

45. "Keeping Alive Cairo Goals for Women," *New York Times,* September 25, 1994.

46. Tim Carrigan, "Viewing Population as a Global Crisis, Cairo Conferees Have Missed the Point," *Wall Street Journal,* September 12, 1994.

47. For the conflicting observations, see B. Sison, "Bangladesh Succeeds with Family Planning," *New York Times,* October 6, 1994, A28; and Betsy Hartmann, "What Success Story?" *New York Times,* September 29, 1994, A25.

48. See Phillip Davis, "The Big O: Zero Population Growth," *Buzzworm,* November–December 1992, 54.

49. Peter J. Donaldson and Amy Ong Tsui, "International Family Planning Movement," *Population Bulletin, 45,* no. 3 (November 1990): 14.

50. P.L. 104–208.

51. Garrett Hardin, "Sheer Numbers," *E Magazine, 1,* no. 6 (November–December 1990): 40–47.

52. Kraft, "Population Policy," 635.

FOR FURTHER READING

Barbara Sundberg Baudot and William R. Moomaw, eds. *People and Their Planet: Searching for Balance.* New York: St. Martin's Press, 1999.

Lester R. Brown. *Beyond Malthus: Nineteen Dimensions of the Population Challenge.* New York: W. W. Norton, 1999.

Audrey R. Chapman, Ed. *Consumption, Population, and Sustainability: Perspectives from Science and Religion.* Covelo, CA: Island Press, 2000.

Garrett J. Hardin. *The Ostrich Factor: Our Population Myopia.* New York: Oxford University Press, 1998.

James W. Hughes and Joseph J. Seneca, eds. *America's Demographic Tapestry: Baseline for the New Millennium.* New Brunswick, NJ: Rutgers University Press, 1999.

Bill McKibben. *Maybe One: A Personal and Environmental Argument for Single-Child Families.* New York: Simon and Schuster, 1998.

John J. Rogers. *People and the Earth: Basic Issues in the Sustainability of Resources and Environment.* New York: Cambridge University Press, 1998.

Anup Shah. *Ecology and the Crisis of Overpopulation: Future Prospects for Global Sustainability.* Northampton, MA: Edward Elgar, 1998.

Michael Tobias. *World War III: Population and the Biosphere at the End of the Millennium.* Portland, OR: Bear and Company, 1998.

WTO TAKE OUR BREAD
BIO WTO TECH

CHAPTER 12

Emerging Issues for the Twenty-First Century

A series of looming crises and ultimate catastrophe can only be averted by a massive increase in political will, We have the technology, but we are not applying it.
— Dr. Klaus Topfer, Executive Director, United Nations Environment Programme[1]

Throughout recorded history there have been prophecies about the fate of humanity and the future of the planet. The majority of those predictions have been negative, "doom-and-gloom" forecasts that envision a world of ruin, whether through the forces of nature or the sins of the people. The predictions are found in religious tracts and holy books, in the mystical visions of seers, in the entrails of animals, in oral histories passed down from generation to generation, and in sophisticated computer models. Predictions are important because they affect behavior — individuals make decisions based on them and policymakers are guided by them.

Contemporary environmental policies are a reflection of the knowledge we have about natural phenomena, mathematical modeling, human needs, economics, and politics. Unfortunately, that knowledge is often biased or incomplete, and as a result, the decisions political leaders make are not always accurate or appropriate.

Many of the negative predictions about population growth and sustainability cited in Chapter 11 are still popular and guide many of the world's leaders in their policy making. By the mid-1990s, however, there emerged a contrarian view of the earth's future. One of the most widely regarded books was journalist Gregg Easterbrook's *A Moment on the Earth: The Coming Age of Environmental Optimism.* Unlike the majority of his colleagues, Easterbrook offered a series of optimistic premises foreshadowing a world that would make significant progress in ending pollution, avoiding runaway global warming, and using efficient technology that would require fewer resources and produce less waste. The doomsday predictions of many environmentalists, Easterbrook says, are placing them on the right side of history but on the wrong side of the present, "risking their credibility by proclaiming emergencies that do not exist. What some

The increasing globalization of trade and environmental issues reached the policy agenda in 1999 as thousands of activists protested the meeting of the World Trade Organization in Seattle, Washington.

doctrinaire environmentalists wish were true for reasons of ideology has begun to obscure the view of what is actually true in 'the laboratory of nature.'"[2]

That optimism was followed by a 1997 article in *The Economist* that debunked many of the gloomier forecasts and argued that the predicted ecological catastrophes (termed "environmental scare stories") followed a seven-year cycle. In the first year, a scientist discovers a potential threat, followed in the second year by a journalist who oversimplifies and exaggerates it. By year three, environmentalists jump on the bandwagon, followed in the fourth year by bureaucratic regulations. The fifth year, the article claims, is when a villain is identified (usually an industrialized nation), and in the sixth year, the skeptics announce that the problem has been exaggerated. In the final year, there is a quiet consensus that the size of the problem is smaller than had been estimated. The cycle represents the argument of H. L. Mencken that "The whole aim of practical politics is to keep the populace alarmed — and hence clamorous to be led to safety — by menacing it with an endless series of hobgoblins, all of them imaginary."[3]

Typical of the journalistic alarums is reporter Ross Gelbspan's book, *The Heat Is On: The Climate Crisis, the Cover-Up, the Prescription*. Gelbspan spins the global climate change debate to a frenzied level, not only providing a frightening series of likely doomsday scenarios, but also pinning the blame for an alleged coverup on fossil fuel producers. He writes:

> In the United States the truth underlying the increasingly apparent changes in global climate has largely been kept out of public view. As a result, what most Americans know about global warming is obsolete and untrue. That is no accident. The reason most Americans don't know what is happening to the climate is that the oil and coal industries have spent millions of dollars to persuade them that global warming isn't happening.[4]

Perhaps the strongest attack on the doomsday scenarios came from the conservative wing of American politics, which has long targeted the environmental movement for its efforts to place more regulations on business and industry. In 1993, the conservative Washington, D.C., think tank the Cato Institute published the strategically worded book, *Apocalypse Not: Science, Economics, and Environmentalism*. The authors argue that "much of the modern environmental movement is a broad-based assault on reason and, not surprisingly, a concomitant assault on freedom." They then go on to critique the government's efforts to control and regulate a laundry list of issues ranging from population, chemicals, radon, the greenhouse effect, and ozone to acid rain and nuclear power.[5]

Given these widely conflicting views of our environmental future, how does one determine which scenario is correct, and what action should then be taken, if any? How can we expect our political leaders to make the "right" choices when there appears to be so little consensus on what progress, if any, has been made so far?

The group Resources for the Future has offered several explanations as to why the negative predictions have been so far off the mark. First, it notes, is a misunderstanding of how the market works, especially in the face of growing scarcity of exhaustible resources. New technologies have allowed resources to be "stretched" and in some cases (such as oil, gas, coal, copper, and timber), prices have actually been reduced. Second, new institutions have been created that are helping to better manage access to common pool resources such as grazing lands, fisheries, and water, although there are some problems, such as the protection of the world's rain forests, that have yet to be solved. The challenge, the authors note, is "to focus our attention on real (not imagined) problems, giving them their proper priority, and through careful analysis to find effective ways to resolve them."[6]

So far, this book has focused on environmental issues and problems that have developed over the last 150 years, the majority of which have made their way to the domestic and international political agenda since 1960. The early legislative efforts dealing with environmental problems have been called the "react and cure" phase of environmental politics. Some global environmental problems, such as air and water pollution, are likely to be around well into the next century in the "anticipate and prevent" stage of policy making.[7] Many observers believe that the framework for environmental legislation has been in place in the United States for over thirty years and subsequent changes to domestic policy amount to only a fine-tuning of those efforts. The decade of the 1990s has seen an emphasis on the globalization of environmental issues, as new problems are recognized and placed on the policy agenda. This last chapter reflects on those issues that are likely to become the focus of twenty-first century activists and policymakers.

SCIENCE AND POLITICS

Two different mechanisms have been widely discussed as a way of approaching environmental problem solving from a different perspective, regardless of whether the predictions are accurate or not. Both involve a measure of cooperation and collaboration that has been missing from much of the political debate over the environment. One approach, as the subtitle to an influential book calls it, is to integrate science and politics. Using the metaphor of a compass and gyroscope, Kai N. Lee explains that sustainable management of the world's resources is possible, and he believes that humanity can direct itself away from its current course of destruction. "Rigorous science can act as our compass, pointing us toward greater and more useful knowledge, and practical politics can serve as our gyroscope, keeping us balanced among competing interest groups."[8]

Lee's metaphor is augmented by Lynton Keith Caldwell, who explores the possibility of attaining "the ideal of a harmonious, productive, and sustainable society of man-in-biosphere." Caldwell argues that the role of science in policy making "is too important to be left to inadvertence, and clearly it is not being left to chance. How science is developed and applied will be a major determining factor in mankind's environmental future."[9] What appears to be essential to this approach is that there be some formalized mechanism for bringing scientists to the political table when decisions are made. Policymakers, whether members of city councils, Congress, or regulatory agencies, must be afforded the opportunity to be informed — to have available the best scientific expertise. Practically speaking, this means allocating additional funding for research and technology so that reasoned decisions can be made away from the spotlight of partisan posturing.

A typical example where "more and better science" might have made a difference in policy outcomes is the case of asbestos. In the early 1950s, researchers determined that asbestos was a potentially carcinogenic substance, based largely on studies of miners who later developed lung cancer. Asbestos, once known as "the wonder fiber," was widely used as a building material in the first half of the twentieth century, and was found in an estimated three-quarters of a million schools, homes, and commercial facilities. The resulting cancer scare led to regulations and laws in the 1980s that created its own industry — asbestos removal and abatement. Almost overnight, companies pestered school district officials to protect children's lives by closing schools down while workers in protective clothing went through the arduous (and expensive) task of removing all asbestos from ceilings, floors, and insulation around pipes.

But by 1990, the EPA changed its policies on asbestos when additional research found that removal was not always necessary as long as the asbestos was not friable (crumbling) and capable of releasing fibers into the air. Other studies showed that the type of asbestos found in most buildings was more benign, and could be controlled by coating, encapsulation, or encasement rather than through removal. Eventually, a U.S. District Court of Appeals struck down the EPA's ban on asbestos products by ruling that the agency had not properly weighed the costs and benefits of the risk.[10] Meanwhile, millions of dollars had been spent on asbestos removal at a time when educational dollars were already being stretched thin.

The primary issue is how science can adapt its methodology to the adversarial arenas that are common to politics. Researcher Lawrence Susskind answers that question by identifying five roles that scientific advisors can play in the policy process: trend spotters, theory builders, theory testers, science communicators, and applied-policy analysts. The key to effective policy making, he argues, is not only to bring together each of the five types of scientists at each step in the process, but to also force them to confront the sources of their disagreement.[11]

When there is scientific uncertainty or differences over the reliability of data, policy is more likely to be challenged. In the case of the Endangered Species Act (ESA), for instance, biologists are often at the forefront of the problem identification phase of policy making discussed throughout this book. In making estimates of a species' population and habitat, biologists make a reasoned decision as to whether or not they should petition the federal government for protected status for a species. Since the ESA was first enacted, several species have been delisted because original estimates of their population were incorrect. In the case of the Northern spotted owl, uncertainty over the methodology used to calculate the extent of the bird's habitat led to controversy when timber companies argued that the number of remaining birds was actually greater than had been originally estimated. Several firms engaged their own experts to challenge the U.S. Forest Service's findings, thus extending the listing process and eventually bringing the issue to federal court.

Internationally, studies have shown that science has been of limited value in global environmental negotiations. While reports by researchers have helped to call attention to issues such as acid rain, biodiversity, and ozone depletion, science has had little impact in the development of treaties dealing with whaling, migratory species protection, trade in hazardous waste, tropical deforestation, Antarctic mineral exploration, trade in African elephant ivory, ocean dumping, and wetlands and world heritage site designations.[12]

A number of reasons have been identified as to why science is often ignored or given little credibility during the policy-making process. First, stakeholders in the policy process often make decisions based on their own self-interest and reject any scientific findings that are contrary to those interests. Some environmental groups argue that the EPA has failed to enforce sections of the 1990 Clean Air Act because of pressure from powerful utility lobbyists, ignoring evidence of permit and emissions violations. Sometimes, the difficulty lies in that the professional goals of scientists and policymakers appear to be extremely different. In considering ways to deal with the issue of climate change, for instance, scientists developed and tested plausible explanations and subjected their findings to peer review, publication, and replication. Policymakers, in contrast, are more likely to interpret scientific findings in terms of their own political ambitions or agendas, and they may value public opinion, budget priorities, or the costs and risks of taking action.[13]

Second, science is often complex and inexact, and so policymakers may disregard what they do not understand. Long-term models that predict trends in population growth have often been inaccurate because of the methodology used to predict birth and mortality rates. The apocalyptic warnings of some researchers have later been found to be unfounded, leading political leaders to disregard a perceived threat as unlikely.

Third, there are many areas of scientific inquiry that have been inconsistent or contradictory, making it difficult for decision makers to choose which course of action is most desirable. In the case of climate change, for example, scientists first warned of a coming ice age, then later theorized that global warming was imminent. As a result, some policymakers were hesitant to make abrupt (and costly) changes in resource use for fear the science community might change its mind again.

Controversy may also arise over the issue of which scientists should be invited to participate in the policy-making process and at which phase their input should be solicited. The drafting of the London Dumping Convention, which included the issue of ocean dumping of low-level radioactive waste, is an example of how this conflict arises. Several nations that had been signatories to the original 1972 treaty proposed that the International Atomic Energy Association and the International Council of Scientific Unions be included in the original provisions of the ban, while other countries sought the creation of a panel comprised of represented nations and international organizations. After considerable deliberation, a two-part review was agreed on, but the experts were unable to come to a consensus to submit to the political leadership, and thus decisions about the future of the convention were made in what was essentially a scientific vacuum.[14]

The emerging issues that confront both domestic and global environmental policymakers are becoming increasing complex and involve more and more stakeholders. In order to begin to solve those problems, it is likely that the role of scientists and scientific inquiry will be revisited. It is doubtful that any real progress will be made if those in the political arena ignore science and allow decisions to be made on the basis of partisanship, popularity, and prejudice.

COLLABORATIVE DECISION MAKING AND CIVIC ENVIRONMENTALISM

A second approach to solving environmental problems, and one that has received more direct public support, is for more of an emphasis on collaborative environmental decision making. This broad term refers to attempts to change the decision-making process from an adversarial one, pitting environmental organizations against a perceived "enemy" (whether corporate or governmental) to one where the parties agree to discuss their differences in hopes of reaching consensus. Collaborative decision making does not necessarily mean that both sides will be in agreement or that they will accept the other side's point of view, but it does imply a willingness to try to find solutions and to enter into a dialogue rather than litigating, protesting, or using violence to express grievances.

Part of that strategy means redefining the nature of "community" and how people who disagree can come together when difficult and controversial problems are involved. The Northern Lights Institute, based in Missoula, Montana, uses the emerging and changing ideas about community in the Western United States to mean "the interdependence of people living in a particular place, the efforts they make to pursue common goals despite diverse individual values, and the ways in which they are able to build upon their relationships with one another to seek the best long-term uses of the land that sustains them."[15]

This process takes many forms, depending upon the size of the community involved and the scale of the problem being addressed. One of the most highly publicized has been the Quincy Library Group in the small mill town of Quincy, California. It is a community coalition that was formed partially in response to a 1991 judicial decision to protect the Northern spotted owl by reducing logging in the Pacific Northwest. Employees of a local mill began assessing what might happen to their town, and realized that they might find an answer in a proposal by a local group, Friends of Plumas Wilderness, that involved selected logging. In early 1993 a core group of about thirty area residents began meeting in the back of the Quincy Library (hence the group's name) and eventually agreed upon a

Community Stability Proposal that was endorsed by timber industry organizations and environmental groups. The plan was presented to the U.S. Forest Service in Washington, D.C., which then began experimenting with the group's proposals and providing funding. The collaboration has not been without controversy, however. National environmental organizations charged that the group was protimber and did not include any of the major environmental organizations. Agency officials were concerned about the amount of control they would be giving to an unknown and untried grass-roots group. But the effort marked a change in strategy from confrontation to creative cooperation, and has inspired similar efforts elsewhere around the country.[16]

In August 1999, the U.S. Forest Service announced its new timber regulations based on the Quincy model — a process that had taken six years of negotiations. The plan doubled logging on 2.4 million acres in three northern California national forests, barred new logging roads on 500,000 acres, and prohibited the harvesting of trees more than thirty inches in diameter. While Wilderness Society officials expressed dismay at the announcement, saying it was "a bitter disappointment," most viewed the plan as a compromise that would help heal the long-standing political wars between loggers and environmentalists.[17]

The process goes by a number of different names, such as collaborative planning and seeking common ground, but the idea is the same — bringing together differing factions within a community to solve environmental problems.[18] In Ohio, the Environmental Protection Agency teamed up with local residents to form the Ashtabula River Partnership, a joint endeavor of environmental groups, polluting industries, regulators, and local officials. Layers of heavy metals and contaminants had clogged the river in the northeast corner of the state, and the parties sought a resolution that would avoid the costs and delays had the site been added to the national priorities list under Superfund. The partnership is designed to avoid years of lawsuits and studies that typically delay any real cleanup.[19] In northern Arizona, the Grand Canyon Forests Partnership brings competing groups together to avoid, as one leader said, letting "this become a technical process, and just have a different set of experts tell us how to do forestry better."[20] In Wyoming, Coordinated Resource Management, an approach that originated in the 1950s, is being used to resolve specific conflicts over resource management — specifically, the tensions among ranchers, federal authorities, and environmental groups. The goal is to encourage ranchers, including the half-million acre Sun family ranch in south-central Wyoming, to move toward voluntary stewardship that is landowner initiated.[21]

One strategy takes its cue from criminal justice policy. In several developing nations, government leaders have attempted to institute community-based forest management, returning control of a region's natural resources to the people who live there. This concept has been applied in Indonesia, the Philippines, Thailand, India, Nepal, Sri Lanka, and Papua New Guinea, with varying degrees of success. As yet there is no "boilerplate" model that can be used by countries seeking to allow for these initiatives to be introduced, and there are significant roadblocks because of differences in culture and legal and political systems. But by allowing the indigenous populations to have a voice in decisions about the use of forest resources, policymakers often circumvent the types of civil unrest and revolt usually associated with the timber industry.[22] Other applications have been made to protecting species diversity, especially in rural areas,[23] and in promoting sustainable coral reef management.[24]

Local management of property does not necessarily mean a complete turnover of lands or resources, as has been advocated by members of the environmental opposition's county supremacy groups. Rather, it can mean that lands are viewed from a multiple-use perspective in which all stakeholders are invited to decide how lands should be managed. Success stories abound, both domestically and globally. For example, since 1898, efforts to preserve the resources of the Black Hills National Forest in South Dakota have been mired in controversy between local residents and the U.S. Forest Service. But when government officials agreed to allow community members to participate in the process of deciding *what* uses were compatible with the area's overall management plans, resources were enhanced rather than degraded.[25]

One other strategy, and perhaps the one most likely to be used in the United States, is termed "civic environmentalism." The concept was initially proposed by two researchers, Stan Johnson and DeWitt John, who sought to develop a new style of environmental politics that would replace the traditional command-and-control, top-down style of environmental regulation with "decentralized, bottom-up initiatives using new tools to address newly recognized environmental problems."[26] In this paradigm, state and local officials and citizens, rather than the federal government, take primary responsibility for pollution prevention and ecosystem management.

Civic environmentalism is an outgrowth of the frustration that both government regulators and environmental activists felt during the administrations of presidents Ronald Reagan, George Bush, and even Bill Clinton, when environmental policy making was hampered by congressional gridlock. It is viewed as a complement to, rather than a substitute for, federal regulation. The idea of crafting a new approach to environmental policy has won the support of mainstream environmental groups such as the World Resources Institute as well as the bipartisan National Commission on the Environment, which includes agency representatives appointed under both Republican and Democratic administrations.

Because civic environmentalism involves a style of decision making that is collaborative, it reduces the potential for conflict. Examples of successful implementation of the model already abound in the United States. Iowa, for example, has relied almost exclusively on voluntary, nonregulatory tools to deal with the issues of nonpoint source pollution by farm chemicals, winning praise for its 1987 Groundwater Act and a 1992 EPA award for pollution prevention.[27] Other attempts at finding common ground include the efforts made to restore the Florida Everglades[28] and Oregon's Applegate Partnership.[29]

What is becoming more and more clear is that traditional decision-making strategies for protecting the environment are no longer effective. Years of backroom political deals, militancy on both ends of the environmental spectrum, sparsely attended regulatory hearings and a need to approach problems from a global, rather than merely localized, perspective have changed the way problems are framed and solutions are developed. The situation is well stated by Michael W. Robbins, editor of *Audubon,* in an editorial that tells the story of an activist who was concerned about his personal safety when he was deciding whether or not to attend a hearing at a regional federal agency. Recognizing that those types of fears, and the passions which accompany them lead nowhere, Robbins suggests the following:

> What will point towards resolution is the recognition of areas of common interest—and some understanding of the other's interests and strong feelings. It's easy for loggers and ranchers and commercial fishers to dismiss environmentalists as Druidical wackos who can't grasp the importance of making a living. And it's just as facile for enviros to label as shortsighted greed what others feel is simply making a living. With some mutual appreciation of the strong feelings, then maybe there can be a civil dialogue about common interests like sustainable forestry and fishery—even if that means attending a hostile hearing.[30]

AGRICULTURE AND GENETICALLY ENGINEERED PRODUCTS

The challenge of producing sufficient food resources to feed the planet's growing population is not a new one — it has been a part of the environmental sustainability agenda for decades. But it gained new prominence toward the end of the twentieth century as hundreds of private sector firms and researchers sought to capitalize on new approaches to increasing agricultural production. As the Union of Concerned Scientists (UCS) notes: "Agricultural practices have ramifications for food security, environmental protection, and economic prosperity. To reduce agriculture's impact on the environment and ensure the economic and food security benefits into the next century, UCS advocates sustainable agricultural policies and practices."[31]

The Massachusetts-based group works to promote agricultural practices that minimize pesticide, fertilizer, and energy use, and researches and evaluates the risks and benefits of biotechnology in agriculture. Their concern is that today's industrial agriculture produces a bountiful harvest for both U.S. consumers and export abroad, but with serious environmental and social costs: damaged soil, depleted groundwater, polluted rivers, and impoverished rural communities. Many of these problems are caused by a heavy reliance upon chemical pesticides and fertilizers, on growing only a few commercial crops, and on planting only one crop per field.

The problem moved up the policy agenda in response to several critical developments. In Scotland, scientists were able to clone a sheep named Dolly, producing an animal that is genetically identical to its "parent." While humans have used plant cloning for thousands of years (and it is a process that occurs naturally in nature), the sheep experiment raised the specter that similar technology could be applied to produce a cloned human baby which would be genetically identical to its donor "parent." The ethical and moral debate over the ramifications of such a process had been discussed from a theoretical perspective, but took on new urgency when a few scientists proposed human experimentation.

Other environmental groups such as OneWorld warned of xenotransplants — the transplantation of an organ of one species to another, unrelated species, such as placing a pig's heart into a human body. Some researchers in the field called for a moratorium on human trials because they believe "that the risks are sufficient to warrant refraining from human xenotransplanation until public deliberations on the ethical issues have occurred." One concern was that pig retroviruses are known to infect human cells in the test tube — a potential hazard with unknown environmental consequences. The group also warns of the danger of biopollution, a term used to describe the unwanted escape of transgenic organisms which then interbreed with other natural organisms resulting in wild progeny which may contain some of the transgenic attributes, such as resistance to weedkillers or antibiotics. In Canada, farmed transgenic salmon with deformities escaped into the wild and began interbreeding with the natural stock.[32]

Another development that brought greater attention to agricultural practices and the resulting environmental consequences is biopiracy. One of the central elements of the revolution taking place in agricultural genetics is the increase in the number of patents sought by industrialized countries for genetic material found in poor, developing nations with few regulations over "intellectual property rights."

But by far the most controversial issue is over the development of genetically altered products and the companies that develop and market them. Genetic engineering (GE), used generically to describe the process that involves the modification of a plant or animal's genes, grew substantially after 1995 both in the United States and abroad. In 1999, about half the U.S. soybeans and one-third of the corn crop were genetically engineered as a way of increasing yield and insect resistance. Supporters of the process, such as Indiana senator Richard Luger, argue that such practices are essential if the world's hungry are to be fed. Opponents, such as Greenpeace and Britain's Prince Charles, point out that GE has the potential of releasing organisms into the environment that are potentially irreversible, untraceable, and uncontrollable. Other critics note that many GE seeds do not significantly increase the yield of crops. In a trial of seeds produced by Monsanto that are genetically engineered to withstand herbicide or produce its own insecticide, fewer bushels of soybeans were produced than from natural varieties, according to one study.[33]

It will take decades of additional research before there are answers to the questions posed by these issues. But more important for the beginning of the twenty-first century is how well U.S. and international institutions are prepared to deal with the advent of technologies like GE. Most analysts believe that government agencies are not yet prepared to openly evaluate the environmental impact of these developments prior to their implementation. As a result, says the Union of Concerned Scientists, "decisions about technologies are largely left to the private sector, which is given full latitude to produce whatever can be sold, subject only to regulation to avoid harm to health and environment."[34]

In the United States, three agencies are responsible for genetic engineered products: the Environmental Protection Agency, the Food and Drug Administration, and the U.S. Department of Agriculture. Their jurisdictions occasionally cross over one another because they are operating under older statutes originally designed to regulate products before GE was even conceptualized. The EPA, for example, gets its regulatory authority under the Federal Insecticide, Fungicide, and Rodenticide Act (FIFRA) and the Toxic Substances Control Act (TSCA). Organisms that are controlled under FIFRA are subject to permit standards under which the EPA can require that studies be undertaken to determine any potential harm to health and the environment. Under TSCA, however, companies need only provide EPA with 90-days notice before they begin the manufacturing process, with few provisions for risk analysis.

The FDA, in contrast, has the legal authority to regulate all GE foods under the Federal Food, Drug, and Cosmetic Act. However, GE food crops are not subject to regulation under current policies, although there is a voluntary program which encourages companies to consult with the FDA. The firms do not, however, have to conduct any standardized safety testing on GE products, and even those that do submit only summaries to the agency, not full data sets. The FDA does not publish any conclusions on the safety of individual GE foods, although it is considering regulations on engineered fish under the category of "animal drugs."

The U.S. Department of Agriculture does have considerably more latitude to regulate GE products, under the Plant Pest Act, the Virus, Serums and Toxin Act, and various meat inspection statutes. Some products have been studied in more depth because they fall under the National Environmental Policy Act, which requires an environmental assessment. Field tests have also been conducted on various GE crops, most of which have been approved for commercial use, including corn, cotton, soybeans, and various fruits and vegetables.

Many environmental organizations have called for a new regulatory framework to deal with GE organisms, especially because so few premarket controls exist. Of particular importance is the range and levels of public participation in GE policy. Most of the statutes grant companies broad privileges to withhold data and information, including health and safety information, from the public. While the agencies almost always hear from the regulated industries on pending policies, most decisions about GE have been dominated by multinational corporations who are the developers of the products.[35]

The regulation of GE products and their role in sustainable agriculture appears to be too new and complex an issue to have yet gained the public's attention, advancing it to the policy agenda. As researchers begin to publish more of their findings, as interest groups take the issue to the political arena, and as public awareness begins to grow and solidify, there is little doubt that GE will become an important part of the environmental policy agenda. Thus far, it is only at the initial stages of being defined as a problem, even though biotechnology as a sector moves forwards with increasing momentum.

TRADE AND THE ENVIRONMENT

The newspaper headlines and photographs at the end of the twentieth century were filled with provocative images of the World Trade Organization (WTO) conference in Seattle, Washington — of protestors being tear-gassed, of the delegates from 135 member nations being turned away from conference facilities, of broken or boarded-up store windows, and of labor leaders marching arm-in-arm through the streets with environmental group activists. The city's downtown was placed under curfew as the National Guard was called in to quell the disturbance against the WTO — a semisecretive organization whose mission is to resolve trade disputes and promote free trade.

Over five hundred groups registered as nongovernmental organizations as part of the forums associated with the meeting, making it what one *Wall Street Journal* reporter called "the Woodstock of antiglobalization."[36] Protestors from Dyke Action criticized the WTO of oppression, charging the group does not care about women's rights. A member of an indigenous people's group, the Kuna Youth Movement of Panama, accused the WTO of destroying biodiversity, liberalizing tourism, and stealing knowledge. Other groups ranged from the Memphis Audubon Society, to the Fourth World Association of Finland, the Ruckus Society, and the Rainforest Action Network.

Among the issues facing both delegates and nondelegates were government subsidies that some say give farmers an unfair edge in global markets, especially those that accept imports of genetically engineered crops; renegotiation of agreements that defend U.S. companies against those countries that dump surplus goods like steel into the U.S. market; maintaining animal welfare standards to ensure food safety for consumers, especially hormone-treated beef; whether more environmental protections should be built into trade agreements such as NAFTA; and changes in import bans on shrimp that threaten endangered sea turtles.

The WTO was established on January 1, 1995, as the successor organization to the General Agreement on Tariffs and Trade (GATT), which had last held a round of negotiations in Uruguay in 1986. Initially, there were 76 charter members; currently 135 are members, with another 31, including China, Russia, and Saudi Arabia, applying to join. Those who do become members agree to abide by a series of regulations on how they conduct international trade, so that it flows as smoothly, predictably, and freely as possible. Headquartered in Geneva, the organization has been heavily criticized because it is perceived as being controlled by large international organizations. Many of the demonstrators used the trade talks as an opportunity to vent their emotions for almost any cause — but clearly, the focus was on the increasing globalization of trade and environmental issues.[37] (See "Another View, Another Voice: Michael Moore: Director General, World Trade Organization.")

By the end of the conference, reform of the organization itself replaced the emphasis on environmental problems and trade. Most agreed the Seattle meeting had been a failure, producing more bitterness than agreement on any substantive

Another View, Another Voice

MICHAEL MOORE
Director General, World Trade Organization

Michael Moore's job description for his position as director general of the WTO probably never included skills like dodging tear-gas canisters, convincing protesters that he would not meet with them after they chained themselves to a staircase where he works, or convincing representatives from small developing countries that his employer is not part of an American conspiracy to control global trade. But after his installation in September 1999, Moore found that the first four months on the job were certainly more than he had expected.

Born into a farming family in New Zealand fifty years ago, Moore brings a unique combination of experiences to his position as head of the trade body. He has worked in construction, in the meat-packing industry, as a printer, social worker, and boxer — the latter occupation good experience for his current job. As prime minister of New Zealand, he was a strong supporter of internationalizing trade, and a patient politician who has gained the respect of many of those who initially opposed his candidacy for the WTO's top administrative job. It took him ten months to land the job after a divisive battle within the organization over a new leader. He had been supported by the United States and several other industrialized trading nations against a Thai rival, who will succeed him in the job when Moore's three-year term expires in 2002.

After finally accepting the position, Moore had only a short time to organize the Seattle round of trade negotiations. Just a week prior to the scheduled start of the conference, the WTO was unable to agree upon an agenda. At the same time, Moore was fielding accounts that as many as 50,000 demonstrators might show up in Seattle to protest the WTO's perceived lack of concern for the environmental, safety, and labor aspects of trade. While trying to meet the needs of diplomats and trade representatives, he was also obliged to acknowledge the concerns of the activists, especially the estimated 20,000 union members representing U.S. labor organizations who showed up to rally in Seattle.

Some observers believe Moore deserves good marks for his handling of the disappointing meeting, with Brazil's trade negotiator, Celso Amorim, calling him incredibly patient. Pakistan's representative, Munir Akram, congratulated the director general for building bridges, while Moroccan representative Nacer Benjelloun-Touimi noted that Moore had been honest and did not try to play games with the delegates. But others were concerned less about Moore's folksy style and more about the entrenched political differences that typify the WTO. He was unable to get the members of the European Union to budge over their demands that farm products must be treated differently because their

(continued)

production contributes to maintaining the rapidly vanishing countryside. This view is considered pure protectionism by the United States.

Moore's position is more symbolic than substantive, most believe. As director general, he represents the WTO but has little power because members can ultimately defy the organization's decisions. A skilled communicator, he is also the focal point for criticism on WTO policies on child labor, financial penalties against those who violate the membership agreement, and the weakening of environmental laws. He clearly was disappointed in the direction of the negotiations, telling reporters: "This is a sad day. To those who argue that we should stop our work, I say: tell that to the poor, to the marginalized around the world, who are looking to us to help them."[1]

Notes

1. Sam Howe Verhovek and Steven Greenhouse, "Seattle Is under Curfew after Disruptions," *New York Times,* December 1, 1999, A14.

issues. The chasm of acrimony that had characterized the gap between the interests of nations of the Northern and Southern hemispheres in the 1990s seemed to grow larger. Even European and American negotiators could not come to an agreement on agricultural trade barriers, and many developing nations' delegates blamed the Clinton administration for promoting a too-ambitious trade agenda. At the end, the WTO's talks were scheduled to move back to Geneva for more limited discussions, primarily on agriculture. Any overhaul, partial or complete, of the WTO itself is in the hands of advanced industrial countries rather than the protestors and activists who made trade and the environment into headline news at the end of the twentieth century.

NOTES

1. Quoted by Paul Brown, "UN Report Warns of Environmental Crisis," *Guardian Weekly,* September 23–29, 1999, 14.
2. Gregg Easterbrook, *A Moment on the Earth: The Coming Age of Environmental Optimism* (New York: Viking, 1995), xvi.
3. "Environmental Scares: Plenty of Gloom," *The Economist,* December 20, 1997, 21.
4. Ross Gelbspan, *The Heat Is On: The Climate Crisis, the Cover-Up, the Prescription,* updated ed. (Reading, MA: Perseus Books, 1998), 5.
5. Ben Bolch and Harold Lyons, *Apocalypse Not: Science, Economics, and Environmentalism* (Washington, DC: The Cato Institute, 1993).
6. Paul R. Portney and Wallace E. Oates, "On Prophecies of Environmental Doom," *Resources, 131* (Spring 1998): 17.
7. See Michael Potier, "Towards a Better Integration of Environmental, Economic, and Other Governmental Policies," in *Maintaining a Satisfactory Environment: An Agenda for International Environmental Policy,* ed. Nordal Akerman (Boulder, CO: Westview Press, 1990), 69–81.
8. Kai N. Lee, *Compass and Gyroscope: Integrating Science and Politics for the Environment* (Washington, DC: Island Press, 1993), flyleaf.

9. Lynton Keith Caldwell, *Between Two Worlds: Science, the Environmental Movement and Policy Choice* (New York: Cambridge University Press, 1992).

10. There are numerous accounts of the asbestos issue and the conflict between science and policy that occurred. See, for example, Paul Brodeur, *Outrageous Misconduct: The Asbestos Industry on Trial* (New York: Pantheon Books, 1985); Diana Goodish, "Asbestos Exposure in Schools," *Journal of School Health, 59,* no. 8 (October 1989): 362–363; Louis S. Richman, "Why Throw Money on Asbestos?" *Fortune,* June 6, 1988, 155; Michael Bennett, *The Asbestos Racket: An Environmental Parable* (Bellevue, WA: Free Enterprise Press, 1991); and Jay Mathews, "To Yank or Not to Yank?" *Newsweek,* April 13, 1992, 59.

11. Lawrence Susskind, *Environmental Diplomacy: Negotiating More Effective Global Agreements* (New York: Oxford University Press, 1994), 76–78.

12. Ibid., 62–63.

13. Lamont C. Hempel, *Environmental Governance: The Global Challenge* (Washington, DC: Island Press, 1996), 103.

14. Susskind, *Environmental Diplomacy,* 68–69.

15. *Chronicle of Community,* 1, no. 2 (Winter 1997): 3.

16. For background and a variety of perspectives on the Quincy Library Group, see Ed Marston, "The Timber Wars Evolve into a Divisive Attempt at Peace," *High Country News,* September 29, 1997, 1; and Tim Fitzgerald, "The Quincy Library Affair," *PERC Reports,* March 1998. The Quincy Library Group maintains a website at <http://www.qlg.org>, March 18, 1999.

17. "U.S. Forest Officials Sign Timber Decision for Northern Sierra," *San Francisco Chronicle,* August 21, 1999, C1.

18. See Marvin R. Weisbord, *Discovering Common Ground* (San Francisco, CA: Berrett-Koehler Publishers, 1992); Dennis C. Le Master and John H. Beuter, eds., *Community Stability in Forest-based Economies* (Portland, OR: Timber Press, 1989); and Margaret G. Thomas, *Forest Resource Strategies for Rural Development* (Washington, DC: U.S. Department of Agriculture, 1990).

19. "Polluters, Government Team Up to Clean Up," *San Francisco Chronicle,* January 2, 1999, A2.

20. Michelle Nijhuis, "Flagstaff Searches For Its Forests' Future," *High Country News,* March 1, 1999, 9.

21. Sarah B. Van de Wetering, "Enlightened Self Interest," *Chronicles of Community,* 1, no. 2 (Winter 1997): 17–25.

22. See Owen J. Lynch and Kirk Talbott, with Marshall S. Berdan, *Balancing Acts: Community-based Forest Management and National Law in Asia and the Pacific* (Washington, DC: World Resources Institute, 1995).

23. See Jeffrey A. McNeely, ed., *Expanding Partnership in Conservation* (Cambridge: World Conservation Union, 1995); and David Western and R. Michael Wright, *Natural Connections: Perspectives on Community-based Conservation* (Washington, DC: Island Press, 1994).

24. Alan T. White et al., eds. *Collaborative and Community-based Management of Coral Reefs* (West Hartford, CT: Kumarian Press, 1994).

25. Martha E. Geores, *Common Ground: The Struggle for Ownership of the Black Hills National Forest* (Lanham, MD: Rowman and Littlefield, 1996).

26. De Witt John, *Civic Environmentalism: Alternatives to Regulation in States and Communities* (Washington, DC: Congressional Quarterly Press, 1994), xiv.

27. Ibid., 85–86.

28. See David Gluckman, "The Margery Stoneman Douglas Everglades Protection Act," *Environmentalism and Urban Issues,* Fall 1991, 17–27; James Webb, "Managing Nature in the Everglades," *EPA Journal,* November–December 1990, 50; and Marjory Douglas, *The Everglades: River of Grass* (Sarasota, FL: Pineapple Press, 1988).

29. For a discussion of the Applegate Partnership's attempt to reach consensus over the issues of logging in sensitive species' habitats, see Brett KenCairn, "Peril on Common Ground: The Applegate Experiment," in *A Wolf in the Garden: The Land Rights Movement*

and the New Environmental Debate, ed. Philip D. Brick and R. McGreggor Cawley (Lanham, MD: Rowman and Littlefield, 1996), 261–277.

30. Michael W. Robbins, "A Place for Feelings," *Audubon,* May–June 1996, 4.

31. Union of Concerned Scientists, "Shaping an Agriculture for the Twenty-First Century," statement, available at <http://www.ucsusa.org/agriculture>, November 22, 1999.

32. "Genetic Engineering," available at <http://www.oneworld.org>, November 22, 1999.

33. Peter Rosset, "Genetically Altered Food Won't Conquer World Hunger," *Seattle Post-Intelligencer,* September 3, 1999.

34. Union of Concerned Scientists, "Biotechnology Policy Briefing," statement, available at <http://www.ucsusa.org/agriculture>, November 22, 1999.

35. Ibid.

36. Helene Cooper, "Some Hazy, Some Erudite and All Angry, WTO Protestors Are Hard to Dismiss," *Wall Street Journal,* November 30, 1999, 1.

37. There is a massive amount of coverage of the WTO meeting in print and electronic formats. For information on the WTO, visit the organization's website at <www.wto.org>. Material on the Seattle meeting is available at <www.wtoseattle.org>, March 18, 2000.

FOR FURTHER READING

Marian Chertow and Daniel C. Esty, eds.. *Thinking Ecologically: The Next Generation of Environmental Policy*. New Haven, CT: Yale University Press, 1997.

Allen Hammond. *Which World? Scenarios for the 21st Century*. Washington, DC: Island Press, 1998.

Uwe Kracht and Manfred Schulz, eds. *Food Security and Nutrition: The Global Challenge*. New York: St. Martin's Press, 1999.

Anne O. Krueger, ed. *The WTO as an International Organization*. Chicago: University of Chicago Press, 1998.

William Anthony Lovett. *U.S. Trade Policy: History, Theory, and the WTO*. Armonk, NY: M. E. Sharpe, 1999.

Jeremy Rifkin. *The Biotech Century: Harnessing the Gene and Remaking the World*. New York: Putnam, 1998.

Ken Sexton et al., eds. *Better Environmental Decisions: Strategies for Governments, Businesses, and Communities*. Washington, DC: Island Press, 1999.

Jon Turney. *Frankenstein's Footsteps: Science, Genetics and Popular Culture*. New Haven, CT: Yale University Press, 1998.

United Nations Environment Programme. *Global Environment Outlook 2000*. London: Earthscan, 1999.

Ken Worpole. *Richer Futures: Fashioning a New Politics*. London: Earthscan, 1999.

APPENDIX A

Major U.S. Environmental Legislation, 1947–2000

Year	Air Quality	Water Quality	Pesticides—Toxics	Solid Waste	Land	Other
1947 Truman			Federal Insecticide, Fungicide, and Rodenticide Act			
1956 Eisenhower		Water Pollution Control Act				
1963 Kennedy	Clean Air Act					
1964 Johnson					Land and Water Conservation Fund Act	
1965 Johnson		Water Quality Act				Highway Beautification Act
1966 Johnson						Endangered Species Preservation Act
1967 Johnson	Air Quality Act					
1968 Johnson					National Wild and Scenic Rivers Act/National Trails System Act	
1969 Nixon						National Environmental PolicyAct/Endangered Species Act Amendments

Year	Air Quality	Water Quality	Pesticides—Toxics	Solid Waste	Land	Other
1970 Nixon	Clean Air Act Amendments	Water Quality Improvement Act		Resources Recovery Act		Environment Education Act
1971 Nixon					Alaska Native Claims Settlement Act	
1972 Nixon		Federal Water Pollution Control Act	Federal Environmental Pesticides Control Act	Coastal Zone Management Act		Marine Protection Research and Sanctuaries Act/ Noise Control Act
1973 Nixon						Endangered Species Act
1974 Nixon		Safe Drinking Water Act				
1976 Ford			Toxic Substances Control Act	Resource Conservation and Recovery Act	Federal Land Policy and Management Act/National Forest Management Act	
1977 Carter	Clean Air Act Amendments	Clean Water Act Amendments			Surface and Mining Control and Reclamation Act/Soil and Water Conservation Act	
1978 Carter						Public Utility Regulatory Policies Act/National Energy Act
1980 Carter			Comprehensive Environmental Response, Compensation, and Liability Act (Superfund)		Alaska National Interest Lands Conservation Act	Fish and Wildlife Conservation Act

Year	Air Quality	Water Quality	Pesticides—Toxics	Solid Waste	Land	Other
1982 Reagan						Nuclear Waste Policy Act
1984 Reagan				Resource Conservation and Recovery Act Amendments		
1985 Reagan						Food Security Act
1986 Reagan		Safe Drinking Water Act	Superfund Amendments			
1987 Reagan		Clean Water Act Amendments				Nuclear Waste Policy Act Amendments/Global Climate Protection Act
1988 Reagan				Federal Insecticide, Fungicide, and Rodenticide Act Amendments		Ocean Dumping Act
1990 Bush	Clean Air Act Amendments					
1992 Bush						Energy Policy Act
1994 Clinton					California Desert Protection Act	
1996 Clinton		Safe Drinking Water Act Amendments				Food Quality Protection Act

Appendix B

Major International Environmental Agreements, 1900–2000

1902	International Convention for the Protection of Birds Useful to Agriculture
1906	Convention Concerning the Equitable Distribution of the Waters of the Rio Grande for Irrigation
1916	Convention for the Protection of Migratory Birds
1933	Convention on the Preservation of Fauna and Flora in Their Natural State
1946	International Convention for the Regulation of Whaling
1947	General Agreement on Tariffs and Trade
1951	International Plant Protection Convention
1954	International Convention for the Protection of the Seas by Oil
1958	Convention on the Continental Shelf
1958	Convention on Fishing and Conservation of the Living Resources of the High Seas
1959	Antarctic Treaty
1963	Berne Convention on the International Commission for the Protection of the Rhine Against Pollution
1963	Treaty Banning Nuclear Weapons Tests
1964	Convention for the International Council for the Exploration of the Sea
1968	African Convention on the Conservation of Nature and Natural Resources
1971	Convention on Wetlands of International Importance Especially as Waterfowl Habitat
1972	Convention Concerning the Protection of the World Cultural and Natural Heritage
1972	Convention on the Prevention of Marine Pollution by Dumping of Wastes and Other Matter
1972	Stockholm Declaration of the United Nations Conference on the Human Environment

1973	Convention on International Trade in Endangered Species of Wild Fauna and Flora
1973	International Convention for the Prevention of Pollution from Ships
1979	International Convention on Long-Range Transboundary Air Pollution
1982	United Nations Convention on the Law of the Sea
1985	Vienna Convention for the Protection of the Ozone Layer
1987	Montreal Protocol on Substances That Deplete the Ozone Layer
1989	Basel Convention on the Control of Transboundary Movements of Hazardous Wastes and Their Disposal
1991	Bamako Convention on the Ban of Import Into Africa and the Control of Transboundary Movement and Management of Hazardous Wastes Within Africa
1992	United Nations Framework Convention on Climate Change
1992	Convention on Biological Diversity
1992	North American Free Trade Agreement
1992	Rio Declaration on Environment and Development
1994	International Tropical Timber Agreement
1994	United Nations Convention to Combat Desertification
1997	Kyoto Protocol to the United Nations Framework Convention on Climate Change
1998	Convention on Access to Information, Public Participation in Decision Making and Access to Justice in Environmental Matters

APPENDIX C

Environmental Film Resources

An Act of Congress (1979) 59 minutes

Uses the Clean Air Act Amendments of 1977 as a legislative case study to illustrate the process of how legislators balance interests to deal with air pollution. Simon and Schuster Communications (Northbrook, IL)

Alaska: The Last Frontier? (1996) 27 minutes

Shows the difficulties of balancing the needs of indigenous peoples and the wilderness with economic development and modern life in Alaska. Annenberg/CPB Collection (South Burlington, VT)

An American Nile (1997) 55 minutes

Charts the dramatic transformation of the Colorado River from a wild desert waterway, including the construction of Hoover Dam and environmental battles over potential damming of the Grand Canyon. Home Vision Cinema: Public Media Incorporated (Chicago, IL)

Borderline Cases: Environmental Matters at the U.S.–Mexico Border (1997) 65 minutes

Describes problems caused by factories along the U.S.–Mexico border which did not need to comply with environmental regulations. Bullfrog Films (Oley, PA)

Cadillac Desert (1997) 55 minutes

Traces the fierce political and environmental battles that raged around the transformation of California's Central Valley and the recent trend of diverting water away from agriculture and towards cities and wildlife. Home Vision Cinema: Public Media Incorporated (Chicago, IL).

Ecofeminism Now! (1996) 37 minutes

Offers an introduction to the theory and practice of ecofeminism. Medusa Productions (Minnesota)

Environment (1994) 60 minutes

Looks at the international dimension of environmental problems, focusing on transnational pollution and international property rights. Annenberg/CPB Collection (South Burlington, VT)

Fooling with Nature (1998) 60 minutes

Examines new evidence in the controversy over the danger of chemicals to human health and the environment. PBS Video (Alexandria, VA)

Full Circle (1993) 55 minutes

Discusses environmental issues from the perspective of women's spirituality. Direct Cinema (Santa Monica, CA)

Fury for the Sound: The Women at Clayoquot (1997) 86 minutes

Reveals the important role of women in establishing grass-roots social movements to protest logging in Clayoquot Sound in British Columbia. TellTale Productions (Vancouver, BC)

Healing the Earth (1995) 28 minutes

Shows how we can help heal the earth through cooperation between communities and the government on Superfund projects and the use of bioremediation. National Geographic Society (Washington, DC)

Hoover Dam (1999) 60 minutes

Describes the making of a national monument and the environmental conflicts involved, using archival footage and photographs. PBS Video (Alexandria, VA)

How Serious Is Global Warming? (1996) 31 minutes

Commentaries by a series of researchers in energy policy and climate on the nature and implications of global warming. Hawkhill Video (Madison, WI)

Keepers of the Coast (1996) 31 minutes

Shows the work of local surfers through the Surfrider Foundation to educate the public and protest the pollution of coastlines. Bullfrog Films (Oley, PA)

In Our Children's Food (1993) 56 minutes

Traces the 30-year history of U.S. pesticide use, regulation, and scientific study and explores what is known and not known about the risks of agricultural chemicals in our food. PBS Video (Alexandria, VA)

Laid to Waste (1996) 52 minutes

Shows how the residents of Chester, PA, fight the location of another waste treatment plant in their city through community action. University of California (Berkeley, CA)

Last Oasis (1997) 55 minutes

The story of how America's large dams became examples for water projects in developing countries. Home Vision Cinema: Public Media Incorporated (Chicago, IL)

The Last Rivermen (1991) 31 minutes

Details the activism of the fishermen along the Hudson River to stop chemical pollution that has decimated their livelihood. Riverkeeper (Garrison, NY)

Logs, Lies, and Videotape (1996) 12 minutes

Looks at the impact of a logging measure passed by Congress that directs the Forest Service and Bureau of Land Management to accelerate salvage logging. Green Fire Productions (Eugene, OR)

Mexico City (1994) 14 minutes

Discusses the problem of water pollution in Mexico City. New Dimension Media (Eugene, OR)

Mulholland's Dream (1997) 85 minutes

Tells of William Mulholland's search for water for the people of Los Angeles and the building of the aqueduct 250 miles from the Owens Valley to southern California. Home Vision Cinema: Public Media Incorporated (Chicago, IL)

Ozone: Protecting the Invisible Shield (1994) 28 minutes

Explains the history of the ozone hole and the chemistry behind the phenomenon, including how groups are working together to halt any further destruction. National Geographic Society (Washington, DC)

The Politics of Trees (1992) 58 minutes

Looks at the on-going debate on how we manage the rapidly disappearing old-growth forest of the Pacific Northwest. PBS Video (Alexandria, VA)

Rachel Carson's Silent Spring (1993) 57 minutes

Focuses on Carson's book and the chemical poisoning of the environment to show how one scientist's courage changed the way we think about our world. PBS Video (Alexandria, VA)

Restoring the Everglades (1998) 15 minutes

Reviews issues of wetland conservation, agricultural pollution, and efforts to restore the National Park. National Parks and Conservation Association (Washington, DC)

Subdivide and Conquer (1999) 57 minutes

Looks at the issue of urban and suburban sprawl in the United States, its effects on the sense of community and the environment. Bullfrog Films (Oley, PA)

Sustainable Environments (1994) 30 minutes

An exploration of the concept of sustainability, with sections on transportation, buildings and landscapes, diet and agriculture. San Luis Video Publishing (Los Osos, CA)

The Search for Clean Air (1994) 57 minutes

A thorough explanation of the problems of air pollution, including its effects on forests, streams, and human health, and thew issues involved in correcting the problems. Films for the Humanities and Sciences (Princeton, NJ)

Thinking Green: Ecofeminists and the Greens (1994) 35 minutes

Discusses the links between the feminist movement, the green movement, as well as other progressive issues regarding the future of the planet. Green Party USA (New York)

Times Beach, Missouri (1994) 57 minutes

Uses archival footage and interviews with former residents to recount the story of a small town in the Midwest extensively contaminated with dioxin. Video Project (Oakland, CA)

Toxic Racism (1994) 60 minutes

Explores the grass-roots war against those responsible for the high levels of toxic waste dumping and industrial pollution in poor and minority neighborhoods. Films for the Humanities and Sciences (Princeton, NJ)

Trinkets and Beads (1996) 53 minutes

Documents the lives of the Huaorani, a small tribe of Ecuadorian Indians, who after pressure from foreign oil companies, agreed to allow oil drilling on their land. First Run/Icarus Films (New York)

Voices from the Frontlines (1997) 38 minutes

Profiles the Los Angeles-based Labor/Community Strategy Center, a grass-roots nonprofit political organization that is involved in environmental issues. Cinema Guild (New York)

Index